THE NEW BOOK OF
AMERICAN RANKINGS

REVISED EDITION

THE NEW BOOK OF AMERICAN RANKINGS

REVISED EDITION

Ellen Meltzer

☑® Facts On File, Inc.

The New Book of American Rankings, Revised Edition

Copyright © 1998 by Ellen Meltzer

Facts On File, Inc.
11 Penn Plaza
New York NY 10001

Library of Congress Cataloging-in-Publication Data

Meltzer, Ellen.
    The New Book of American rankings / Ellen Meltzer. — Rev. ed.
      p. cm.
    Rev. ed. of: New book of American rankings, 1984.
    Includes index.
    ISBN 0-8160-2878-8
    United States—Statistics. I. Title.
  HA214.N49 1997
  317.3—dc21   97-7932

Text design by Cathy Rincon

Cover design by Richard Adelson

This book is printed on acid-free paper.

Printed in the United States of America

VB COM 10 9 8 7 6 5 4 3 2

CONTENTS

PREFACE

In almost 250 tables *The New Book of American Rankings* illustrates the enormous geographic, demographic and cultural variety found in the United States of America. A handy collection of reference materials, the book presents, in tabular form, comparisons of the 50 states in over 400 different categories.

Serving both the casual browser and the serious student, *American Rankings* offers in a concise format a wide range of information, including data on natural resources, federal programs and population and covering topics such as housing, income and religion. Students in particular will discover a useful introduction to the general issue of regional differentiation and variation in the United States.

While the coverage is broad in scope, it is necessarily selective. Some categories of data are now available almost continuously; conversely in other areas, data are updated once in a decade. The primary source for *American Rankings* was the *Statistical Abstract of the United States*.

The information presented endeavors to raise questions, not to have the last word on interpretation of evidence. Skepticism and caution are the watch words for any serious reader of statistical data.

Many existing generalizations about the United States are contested here and challenge the reader to make use of the data to extend his or her own vision of the nation. For example, the United States is often said to be a wealthy and a well-educated nation. The specific data presented in this book allow readers to examine equally the extent to which such general statements may prove inconsistent in different parts of the country.

The tables in the book are arranged into broad subject categories, such as education, agriculture and religion. Each section begins with a brief introduction. Prefacing each table is a short explanation in which statistical indicators are defined and specific cautions against misinterpretation are introduced.

Included in tables, along with data for particular states or metropolitan areas (cities and metropolitan areas are defined in the section on population), are national totals or averages and in some cases state median or middle values (i.e., the states ranking at positions 25 and 26 in the category being measured). The ranking order of the states in a table depends on the topic or item in question. If the topic is land area, for example, Alaska ranks as number one and Rhode Island as number 50.

Data are presented in a form—generally involving the use of percentages and per capita rates—that allows for meaningful comparisons among the states. When states differ by a wide margin on basic variables like population and area, comparisons based on simple counts can be deceptive. If, for example, we rank states by the *number* of residents age 5 to 17 years old, we will produce a listing that closely corresponds to the ranking of states by population. This makes only the trivial point that states with large populations also have many school age residents. If the states are ranked by *percentage* of residents age 5 to 17 years old, however, we obtain a ranking independent of population size that gives a more useful indication of the proportion of each state's population which is school age.

The last section in the book provides a profile of each state highlighting specific data presented in the earlier sections of the book.

The aim of *American Rankings* is to provide useful and accurate information on a range of subjects pertaining to the 50 United States in manner that is both accessible and instructive.

I wish to acknowledge the enormous contribution of all the men and women responsible for the research that lead to the results reported here. Most of these people are employed in the various departments of the federal government. For her good counsel, humor and patience, a special thanks to Eleanora von Dehsen, special projects director at Facts On File. Thanks to Eric Schneider for his ever present support.

—Ellen Meltzer
Brookline, Massachusetts

The New Book of American Rankings

American Rankings

REVISED EDITION

STATE
PROFILES

STATE PROFILES

Profiles of each state indicate the ranking of the state according to 42 separate categories. For example, a comparison of the data for all 50 states and Washington, D.C. ranks Alabama first in number of single families headed by women and 40th in mean elevation.

GEOGRAPHY

Geographically, the United States is a giant among nations, ranking third in total area after Canada and China. The nation spans the continent of North America from east to west and reaches out into the heart of the Pacific, thus incorporating immense geographical variety. The dense settlement of the states of the eastern shore stands in sharp contrast to the sparsity of areas of human habitation separated by vast distances in Alaska and many western states.

The great variety of American lifestyles is based in part on the variety of geographical conditions. In any given state, geographical and other environmental conditions help to determine the range of available occupations and leisure pursuits. The resources of the earth, the air and the water set limits upon what can be done in a given state, and thus provide the framework for the political process of discussion and decision as to what should be done. Natural conditions also have a profound effect on everyday experiences and attitudes. Recognition of the effects of geographical factors on lifestyles has become an increasingly important factor both for families and for economic enterprises faced with relocation decisions.

The tables in this section describe the states as physical entities. They provide a concise overview of the major interactions between inhabitants and environments that set the stage for studying other patterns of variation among the states.

TOTAL AREA

The familiar jumble of sizes and shapes on a map of the United States reminds even the casual observer that no two states are alike. Comparing extremes, it seems that Alaska could be broken up into as many as 487 districts the size of Rhode Island, or into two states of Texas plus one Illinois. The 20 largest states are west of the Mississippi. The 20 smallest states (except Hawaii) lie to the east of or, in the case of Louisiana, astride that river.

National territory increased by nearly 20% when Alaska and Hawaii entered the Union in 1959. The 49th and 50th states are presently the only ones without neighboring borders, but this situation is not historically unique. California, which entered the Union in 1850, was isolated until the entry of Oregon in 1859. Nevada was added as a neighbor to both states in 1864, but this western group remained isolated until the admission of Idaho and Wyoming in 1890 added the final links in a chain of states joining the West Coast to the East.

In the East, state boundary lines are generally irregular; in the West, most state lines are straight. There is a story behind every state line. In the East and South, the political map was fashioned by colonial charters, border disputes and the Indian wars of the 17th and 18th centuries. Arrangements with foreign powers have shaped the borders of many states, including Alaska (purchased from Russia in 1867), Florida (ceded by Spain in 1819), Montana and North Dakota (acquired by treaty with Great Britain in 1818), and the states of the Southwest (acquired from Mexico in the mid-19th century). National issues have also shaped state lines. The politics of slavery helped fix the Kansas-Nebraska border. Efforts to contain Mormon influence led to the formation of Utah. Texas, which after breaking away from Mexico, had claimed the status of an independent nation from 1836 to 1845, received its final form in the give and take of domestic politics.

TABLE: Total Area
DATE: 1990
SOURCE: U.S. Bureau of the Census, *1990 Census of Population and Housing*
DESCRIPTION: Total land and water area of each state and percent of total U.S. area.
UNITED STATES TOTAL: 3,717,522 square miles

Rank	State	Square miles	Percent of total area
1	Alaska	615,230	17
2	Texas	267,277	7
3	California	158,869	4
4	Montana	147,046	4
5	New Mexico	121,598	3

Rank	State	Square miles	Percent of total area
6	Arizona	114,006	3
7	Nevada	110,567	3
8	Colorado	104,100	3
9	Wyoming	97,819	3
10	Oregon	97,093	3
11	Michigan	96,705	3
12	Minnesota	86,943	2
13	Utah	84,904	2
14	Idaho	83,574	2
15	Kansas	82,282	2
16	Nebraska	77,359	2
17	South Dakota	77,121	2
18	North Dakota	70,704	2
19	Washington	70,637	2
20	Oklahoma	69,903	2
21	Missouri	69,709	2
22	Wisconsin	65,500	2
23	Florida	59,988	2
24	Georgia	58,977	2
25	Illinois	57,918	2
26	Iowa	56,276	2
27	New York	53,989	1
28	Arkansas	53,182	1
29	North Carolina	52,672	1
30	Alabama	52,237	1
31	Louisiana	49,650	1
32	Mississippi	48,286	1
33	Pennsylvania	45,759	1
34	Ohio	44,828	1
35	Virginia	42,326	1
36	Tennessee	42,145	1
37	Kentucky	40,411	1
38	Indiana	36,420	1
39	Maine	33,741	1
40	South Carolina	31,189	1
41	West Virginia	24,232	1
42	Maryland	12,297	0
43	Vermont	9,615	0
44	New Hampshire	9,283	0
45	Massachusetts	9,241	0
46	New Jersey	8,215	0
47	Hawaii	6,459	0
48	Connecticut	5,544	0
49	Delaware	2,397	0
50	Rhode Island	1,231	0
51	Washington, DC	68	0

LAND AREA

Twelve states contain half the nation's land. Alaska, Texas, California and Montana total over 30% of the land area of the United States; the next eight largest states another 20%. Forty percent of the United States is comprised of 12 contiguous western states: Texas, California, Montana, New Mexico, Arizona, Nevada, Colorado, Wyoming, Oregon, Idaho, Utah and Washington.

Some states that rank high in total area drop dramatically in ranking if only land area is considered. Michigan, which ranks 11th in total area—water and land combined—drops to 22nd in land area exclusive of water. Over 40% of Michigan is water.

TABLE: Land Area
DATE: 1990
SOURCE: U.S. Bureau of the Census, *1990 Census of Population and Housing*
DESCRIPTION: Total land area of each state in square miles and percent of total U.S. area.
UNITED STATES TOTAL: 3,536,338 square miles

Rank	State	Square miles	Percent of total U.S area
1	Alaska	570,374	16.10
2	Texas	261,914	7.40
3	California	155,973	4.40
4	Montana	145,556	4.00
5	New Mexico	121,364	3.40
6	Arizona	113,642	3.20
7	Nevada	109,806	3.00
8	Colorado	103,729	2.90
9	Wyoming	97,105	2.70
10	Oregon	96,002	2.70
11	Idaho	82,751	2.30
12	Utah	82,168	2.30
13	Kansas	81,823	2.30
14	Minnesota	79,617	2.30
15	Nebraska	76,878	1.00
16	South Dakota	75,896	2.10
17	North Dakota	68,994	2.00
18	Missouri	68,898	1.90
19	Oklahoma	68,679	1.90
20	Washington	66,581	1.90
21	Georgia	57,919	1.60
22	Michigan	56,809	1.60
23	Iowa	55,875	1.60
24	Illinois	55,593	1.60
25	Wisconsin	54,314	1.50
26	Florida	53,997	1.50
27	Arkansas	52,075	1.50
28	Alabama	50,750	1.40
29	North Carolina	48,718	1.40
30	New York	47,224	1.30
31	Mississippi	46,914	1.30
32	Pennsylvania	44,820	0.33
33	Louisiana	43,566	0.50
34	Tennessee	41,219	0.50
35	Ohio	40,953	1.20
36	Kentucky	39,732	1.10
37	Virginia	39,598	1.10
38	Indiana	35,870	1.00

Rank	State	Square miles	Percent of total U.S area
39	Maine	30,865	0.90
40	South Carolina	30,111	0.90
41	West Virginia	24,087	0.70
42	Maryland	9,775	0.30
43	Vermont	9,249	0.30
44	New Hampshire	8,969	0.30
45	Massachusetts	7,838	0.20
46	New Jersey	7,419	0.20
47	Hawaii	6,423	0.20
48	Connecticut	4,845	0.10
49	Delaware	1,955	0.05
50	Rhode Island	1,045	0.03

TOTAL WATER AREAS

Surface water resources are an important element in the economic geography of the states. Centers of commerce are found on the coasts and around the Great Lakes, but also along such inland waterways as the Mississippi and Ohio rivers and on the routes of the great 19th-century canals, of which the Erie Canal in New York is the foremost example. Natural and artificial lakes are the sites of many resort areas and also furnish water for metropolitan centers. The scarcity of water looms as an important constraint on the further development of the American Southwest. Plans to carry the waters of northern California to the booming but thirsty cities of the southern part of the state by means of a grand canal have touched off political disputes involving sectional interests as well as the issues of environmental integrity versus economic development.

When the states are ranked by percentage of total area occupied by open water, the top of the list is dominated by states along the eastern coast and in the district of the glacial lakes along the northern border: Michigan and Wisconsin eastward. The inland waters of the 10 East Coast states at the head of the list include extensive estuaries and other coastal waters.

The complex interplay of weather and geology that determines the amount of surface water in a given state is suggested by the geographical variety at the bottom of the list. Here, mountainous West Virginia and Hawaii, with its volcanic terrain, join desert states and states of the Central Plains.

In this table coastal, Great Lakes and inland waters are combined in determining the total water area of each state.

TABLE: Total Water Areas
DATE: 1990
SOURCE: U.S. Bureau of the Census, *1990 Census of Population and Housing*, series

DESCRIPTION: Total water area of each state in square miles and percent of total state area.
UNITED STATES TOTAL: 181,184 square miles

Rank	State	Square miles	Percent of total state area
1	Michigan	39,896	41.3
2	Maryland	2,522	20.5
3	Delaware	442	18.4
4	Wisconsin	11,186	17.1
5	Massachusetts	1,403	15.2
6	Rhode Island	186	15.1
7	Connecticut	699	12.6
8	New York	6,765	12.5
9	Louisiana	6,084	12.3
10	Washington, DC	7	10.3
11	Florida	5,991	10.0
12	New Jersey	796	9.7
13	Ohio	3,875	8.6
14	Maine	2,876	8.5
15	Minnesota	7,326	8.4
16	North Carolina	3,954	7.5
17	Alaska	44,856	7.3
18	Virginia	2,728	6.4
19	Washington	4,056	5.7
20	Illinois	2,325	4.0
21	Vermont	366	3.8
22	South Carolina	1,078	3.5
23	New Hampshire	314	3.4
24	Utah	2,736	3.2
25	Alabama	1,487	2.8
26	Mississippi	1,372	2.8
27	North Dakota	1,710	2.4
28	Tennessee	926	2.2
29	Arkansas	1,107	2.1
30	Pennsylvania	939	2.1
31	Texas	5,363	2.0
32	California	2,896	1.8
33	Georgia	1,058	1.8
34	Oklahoma	1,224	1.8
35	Kentucky	679	1.7
36	South Dakota	1,225	1.6
37	Indiana	550	1.5
38	Missouri	811	1.2
39	Oregon	1,091	1.1
40	Montana	1,490	1.0
41	Idaho	823	1.0
42	Wyoming	714	0.7
43	Iowa	401	0.7
44	Nevada	761	0.7
45	Nebraska	481	0.6
46	West Virginia	145	0.6
47	Kansas	459	0.6
48	Hawaii	36	0.6
49	Colorado	371	0.4
50	Arizona	364	0.3
51	New Mexico	234	0.2

TOTAL INLAND WATER AREA

Total inland waters are found in several forms: lakes, rivers, canals, streams and ponds; coastal waters and the Great Lakes are excluded. Swamps, bogs, marshlands and wetlands are classified as land area and are not included under the inland water designation.

TABLE: Total Inland Water Area
DATE: 1990
SOURCE: U.S. Bureau of the Census, *1990 Census of Population and Housing*
DESCRIPTION: Total inland water area of each state in square miles and percent of total area of the state.
UNITED STATES TOTAL*: 78,641 square miles

Rank	State	Square miles	Percent of total area of the state
1	Rhode Island	168	13.6
2	Louisiana	4,153	8.4
3	Florida	4,683	7.8
4	North Carolina	3,954	7.5
5	Maine	2,263	6.7
6	Maryland	680	5.5
7	Minnesota	4,780	5.5
8	Massachusetts	424	4.6
9	New Jersey	371	4.5
10	Vermont	366	3.8
11	New York	1,888	3.5
12	New Hampshire	314	3.4
13	South Carolina	1,006	3.2
14	Utah	2,736	3.2
15	Delaware	71	3.0
16	Connecticut	161	2.9
17	Alaska	17,501	2.8
18	Wisconsin	1,831	2.8
19	North Dakota	1,710	2.4
20	Virginia	1,000	2.4
21	Tennessee	926	2.2
22	Washington	1,545	2.2
23	Arkansas	1,107	2.1
24	Texas	4,959	1.9
25	Alabama	968	1.9
26	Michigan	1,704	1.8
27	Oklahoma	1,224	1.8
28	Georgia	1,011	1.7
29	California	2,674	1.7
30	Kentucky	679	1.7
31	Mississippi	781	1.6
32	South Dakota	1,225	1.6
33	Illinois	750	1.3
34	Missouri	811	1.2
35	Oregon	1,050	1.1
36	Montana	1,490	1.0
37	Idaho	823	1.0
38	Indiana	315	0.9
39	Ohio	376	0.8
40	Wyoming	714	0.7
41	Iowa	401	0.7
42	Nevada	761	0.7
43	Nebraska	481	0.6
44	West Virginia	145	0.6
45	Kansas	459	0.6
46	Hawaii	36	0.6
47	Pennsylvania	190	0.4
48	Colorado	371	0.4
49	Arizona	364	0.3
50	New Mexico	234	0.2

*Includes Washington, DC

COASTAL WATERS

Alaska incorporates over half of the nation's coastal waters. Puget Sound is an example of coastal waters and makes up the bulk of the Washington state's 2,511 square miles of coastal waters. The measurement is used by the National Oceanic and Atmospheric Agency (NOAA) for coastal areas where water goes into land, for example, bays, sounds and inlets.

TABLE: Coastal Waters
DATE: 1990
SOURCE: U.S. Bureau of the Census, *1990 Census of Population and Housing*
DESCRIPTION: Coastline of states and percent of total U.S. coastline. Table excludes Hawaii. Percentage may not add up to 100% because of rounding.
UNITED STATES TOTAL: 42,491 square miles

Rank	State	Square miles	Percent of U.S. coastline
1	Alaska	27,355	64.38
2	Washington	2,511	5.91
3	Louisiana	1,931	4.54
4	Maryland	1,842	4.34
5	Virginia	1,728	4.07
6	Florida	1,308	3.08
7	Massachusetts	979	2.30
8	New York	976	2.30
9	Maine	613	1.44
10	Mississippi	591	1.39
11	Connecticut	538	1.27
12	Alabama	519	1.22
13	New Jersey	425	1.00
14	Texas	404	0.95
15	Delaware	371	0.87
16	California	222	0.52
17	South Carolina	72	0.17

Rank	State	Square miles	Percent of U.S. coastline
18	Georgia	47	0.11
19	Oregon	41	0.10
20	Rhode Island	18	0.04

HIGHEST POINT IN THE STATE

The highest points in the United States all occur west of the Mississippi River. Mount Mitchell in North Carolina, ranked number 16, is the highest point in the East. Florida is last, its highest point of elevation 345 feet in Walton County.

TABLE: Highest Point in the State
DATE: 1989
SOURCE: U.S. Geological Survey, *Elevations and Distances in the United States*
DESCRIPTION: Highest point in the state. States report either highest county or highest point.

Rank	State	Highest point	Elevation (feet)
1	Alaska	Mount McKinley	20,320
2	California	Mount Whitney	14,494
3	Colorado	Mt. Elbert	14,433
4	Washington	Mount Rainier	14,410
5	Wyoming	Gannett Peak	13,804
6	Hawaii	Puu Wekiu	13,796
7	Utah	Kings Peak	13,528
8	New Mexico	Wheeler Peak	13,161
9	Nevada	Boundary Peak	13,140
10	Montana	Granite Peak	12,799
11	Idaho	Borah Peak	12,662
12	Arizona	Humphreys Peak	12,633
13	Oregon	Mount Hood	11,239
14	Texas	Guadalupe Peak	8,749
15	South Dakota	Harney Peak	7,242
16	North Carolina	Mount Mitchell	6,684
17	Tennessee	Clingmans Dome	6,643
18	New Hampshire	Mount Washington	6,288
19	Virginia	Mount Rogers	5,729
20	Nebraska	Johnson Twp., Kimball County	5,424
21	New York	Mount Marcy	5,344
22	Maine	Mount Katahdin	5,267
23	Oklahoma	Black Mesa	4,973
24	West Virginia	Spruce Knob	4,861
25	Georgia	Brasstown Bald	4,784
26	Vermont	Mount Mansfield	4,393
27	Kentucky	Black Mountain	4,139
28	Kansas	Mount Sunflower	4,039
29	South Carolina	Sassafras Mountain	3,560
30	North Dakota	White Butte, Slope County	3,506
31	Massachusetts	Mount Greylock	3,487
32	Maryland	Backbone Mountain	3,360
33	Pennsylvania	Mount Davis	3,213
34	Arkansas	Magazine Mountain	2,753
35	Alabama	Cheaha Mountain	2,405
36	Connecticut	Mt. Frissell	2,380
37	Minnesota	Eagle Mountain	2,301
38	Michigan	Mount Arvon	1,979
39	Wisconsin	Timms Hill	1,951
40	New Jersey	High Point	1,803
41	Missouri	Taum Sauk Mountain	1,772
42	Iowa	Osceola County	1,670
43	Ohio	Campbell Hill	1,549
44	Indiana	Franklin Twp., Wayne County	1,257
45	Illinois	Charles Mound	1,235
46	Rhode Island	Jerimoth Hill	812
47	Mississippi	Woodall Mountain	806
48	Louisiana	Driskill Mountain	535
49	Delaware	New Castle County	442
50	Florida	Walton County	345

LOWEST POINT IN THE STATE

The top-ranking lowest points in the United States are found in the East and Midwest, except for Death Valley in California and the Colorado River in Colorado and Arizona. The low points are the mirror opposite of the high points, which are all located in the West. Death Valley is in a category by itself at −282 feet below sea level, followed by the city of New Orleans in Louisiana at −8 feet below sea level.

TABLE: Lowest Point in the State
DATE: 1989
SOURCE: U.S. Geological Survey, *Elevations and Distances in the United States*
DESCRIPTION: Lowest point in the state.

Rank	State	Lowest point	Elevation (feet)*
1	California	Death Valley	-282
2	Louisiana	New Orleans	-8
3	Alabama	Gulf of Mexico	0
4	Alaska	Pacific Ocean	0
5	Connecticut	Long Island Sound	0
6	Delaware	Atlantic Ocean	0
7	Florida	Atlantic Ocean	0
8	Georgia	Atlantic Ocean	0
9	Hawaii	Pacific Ocean	0
10	Maine	Atlantic Ocean	0
11	Maryland	Atlantic Ocean	0
12	Massachusetts	Atlantic Ocean	0

Rank	State	Lowest point	Elevation (feet)*
13	Mississippi	Gulf of Mexico	0
14	New Hampshire	Atlantic Ocean	0
15	New Jersey	Atlantic Ocean	0
16	New York	Atlantic Ocean	0
17	North Carolina	Atlantic Ocean	0
18	Oregon	Pacific Ocean	0
19	Pennsylvania	Delaware River	0
20	Rhode Island	Atlantic Ocean	0
21	South Carolina	Atlantic Ocean	0
22	Texas	Gulf of Mexico	0
23	Virginia	Atlantic Ocean	0
24	Washington	Pacific Ocean	0
25	Arkansas	Ouachita River	55
26	Arizona	Colorado River	70
27	Vermont	Lake Champlain	95
28	Tennessee	Mississippi River	178
29	Missouri	St. Francis River	230
30	West Virginia	Potomac River	240
31	Kentucky	Mississippi River	257
32	Illinois	Mississippi River	279
33	Oklahoma	Little River	289
34	Indiana	Ohio River	320
35	Ohio	Ohio River	455
36	Nevada	Colorado River	479
37	Iowa	Mississippi River	480
38	Michigan	Lake Erie	571
39	Wisconsin	Lake Michigan	579
40	Minnesota	Lake Superior	600
41	Kansas	Verdigris River	679
42	Idaho	Snake River	710
43	North Dakota	Red River	750
44	Nebraska	Missouri River	840
45	South Dakota	Big Stone Lake	966
46	Montana	Kootenai River	1,800
47	Utah	Beaverdam Wash	2,000
48	New Mexico	Red Bluff Reservoir	2,842
49	Wyoming	Belle Fourche River	3,099
50	Colorado	Arkansas River	3,350

*Zero equals sea level.

MEAN ELEVATION

Mean elevation figures smooth out sharp local variations within the states. Consider the case of California. Ranked 11th overall, California includes both the highest point in the 48 contiguous states (Mt. Whitney) and the lowest point in the entire nation (Death Valley). The highest point in all 50 states is in Alaska (Mt. McKinley), but the state also includes large coastal areas at sea level and thus ranks only 15th in mean elevation. Louisiana is the only state except California with territory below sea level (the city of New Orleans, −8 ft.). It is also a relatively flat state, with no elevation above 535 ft., and thus it is found at the bottom of

this list along with the two lowest and flattest states in the nation: Florida and Delaware.

The top states on the list all include parts of the Rockies. The first five are over one mile high on the average. Volcanic Hawaii stands high on the list, but the only eastern states found in the top half are West Virginia and Pennsylvania, with their Appalachian mountain ranges.

TABLE: Mean Elevation
DATE: 1990
SOURCE: U.S. Geological Survey, *Elevations and Distances in the United States*
DESCRIPTION: Mean elevation for each state.

Rank	State	Mean elevation (feet)
1	Colorado	6,800
2	Wyoming	6,700
3	Utah	6,100
4	New Mexico	5,700
5	Nevada	5,500
6	Idaho	5,000
7	Arizona	4,100
8	Montana	3,400
9	Oregon	3,300
10	Hawaii	3,030
11	California	2,900
12	Nebraska	2,600
13	South Dakota	2,200
14	Kansas	2,000
15	Alaska	1,900
16	North Dakota	1,900
17	Texas	1,700
18	Washington	1,700
19	West Virginia	1,500
20	Oklahoma	1,300
21	Minnesota	1,200
22	Iowa	1,100
23	Pennsylvania	1,100
24	Wisconsin	1,050
25	New Hampshire	1,000
26	New York	1,000
27	Vermont	1,000
28	Virginia	950
29	Michigan	900
30	Tennessee	900
31	Ohio	850
32	Missouri	800
33	Kentucky	750
34	Indiana	700
35	North Carolina	700
36	Arkansas	650
37	Georgia	600
38	Illinois	600
39	Maine	600
40	Alabama	500
41	Connecticut	500

Rank	State	Mean elevation (feet)
42	Massachusetts	500
43	Maryland	350
44	South Carolina	350
45	Mississippi	300
46	New Jersey	250
47	Rhode Island	200
48	Washington, DC	150
49	Florida	100
50	Louisiana	100
51	Delaware	60

INDIAN LANDS

The native peoples who once dominated this continent now control only about 2% of the land, and this land stands under the legal jurisdiction of the U.S. Bureau of Indian Affairs. Established under hundreds of specific treaties, Indian lands are scattered across 37 states. The affairs of Native Alaskans, organized in corporations that are receiving distributions of federal lands, are managed separately under the Native Claims Settlement Act of 1971.

The principal Indian reservations are in the West, a geographical legacy of numerous campaigns of forced resettlement. The most radical of these campaigns (mandated by Congress under the terms of the Indian Removal Act of 1830) transferred all Indians east of the Mississippi River to lands in the West. The extent of these lands was in turn reduced following a series of military operations that culminated in the battle of Wounded Knee, in 1890.

The largest reservation belongs to the Navajo. It occupies over 20,000 square miles in parts of Arizona, New Mexico and Utah. Indian lands make up 27% of the territory of Arizona, 10% of New Mexico and South Dakota, 5% of Montana (where Custer was defeated at the battle of Little Bighorn in 1876), and much smaller fractions elsewhere.

About 80% of the Indian lands are owned collectively by tribal authorities. Almost all of the Indian lands in Arizona and 90% of those in New Mexico are owned in common. Federal efforts to turn Indians into farmers, under the Dawes Act of 1887, were finally abandoned in 1934, but not before 20% of present Indian lands had been carved out and assigned to individual proprietors. Individual ownership is predominant in Oklahoma. Montana (with 60% individual ownership) and South Dakota (where the two forms are about evenly split) stand between the extremes.

TABLE: Indian Lands
DATE: 1990
SOURCE: Bureau of Indian Affairs
DESCRIPTION: Lands under jurisdiction of the Bureau of Indian Affairs (BIA), for 34 states. Percent may not add up to 100% because of rounding.
UNITED STATES TOTAL: 56,611,472 acres

Rank	State	Acres	Percent of total BIA land
1	Arizona	20,178,235	35.64
2	New Mexico	8,152,895	14.40
3	Montana	5,551,343	9.81
4	South Dakota	4,522,324	7.99
5	Washington	2,568,791	4.54
6	Utah	2,319,373	4.10
7	Nebraska	2,185,211	3.86
8	Wyoming	2,010,929	3.55
9	Nevada	1,230,562	2.17
10	Oklahoma	1,099,301	1.94
11	Alaska	970,873	1.71
12	Idaho	969,454	1.71
13	North Dakota	841,918	1.49
14	Minnesota	829,578	1.47
15	Colorado	798,048	1.41
16	Oregon	795,797	1.41
17	California	587,626	1.04
18	Wisconsin	418,443	0.74
19	Maine	163,570	0.29
20	Florida	154,208	0.27
21	New York	118,199	0.21
22	North Carolina	56,621	0.10
23	Kansas	30,982	0.05
24	Michigan	23,687	0.04
25	Mississippi	20,679	0.04
26	Texas	4,629	0.01
27	Iowa	3,550	0.01
28	Rhode Island	1,800	less than 0.01
29	Connecticut	1,638	less than 0.01
30	Louisiana	415	less than 0.01
31	Missouri	374	less than 0.01
32	Alabama	213	less than 0.01
33	Massachusetts	157	less than 0.01
34	Arkansas	3	less than 0.01

FEDERALLY OWNED LAND

The federal government holds title to almost 29% of all land in the United States. The rest of the land is divided among private interests, state and local governments and native Americans. In 1979, Alaska was almost exclusively a federal preserve; nonfederal Alaska was no larger than the state of Maryland (ranked 42nd see Total Area table on page 3). This situation has changed considerably, as distributions of land to state government and native corporations has occurred. With the drop in federal ownership, nonfederal Alaska is closer to the size of Texas.

Federal holdings are concentrated in the West. This present pattern of federal holdings was established early in the 20th century under President Theodore Roosevelt. Surveys of the western lands by John Wesley Powell, published in 1879, had shown that traditional farming patterns were unsuited to conditions in much of the area. Under Roosevelt land sales to private individuals, as provided under the Homestead Act of 1862, were suspended. The new federal policy, guided by presidential aide and prominent conservationist Gifford Pinchot, called for retaining title to public lands and introducing coordinated resource management. Private use of federal land was regulated under leasing arrangements. The scope of federal resource management tasks has since expanded, and other policy aims have been developed, such as preservation of forests, wildlife and endangered species and the provision of sites under national defense.

A dramatic shift in the ideas that have guided federal land policy for over 75 years is under way. This new course advocates the sale of federal land to private concerns, allowing short-term revenue to the Treasury and increased long-run increases in national output by more efficiently managing the land. There have been similar arguments made in regard to wildlife and endangered species policies, which historically have inhibited the full utilization of the land for commercial purposes.

TABLE: Federally Owned Land
DATE: 1991
SOURCE: U.S. General Services Administration, *Inventory Report on Real Property Owned by the United States Throughout the World*, annual
DESCRIPTION: Federally owned land and percent of total state land area federally owned.

Rank		Total (thousand acres)	Percent of total area
	United States	649,346	28.6
1	Nevada	58,265	82.9
2	Alaska	248,021	67.9
3	Utah	33,661	63.9
4	Idaho	32,614	61.6
5	Oregon	32,291	52.4
6	Wyoming	30,477	48.9
7	Arizona	34,308	47.2
8	California	44,707	44.6
9	Colorado	24,154	36.3
10	New Mexico	25,203	32.4
11	Washington	12,080	28.3
12	Montana	26,142	28.0
13	Washington, DC	10	26.1
14	Hawaii	634	15.5
15	New Hampshire	734	12.7
16	Michigan	4,589	12.6
17	Minnesota	5,367	10.5
18	Wisconsin	3,537	10.1
19	Florida	3,114	9.0
20	Arkansas	2,762	8.2
21	West Virginia	1,028	6.7
22	North Carolina	1,970	6.3
23	Virginia	1,597	6.3
24	Vermont	358	6.0
25	South Dakota	2,806	5.7
26	Missouri	2,096	4.7

Rank		Total (thousand acres)	Percent of total area
27	Mississippi	1,306	4.3
28	Kentucky	1,080	4.2
29	North Dakota	1,879	4.2
30	Georgia	1,488	4.0
31	South Carolina	722	3.7
32	Tennessee	994	3.7
33	Alabama	1,075	3.3
34	New Jersey	149	3.1
35	Maryland	187	3.0
36	Illinois	961	2.7
37	Louisiana	745	2.6
38	Delaware	27	2.2
39	Pennsylvania	608	2.1
40	Indiana	401	1.7
41	Oklahoma	705	1.6
42	Nebraska	710	1.4
43	Texas	2,245	1.3
44	Massachusetts	66	1.3
45	Ohio	342	1.3
46	Iowa	336	0.9
47	Kansas	422	0.8
48	Maine	155	0.8
49	New York	209	0.7
50	Rhode Island	2	0.3
51	Connecticut	6	0.2

Rural Land

In the seven Great Plains states, Nebraska, Kansas, Iowa, Texas, Oklahoma, North Dakota and South Dakota, over 90% of the nonfederally owned land is rural. Rural land is defined as: land for cultivating crops; land for pasture animals; land for feeding cattle; and forest land. Rural land accounts for over 70% of land use in the United States.

TABLE: Rural Land
DATE: 1987
SOURCES: U.S. Dept. of Agriculture, Soil Conservation Service, and Iowa State University, Statistical Laboratory, *Statistical Bulletin No. 790, Summary Report, 1987 National Resources Inventory*, December 1989
DESCRIPTION: Total nonfederally owned rural land and percent of total state area in nonfederally owned rural land. Table excludes Washington, DC and Alaska.

Rank		Total area (thousand acres)	Percent of total area
	United States	1,406,851	73
1	Nebraska	46,967	95
2	Kansas	49,592	94
3	Iowa	33,699	94

Rank		Total area (thousand acres)	Percent of total area
4	Texas	156,768	92
5	Oklahoma	40,715	91
6	North Dakota	41,013	91
7	South Dakota	44,403	90
8	Alabama	29,591	89
9	Maine	19,009	89
10	Illinois	32,000	89
11	Indiana	20,522	89
12	Missouri	39,491	89
13	West Virginia	13,695	88
14	Kentucky	22,799	88
15	Mississippi	26,884	88
16	Vermont	5,348	87
17	New York	27,297	87
18	Pennsylvania	25,027	86
19	Ohio	22,762	86
20	Wisconsin	30,820	86
21	Georgia	32,289	86
22	Tennessee	23,090	86
23	Hawaii	3,500	85
24	Arkansas	28,672	84
25	Minnesota	44,941	83
26	South Carolina	16,363	82
27	Louisiana	25,016	82
28	Virginia	21,150	81
29	Michigan	30,130	80
30	Delaware	1,048	80
31	North Carolina	26,135	78
32	New Hampshire	4,599	77
33	Maryland	5,111	76
34	Connecticut	2,362	74
35	Florida	27,059	72
36	Massachusetts	3,786	71
37	Montana	64,682	69
38	Washington	28,383	65
39	New Jersey	3,239	65
40	New Mexico	50,445	65
41	Rhode Island	500	64
42	Colorado	40,945	61
43	Arizona	40,878	56
44	Wyoming	32,075	51
45	California	49,033	48
46	Oregon	27,977	45
47	Idaho	19,152	36
48	Utah	15,975	29
49	Nevada	9,916	14

CROPLAND

Cultivated or cropland accounts for 22% of total land usage of nonfederally owned land. Over 30,000 acres of land are under cultivation in Texas, but that accounts for only 19% of the state's nonfederally owned land.

TABLE: Cropland
DATE: 1987
SOURCES: U.S. Dept. of Agriculture, Soil Conservation Service, and Iowa State University, *Statistical Laboratory, Statistical Bulletin No.790, Summary Report, 1987 National Resources Inventory, December 1989*
DESCRIPTION: Total nonfederally owned cropland and percent of total state area in nonfederally owned cropland. Table excludes Washington, DC and Alaska.

Rank		Total area (thousand acres)	Percent of total area
	United States	422,416	22
1	Iowa	27,031	75
2	Illinois	25,121	70
3	North Dakota	28,064	62
4	Indiana	13,930	60
5	Kansas	29,119	55
6	Ohio	12,537	47
7	Minnesota	22,990	43
8	Nebraska	20,601	42
9	Delaware	521	40
10	South Dakota	17,819	36
11	Missouri	15,090	34
12	Wisconsin	11,671	32
13	Maryland	1,795	27
14	Oklahoma	11,557	26
15	Michigan	9,484	25
16	Arkansas	8,182	24
17	Mississippi	7,078	23
18	Kentucky	5,818	22
19	Tennessee	5,765	21
20	Louisiana	6,484	21
21	Pennsylvania	5,774	20
22	North Carolina	6,548	19
23	Montana	17,881	19
24	Texas	31,944	19
25	New York	5,774	18
26	Washington	7,758	18
27	South Carolina	3,371	17
28	Georgia	6,307	17
29	Colorado	10,967	16
30	New Jersey	673	13
31	Alabama	4,210	13
32	Virginia	3,309	13
33	Idaho	6,532	12
34	Vermont	653	11
35	California	10,209	10
36	Florida	3,592	10
37	Hawaii	348	8
38	Connecticut	239	7
39	Oregon	4,348	7
40	West Virginia	1,053	7
41	Massachusetts	291	5
42	Maine	943	4
43	Wyoming	2,362	4

Rank		Total area (thousand acres)	Percent of total area
44	Utah	2,002	4
45	New Mexico	2,297	3
46	Rhode Island	22	3
47	New Hampshire	163	3
48	Arizona	1,306	2
49	Nevada	889	1

Rank		Total area (thousand acres)	Percent of total area
23	Maryland	2,415	36
24	Hawaii	1,419	34
25	Florida	12,088	32
26	Washington	12,634	29
27	Delaware	357	27
28	Minnesota	13,952	26
29	Missouri	10,959	25
30	Ohio	6,426	24
31	Oregon	11,857	19
32	Indiana	3,698	16
33	California	15,073	15
34	Oklahoma	6,505	15
35	Illinois	3,447	10
36	Idaho	4,071	8
37	Arizona	4,912	7
38	Colorado	4,079	6
39	New Mexico	4,685	6
40	Utah	3,194	6
41	Montana	5,253	6
42	Texas	9,476	6
43	Iowa	1,841	5
44	Wyoming	984	2
45	Nebraska	728	1
46	Kansas	681	1
47	South Dakota	565	1
48	North Dakota	428	1
49	Nevada	356	1

FORESTLAND

Maine ranks first in percentage of state area in forestland. California is 48th. Yet forestland accounts for approximately equal acreage in both states. New England is the most heavily forested region in the country on a percentage basis, although the total amount of forest here is but a small part of the national total.

TABLE: Forestland
DATE: 1987
SOURCES: U.S. Dept. of Agriculture, Soil Conservation Service, and Iowa State University, Statistical Laboratory, *Statistical Bulletin No.790, Summary Report, 1987 National Resources Inventory, December 1989*
DESCRIPTION: Total nonfederally owned forestland and percent of total state area in nonfederally owned forestland. Table excludes Washington, DC, and Alaska.

Rank		Total area (thousand acres)	Percent of total area
	United States	393,904	20
1	Maine	16,933	80
2	New Hampshire	4,052	68
3	Vermont	4,184	68
4	West Virginia	10,466	67
5	Alabama	21,017	64
6	Georgia	21,860	58
7	Connecticut	1,797	56
8	South Carolina	11,073	56
9	Massachusetts	2,937	55
10	Pennsylvania	15,398	53
11	New York	16,650	53
12	Virginia	13,622	52
13	Rhode Island	404	52
14	Mississippi	15,443	51
15	North Carolina	16,528	49
16	Tennessee	11,601	43
17	Arkansas	14,268	42
18	Louisiana	12,736	42
19	Michigan	15,483	41
20	Kentucky	10,054	39
21	New Jersey	1,890	38
22	Wisconsin	13,428	37

TOTAL AREA OF NATIONAL FORESTLANDS

President Theodore Roosevelt inaugurated the National Forest System in 1905, and he set up the U.S. Forest Service to administer it. Today there are 56 National Forests, which are separate and distinct from the national and state parks system. These lands are under the jurisdiction of the U.S. Department of Agriculture which uses them for research and experimentation as well as public recreation. Six states have no national forests: Delaware, Iowa, Maryland, Massachusetts, New Jersey and Rhode Island. The table below includes both publicly and privately owned land within the forest.

TABLE: Total Area of the National Forestlands
DATE: 1991
SOURCE: U.S. Forest Service, *Land Areas of the National Forest System*, annual
DESCRIPTION: Total publicly and privately owned land

within authorized boundaries of national forests and
percent of total national forestland.
UNITED STATES TOTAL: 231,502,000 acres

Rank	State	Total area (thousand acres)	Percent of total national forest
1	California	24,401	11
2	Alaska	24,345	11
3	Idaho	21,674	9
4	Montana	19,102	8
5	Oregon	17,504	8
6	Colorado	16,037	7
7	Arizona	11,887	5
8	New Mexico	10,367	4
9	Washington	10,061	4
10	Wyoming	9,704	4
11	Utah	9,186	4
12	Nevada	6,275	3
13	Minnesota	5,467	2
14	Michigan	4,895	2
15	Arkansas	3,490	2
16	Virginia	3,223	1
17	North Carolina	3,165	1
18	Missouri	3,082	1
19	South Dakota	2,352	1
20	Mississippi	2,310	1
21	Kentucky	2,102	1
22	Wisconsin	2,023	1
23	Texas	1,994	1
24	West Virginia	1,863	1
25	Georgia	1,846	1
26	South Carolina	1,376	1
27	Alabama	1,288	1
28	Florida	1,254	1
29	Tennessee	1,212	1
30	North Dakota	1,106	less than 1%
31	Louisiana	1,022	less than 1%
32	Illinois	840	less than 1%
33	Ohio	833	less than 1%
34	New Hampshire	825	less than 1%
35	Vermont	816	less than 1%
36	Pennsylvania	744	less than 1%
37	Indiana	644	less than 1%
38	Oklahoma	465	less than 1%
39	Nebraska	442	less than 1%
40	Kansas	116	less than 1%
41	Maine	93	less than 1%
42	New York	13	less than 1%
43	Connecticut	Less than 500 acres	less than 1%
44	Hawaii	Less than 500 acres	less than 1%
45	Delaware	0	0
46	Iowa	0	0
47	Maryland	0	0
48	Massachusetts	0	0
49	New Jersey	0	0
50	Rhode Island	0	0

STATE PARKS AND RECREATION AREAS

At the turn of the century, progressives, responding to the closing of the frontier and to the environmental inefficiencies and damages resulting from prevailing patterns of private land use, pressed for greater public control over land. Conservationists successfully promoted federal legislation that permanently removed public lands from the marketplace by creating the National Park Service. States, too, protected lands from development. State parks and recreation areas are administered independently by each state, and total over 11 million acres across the nation.

TABLE: State Parks and Recreation Areas
DATE: 1991
SOURCE: National Association of State Park Directors, Tallahassee, FL, *Annual Information Exchange*
DESCRIPTION: Total area of state parks and recreation areas and percentage of total area of the state.
UNITED STATES TOTAL: 11,148,000 acres

Rank	State	Total (thousand acres)	Percent of total area of the state
1	New Jersey	303	6.30
2	Connecticut	172	5.49
3	Massachusetts	273	5.42
4	Maryland	226	3.58
5	Vermont	90	0.02
6	West Virginia	202	0.03
7	California	1,314	0.03
8	Rhode Island	9	0.03
9	Florida	444	0.04
10	Illinois	405	1.13
11	Delaware	13	0.20
12	Pennsylvania	277	0.96
13	Alaska	3,169	0.87
14	New York	260	0.85
15	Ohio	208	0.79
16	Michigan	264	0.72
17	Hawaii	25	0.61
18	Washington	241	0.56
19	New Hampshire	31	0.54
20	Tennessee	133	0.50
21	Colorado	307	0.46
22	Minnesota	231	0.45
23	North Carolina	134	0.43
24	South Carolina	80	0.41
25	Wisconsin	139	0.40
26	Maine	75	0.38
27	Texas	499	0.30
28	Nebraska	142	0.29
29	Missouri	117	0.27
30	Indiana	57	0.24

Rank	State	Total (thousand acres)	Percent of total area of the state	Rank	State	Total (thousand acres)	Percent of total area of the state
31	Virginia	59	0.23	41	Alabama	50	0.15
32	Iowa	82	0.23	42	Oregon	90	0.15
33	Nevada	142	0.20	43	Arkansas	47	0.14
34	Wyoming	120	0.19	44	Louisiana	39	0.13
35	South Dakota	92	0.19	45	Idaho	42	0.08
36	Utah	97	0.18	46	Mississippi	23	0.08
37	Oklahoma	77	0.18	47	Arizona	42	0.06
38	Kentucky	42	0.16	48	Kansas	30	0.06
39	New Mexico	123	0.16	49	North Dakota	19	0.04
40	Georgia	57	0.15	50	Montana	32	0.03

CLIMATE

Although the 48 contiguous states all lie in the Temperate Zone, the variety of climates found here would guarantee that some of the most severe as well as some of the most pleasant weather conditions in the world lie within the American experience—even if arctic Alaska and sub-tropical Hawaii were not members of the Union. Contrasts between warm and chilly, wet and dry climates have become a part of our national folklore. We know where hurricanes rage and tornadoes whirl, where snow piles up winter after winter, and where to find our place in the sun.

This chapter gives weather information for those cities among the most populous urban centers in the nation for which data is available. The big cities have the best historical data series, and the local variations in many states are so great that average values would not be very informative in any case. (Compare, for example, rainfall in El Paso and Houston in Texas.)

The National Oceanic and Atmospheric Agency (NOAA), through the National Weather Service and the National Environmental Satellite, Data and Information Service, is responsible for data on climate. The climatological temperatures, precipitation and degree days listed are averages for the 30-year period from 1961 to 1990. The information for all other tables is based on data from the beginning of the record in that city through the year given.

Climactic conditions are represented as long-term averages that discount variations in the weather from year to year. The major influences on local climate are latitude and geography (altitude, position with respect to the oceans or other large bodies of water, the location of mountains, etc.). Weather obviously influences the agricultural economy of the area, but also has important effects on other aspects of the economy (e.g., on energy costs for heating and cooling) and on lifestyles.

SUNSHINE

Cities have kept records for years of the amount of sunshine that reaches the surface of the Earth. These figures are expressed as a percentage of the maximum amount of sun-shine (which varies by latitude as well as by season) that would reach the surface between dawn and dusk in the absence of clouds, fog, smoke and other blockages in the atmosphere.

The five cities at the top of the list, all west of the Rockies, maintain over 75% reception of sunlight. The minimum value for all big cities is 46%, except for Juneau at 30%. The cities at the low end of the ranking are found in two regions: the Great Lakes and the Northwest, although there are great variations among Texas cities according to their location—in the desert or near the Gulf. Boston and New York are the sunniest of the northeastern cities.

TABLE: Sunshine
DATE: For period of record through 1991
SOURCE: U.S. National Oceanic and Atmospheric Administration, *Comparative Climatic Data*, annual
DESCRIPTION: Average percentage of possible sunshine and length of years recorded in selected cities.

Rank	City	Number of years recorded	Percent of possible sunshine
1	Phoenix, AZ	96	86
2	El Paso, TX	49	84
3	Reno, NV	43	79
4	Sacramento, CA	43	78
5	Albuquerque, NM	52	76
6	Los Angeles, CA	32	73
7	Miami, FL	15	72
8	Denver, CO	42	70
9	Honolulu, HI	39	69
10	San Diego, CA	51	68
11	Salt Lake City, UT	53	66
12	San Juan, PR	36	66
13	Wichita, KS	38	65
14	Cheyenne, WY	52	65
15	Boise, ID	49	64
16	Columbia, SC	38	64
17	Memphis, TN	35	64
18	Jacksonville, FL	40	63
19	Charlotte, NC	41	63

Rank	City	Number of years recorded	Percent of possible sunshine
20	Dallas-Fort Worth, TX	13	63
21	Little Rock, AR	32	62
22	Kansas City, MO	19	62
23	Richmond, VA	41	62
24	Atlanta, GA	56	61
25	Great Falls, MT	46	61
26	Norfolk, VA	27	61
27	Jackson, MS	27	60
28	Omaha, NE	55	60
29	Mobile, AL	41	59
30	Des Moines, IA	41	59
31	New Orleans, LA	18	59
32	Raleigh, NC	37	59
33	Bismarck, ND	52	59
34	Boston, MA	56	58
35	Minneapolis-St. Paul, MN	53	58
36	New York, NY	105	58
37	Providence, RI	38	58
38	Peoria, IL	48	57
39	Portland, ME	51	57
40	Baltimore, MD	40	57
41	St. Louis, MO	32	57
42	Hartford, CT	37	56
43	Washington, DC	43	56
44	Louisville, KY	44	56
45	Atlantic City, NJ	31	56
46	Philadelphia, PA	49	56
47	Nashville, TN	49	56
48	Houston, TX	22	56
49	Indianapolis, IN	47	55
50	Chicago, IL	11	54
51	Concord, NH	50	54
52	Spokane, WA	43	54
53	Milwaukee, WI	51	54
54	Detroit, MI	26	53
55	Duluth, MN	41	52
56	Albany, NY	53	52
57	Cincinnati, OH	8	52
58	Buffalo, NY	48	49
59	Cleveland, OH	48	49
60	Columbus, OH	40	49
61	Burlington, VT	48	49
62	Portland, OR	42	48
63	Sault Ste. Marie, MI	50	47
64	Pittsburgh, PA	39	46
65	Seattle, WA	25	46
66	Juneau, AK	33	30
67	San Francisco, CA	NA	NA
68	Wilmington, DE	NA	NA
69	Oklahoma City, OK	NA	NA
70	Sioux Falls, SD	NA	NA
71	Charleston, WV	NA	NA

NA Not Available

DAILY MEAN TEMPERATURE FOR JANUARY

Not surprisingly, the cities with the warmest temperatures are in Hawaii, California and the South. The coldest cities are around the Great Lakes or in the Great Plains. Juneau is comparatively far down the list, with a mean temperature similar to Hartford. That dubious honor of having the lowest mean goes to Duluth, with a mean temperature of only 7°.

Some cities experience very little variation in temperature from January to June. (Compare the data on this table with the Daily Mean Temperature table on page 17). Honolulu, for example, experiences no seasons as mainlanders know them. In contrast, some cities maintain a 30-degree or more difference from January to June, among them Chicago, Des Moines and Omaha.

TABLE: Daily Mean Temperature for January
DATE: 1961–1990
SOURCE: U.S. National Oceanic and Atmospheric Administration, *Climatography of the United States*
DESCRIPTION: Daily mean temperature for January for a 30-year period in selected U.S. cities.

Rank	City	Temperature (Fahrenheit)
1	Honolulu, HI	72.9
2	Miami, FL	67.2
3	San Diego, CA	57.4
4	Los Angeles, CA	56.8
5	Phoenix, AZ	53.6
6	Jacksonville, FL	52.4
7	New Orleans, LA	51.3
8	Houston, TX	50.4
9	Mobile, AL	49.9
10	San Francisco, CA	48.7
11	Sacramento, CA	45.2
12	Jackson, MS	44.1
13	Columbia, SC	43.8
14	Dallas-Fort Worth, TX	43.4
15	El Paso, TX	42.8
16	Atlanta, GA	41.0
17	Seattle-Tacoma, WA	40.1
18	Memphis, TN	39.7
19	Portland, OR	39.6
20	Charlotte, NC	39.3
21	Norfolk, VA	39.1
22	Little Rock, AR	39.1
23	Raleigh, NC	38.9
24	Nashville, TN	36.2
25	Oklahoma City, OK	35.9
26	Richmond, VA	35.7
27	Washington, DC	34.6

Rank	City	Temperature (Fahrenheit)
28	Albuquerque, NM	34.2
29	Reno, NV	32.9
30	Charleston, WV	32.1
31	Baltimore, MD	31.8
32	Louisville, KY	31.7
33	New York, NY	31.5
34	Atlantic City, NJ	30.9
35	Wilmington, DE	30.6
36	Philadelphia, PA	30.4
37	Denver, CO	29.7
38	Wichita, KS	29.5
39	St. Louis, MO	29.3
40	Boise, ID	29.0
41	Boston, MA	28.6
42	Cincinnati, OH	28.1
43	Salt Lake City, UT	27.9
44	Providence, RI	27.9
45	Spokane, WA	27.1
46	Cheyenne, WY	26.5
47	Columbus, OH	26.4
48	Pittsburgh, PA	26.1
49	Kansas City, MO	25.7
50	Indianapolis, IN	25.5
51	Cleveland, OH	24.8
52	Hartford, CT	24.6
53	Juneau, AK	24.2
54	Buffalo, NY	23.6
55	Detroit, MI	22.9
56	Peoria, IL	21.6
57	Great Falls, MT	21.2
58	Omaha, NE	21.1
59	Chicago, IL	21.0
60	Portland, ME	20.8
61	Albany, NY	20.6
62	Des Moines, IA	19.4
63	Milwaukee, WI	18.9
64	Concord, NH	18.6
65	Burlington, VT	16.3
66	Sioux Falls, SD	13.8
67	Sault Ste. Marie, MI	12.9
68	Minneapolis-St. Paul, MN	11.8
96	Bismarck, ND	9.2
70	Duluth, MN	7.0

DAILY MEAN TEMPERATURE FOR JULY

In the words of Mark Twain, "The coldest winter I ever spent was a summer in San Francisco." The data confirms this. San Francisco is the coldest city in the continental United States in July with a mean temperature of only 62°. Phoenix, in contrast, has an average temperature over 90°.

Days when the thermometer goes over 100° are not uncommon.

TABLE: Daily Mean Temperature for July
DATE: 1961–1990
SOURCE: U.S. National Oceanic and Atmospheric Administration, *Climatography of the United States*
DESCRIPTION: Daily mean temperature for July for a 30-year period in selected U.S. cities.

Rank	City	Temperature (Fahrenheit)
1	Phoenix, AZ	93.5
2	Dallas-Fort Worth, TX	85.3
3	Miami, FL	82.6
4	Memphis, TN	82.6
5	Houston, TX	82.6
6	Mobile, AL	82.3
7	El Paso, TX	82.3
8	Oklahoma City, OK	82.0
9	Little Rock, AR	81.9
10	New Orleans, LA	81.9
11	Jacksonville, FL	81.6
12	Jackson, MS	81.5
13	Wichita, KS	81.4
14	Columbia, SC	80.8
15	Honolulu, HI	80.5
16	Washington, DC	80.0
17	St. Louis, MO	79.8
18	Charlotte, NC	79.3
19	Nashville, TN	79.3
20	Atlanta, GA	78.8
21	Kansas City, MO	78.5
22	Albuquerque, NM	78.5
23	Norfolk, VA	78.2
24	Raleigh, NC	78.1
25	Richmond, VA	78.0
26	Salt Lake City, UT	77.9
27	Louisville, KY	77.2
28	Baltimore, MD	77.0
29	Omaha, NE	76.9
30	New York, NY	76.8
31	Philadelphia, PA	76.7
32	Des Moines, IA	76.6
33	Wilmington, DE	76.4
34	Sacramento, CA	75.7
35	Peoria, IL	75.5
36	Indianapolis, IN	75.4
37	Cincinnati, OH	75.1
38	Charleston, WV	75.1
39	Atlantic City, NJ	74.7
40	Sioux Falls, SD	74.3
41	Boise, ID	74.0
42	Hartford, CT	73.7
43	Minneapolis-St Paul, MN	73.6
44	Denver, CO	73.5
45	Boston, MA	73.5

Rank	City	Temperature (Fahrenheit)
46	Chicago, IL	73.2
47	Columbus, OH	73.2
48	Providence, RI	72.7
49	Detroit, MI	72.3
50	Pittsburgh, PA	72.1
51	Cleveland, OH	71.9
52	Albany, NY	71.8
53	Reno, NV	71.6
54	Buffalo, NY	71.1
55	San Diego, CA	71.0
56	Milwaukee WI	70.9
57	Burlington, VT	70.5
58	Bismarck, ND	70.4
59	Concord, NH	69.5
60	Los Angeles, CA	69.1
61	Spokane, WA	68.8
62	Portland, ME	68.6
63	Cheyenne, WY	68.4
64	Great Falls, MT	68.2
65	Portland, OR	68.2
66	Duluth, MN	66.1
67	Seattle-Tacoma, WA	65.2
68	Sault Ste. Marie, MI	63.8
69	San Francisco, CA	62.7
70	Juneau, AK	56.0

HIGHEST TEMPERATURE OF RECORD FOR JULY

As could be expected, Phoenix leads the list with 118°. This is not the highest temperature recorded in the United States. That honor is held by Death Valley. On July 10, 1913, at Greenland Ranch, a temperature of 134° was recorded.

TABLE: Highest Temperature of Record for July
DATE: For period of record through 1992
SOURCE: U.S. National Oceanic and Atmospheric Administration, *Comparative Climatic Data*, annual
DESCRIPTION: Highest temperature of record for July in selected U.S. cities

Rank	City	Number of years recorded	Temperature (Fahrenheit)
1	Phoenix, AZ	55	118
2	Omaha, NE	56	114
3	Sacramento, CA	42	114
4	Wichita, KS	40	113
5	El Paso, TX	53	112
6	Little Rock, AR	51	112
7	Boise, ID	53	111
8	Dallas-Fort Worth, TX	39	110
9	Oklahoma City, OK	39	109
10	Raleigh, NC	53	109
11	Memphis, TN	51	108
12	Sioux Fall, SD	47	108
13	Columbia, SC	45	107
14	Kansas City, MO	20	107
15	Nashville, TN	53	107
16	Portland, ME	52	107
17	Salt Lake City, UT	64	107
18	St. Louis, MO	35	107
19	Jackson, MS	29	106
20	New York, NY	124	106
21	Albuquerque, NM	53	105
22	Atlanta, GA	44	105
23	Bismarck, ND	48	105
24	Des Moines, IA	53	105
25	Great Falls, MT	55	105
26	Jacksonville, FL	51	105
27	Louisville, KY	45	105
28	Minneapolis-St. Paul, MN	54	105
29	Richmond, VA	63	105
30	San Francisco, CA	65	105
31	Atlantic City, NJ	49	104
32	Baltimore, MD	42	104
33	Charleston, WV	45	104
34	Denver, CO	58	104
35	Houston, TX	23	104
36	Indianapolis, IN	53	104
37	Mobile, AL	51	104
38	Philadelphia, PA	51	104
39	Reno, NV	51	104
40	Washington, DC	51	104
41	Charlotte, NC	53	103
42	Cincinnati, OH	31	103
43	Cleveland, OH	51	103
44	Norfolk, VA	44	103
45	Peoria, IL	53	103
46	Pittsburgh, PA	40	103
47	Spokane, WA	45	103
48	Boston, MA	41	102
49	Chicago, IL	34	102
50	Concord, NH	51	102
51	Detroit, MI	34	102
52	Hartford, CT	38	102
53	Providence, RI	39	102
54	Wilmington, DE	45	102
55	Milwaukee, WI	52	101
56	New Orleans, LA	46	101
57	Albany, NY	46	100
58	Cheyenne, WY	57	100

Rank	City	Number of years recorded	Temperature (Fahrenheit)
59	Columbus, OH	53	100
60	Burlington, VT	49	99
61	Portland, OR	52	99
62	Seattle-Tacoma, WA	48	99
63	Miami, FL	50	98
64	Buffalo, NY	49	97
65	Duluth, MN	51	97
66	Los Angeles, CA	57	97
67	Sault Ste. Marie, MI	52	97
68	San Diego, CA	52	95
69	Honolulu, HI	23	92
70	Juneau, AK	48	90

LOWEST TEMPERATURE OF RECORD FOR JANUARY

The coldest January temperature in 53 years of government charting occurred in Duluth, –39°. Some of the cities traditionally considered temperate have recorded dramatic low temperatures: Louisville, Nashville and Charleston all reported temperatures of below –15°. Juneau, by contrast, ranks only 20th out of 70 cities listed with a record temperature of –22° in 48 years of charting.

TABLE: Lowest Temperature of Record for January
DATE: For period of record through 1992
SOURCE: U.S. National Oceanic and Atmospheric Administration, *Comparative Climatic Data*, annual
DESCRIPTION: Lowest temperature of record for January in selected U.S. cities.

Rank	City	Number of years recorded	Temperature (Fahrenheit)
1	Duluth, MN	51	-39
2	Great Falls, MT	55	-37
3	Sault Ste. Marie, MI	52	-36
4	Sioux Falls, SD	47	-36
5	Minneapolis-St. Paul, MN	54	-34
6	Concord, NH	51	-33
7	Burlington, VT	49	-30
8	Cheyenne, WY	57	-29
9	Albany, NY	46	-28
10	Chicago, IL	34	-27
11	Hartford, CT	38	-26
12	Milwaukee, WI	52	-26
13	Portland, OR	52	-26
14	Cincinnati, OH	31	-25
15	Denver, CO	58	-25

Rank	City	Number of years recorded	Temperature (Fahrenheit)
16	Peoria, IL	53	-25
17	Des Moines, IA	53	-24
18	Omaha, NE	56	-23
19	Indianapolis, IN	53	-22
20	Juneau, AK	48	-22
21	Salt Lake City, UT	64	-22
22	Spokane, WA	45	-22
23	Detroit, MI	34	-21
24	Louisville, KY	45	-20
25	Cleveland, OH	51	-19
26	Columbus, OH	53	-19
27	Pittsburgh, PA	40	-18
28	St. Louis, MO	35	-18
29	Albuquerque, NM	53	-17
30	Boise, ID	53	-17
31	Kansas City, MO	20	-17
32	Nashville, TN	53	-17
33	Buffalo, NY	49	-16
34	Reno, NV	51	-16
35	Charleston, WV	45	-15
36	Wilmington, DE	45	-14
37	Providence, RI	39	-13
38	Boston, MA	41	-12
39	Richmond, VA	63	-12
40	Wichita, KS	40	-12
41	Atlantic City, NJ	49	-10
42	Bismarck, ND	48	-9
43	Atlanta, GA	44	-8
44	El Paso, TX	53	-8
45	Raleigh, NC	53	-7
46	Baltimore, MD	42	-7
47	Philadelphia, PA	51	-7
48	New York, NY	124	-6
49	Charlotte, NC	53	-5
50	Washington, DC	51	-5
51	Little Rock, AR	51	-4
52	Memphis, TN	51	-4
53	Oklahoma City, OK	39	-4
54	Norfolk, VA	44	-3
55	Portland, ME	52	-2
56	Columbia, SC	45	-1
57	Seattle-Tacoma, WA	48	0
58	Jackson, MS	29	2
59	Mobile, AL	51	3
60	Dallas-Fort Worth, TX	39	4
61	Jacksonville, FL	51	7
62	Houston, TX	23	12
63	New Orleans, LA	46	14
64	Phoenix, AZ	55	17
65	Los Angeles, CA	57	23
66	Sacramento, CA	42	23
67	San Francisco, CA	65	24
68	San Diego, CA	52	29
69	Miami, FL	50	30
70	Honolulu, HI	23	53

MEAN NUMBER OF DAYS WITH TEMPERATURES OF 32 DEGREES OR LESS

There are few surprises on this list. Bismarck, Duluth and Sault Ste. Marie, which had low temperatures in other categories, averaged 18 days of temperatures at or below 32°. Reno is surprising; it ranks fourth while Juneau ranks 14th.

The figures below are misleading. Obviously cities such as Bismarck, which has a mean January temperature of 7°, experiences more than 18 days of temperatures below 32°. The calculations in the table are derived by taking the temperatures for each of the 365 days of the year for all the years charted. Therefore the warm temperatures of summer will modify the winter figures.

TABLE: Mean Number of Days with Temperature of 32 Degrees or Less
DATE: For period of record through 1991
SOURCE: U.S. National Oceanic and Atmospheric Administration, *Comparative Climatic Data,* annual
DESCRIPTION: Mean number of days with temperature of 32 degrees or less for selected U.S. cities.

Rank	City	Number of years recorded	Mean number of days
1	Bismarck, ND	32	18.62
2	Duluth, MN	30	18.52
3	Sault Ste. Marie, MI	50	18.05
4	Reno, NV	28	17.35
5	Concord, NH	26	17.26
6	Cheyenne, WY	32	17.17
7	Sioux Falls, SD	28	16.79
8	Great Falls, MT	30	15.70
9	Portland, ME	51	15.67
10	Denver, CO	31	15.65
11	Minneapolis-St. Paul, MN	32	15.62
12	Burlington, VT	27	15.51
13	Albany, NY	26	14.85
14	Juneau, AK	47	14.14
15	Milwaukee, WI	31	14.05
16	Spokane, WA	32	13.93
17	Omaha, NE	37	13.72
18	Detroit, MI	33	13.61
19	Des Moines, IA	30	13.51
20	Hartford, CT	32	13.48
21	Chicago, IL	33	13.25
22	Buffalo, NY	31	13.21
23	Peoria, IL	32	12.91
24	Salt Lake City, UT	32	12.46
25	Boise, ID	52	12.43
26	Cleveland, OH	31	12.34

Rank	City	Number of years recorded	Mean number of days
27	Pittsburgh, PA	32	12.31
28	Albuquerque, NM	31	11.89
29	Columbus, OH	32	11.85
30	Providence, RI	28	11.82
31	Indianapolis, IN	32	11.78
32	Wichita, KS	38	11.12
33	Kansas City, MO	19	11.04
34	Atlantic City, NJ	27	10.97
35	Cincinnati, OH	29	10.77
36	Wilmington, DE	44	10.01
37	St. Louis, MO	31	9.98
38	Charleston, WV	44	9.97
39	Boston, MA	27	9.76
40	Baltimore, MD	41	9.73
41	Philadelphia, PA	32	9.67
42	Louisville, KY	31	8.90
43	Richmond, VA	62	8.46
44	New York, NY	78	7.93
45	Raleigh, NC	27	7.75
46	Oklahoma City, OK	26	7.67
47	Nashville, TN	26	7.60
48	Washington, DC	31	7.02
49	Charlotte, NC	31	6.58
50	El Paso, TX	31	6.45
51	Columbia, SC	25	6.03
52	Little Rock, AR	31	5.99
53	Memphis, TN	50	5.66
54	Norfolk, VA	43	5.39
55	Atlanta, GA	31	5.27
56	Jackson, MS	28	4.95
57	Portland, OR	51	4.25
58	Dallas-Fort Worth, TX	28	4.01
59	Seattle-Tacoma, WA	32	3.09
60	Mobile, AL	29	2.23
61	Houston, TX	22	2.08
62	Sacramento, CA	41	1.69
63	Jacksonville, FL	50	1.50
64	New Orleans, LA	45	1.30
65	Phoenix, AZ	31	0.75
66	Miami, FL	27	0.02
67	Honolulu, HI	22	Less than one-half a day
68	Los Angeles, CA	51	Less than one-half a day
69	San Diego, CA	31	Less than one-half a day
70	San Francisco, CA	55	Less than one-half a day

NORMAL ANNUAL PRECIPITATION

Mobile is the wettest among the 70 cities ranked, receiving 63.96 inches of rainfall on the average. Ironically, the other cities that lead the list in rainfall—New Orleans,

Rank	City	Precipitation (inches)
41	Albany, NY	36.17
42	Chicago, IL	35.82
43	Burlington, VT	34.47
44	Sault Ste. Marie, MI	34.23
45	Dallas-Fort Worth, TX	33.70
46	Oklahoma City, OK	33.36
47	Des Moines, IA	33.12
48	Milwaukee, WI	32.93
49	Detroit, MI	32.62
50	Duluth, MN	30.00
51	Omaha, NE	29.86
52	Wichita, KS	29.33
53	Minneapolis-St. Paul, MN	28.32
54	Sioux Falls, SD	23.86
55	Honolulu, HI	22.02
56	San Francisco, CA	19.70
57	Sacramento, CA	17.52
58	Spokane, WA	16.49
59	Salt Lake City, UT	16.18
60	Bismarck, ND	15.47
61	Denver, CO	15.40
62	Great Falls, MT	15.21
63	Cheyenne, WY	14.40
64	Boise, ID	12.11
65	Los Angeles, CA	12.01
66	San Diego, CA	9.90
67	Albuquerque, NM	8.88
68	El Paso, TX	8.81
69	Phoenix, AZ	7.66
70	Reno, NV	7.53

Miami, Jackson—are also in the Sunbelt, the South and the Southwest.

Reno, located near a desert, is the nation's driest large city, with an average of only 7.53″ of precipitation per year. Honolulu, despite its reputation as a lush, subtropical paradise, received only 22.02″, less than New York, Chicago or Detroit.

TABLE: Normal Annual Precipitation
DATE: 1961–1990
SOURCE: U.S. National Oceanic and Atmospheric Administration, *Comparative Climatic Data*, annual
DESCRIPTION: Normal annual precipitation over a 30-year period.

Rank	City	Precipitation (inches)
1	Mobile, AL	63.96
2	New Orleans, LA	61.88
3	Miami, FL	55.91
4	Jackson, MS	55.37
5	Juneau, AK	54.31
6	Memphis, TN	52.10
7	Jacksonville, FL	51.32
8	Little Rock, AR	50.86
9	Atlanta, GA	50.77
10	Columbia, SC	49.91
11	Nashville, TN	47.30
12	New York, NY	47.25
13	Houston, TX	46.07
14	Providence, RI	45.53
15	Norfolk, VA	44.64
16	Louisville, KY	44.39
17	Portland, ME	44.34
18	Hartford, CT	44.14
19	Richmond, VA	43.16
20	Charlotte, NC	43.09
21	Charleston, WV	42.53
22	Boston, MA	41.51
23	Raleigh, NC	41.43
24	Philadelphia, PA	41.41
25	Cincinnati, OH	41.33
26	Wilmington, DE	40.84
27	Baltimore, MD	40.76
28	Atlantic City, NJ	40.29
29	Indianapolis, IN	39.94
30	Washington, DC	38.63
31	Buffalo, NY	38.58
32	Columbus, OH	38.09
33	Kansas City, MO	37.62
34	St. Louis, MO	37.51
35	Seattle-Tacoma, WA	37.19
36	Pittsburgh, PA	36.85
37	Cleveland, OH	36.63
38	Concord, NH	36.37
39	Portland, OR	36.30
40	Peoria, IL	36.25

SNOW AND ICE PELLETS

Snowfall data, like those for sunshine, are long-term averages, covering at least 29 years for all 70 cities with available information. Sault Ste. Marie is the snow capital of the United States, averaging just under 10 ft. per annum since 1944. Juneau and Buffalo, famous for snowy winters, follow at approximately 8 ft. and 7 1/2 ft. respectively. Honolulu and Miami, on the other hand, have never recorded snow. Snow is not unknown in Southern California and the Florida peninsula. Los Angeles, San Diego and Jacksonville have all had traces of snow.

TABLE: Snow and Ice Pellets
DATE: For period of record through 1992
SOURCE: U.S. National Oceanic and Atmospheric Administration, *Comparative Climatic Data*, annual
DESCRIPTION: Snow and ice pellets in inches in selected cities.

Rank	City	Number of years recorded	Snow and ice (inches)
1	Sault Ste. Marie, MI	51	116.7
2	Juneau, AK	48	99.1
3	Buffalo, NY	49	90.9
4	Duluth, MN	49	77.6
5	Burlington, VT	49	76.0
6	Portland, ME	52	69.3
7	Albany, NY	46	62.9
8	Concord, NH	51	62.5
9	Denver, CO	58	60.4
10	Great Falls, MT	55	59.2
11	Salt Lake City, UT	64	57.5
12	Cheyenne, WY	57	54.7
13	Cleveland, OH	51	54.6
14	Spokane, WA	45	50.5
15	Minneapolis-St. Paul, MN	54	49.8
16	Hartford, CT	38	46.7
17	Milwaukee, WI	52	46.6
18	Pittsburgh, PA	40	42.1
19	Raleigh, NC	53	41.5
20	Detroit, MI	34	41.0
21	Boston, MA	57	40.2
22	Sioux Falls, SD	47	39.4
23	Chicago, IL	34	38.0
24	Providence, RI	39	35.4
25	Des Moines, IA	53	33.3
26	Charleston, WV	45	31.8
27	Omaha, NE	57	29.9
28	Charlotte, NC	124	28.1
29	Columbus, OH	45	27.5
30	Peoria, IL	49	25.0
31	Reno, NV	50	24.4
32	Cincinnati, OH	45	22.9
33	Indianapolis, IN	61	22.5
34	Philadelphia, PA	50	20.9
35	Boise, ID	53	20.8
36	Baltimore, MD	42	20.5
37	Wilmington, DE	45	20.2
38	Kansas City, MO	58	19.9
39	St. Louis, MO	56	19.7
40	Washington, DC	49	16.7
41	Atlantic City, NJ	48	16.2
42	Louisville, KY	45	16.1
43	Wichita, KS	39	16.1
44	Richmond, VA	55	13.9
45	Seattle-Tacoma, WA	48	12.0
46	Albuquerque, NM	53	11.3
47	Nashville, TN	51	10.3
48	Oklahoma City, OK	53	9.3
49	Norfolk, VA	44	7.5
50	Bismarck, ND	48	7.0
51	Portland, OR	52	6.4
52	El Paso, TX	53	5.6
53	New York, NY	53	5.6
54	Memphis, TN	42	5.5
55	Little Rock, AR	50	5.2
56	Dallas-Fort Worth, TX	39	2.7
57	Atlanta, GA	58	2.0
58	Columbia, SC	45	1.7
59	Jackson, MS	29	0.9
60	Houston, TX	58	0.4
61	Mobile, AL	51	0.4
62	New Orleans, LA	46	0.2
63	Honolulu, HI	46	0.0
64	Jacksonville, FL	51	0.0
65	Los Angeles, CA	57	0.0
66	Miami, FL	50	0.0
67	Phoenix, AZ	55	0.0
68	Sacramento, CA	44	0.0
69	San Diego, CA	52	0.0
70	San Francisco, CA	65	0.0

POLLUTION

National concern for environmental quality emerged in the 1960s. Enactment of federal legislation, primarily the Clean Air and Clean Water acts passed in 1963 marked the beginning of a continuing focus on environmental pollution. In 1970 the Environmental Protection Agency (EPA) was created to set pollution standards, monitor the nation's air and water and enforce legislation and regulations that impact the environment. The agency came under increasing attack in the 1990s as conservatives, anxious to cut the size and scope of government, attempted to reduce its power.

Comparative data on pollution are relatively hard to find. The tables in this section provide only a glimpse of the overall situation. They deal with hazardous waste sites, air quality and waste treatment facilities. The EPA and Bureau of the Census compiled the information used in this section.

HAZARDOUS WASTE SITES

The data in this table include both proposed and final sites listed on the National Priorities List for the Superfund program. Enacted by Congress, this program provides money to states to clean up hazardous waste sites.

New Jersey tops the list with 109 separate sites. This figure represents over 8% of all the sites in the United States. Large population and heavy industrialization characterizes nine of the top 10 states, all of which have more than 35 hazardous waste sites. The exception is Washington state. It ranks 47th in population but sixth in total hazardous waste sites. That state's high ranking can be attributed to the large amount of government research into nuclear energy carried on there. One third of Washington's 55 hazardous waste sites are located on federal land.

TABLE: Hazardous Waste Sites
DATE: 1993
SOURCE: U.S. Environmental Protection Agency, *Supplementary Materials: National Priorities List*

DESCRIPTION: Hazardous waste sites on the national priority list and percent of total sites in a state.
UNITED STATES TOTAL: 1,258

Rank	State	Total sites	Percent of total sites
1	New Jersey	109	8.7
2	Pennsylvania	99	7.9
3	California	95	7.6
4	New York	85	6.8
5	Michigan	76	6.0
7	Florida	55	4.4
6	Washington	55	4.4
8	Minnesota	41	3.3
9	Wisconsin	40	3.2
10	Illinois	37	2.9
11	Ohio	36	2.9
12	Indiana	33	2.6
13	Massachusetts	31	2.5
14	Texas	30	2.4
15	South Carolina	24	1.9
15	Virginia	24	1.9
17	Missouri	23	1.8
18	North Carolina	22	1.7
19	Iowa	20	1.6
19	Kentucky	20	1.6
21	Delaware	19	1.5
22	Colorado	18	1.4
23	New Hampshire	17	1.4
24	Connecticut	15	1.2
24	Tennessee	15	1.2
26	Alabama	14	1.1
27	Georgia	13	1.0
27	Utah	13	1.0
29	Arkansas	12	1.0
29	Louisiana	12	1.0
29	Maryland	12	1.0
29	Oregon	12	1.0
29	Rhode Island	12	1.0
34	New Mexico	11	0.9
34	Oklahoma	11	0.9
36	Arizona	10	0.8
36	Idaho	10	0.8

Rank	State	Total sites	Percent of total sites
36	Kansas	10	0.8
36	Maine	10	0.8
36	Nebraska	10	0.8
41	Alaska	8	0.6
41	Montana	8	0.6
41	Vermont	8	0.6
44	West Virginia	6	0.5
45	Mississippi	4	0.3
45	South Dakota	4	0.3
47	Hawaii	3	0.2
47	Wyoming	3	0.2
49	North Dakota	2	0.2
50	Nevada	1	0.1

HAZARDOUS WASTE SITES ON FEDERAL AND NONFEDERAL LAND

Primarily found on nonfederal land, hazardous waste sites exist in all 50 states. The Environmental Protection Agency is charged with the mission of identifying the parties responsible for the initial pollution, conducting settlement negotiations for clean-up and enforcing the settlement.

California and Washington lead the country in number of hazardous waste sites on federal land. Their combined total of 40 represents more than one quarter of all hazardous waste sites on federal land.

TABLE: Hazardous Waste Sites on Federal and Nonfederal Land
DATE: 1993
SOURCE: U.S. Environmental Protection Agency, *Supplementary Materials: National Priorities List*
DESCRIPTION: Hazardous waste sites on the national priority list, on federal and nonfederal land, ranked by total sites.

Rank	State	Federal	Nonfederal	Total
	United States	141	1,117	1,258
1	New Jersey	6	103	109
2	Pennsylvania	4	95	99
3	California	22	73	95
4	New York	4	81	85
5	Michigan	0	76	76
6	Florida	4	51	55
7	Washington	18	37	55
8	Minnesota	2	39	41
9	Wisconsin	0	40	40
10	Illinois	4	33	37
11	Ohio	3	33	36
12	Indiana	0	33	33

Rank	State	Federal	Nonfederal	Total
13	Massachusetts	8	23	31
14	Texas	4	26	30
15	South Carolina	1	23	24
16	Virginia	5	19	24
17	Missouri	3	20	23
18	North Carolina	1	21	22
19	Iowa	1	19	20
20	Kentucky	1	19	20
21	Delaware	1	18	19
22	Colorado	3	15	18
23	New Hampshire	1	16	17
24	Connecticut	1	14	15
25	Tennessee	3	12	15
26	Alabama	3	11	14
27	Georgia	2	11	13
28	Utah	4	9	13
29	Arkansas	0	12	12
30	Louisiana	1	11	12
31	Maryland	3	9	12
32	Oregon	2	10	12
33	Rhode Island	2	10	12
34	New Mexico	2	9	11
35	Oklahoma	1	10	11
36	Arizona	3	7	10
37	Idaho	2	8	10
38	Kansas	1	9	10
39	Maine	3	7	10
40	Nebraska	1	9	10
41	Alaska	6	2	8
42	Montana	0	8	8
43	Vermont	0	8	8
44	West Virginia	1	5	6
45	Mississippi	0	4	4
46	South Dakota	1	3	4
47	Hawaii	2	1	3
48	Wyoming	1	2	3
49	North Dakota	0	2	2
50	Nevada	0	1	1

OZONE

Ozone is necessary in the upper atmosphere, where it forms a thin layer around the Earth that screens out harmful ultraviolet light from the Sun. However, on Earth, ozone is the most significant component of smog. It causes respiratory and eye irritation. Produced by unburned hydrocarbons, ozone's primary sources include cars and power plants.

The air in Los Angles exceeded the Environmental Protection Agency's standard for ozone in the air on more days than any other metropolitan area in the nation. The top four metropolitan areas were located in California. Over the years there has been significant improvement in the atomosphere. Of 78 metropolitan areas ranked, only the first five are in the double digits for the two-year period 1990–1992.

Good
* Oklahoma not on List

TABLE: Ozone
DATE: 1990–1992
SOURCE: U.S. Environmental Protection Agency, *1992 Air Quality Update*
DESCRIPTION: Number of days selected metropolitan areas failing to meet National Ambient Air Quality Standards for ozone from 1990 to 1992.

Rank	Metropolitan Area	1990–1992 average days
1	Los Angeles South Coast Air, CA	106.1
2	Southeast Desert, CA**	52.9
3	San Joaquin Valley, CA	22.6
4	Ventura Co, CA	17.6
5	Houston-Galveston-Brazoria, TX	13.0
6	Phoenix, AZ	9.4
7	Philadelphia-Wilmington-Trenton, PA-NJ-MD	8.4
8	Greater Connecticut, CT	8.3
9	San Diego, CA	7.3
10	Sacramento, CA	6.1
11	Providence, RI	5.5
12	Baton Rouge, LA	5.1
13	Baltimore, MD	4.9
14	Chicago-Gary-Lake County, IL-IN-WI	4.7
15	Milwaukee-Racine, WI	4.7
16	Portland, ME	4.5
17	Atlanta, GA	4.4
18	El Paso, TX	3.7
19	Beaumont-Port Arthur, TX	3.6
20	Springfield, MA	3.6
21	Grand Rapids, MI	3.4
22	New York-No. NJ-Long Island, NY-NJ-CT	3.4
23	Sheboygan, WI	3.2
24	Dallas-Fort Worth, TX	3.1
25	Muskegon, MI	3.0
26	Boston-Lawrence-Salem, MA-NH	2.9
27	Atlantic City, NJ	2.8
28	Knox Co and Lincoln Co, ME*	2.8
29	Manitowoc Co, WI	2.8
30	San Francisco-Oakland-San Jose, CA	2.8
31	Door Co, WI*	2.7
32	Kent Co and Queen Anne's Co, MD*	2.4
33	Portland-Vancouver, OR-WA	2.4
34	Washington, DC-MD-VA	2.4
35	Cincinnati-Hamilton, OH-KY-IN	2.3
36	Nashville, TN	2.3
37	Birmingham, AL	2.1
38	Essex County, NJ*	2.1
39	Portsmouth-Dover-Rochester, NH-ME	2.1
40	Cleveland-Akron-Lorain, OH	2.0
41	Louisville, KY-IN	1.8
42	Huntington-Ashland, WV-KY-OH	1.5
43	Lake Charles, LA	1.5
44	Reno, NV	1.4
45	St. Louis, MO-IL	1.4
46	Sussex County, DE*	1.4
47	Hancock and Waldo County, ME*	1.3
48	Santa Barbara-Santa Maria-Lompoc, CA	1.3
49	Poughkeepsie, NY	1.1
50	Seattle-Tacoma, WA	1.1
51	Detroit-Ann Arbor, MI	1.0
52	Manchester, NH	1.0
53	Owensboro, KY	1.0
54	Kewaunee County, WI*	0.8
55	Norfolk-Virginia Beach-Newport News, VA	0.7
56	Columbus, OH	0.7
57	Jersey Co, IL*	0.7
58	Richmond-Petersburg, VA	0.7
59	Albany-Schenectady-Troy, NY	0.6
60	Pittsburgh-Beaver Valley, PA	0.6
61	Scranton-Wilkes-Barre, PA	0.6
62	Lewiston-Auburn, ME	0.5
63	Tampa-St. Petersburg-Clearwater, FL	0.5
64	Greenbrier County, WV*	0.4
65	Monterey Bay, CA	0.4
66	Allentown-Bethlehem, PA-NJ	0.3
67	Canton, OH	0.3
68	Charleston, WV	0.3
69	Charlotte-Gastonia-Rock Hill, NC-SC*	0.3
70	Harrisburg-Lebanon-Carlisle, PA	0.3
71	Indianapolis, IN	0.3
72	Lexington-Fayette, KY	0.3
73	Miami-Fort Lauderdale, FL	0.3
74	Reading, PA	0.3
75	Salt Lake City-Ogden, UT	0.3
76	Walworth Co, WI	0.3
77	York, PA	0.3
78	Youngstown-Warren, OH	0.3

*Not a metropolitan area.
**Represents primarily San Joaquin, Turlock, Merced, Madera, Fresno, Kings, Tulare and Kern counties.

CARBON MONOXIDE

Carbon monoxide is released into the air when fuel does not burn completely. It principally comes from car and truck emissions. There has been significant improvement in meeting air quality standards in this cateogry. In 1992 only the first 13 metropolitan areas listed any days in which they exceeded the Environmental Protection Agency standards as opposed to 33 in 1987. Of those exceeding standards in 1992, only six metropolitan areas exceeded two days of emissions.

Air quality has improved as a result of a reduction in carbon monoxide emissions due to several factors, car control systems, the manufacture of cleaner fuels and car inspection programs administered individually by many cities and some states—all these factors were mandated by the Clean Air Act of 1990.

TABLE: Carbon Monoxide
DATES: 1987 and 1992
SOURCE: U.S. Environmental Protection Agency, *1992 Air Quality Update*
DESCRIPTION: Number of days selected metropolitan areas failing to meet National Ambient Air Quality Standards for carbon monoxide for 1987 and 1992.

Rank	Metropolitan Area	1987	1992
1	Los Angeles-Anaheim-Riverside, CA	48	35
2	Denver-Boulder, CO	24	7
3	Spokane, WA	66	6
4	Phoenix, AZ	24	5
5	El Paso, TX	11	3
6	Provo-Orem, UT	20	3
7	Anchorage, AK	4	2
8	Fairbanks, AK*	18	2
9	Las Vegas, NV	4	2
10	New York-No. NJ-Long Island, NY-NJ-CT	69	2
11	Hartford, CT	7	1
12	Memphis, TN-AR-MS	3	1
13	Seattle-Tacoma, WA	9	1
14	Minneapolis-St. Paul, MN-WI	5	0
15	San Francisco-Oakland-San Jose,CA	1	0
16	Albuquerque, NM	14	0
17	Baltimore, MD	1	0
18	Boston-Lawrence-Salem, MA-NH	2	0
19	Chico, CA	0	0
20	Cleveland-Akron-Lorain, OH	2	0
21	Colorado Springs, CO	1	0
22	Fort Collins, CO	5	0
23	Fresno, CA	3	0
24	Medford, OR	3	0
25	Missoula County, MT*	4	0
26	Modesto, CA	0	0
27	Portland-Vancouver, OR-WA	4	0
28	Raleigh-Durham, NC	2	0
29	Reno, NV	1	0
30	Sacramento, CA	12	0
31	San Diego, CA	0	0
32	San Jose, CA	1	0
33	Washington, DC-MD-VA	2	0

* Not a metropolitan area.

FEDERAL AID FOR CONSTRUCTION OF WASTE TREATMENT FACILITIES

This table documents federal monies administered by the Environmental Protection Agency and distributed to state and local governments for construction of waste treatment facilities. The purpose of these facilities is to control waste in compliance with environmental standards regulations. The top five recipients—New York, Massachusetts, California, Illinois and Ohio—account for almost one third of all federal monies distributed.

TABLE: Federal Aid for Construction of Waste Treatment Facilities
DATE: 1993
SOURCE: U.S. Bureau of the Census, *Federal Expenditures by State for Fiscal Year 1993*
DESCRIPTION: Federal aid for construction of waste treatment.
UNITED STATES TOTAL IN MILLIONS: $2,126

Rank	State	$ millions
1	New York	245
2	Massachusetts	166
3	California	137
4	Illinois	127
5	Ohio	124
6	Texas	98
7	Michigan	89
8	Wisconsin	86
9	Florida	77
10	Pennsylvania	71
11	New Jersey	60
12	Washington	56
13	Maryland	53
14	Missouri	52
15	North Carolina	43
16	Virginia	35
17	Indiana	33
18	Kentucky	33
19	Minnesota	33
20	Tennessee	30
21	Connecticut	29
22	Oregon	29
23	Georgia	24
24	Alabama	23
25	Louisiana	23
26	Hawaii	22
27	Nevada	22
28	Iowa	21
29	Kansas	20
30	New Hampshire	20
31	Maine	19
32	Arizona	17
33	Arkansas	16
34	Mississippi	16
35	West Virginia	16
36	South Carolina	15
37	Colorado	14
38	Oklahoma	14
39	South Dakota	14

Rank	State	$ millions
40	Washington, DC	11
41	Montana	11
42	New Mexico	9
43	Nebraska	8
44	Vermont	8
45	North Dakota	7

Rank	State	$ millions
46	Rhode Island	7
47	Utah	7
48	Alaska	6
49	Delaware	6
50	Idaho	4
51	Wyoming	4

LABOR

This section reports on the composition of the labor force and the type of work Americans perform. It is based on two primary sources of data, the Bureau of Labor Statistics (BLS) and by the U.S. Bureau of the Census.

The Census Bureau defines the civilian labor force as all civilians in the noninstitutional population 16 years and over classified as "employed" or "unemployed." Employed civilians are:

(1) All, who, during the week surveyed, did any work for pay or profit or worked 15 hours or more as unpaid workers in a family enterprise, and

(2) All who were temporarily absent for noneconomic reasons: illness, weather conditions, vacation, labor-management disputes, etc., whether they were paid for time off or seeking other jobs. The total labor force includes the civilian labor force and members of the armed forces stationed in the United States.

In 1993 there were over 100 million Americans in the workforce. Women continued to enter the workforce at rapidly increasing rates. In 1960, 18.6% of married women with children worked, by 1980 the number grew to 45.1%, and by 1993, 59.6% of married women with children were working.

The tables below analyze the geographical movement of the workforce and analyze its composition. They are designed to show long-term trends and patterns and should not be used for absolute values, which the government updates frequently.

EMPLOYEES 1980 AND 1993

Over the period under consideration job growth was strongest in the South and the West (with the exception of Wyoming). Growth was low in the Northeast and the Midwest (the Rust Belt). Job growth is an indication of the health of a state's economy. The states at the top of this ranking also had the greatest increase in population from 1980 to 1990 as people moved to job opportunities.

The average annual number of employees increased in Nevada, Florida and Arizona by greater than 50% between 1980 and 1993. These three states also had the greatest increase in population from 1980 to 1990 (Alaska was also in the top four see Population Change table on page 116).

The table also shows long-term trends in job creation. It is not designed as an indication of current employment rates.

TABLE: Employees 1980 and 1993
DATE: 1993
SOURCE: U.S. Bureau of Labor Statistics, *Employment and Earnings*
DESCRIPTION: Total employees for 1980 and 1993 and percent change. National totals differ from the sum of the state figures because of differing means of calculation.

Rank		1980 (thousands)	1993 (thousands)	Percent change
	United States	90,406	110,178	22
1	Nevada	400	670	68
2	Florida	3,576	5,567	56
3	Arizona	1,014	1,571	55
4	Alaska	169	253	49
5	Utah	551	810	47
6	Georgia	2,159	3,106	44
7	Washington	1,608	2,250	40
8	North Carolina	2,380	3,245	36
9	Virginia	2,157	2,920	35
10	Delaware	259	348	34
11	New Mexico	465	624	34
12	South Dakota	238	318	34
13	Arkansas	742	990	33
14	Tennessee	1,747	2,328	33
15	Hawaii	405	539	33
16	Colorado	1,251	1,666	33
17	Idaho	330	437	32
18	South Carolina	1,189	1,570	32
19	New Hampshire	385	500	30

Rank		1980 (thousands)	1993 (thousands)	Percent change
20	Vermont	200	256	28
21	Texas	5,851	7,479	28
22	Kentucky	1,210	1,534	27
23	Minnesota	1,770	2,242	27
24	Alabama	1,356	1,712	26
25	Oregon	1,045	1,310	25
26	Wisconsin	1,938	2,407	24
27	Maine	418	519	24
28	Maryland	1,712	2,100	23
29	California	9,849	12,000	22
30	Indiana	2,130	2,589	22
31	Missouri	1,970	2,395	22
32	Nebraska	628	763	22
33	Mississippi	829	998	20
34	Kansas	945	1,135	20
35	Montana	280	326	16
36	North Dakota	245	285	16
37	Michigan	3,443	3,982	16
38	Iowa	1,110	1,277	15
39	New Jersey	3,060	3,493	14
40	Ohio	4,367	4,905	12
41	Illinois	4,850	5,316	10
42	Oklahoma	1,138	1,240	9
43	Washington, DC	616	670	9
44	Rhode Island	398	429	8
45	Pennsylvania	4,753	5,110	8
46	New York	7,207	7,736	7
47	Connecticut	1,427	1,529	7
48	Massachusetts	2,652	2,842	7
49	Louisiana	1,579	1,643	4
50	West Virginia	646	652	1
51	Wyoming	210	210	0

EMPLOYEES IN CONSTRUCTION

Nevada's substantial population growth (see the Employees for 1980 and 1993 table on page 28) and the accompanying demand for housing, infrastructure and commercial development have driven it to the top rank in percent of workers employed in construction. The booming gambling and tourist industries, with increased demand for new facilities, also contributed to the ranking. In actual numbers California and Texas employ more workers in construction, but this represents only 4% and 5% of all the workers surveyed, respectively.

TABLE: Employees in Construction
DATE: 1993
SOURCE: U.S. Bureau of Labor Statistics, *Employment and Earnings*
DESCRIPTION: Employees in construction and percent of total workforce in construction.

Rank		Employees (thousands)	Percent of total workers in construction
	United States	4,574	4
1	Nevada	46	7
2	Hawaii*	32	6
3	Louisiana	97	6
4	Wyoming	12	6
5	Maryland	120	6
6	New Mexico	36	6
7	Arizona	89	6
8	Idaho	25	6
9	Washington	118	5
10	Virginia	153	5
11	Delaware	18	5
12	South Carolina	82	5
13	Florida	287	5
14	Colorado	84	5
15	Utah	40	5
16	West Virginia	31	5
17	North Carolina	153	5
18	Texas	351	5
19	Indiana	119	5
20	Alabama	78	5
21	Kentucky	69	5
22	Alaska	11	5
23	Vermont	11	4
24	Montana	14	4
25	South Dakota	13	4
26	Oregon	54	4
27	Georgia	128	4
28	North Dakota	12	4
29	Nebraska	31	4
30	Kansas	47	4
31	Tennessee	94	4
32	Maine	21	4
33	Missouri	95	4
34	Mississippi	39	4
35	Wisconsin	93	4
36	Pennsylvania	197	4
37	Iowa	48	4
38	Arkansas	37	4
39	Ohio	184	4
40	Illinois	198	4
41	California	446	4
42	Minnesota	79	4
43	Oklahoma	42	3
44	New Hampshire	17	3
45	Michigan	133	3
46	New Jersey	115	3
47	New York	239	3
48	Connecticut	47	3
49	Massachusetts	81	3
50	Rhode Island	12	3
51	Washington, DC	8	1

*Hawaii includes mining with construction.

EMPLOYEES IN MANUFACTURING

Manufacturing employed 60% of workers in 1960, but only 16% in 1993, documenting the erosion of the manufacturing or "blue collar" segment of the labor force. Manufacturing still accounts for approximately one quarter of the workforce in the Midwest, where the auto industry is a major employer, and in the South, where unions are not as prevalent and automakers have opened new facilities.

TABLE: Employees in Manufacturing
DATE: 1993
SOURCE: U.S. Bureau of Labor Statistics, *Employment and Earnings*
DESCRIPTION: Employees in manufacturing and percent of total workforce in manufacturing.

Rank		Employees (thousands)	Percent of total workers in manufacturing
	United States	17,802	16
1	North Carolina	846	26
2	Mississippi	255	25
3	Indiana	639	25
4	Arkansas	243	25
5	South Carolina	374	24
6	Wisconsin	559	23
7	Tennessee	528	23
8	Michigan	902	23
9	Alabama	383	22
10	Ohio	1,049	21
11	Rhode Island	88	20
12	New Hampshire	97	19
13	Connecticut	294	19
14	Kentucky	292	19
15	Delaware	65	19
16	Iowa	236	18
17	Pennsylvania	940	18
18	Minnesota	405	18
19	Georgia	555	18
20	Maine	91	18
21	Illinois	933	18
22	Missouri	411	17
23	Vermont	43	17
24	Oregon	211	16
25	Kansas	182	16
26	Massachusetts	454	16
27	Idaho	69	16
28	Washington	340	15
29	California	1,804	15
30	New Jersey	516	15
31	Virginia	405	14
32	Utah	111	14
33	Oklahoma	168	14
34	Nebraska	103	13
35	Texas	987	13

Rank		Employees (thousands)	Percent of total workers in manufacturing
36	West Virginia	83	13
37	New York	982	13
38	South Dakota	39	12
39	Colorado	188	11
40	Louisiana	186	11
41	Arizona	174	11
42	Florida	484	9
43	Maryland	180	9
44	Montana	23	7
45	New Mexico	43	7
46	North Dakota	19	7
47	Alaska	17	7
48	Wyoming	10	5
49	Nevada	30	4
50	Hawaii	19	4
51	Washington, DC	14	2

EMPLOYEES IN TRANSPORTATION AND PUBLIC UTILITIES

Transportation and public utilities accounted for 5% or less of the employment in the majority of states surveyed. Alaska ranks number one due to the state's unique geography and climate and the major role of public sector employment.

TABLE: Employees in Transportation and Public Utilities
DATE: 1993
SOURCE: U.S. Bureau of Labor Statistics, *Employment and Earnings*
DESCRIPTION: Employees in transportation and public utilities and percent of total workforce in transportation and public utilities.

Rank		Employees (thousands)	Percent of total workers in transportation and public utilities
	United States	5,708	5
1	Alaska	23	9
2	Hawaii	41	8
3	Wyoming	15	7
4	New Jersey	235	7
5	Georgia	202	6
6	Louisiana	105	6
7	Missouri	153	6
8	North Dakota	18	6
9	Colorado	104	6
10	Montana	20	6
11	Nebraska	47	6
12	West Virginia	39	6

Rank		Employees (thousands)	Percent of total workers in transportation and public utilities
13	Texas	437	6
14	Utah	47	6
15	Illinois	310	6
16	Kansas	66	6
17	Oklahoma	72	6
18	Arkansas	57	6
19	Tennessee	126	5
20	Kentucky	82	5
21	Nevada	35	5
22	Pennsylvania	267	5
23	New York	401	5
24	Indiana	134	5
25	Florida	286	5
26	Virginia	149	5
27	Washington	114	5
28	Oregon	66	5
29	California	602	5
30	Alabama	85	5
31	Arizona	78	5
32	Minnesota	109	5
33	North Carolina	156	5
34	Idaho	21	5
35	Wisconsin	113	5
36	Maryland	98	5
37	New Mexico	29	5
38	South Dakota	15	5
39	Mississippi	46	5
40	Connecticut	69	5
41	Iowa	57	4
42	Vermont	11	4
43	Ohio	214	4
44	Massachusetts	124	4
45	Delaware	15	4
46	South Carolina	66	4
47	Maine	22	4
48	Michigan	156	4
49	New Hampshire	18	4
50	Rhode Island	14	3
51	Washington, DC	21	3

EMPLOYEES IN WHOLESALE AND RETAIL TRADE

The percentage of employees in wholesale and retail trade is remarkably consistent across the country. The wholesale and retail occupations account for between 20% and 26% of employment in 48 states. Montana, Alaska and Washington, DC, were the exceptions.

TABLE: Employees in Wholesale and Retail Trade
DATE: 1993

SOURCE: U.S. Bureau of Labor Statistics, *Employment and Earnings*
DESCRIPTION: Employees in wholesale and retail trade and percent of total workforce in wholesale and retail trade.

Rank		Employees (thousands)	Percent of total workers in wholesale and retail trade
	United States	25,857	23
1	Montana	87	27
2	North Dakota	75	26
3	Florida	1,452	26
4	New Hampshire	128	26
5	South Dakota	81	26
6	Nebraska	193	25
7	Maine	130	25
8	Idaho	110	25
9	Iowa	320	25
10	Oregon	327	25
11	Georgia	773	25
12	Hawaii	133	25
13	Arizona	385	25
14	Colorado	403	24
15	Washington	545	24
16	Texas	1,808	24
17	Kansas	274	24
18	Minnesota	537	24
19	Ohio	1,173	24
20	Maryland	499	24
21	Missouri	569	24
22	Utah	192	24
23	New Mexico	147	24
24	Indiana	608	23
25	Michigan	935	23
26	Kentucky	360	23
27	Vermont	60	23
28	Illinois	1,245	23
29	New Jersey	815	23
30	Louisiana	382	23
31	California	2,787	23
32	Oklahoma	288	23
33	Wisconsin	553	23
34	Tennessee	534	23
35	Wyoming	48	23
36	West Virginia	149	23
37	Massachusetts	644	23
38	North Carolina	730	22
39	Pennsylvania	1,147	22
40	South Carolina	351	22
41	Virginia	648	22
42	Arkansas	220	22
43	Alabama	376.3	22
44	Delaware	76	22
45	Rhode Island	93	22
46	Connecticut	329	21
47	Mississippi	209	21
48	New York	1,553	20

Rank		Employees (thousands)	Percent of total workers in wholesale and retail trade
49	Nevada	133	20
50	Alaska	48.7	19
51	Washington, DC	53	8

EMPLOYEES IN FINANCE, INSURANCE AND REAL ESTATE

Delaware's premier position in this table reflects the state's historically favorable tax structure for business. Nevertheless, finance, insurance and real estate account for only 10% of the state's employment. New York and Connecticut, with their concentration of financial and insurance institutions, are second and third, respectively, at approximately 9%.

TABLE: Employees in Finance, Insurance and Real Estate
DATE: 1993
SOURCE: U.S. Bureau of Labor Statistics, *Employment and Earnings*
DESCRIPTION: Employees in finance, insurance and real estate and percent of total workforce in finance, insurance and real estate.

Rank		Employees (thousands)	Percent of total workers in finance, insurance and real estate
	United States	6,604	6
1	Delaware	35	10
2	New York	728	9
3	Connecticut	139	9
4	Hawaii	39	7
5	Illinois	382	7
6	Massachusetts	199	7
7	Oregon	91	7
8	Nebraska	50	7
9	California	786	7
10	New Jersey	229	7
11	Florida	357	6
12	Colorado	106	6
13	Arizona	100	6
14	Maryland	129	6
15	Minnesota	136	6
16	New Hampshire	30	6
17	Pennsylvania	303	6
18	Rhode Island	25	6
19	Missouri	141	6
20	Iowa	74	6
21	Texas	428	6
22	South Dakota	18	6

Rank		Employees (thousands)	Percent of total workers in finance, insurance and real estate
23	Wisconsin	131	5
24	Washington	121	5
25	Virginia	157	5
26	Georgia	166	5
27	Ohio	259	5
28	Idaho	23	5
29	Kansas	58	5
30	Utah	41	5
31	Indiana	128	5
32	Oklahoma	61	5
33	Maine	26	5
34	Michigan	192	5
35	Louisiana	78	5
36	North Dakota	14	5
37	Vermont	12	5
38	Washington, DC	31	5
39	Nevada	31	5
40	Montana	15	5
41	Tennessee	104	4
42	Alabama	76	4
43	New Mexico	28	4
44	Alaska	11	4
45	North Carolina	138	4
46	South Carolina	66	4
47	Kentucky	63	4
48	Arkansas	40	4
49	Mississippi	39	4
50	West Virginia	25	4
51	Wyoming	8	4

EMPLOYEES IN SERVICE JOBS

In 1960 service jobs made up 14% of the workforce surveyed. By 1993 that figure had more than doubled to 32%. Service jobs currently account for approximately a quarter of the labor force in over half the states. Forty-four percent of Nevada's workers are employed in service occupations, primarily those associated with the gambling industry and its associated hotels and restaurants. The U.S. Bureau of Labor Statistics projects that the fastest growing occupations for the rest of this century and into the next will be in the service sector, including: home health aides, human service workers, and personal and home care aides.

TABLE: Employees in Service Jobs
DATE: 1993
SOURCE: U.S. Bureau of Labor Statistics, *Employment and Earnings*
DESCRIPTION: Employees in service jobs and percent of total workforce in service jobs.

Rank		Employees (thousands)	Percent of total workers in service jobs
	United States	30,192	32
1	Nevada	294	44
2	Washington, DC	255	38
3	Massachusetts	952	33
4	Florida	1,814	33
5	Rhode Island	135	31
6	Maryland	655	31
7	New York	2,408	31
8	Hawaii	164	30
9	Pennsylvania	1,527	30
10	New Jersey	1,015	29
11	Connecticut	443	29
12	California	3,463	29
13	Vermont	74	29
14	Arizona	448	29
15	Colorado	468	28
16	Illinois	1,465	28
17	Minnesota	615	27
18	Virginia	797	27
19	New Hampshire	136	27
20	North Dakota	77	27
21	Missouri	644	27
22	New Mexico	167	27
23	Montana	88	27
24	Utah	212	26
25	Ohio	1,277	26
26	South Dakota	83	26
27	Maine	134	26
28	Texas	1,926	26
29	Washington	579	26
30	Delaware	89	26
31	West Virginia	167	26
32	Michigan	1,016	26
33	Oregon	327	25
34	Louisiana	409	25
35	Iowa	317	25
36	Wisconsin	595	25
37	Tennessee	574	25
38	Nebraska	188	25
39	Oklahoma	304	25
40	Kansas	269	24
41	Kentucky	363	24
42	Georgia	729	23
43	Alaska	57	22
44	Idaho	98	22
45	Arkansas	220	22
46	Indiana	562	22
47	North Carolina	688	22
48	Alabama	363	21
49	South Carolina	332	21
50	Wyoming	43	20
51	Mississippi	196	20

EMPLOYEES IN GOVERNMENT

Over the last 30 years the percentage of employees who work for all types of government—federal, state and local—has remained comparatively constant, ranging from a low of 15% in 1960 to a high of 19% in 1975. The currently national average is 17%. In Washington, DC, 43% of the workforce is employed by the federal government. These employees have a wide range of occupations, from lawyers and accountants to those who maintain the White House and take tickets at the Smithsonian museums. After the nation's capital, Alaska, Wyoming, New Mexico, North Dakota and Montana have the highest percentage of government workers. All these states are rural. The lack of other employment opportunities means that the federal, state and local governments employ a substantial portion, a quarter or more, of those who work in these states.

TABLE: Employees in Government
DATE: 1993
SOURCE: U.S. Bureau of Labor Statistics, *Employment and Earnings*
DESCRIPTION: Employees in government and percent of total workforce in government.

Rank		Employees (thousands)	Percent of total workers in government
	United States	18,842	17
1	Washington, DC	287	43
2	Alaska	74	29
3	Wyoming	57	27
4	New Mexico	159	25
5	North Dakota	67	24
6	Montana	74	23
7	Oklahoma	270	22
8	Mississippi	210	21
9	South Dakota	67	21
10	Louisiana	341	21
11	Hawaii	112	21
12	Idaho	90	21
13	Virginia	598	20
14	West Virginia	133	20
15	Kansas	230	20
16	Alabama	341	20
17	Maryland	417	20
18	Utah	160	20
19	Nebraska	150	20
20	Washington	429	19
21	South Carolina	297	19
22	Texas	1,377	18
23	New York	1,420	18
24	Maine	95	18
25	Arizona	286	18
26	Kentucky	276	18
27	Colorado	297	18
28	Oregon	233	18
29	Georgia	547	18

Rank		Employees (thousands)	Percent of total workers in government
30	Iowa	223	17
31	California	2,078	17
32	Arkansas	169	17
33	Vermont	44	17
34	North Carolina	529	16
35	New Jersey	566	16
36	Michigan	640	16
37	Florida	882	16
38	Minnesota	354	16
39	Missouri	377	16
40	Tennessee	362	16
41	Indiana	393	15
42	Ohio	737	15
43	Wisconsin	360	15
44	New Hampshire	74	15
45	Illinois	768	14
46	Rhode Island	61	14
47	Delaware	50	14
48	Pennsylvania	708	14
49	Massachusetts	387	14
50	Connecticut	207	14
51	Nevada	89	13

Self-Employed Workers

Historically, being self-employed meant being a farmer or rancher. Farm employment continues to be the major form of self-employment at least in the top six states. However, the transformation of work via computer technology and a fundamental shift in employer-employee relationships has given rise to an increase of self-employed workers. It is predicted that the self-employment model will continue to grow into the next century.

TABLE: Self-Employed Workers
DATE: 1990
SOURCE: U.S. Bureau of the Census, Journey-to-Work and Migration Statistics Branch, Population Division
DESCRIPTION: Total number of workers 16 years and over who are self-employed and percentage of total workforce who are self-employed.

Rank		Self-employed	Percent of total workers
	United States	8,067,483	7.0
1	South Dakota	47,989	14.9
2	North Dakota	42,769	14.6
3	Montana	46,443	13.3
4	Idaho	48,890	11.1
5	Iowa	146,166	11.1
6	Nebraska	85,493	11.0
7	Vermont	29,019	10.5
8	Oregon	122,886	9.5
9	Wyoming	19.834	9.5
10	Kansas	109,162	9.2

Rank		Self-employed	Percent of total workers
11	Maine	52,602	9.2
12	Arkansas	87,371	8.8
13	Oklahoma	121,435	8.8
14	Minnesota	188,123	8.7
15	New Mexico	54,311	8.6
16	California	1,173,375	8.4
17	Colorado	134,204	8.1
18	Washington	179,204	7.8
19	Kentucky	121,120	7.7
20	New Hampshire	43,942	7.7
21	Alaska	20,058	7.6
22	Missouri	178,906	7.6
23	Texas	579,252	7.6
24	Wisconsin	176,255	7.5
25	Tennessee	159,270	7.1
26	Mississippi	72,105	7.0
27	Utah	49,906	6.8
28	Arizona	112,790	6.7
29	Florida	382,511	6.6
30	Louisiana	107,005	6.5
31	North Carolina	212,775	6.4
32	Pennsylvania	337,297	6.3
33	West Virginia	41,259	6.3
34	Connecticut	104,432	6.2
35	Alabama	107,204	6.1
36	Georgia	190,906	6.1
37	Indiana	158,609	6.1
38	Hawaii	34,291	6.0
39	Massachusetts	180,228	6.0
40	New York	495,342	6.0
41	Illinois	314,603	5.9
42	Ohio	281,124	5.8
43	Nevada	33,805	5.6
44	Rhode Island	26,862	5.6
45	South Carolina	91,848	5.6
46	Virginia	176,862	5.6
47	Michigan	223,020	5.5
48	Maryland	133,523	5.3
49	New Jersey	198,651	5.2
50	Washington, DC	15,725	5.1
51	Delaware	16,721	5.0

Working at Home

Farmers are the only group that works "at home" in significant numbers. For almost all other American workers, being on the job means a drive, a ride or a walk to a place of business. The practice of separating the home and the workplace was virtually unknown before the industrial transformation that began some 150 years ago in America. Within 50 years from that beginning, the pattern that we know today had been firmly established. This pattern has been augmented by highway, rail and air transportation systems. Commuting to work has become a fixture in American life. The computer transformation of society may change this. Thanks to new technologies, more and more Americans will be able to "telecommute."

TABLE: Working at Home
DATE: 1990
SOURCE: U.S. Bureau of the Census, Journey-to-Work and Migration Statistics Branch, Population Division
DESCRIPTION: Total number of workers 16 years and over who work at home and percentage of total workforce who work at home.

Rank		Total working at home	Percent of total workers
	United States	3,406,025	2.90
1	South Dakota	30,639	9.45
2	North Dakota	23,950	8.16
3	Iowa	88,750	6.71
4	Montana	21,876	6.26
5	Vermont	16,510	5.97
6	Nebraska	44,234	5.71
7	Minnesota	115,737	5.36
8	Wisconsin	114,167	4.86
9	Idaho	20,703	4.70
10	Wyoming	9,278	4.45
11	Oregon	55,667	4.30
12	Maine	24,428	4.28
13	Alaska	11046	4.19
14	Kansas	48,863	4.14
15	Colorado	67,189	4.10
16	Washington	86,377	3.75
17	New Mexico	23,570	3.72
18	Utah	26,248	3.58
19	Missouri	83,698	3.57
20	New Hampshire	20,175	3.56
21	Hawaii	19,227	3.39

Rank		Total working at home	Percent of total workers
22	Virginia	103,418	3.29
23	California	452,867	3.25
24	Kentucky	47,272	3.02
25	Arizona	48,076	3.00
26	Oklahoma	41,241	3.00
27	Indiana	73,203	2.83
28	Arkansas	27,772	2.81
29	Michigan	110,465	2.71
30	Pennsylvania	144,551	2.70
31	Connecticut	45,120	2.70
32	Illinois	144,245	2.70
33	Maryland	64,835	2.61
34	New York	213,222	2.59
35	Massachusetts	74,855	2.51
36	West Virginia	16,452	2.50
37	Ohio	118,670	2.45
38	Texas	185,380	2.44
39	Delaware	7,980	2.39
40	Tennessee	52,163	2.33
41	Florida	132,084	2.28
42	North Carolina	70,959	2.15
43	Rhode Island	10,166	2.11
44	New Jersey	80,474	2.11
45	Georgia	65,004	2.09
46	Nevada	11,820	1.95
47	South Carolina	31,365	1.92
48	Louisiana	31,213	1.90
49	Mississippi	18,620	1.81
50	Alabama	31,094	1.79
51	Washington, DC	9,116	0

EMPLOYED POPULATION BY GENDER

In 1993, 75% of men and 58% of women were employed nationally. Minnesota had the highest percentage of working women, 67%; West Virginia the lowest, 45%. A state's standing in terms of employment reflects the health of its economy. The difference between the percentage of males and females employed is an indication not only of women's greater difficulty in obtaining work, but also of social conditions that may influence their desire to work outside the home. Many of the states that had a large difference in percentage between men and women workers are in the South, a traditionally conservative region. The figures below should be used as an indication of the different rates of employment between men and women, not as absolutes on unemployment. The federal government updates these figures frequently.

TABLE: Employed Population by Gender
DATE: 1993
SOURCE: U.S. Bureau of Labor Statistics, *Geographic Profile of Employment and Unemployment*, annual
DESCRIPTION: Figures include civilian noninstitutional employed population 16 years old and over. Because of separate processing and weighing procedures, the totals for the United States may differ from the results obtained by totaling the states. Table ranked by percentage difference betweeen males and females employed.

Rank		Females employed (thousands)	Percent of females employed	Males employed (thousands)	Percent of males employed	Percent difference between males and females employed
	United States	54,606	57.9	64,700	75.2	17.3
1	West Virginia	311	45.0	391	66.0	21.0

Rank		Females employed (thousands)	Percent of females employed	Males employed (thousands)	Percent of males employed	Percent difference between males and females employed
2	Louisiana	770	50.2	970	70.8	20.6
3	Oklahoma	640	53.9	792	74.0	20.1
4	California	6,092	55.8	7,761	75.8	20.0
5	Texas	3,758	59.2	4,750	79.0	19.8
6	New Jersey	1,685	56.4	2,021	75.6	19.2
7	Mississippi	490	52.9	645	72.1	19.2
8	South Carolina	778	57.9	907	76.8	18.9
9	New Mexico	310	54.6	390	73.5	18.9
10	Alabama	830	53.6	1,010	72.2	18.6
11	Pennsylvania	2,494	54.7	2,985	73.2	18.5
12	Arizona	779	53.4	944	71.8	18.4
13	Idaho	227	59.2	285	77.6	18.4
14	Indiana	1,297	59.6	1,483	77.7	18.1
15	Michigan	1,967	57.3	2,407	75.2	17.9
16	Ohio	2,360	56.9	2,772	74.7	17.8
17	Utah	391	63.5	484	81.2	17.7
18	Illinois	2,547	59.4	2,991	76.9	17.5
19	New York	3,714	53.5	4,271	70.8	17.3
20	Kentucky	761	54.0	923	71.2	17.2
21	Arkansas	499	55.2	592	72.0	16.8
22	Iowa	676	65.1	812	81.8	16.7
23	Massachusetts	1,383	60.3	1,570	76.4	16.1
24	Connecticut	783	62.6	895	78.7	16.1
25	Florida	2,851	54.4	3,315	70.5	16.1
26	Tennessee	1,110	56.2	1,248	72.3	16.1
27	Georgia	1,558	59.6	1,709	75.4	15.8
28	South Dakota	156	62.4	191	78.1	15.7
29	New Hampshire	265	64.5	314	80.0	15.5
30	Wyoming	103	62.2	123	77.6	15.4
31	Washington	1,146	60.9	1,344	76.2	15.3
32	Missouri	1,148	60.3	1,333	75.5	15.2
33	Alaska	126	66.2	150	81.2	15.0
34	Kansas	570	63.6	683	78.6	15.0
35	Colorado	841	63.7	964	78.5	14.8
36	Delaware	159	62.7	195	77.5	14.8
37	Nevada	309	62.8	383	77.3	14.5
38	North Dakota	143	61.8	162	76.3	14.5
39	Virginia	1,502	62.5	1,706	76.9	14.4
40	North Carolina	1,591	60.4	1,792	74.8	14.4
41	Oregon	672	61.1	801	75.4	14.3
42	Minnesota	1,110	66.7	1,231	81.0	14.3
43	Rhode Island	227	60.6	245	74.7	14.1
44	Hawaii	266	61.8	292	75.4	13.6
45	Montana	182	61.3	219	74.5	13.2
46	Nebraska	396	65.8	434	78.8	13.0
47	Wisconsin	1,223	65.9	1,366	78.4	12.5
48	Maryland	1,218	64.6	1,289	76.8	12.2
49	Washington, DC	139	61.5	141	73.1	11.6
50	Maine	275	60.8	306	72.3	11.5
51	Vermont	146	66.4	153	77.7	11.3

CIVILIAN EMPLOYEES IN THE MILITARY

The military is a significant employer in many states. The statistics below reflect the location of military facilities throughout the country. California, with major army and naval stations, leads the list. Virginia, with the military complexes surrounding the capital, is second.

TABLE: Civilian Employees in the Military

DATE: 1992

SOURCE: U.S. Department of Defense, *Atlas/Data Abstract for the United States and Selected Areas*, annual

DESCRIPTION: Civilian employees in the military in the United States.

Rank		Employees (thousands)
	United States	899.0
1	California	119.9
2	Virginia	106.3
3	Texas	58.2
4	Pennsylvania	48.5
5	Maryland	40.5
6	Georgia	37.3
7	Ohio	34.7
8	Florida	32.3
9	Washington	29.0
10	Alabama	26.0
11	New Jersey	24.7
12	Oklahoma	21.9
13	Utah	19.9
14	Illinois	19.3
15	Missouri	18.3
16	Hawaii	17.9

Rank		Employees (thousands)
17	New York	17.8
18	South Carolina	17.6
19	North Carolina	17.1
20	Washington, DC	16.8
21	Indiana	15.7
22	Kentucky	14.2
23	Colorado	14.0
24	Massachusetts	11.1
25	Michigan	11.1
26	Mississippi	11.0
27	Arizona	9.8
28	New Mexico	9.2
29	Louisiana	9.0
30	Maine	8.3
31	Tennessee	7.6
32	Kansas	6.8
33	Connecticut	4.8
34	Alaska	4.7
35	Arkansas	4.5
36	Rhode Island	4.2
37	Nebraska	3.8
38	Wisconsin	3.4
39	Minnesota	2.9
40	Oregon	2.9
41	Nevada	2.1
42	North Dakota	1.9
43	Delaware	1.8
44	West Virginia	1.7
45	Iowa	1.5
46	Idaho	1.5
47	New Hampshire	1.4
48	South Dakota	1.3
49	Montana	1.2
50	Wyoming	1.1
51	Vermont	0.6

INCOME

This section surveys basic income. The primary source for information on personal income is the *Survey of Current Business*, published by the Bureau of Economic Analysis. Sources of income distribution data come from the U.S. Bureau of the Census's *Current Population Reports*.

The tables below cover total income, average income, average per capita income, change in income and median income. Information on the states' wealthiest follows.

The government includes the District of Columbia in the tables below. However, comparisons between the District and the states are misleading. The figures for the District reflect a small, densely populated city, while those for the states are from larger, more diverse areas.

AVERAGE ANNUAL PAY

This table shows the average annual pay for approximately 90% of the total civilian employment. The highest pay in the nation occurs in Washington, DC, Connecticut, New York, New Jersey and Alaska, all areas with high costs of living. Two out of the top five, the District of Columbia and Alaska, rank high because of unique circumstances. The District's figures are not comparable with the states', which, in part because of greater area, have more diversity in terms of economy and cost of living. Alaska's location and climate make its cost of living high in comparison to the lower forty-eight states. The higher cost of living offsets the increased income. For example, workers in government and the corporate extractive industries receive premium salaries that compensate for the high cost of goods that must be "imported." On the other hand, Alaska is unique in having a program that pays residents an annual stipend out of a state fund.

That leaves the contiguous eastern states of Connecticut, New York and New Jersey, as leading the nation in average annual pay. The ring of suburbs surrounding New York City that are the site of the head-

quarters of many international corporations helps to account for the high ranking of Connecticut, New York and New Jersey. South Dakota, North Dakota, Mississippi, Montana and Arkansas rank 51st through 47th at the bottom end of the scale.

Average annual wage increases ranged from a high of 13% in Washington, DC, New Jersey and Washington state to a low of 6% in Alaska and Wyoming from 1990 to 1992.

TABLE: Average Annual Pay
DATE: 1992
SOURCES: U.S. Bureau of Labor Statistics, *Employment and Wages Annual Averages*, annual; and *Average Annual Pay by State and Industry*, annual
DESCRIPTION: Average annual pay for 1990 and 1992 with percentage increase 1990–1992 in current dollars. Figures are for employees covered by state unemployment insurance laws and for federal civilian workers. Table ranked by 1992 figures.

Rank		1990 average annual pay	1992 average annual pay	1990–1992 percent increase
	United States	23,602	25,903	10
1	Washington, DC	33,717	37,971	13
2	Connecticut	28,995	32,587	12
3	New York	28,873	32,399	12
4	New Jersey	28,449	32,125	13
5	Alaska	29,946	31,825	6
6	Massachusetts	26,699	29,664	11
7	California	26,180	28,934	11
8	Illinois	25,312	27,910	10
9	Michigan	25,376	27,463	8
10	Maryland	24,730	27,145	10
11	Delaware	24,423	26,596	9
12	Pennsylvania	23,457	25,785	10
13	Hawaii	23,167	25,613	11
14	Washington	22,646	25,553	13
15	Minnesota	23,121	25,315	9

Rank		1990 average annual pay	1992 average annual pay	1990–1992 percent increase
16	Texas	22,700	25,080	10
17	Colorado	22,908	25,040	9
18	Virginia	22,750	24,937	10
19	New Hampshire	22,609	24,925	10
20	Ohio	22,844	24,846	9
21	Nevada	22,358	24,743	11
22	Georgia	22,115	24,373	10
23	Rhode Island	22,388	24,315	9
24	Indiana	21,699	23,570	9
25	Missouri	21,716	23,550	8
26	Oregon	21,332	23,514	10
27	Arizona	21,443	23,161	8
28	Florida	21,030	23,144	10
29	Wisconsin	21,101	23,022	9
30	Tennessee	20,611	22,807	11
31	Vermont	20,532	22,347	9
32	Alabama	20,468	22,340	9
33	Louisiana	20,646	22,340	6
34	North Carolina	20,220	22,248	10
35	West Virginia	20,715	22,169	7
36	Kansas	20,238	21,982	9
37	Utah	20,074	21,976	9
38	Kentucky	19,947	21,858	10
39	Maine	20,154	21,808	8
40	Oklahoma	20,288	21,699	7
41	South Carolina	19,668	21,423	9
42	Wyoming	20,049	21,215	6
43	New Mexico	19,347	21,051	9
44	Iowa	19,224	20,937	9
45	Idaho	18,991	20,649	9
46	Nebraska	18,577	20,355	10
47	Arkansas	18,204	20,108	10
48	Montana	17,895	19,378	8
49	Mississippi	17,718	19,237	9
50	North Dakota	17,626	18,945	7
51	South Dakota	16,430	18,016	10

DISPOSABLE PERSONAL INCOME

Disposable personal income, defined as money available to individuals to spend and save, nationally averaged $8,569 in 1980 and $18,177 in 1993. It is given in current dollars so that income can be compared over time.

Ranked here from highest to lowest, Washington, DC, topped the list in 1993 for per capita disposable income. Income in the District more than doubled from 1980; moving from $10,542 to $24,595 in 1993. However, in 1980, Washington, DC, ranked number two; the top spot belonged to Alaska at $11,639. By 1993 that state had dropped to number six at $20,985.

Massachusetts, North Carolina and South Dakota recorded the most significant increases in income; all three states rose 10 places in rank from 1980 to 1993.

Wyoming dropped from number seven in 1980 to 23rd in 1993. Oklahoma, Louisiana, Arizona and Oregon also registered significant declines in personal income large enough to cause these states to drop substantially in rank.

TABLE: Disposable Personal Income
DATE: 1993
SOURCE: U.S. Bureau of Economic Analysis, *Survey of Current Business*, and unpublished data
DESCRIPTION: Disposable personal income per capita in current dollars.

Rank		1980 income ($)	1993 income ($)
	United States	8,569	18,177
1	Washington, DC	10,542	24,595
2	Connecticut	10,321	23,776
3	New Jersey	9,974	23,354
4	Massachusetts	9,052	20,985
5	New York	9,249	20,948
6	Maryland	9,097	20,552
7	Alaska	11,639	20,306
8	New Hampshire	8,611	20,278
9	Hawaii	9,286	20,038
10	Nevada	10,058	19,781
11	Illinois	9,276	19,648
12	Washington	9,317	19,290
13	California	10,084	18,997
14	Virginia	8,443	18,762
15	Pennsylvania	8,549	18,632
16	Colorado	9,130	18,628
17	Florida	8,595	18,513
18	Rhode Island	8,306	18,384
19	Delaware	8,502	18,374
20	Minnesota	8,505	17,907
21	Michigan	8,779	17,886
22	Kansas	8,419	17,635
23	Wyoming	9,705	17,504
24	Nebraska	7,769	17,416
25	Wisconsin	8,401	17,196
26	Ohio	8,405	17,180
27	Missouri	8,030	17,158
28	Texas	8,459	17,116
29	Vermont	7,485	17,076
30	Maine	7,283	16,898
31	Georgia	7,309	16,871
32	Indiana	7,988	16,824
33	Oregon	8,425	16,731
34	Tennessee	7,117	16,705
35	North Carolina	6,939	16,421
36	South Dakota	6,890	15,981
37	Idaho	7,452	15,974
38	Arizona	8,147	15,921
39	Iowa	7,987	15,782

Rank		1980 income ($)	1993 income ($)
40	North Dakota	6,600	15,688
41	Alabama	6,741	15,332
42	Montana	7,565	15,128
43	South Carolina	6,627	15,071
44	Oklahoma	8,017	15,060
45	Kentucky	7,066	15,010
46	Louisiana	7,523	14,947
47	New Mexico	7,246	14,587
48	West Virginia	6,944	14,552
49	Arkansas	6,502	14,424
50	Utah	6,987	14,066
51	Mississippi	6,122	13,631

STATE'S TOTAL PERSONAL INCOME

Personal income is the total compensation received minus the individual's contributions to social insurance programs. The largest portion of personal income is received in the form of wages, salaries and other forms of compensation for labor. A smaller part comes from interest or dividend income and what are called transfer payments (Social Security and other government programs). The smallest portion is rent or income from business.

The ranking below depends a great deal on the number of persons in each state, but differences in average income level (see the Per Capita Personal Income table on page 41) are large enough to shift many states a few positions away from their population ranking. Californians received 681 billion dollars in personal income during 1993, almost a third more than New Yorkers. The figures are important to states because they determine the maximum tax revenue a state could potentially generate from income tax.

TABLE: State's Total Personal Income
DATE: 1993
SOURCE: U.S. Bureau of Economic Analysis, *Survey of Current Business*, and unpublished data
DESCRIPTION: State's total personal income in billions of current dollars.

Rank		1980 total personal income ($ billion)	1993 total personal income ($ billion)
	United States	2,259	5,369
1	California	278	681
2	New York	192	448
3	Texas	141	346
4	Florida	97	285
5	Illinois	124	264
6	Pennsylvania	118	257
7	Ohio	105	218

Rank		1980 total personal income ($ billion)	1993 total personal income ($ billion)
8	New Jersey	86	213
9	Michigan	94	194
10	Massachusetts	61	148
11	Virginia	53	140
12	Georgia	46	133
13	North Carolina	47	130
14	Maryland	46	119
15	Washington	45	115
16	Indiana	51	110
17	Missouri	46	102
18	Wisconsin	46	100
19	Minnesota	41	95
20	Tennessee	37	94
21	Connecticut	38	92
22	Colorado	31	77
23	Alabama	30	72
24	Louisiana	37	72
25	Arizona	25	71
26	Kentucky	30	65
27	South Carolina	24	62
28	Oregon	26	59
29	Oklahoma	28	55
30	Iowa	27	52
31	Kansas	23	51
32	Mississippi	17	39
33	Arkansas	17	39
34	Nebraska	14	32
35	Nevada	9	32
36	Utah	12	30
37	West Virginia	16	30
38	Hawaii	10	27
39	New Mexico	11	26
40	New Hampshire	9	26
41	Maine	9	23
42	Rhode Island	9	21
43	Idaho	8	19
44	Washington, DC	8	17
45	Delaware	6	15
46	Montana	7	15
47	Alaska	6	14
48	South Dakota	5	13
49	Vermont	4	11
50	North Dakota	5	11
51	Wyoming	5	9

AVERAGE ANNUAL PERCENT CHANGE IN PERSONAL INCOME

Across the United States total personal income of all residents from all sources increased an average of 2.2% from 1980 to 1993. Rates were highest in Nevada, Florida and

Georgia. The rate decreased by 3% in Wyoming. This low rate of wage growth, often referred to as "wage stagnation," means a drop in real income after inflation rates are taken into account. Several states, principally in the West, had significant increases in income in 1992–93, but the nation as a whole still experienced stagnation.

It is interesting to compare these rankings with those on the table that follows. A number of the states ranking lowest in personal income per capita for 1993 report substantial gains from 1992 to 1993. For example, Idaho, Montana and New Mexico, rank in the top five in percent of increase in personal income and simultaneously in the bottom fourth in per capita income for 1993 (see the Per Capita Personal Income table on this page).

TABLE: Average Annual Percent Change in Personal Income
DATE: 1993
SOURCES: U.S. Bureau of Economic Analysis, *Survey of Current Business,* and unpublished data
DESCRIPTION: Average annual percent change in personal income in constant (1987) dollars (see the Median Household Income table on page 42 for a definition of constant dollars). Table ranked by 1992–1993 change.

Rank		1980–1993 average annual percent change	1992–1993 average annual percent change
	United States	2.2	2.0
1	Idaho	2.4	6.5
2	Nevada	5.0	6.3
3	Montana	1.3	6.1
4	New Mexico	2.5	4.9
5	Florida	4.0	4.6
6	Colorado	2.6	4.6
7	Arizona	3.6	4.2
8	Mississippi	1.9	4.1
9	Utah	2.9	3.9
10	Oregon	1.9	3.9
11	Hawaii	3.0	3.9
12	North Carolina	3.4	3.6
13	Georgia	3.8	3.4
14	Texas	2.5	3.4
15	Wyoming	-0.3	3.4
16	Tennessee	2.8	3.1
17	Indiana	1.5	2.8
18	South Carolina	3.0	2.8
19	Alabama	2.4	2.8
20	Alaska	2.5	2.8
21	Virginia	3.1	2.4
22	Wisconsin	1.5	2.3
23	Delaware	2.5	2.3
24	Louisiana	0.7	2.3
25	Washington	2.9	2.3
26	Michigan	1.1	2.2
27	Kentucky	1.7	2.1
28	West Virginia	0.5	1.9

Rank		1980–1993 average annual percent change	1992–1993 average annual percent change
29	Illinois	1.4	1.8
30	Kansas	1.6	1.8
31	Arkansas	2.0	1.8
32	Oklahoma	0.7	1.8
33	Vermont	2.8	1.7
34	Nebraska	1.8	1.7
35	Maine	2.7	1.6
36	New Hampshire	3.6	1.6
37	Maryland	3.0	1.6
38	Washington, DC	1.4	1.6
39	Massachusetts	2.4	1.4
40	New Jersey	2.6	1.4
41	Ohio	1.2	1.4
42	Rhode Island	2.1	1.2
43	Pennsylvania	1.6	1.2
44	Minnesota	2.1	1.2
45	South Dakota	2.2	1.0
46	Connecticut	2.4	0.8
47	Missouri	1.8	0.8
48	California	2.5	0.6
49	North Dakota	1.7	0.1
50	New York	2.1	0.0
51	Iowa	0.5	-2.0

PER CAPITA PERSONAL INCOME

The relatively low level of per capita personal income in the South remains the most striking feature of American income distribution in the 1990s. Virginia, with its affluent suburbs adjacent to the nation's capital, and Florida, with its wealthy retirement colonies, are the only states in the southern region where per capita personal income is greater than $20,000. Washington, DC, tops the list with a figure almost $9,000 above the national average and over $1,000 above second-place Connecticut. Several of the high-income states are located in the East, but high incomes are also found in other regions.

TABLE: Per Capita Personal Personal Income
DATE: 1993
SOURCE: U.S. Bureau of Economic Analysis, *Survey of Current Business,* and unpublished data
DESCRIPTION: Personal income per capita in current dollars. Table ranked by 1993 income.

Rank		1980 income ($)	1993 income ($)
	United States	9,940	20,817
1	Washington, DC	12,508	29,438
2	Connecticut	12,170	28,110
3	New Jersey	11,648	26,967

Rank		Income 1980 ($)	Income 1993 ($)
4	New York	10,906	24,623
5	Massachusetts	10,659	24,563
6	Maryland	10,824	24,044
7	Hawaii	10,774	23,354
8	Alaska	13,692	22,846
9	Nevada	11,559	22,729
10	New Hampshire	9,803	22,659
11	Illinois	10,875	22,582
12	Washington	10,716	21,887
13	California	11,681	21,821
14	Virginia	9,857	21,634
15	Colorado	10,616	21,564
16	Delaware	10,356	21,481
17	Pennsylvania	9,923	21,351
18	Rhode Island	9,576	21,096
19	Minnesota	9,982	21,063
20	Florida	9,835	20,857
21	Michigan	10,154	20,453
22	Kansas	9,829	20,139
23	Wisconsin	9,772	19,811
24	Nebraska	8,988	19,726
25	Ohio	9,738	19,688
26	Wyoming	11,356	19,539
27	Vermont	8,546	19,467
28	Missouri	9,256	19,463
29	Oregon	9,863	19,443
30	Georgia	8,353	19,278
31	Indiana	9,215	19,203
32	Texas	9,840	19,189
33	Maine	8,218	18,895
34	North Carolina	8,000	18,702
35	Tennessee	8,010	18,434
36	Iowa	9,346	18,315
37	Arizona	9,272	18,121
38	South Dakota	7,701	17,666
39	Idaho	8,433	17,646
40	North Dakota	7,641	17,488
41	Montana	8,728	17,322
42	Alabama	7,656	17,234
43	Kentucky	8,051	17,173
44	Oklahoma	9,308	17,020
45	South Carolina	7,558	16,923
46	Louisiana	8,672	16,667
47	New Mexico	8,147	16,297
48	West Virginia	7,972	16,209
49	Utah	7,942	16,180
50	Arkansas	7,371	16,143
51	Mississippi	6,868	14,894

MEDIAN HOUSEHOLD INCOME

Median household income is less affected by very high and low incomes than data reported as average income because averages can be skewed by the extreme highs and lows of the figures being averaged. Median household income is money available to households to meet all the daily costs of living.

The median income dropped in the United States from $32,288 in 1988 to $30,786 in 1992. It was $10,000 less than the median income in 1985. While median income in Hawaii, ranked first, is more than double that of West Virginia, ranked 51st, in most states the median range is between $35,000 and $25,000. The only southern state in the top 20 is Virginia, a reflection of the wealthy suburbs surrounding the capital. Median income in Maryland and Rhode Island dropped $6,000 and $4,000, respectively, in four years. No state reported a rise in income of that magnitude during the same time period.

This table is reported in constant dollars. Constant dollar figures are estimates made after removing the effects of price changes. The constant dollar's central concept is constant purchasing power. On this scale a dollar has the same purchasing power regardless of the year reported.

TABLE: Median Household Income
DATE: 1992
SOURCE: U.S. Bureau of the Census, *Current Population Reports*
DESCRIPTION: Median household income in constant 1992 dollars.

Rank		1988 median household income ($)	1992 median household income ($)
	United States	32,288	30,786
1	Hawaii	39,165	42,171
2	Alaska	39,259	41,969
3	Connecticut	42,947	41,059
4	New Hampshire	41,064	39,644
5	New Jersey	43,035	39,227
6	Virginia	38,719	38,223
7	Maryland	43,350	37,287
8	Massachusetts	39,390	36,558
9	Delaware	36,178	35,739
10	California	35,919	35,173
11	Utah	31,206	34,433
12	Washington	38,339	34,064
13	Wisconsin	35,075	33,415
14	Vermont	34,379	32,829
15	Colorado	31,089	32,716
16	Michigan	34,953	32,347
17	Oregon	32,908	32,114
18	Nevada	33,187	32,026
19	Illinois	35,015	31,707
20	Ohio	32,899	31,479
21	New York	34,292	31,254
22	Minnesota	34,496	31,077
23	Rhode Island	35,392	30,636

Rank		1988 median household income ($)	1992 median household income ($)
24	Kansas	30,320	30,447
25	Wyoming	31,332	30,379
26	Washington, DC	31,714	30,357
27	Nebraska	29,838	30,177
28	Pennsylvania	31,715	29,985
29	Maine	31,312	29,705
30	Arizona	31,351	29,593
31	Georgia	31,506	28,889
32	Iowa	28,825	28,880
33	Indiana	31,183	28,663
34	Texas	29,605	28,282
35	North Carolina	28,955	27,835
36	Idaho	27,811	27,784
37	South Carolina	30,281	27,667
38	Missouri	27,803	27,490
39	Florida	30,131	27,456
40	North Dakota	28,572	27,105
41	Montana	26,365	26,602
42	South Dakota	26,440	26,351
43	New Mexico	22,884	26,158
44	Alabama	23,658	25,891
45	Louisiana	24,309	25,479
46	Oklahoma	28,068	25,363
47	Tennessee	24,735	24,339
48	Arkansas	23,923	23,893
49	Kentucky	23,609	23,567
50	Mississippi	21,544	20,585
51	West Virginia	22,952	20,301

TOP WEALTHHOLDERS

Although those classified as the wealthiest Americans live in every state, over 50% of them reside in California, New York, Florida, Texas, New Jersey and Illinois. However, Connecticut, 10th in total population, substantially outpaces every state in rate of wealthholders, with 390 per 10,000. California is second with 306 per 10,000. Delaware and Nevada both register significant rates of wealthholders 264 and 245 per 10,000, respectively.

TABLE: Top Wealthholders
DATE: 1989
SOURCE: U.S. Internal Revenue Service, *Statistics of Income Bulletin, 1993*, and unpublished data
DESCRIPTION: Number of individuals with gross assets of $600,000 or more and net worth under $10 million and rate per 10,000 in current dollars. Figures are based on samples of estate tax returns. Net worth is defined as assets minus debts and mortgages.

Rank		Number (thousands)	Rate (per 10,000 people)
	United States	3,380	184
1	Connecticut	99	390
2	California	662	306
3	Hawaii	22	274
4	New Jersey	162	274
5	Delaware	13	264
6	Washington, DC	13	262
7	Nevada	21	245
8	Florida	241	245
9	New York	325	237
10	Massachusetts	109	233
11	Rhode Island	17	214
12	North Dakota	10	206
13	Wyoming	6	197
14	Maryland	65	182
15	New Hampshire	15	181
16	Alaska	7	180
17	Nebraska	20	178
18	Maine	16	178
19	Colorado	42	176
20	Illinois	148	175
21	Montana	10	172
22	Washington	60	171
23	Vermont	7	168
24	South Carolina	42	164
25	Iowa	33	161
26	Arizona	42	160
27	Kansas	28	156
28	Virginia	69	150
29	Georgia	69	147
30	Missouri	55	146
31	Texas	174	145
32	North Carolina	71	142
33	South Dakota	7	141
34	Pennsylvania	127	140
35	New Mexico	15	139
36	Minnesota	44	139
37	Oklahoma	30	129
38	Michigan	85	125
39	Tennessee	45	125
40	Ohio	99	124
41	Oregon	24	117
42	Kentucky	31	114
43	Idaho	8	112
44	Louisiana	31	102
45	Wisconsin	36	102
46	Alabama	30	101
47	Arkansas	17	99
48	Mississippi	17	92
49	Indiana	37	91
50	Utah	8	70
51	West Virginia	9	67

POVERTY, WELFARE AND HOMELESSNESS

Poverty was a focus of American political discussion during the 1960s, the decade when the legislative structure of anti-poverty programs was established. Faced with rising program costs and newly conservative government, the 1980s produced a political debate regarding the effectiveness and the proper scope of the federal government in addressing the problems of poverty. In 1996 the passage of a new federal welfare bill by Congress initiated the dismantling of over 30 years of federal anti-poverty programs.

The tables below document the changing extent of poverty prior to the passage of this legislation. Two tables review the numbers of poor and homeless in the United States. In 1980, 29.2 million individuals were living below the poverty level; by 1992 the number was 36.9. In 1992 the number of homeless totaled 240,140.

This chapter includes descriptive statistics for the major social welfare programs targeting the poor: Aid to Families with Dependent Children (AFCD), Supplemental Security Income (SSI), Food Stamps and School Lunches. These four programs are mandated and funded primarily by the federal government. Two of the programs (AFDC and SSI) provide cash assistance. In 1980, 6.5% of the population received public aid through AFDC or SSI; that figure reached 7.6% in 1992. Food Stamps and the School Lunch program provide food assistance. The Food Stamps program supplies recipients with redeemable coupons, and the School Lunch program feeds school-age children who qualify. In 1992, 48% of households below the poverty level received food stamps. The federal food stamp program cost $7.9 billion in 1980, $22 billion in 1993. The school lunch program fed 26.4 million children in 1980; by 1993 that number dropped to 25 million. The cost of the program was $2.2 billion in 1980 and $4 billion in 1993.

POPULATION BELOW THE POVERTY LEVEL

People are classified as being above or below the poverty level according to a poverty index devised by the federal government. The poverty index is based solely on money income and does not reflect the receipt of noncash benefits such as food stamps, Medicaid and public housing. The poverty threshold is the same for all states. The index is based on the Department of Agriculture's 1961 Economy Food Plan and reflects the different consumption requirements of families based on their size and composition. The poverty thresholds are updated every year to reflect changes in the Consumer Price Index.

More than 14% of the entire population, almost 37 million Americans, were living in poverty in 1992. Proportions of poor families exceed the national average in all the southern states except Virginia and Florida. In Mississippi and Louisiana approximately one in four persons is poor. Another group of states with high poverty levels extends westward from the South through Missouri, Oklahoma, Texas, New Mexico, Arizona and California. States in other regions with above average poverty levels are New York, Illinois and Idaho.

TABLE: Population Below the Poverty Level
DATE: 1992
SOURCE: U.S. Bureau of the Census, *Current Population Reports*
DESCRIPTION: Percent of population below poverty level.

Rank	State	1992 percent
	United States	14.5
1	Mississippi	24.5
2	Louisiana	24.2
3	West Virginia	22.3
4	New Mexico	21.0
5	Washington, DC	20.3
6	Kentucky	19.7
7	South Carolina	18.9
8	Oklahoma	18.4
9	Georgia	17.8
10	Texas	17.8
11	Arkansas	17.4
12	Alabama	17.1
13	Tennessee	17.0

Rank	State	1992 percent
14	California	15.8
15	North Carolina	15.7
16	Missouri	15.6
17	Florida	15.3
18	Illinois	15.3
19	New York	15.3
20	Arizona	15.1
21	Idaho	15.0
22	South Dakota	14.8
23	Nevada	14.4
24	Montana	13.7
25	Michigan	13.5
26	Maine	13.4
27	Minnesota	12.8
28	Ohio	12.4
29	Rhode Island	12.0
30	North Dakota	11.9
31	Indiana	11.7
32	Pennsylvania	11.7
33	Maryland	11.6
34	Iowa	11.3
35	Oregon	11.3
36	Hawaii	11.0
37	Kansas	11.0
38	Washington	11.0
39	Wisconsin	10.8
40	Colorado	10.6
41	Vermont	10.4
42	Nebraska	10.3
43	Wyoming	10.3
44	Alaska	10.0
45	Massachusetts	10.0
46	New Jersey	10.0
47	Connecticut	9.4
48	Virginia	9.4
49	Utah	9.3
50	New Hampshire	8.6
51	Delaware	7.6

RECIPIENTS OF AFDC AND SSI

The two most important government aid programs, Aid to Families with Dependent Children (AFDC) and Supplemental Security Income (SSI), provide direct cash relief to poor people in the United States. AFDC provides assistance to children under 18 years of age who are being raised by a single parent with low income. The states organize the program and set the eligibility requirements. Federal grants to states cover more than half the total costs. SSI provides assistance to elderly, blind or disabled people who must also qualify on the basis of low income. Although SSI is a federal program, most states operate parallel programs to supplement federal payments.

Almost 14 million individuals received AFDC benefits and over 5 million individuals received SSI benefits in 1992. Persons receiving AFDC or SSI support made up 7.6% of the population that year. Numbers of recipients and costs increased for both programs through the 1980s and the 1990s. In 1980 AFDC payments totaled $12.4 billion, almost half the 1992 total of $22 billion. SSI payments for 1980 amounted to $7.7 billion; in 1992 the cost totaled $21.6 billion.

Variations in the percentage of state populations receiving these forms of support depended on several factors including the extent of poverty, the eligibility requirements set in each state and the willingness of qualified persons to seek support. The District of Columbia ranks first in the percent of people receiving AFDC and SSI benefits. Mississippi, the poorest state in the nation, has the second highest percentage of residents receiving benefits. However, many other states where poverty rates are high are not in the top half of this table. South Carolina, Oklahoma and Texas are examples. In Michigan, Ohio and Rhode Island, Maine, Massachusetts and Vermont a larger fraction of the population is supported by public aid than might be expected given comparatively low poverty rates.

TABLE: Recipients of AFDC and SSI
DATE: 1992
SOURCES: Compiled by the U.S. Bureau of the Census. Data from Social Security Administration, *Social Security Bulletin*, and U.S. Administration for Children and families, *Quarterly Public Assistance Statistics*
DESCRIPTION: Percent of population receiving public assistance from Aid to Families with Dependent Children and Federal Supplemental Security Income.

Rank		1980 percent	1992 percent
	United States	6.5	7.6
1	Washington, DC	15.5	13.3
2	Mississippi	11.4	11.8
3	California	8.8	10.7
4	Louisiana	8.3	10.2
5	Kentucky	7.2	9.8
6	West Virginia	6.0	9.7
7	New York	8.4	9.0
8	Michigan	8.9	9.0
9	Ohio	6.0	8.7
10	Tennessee	6.4	8.6
11	Georgia	6.9	8.5
12	New Mexico	6.1	8.0
13	Rhode Island	7.2	8.0
14	Illinois	7.0	7.9
15	Maine	7.4	7.6
16	Massachusetts	8.3	7.5
17	Vermont	6.4	7.2
18	North Carolina	5.8	7.2
19	Alabama	8.1	7.1

Rank		1980 percent	1992 percent
20	Wisconsin	6.1	6.9
21	Washington	4.9	6.9
22	Pennsylvania	6.7	6.9
23	Florida	4.4	6.8
24	Arkansas	7.2	6.8
25	Missouri	5.9	6.8
26	South Carolina	7.6	6.7
27	Alaska	4.6	6.7
28	Arizona	3.0	6.4
29	Oklahoma	5.2	6.4
30	Texas	4.0	6.3
31	New Jersey	7.4	6.1
32	Connecticut	5.2	6.0
33	Maryland	6.1	6.0
34	Hawaii	7.3	5.9
35	Minnesota	4.2	5.7
36	Montana	3.4	5.4
37	Oregon	4.9	5.2
38	Wyoming	1.9	5.2
39	Delaware	6.6	5.2
40	Iowa	4.6	5.0
41	Colorado	3.7	5.0
42	Indiana	3.7	5.0
43	Virginia	4.6	4.8
44	Kansas	3.8	4.6
45	South Dakota	4.2	4.6
46	North Dakota	3.0	4.3
47	Nebraska	3.2	4.2
48	Utah	3.2	3.8
49	Nevada	2.3	3.6
50	New Hampshire	3.0	3.4
51	Idaho	3.1	3.2

RECIPIENTS OF AID TO FAMILIES WITH DEPENDENT CHILDREN (AFDC)

In the 12-year period covered here, California and New York led the nation in numbers of AFDC recipients. However, California's numbers grew at a far more rapid rate. Similarly in Texas, Florida, Tennessee, Nevada, Alaska and Wyoming numbers of recipients more than doubled from 1980 to 1992. In Arizona they tripled. Ohio, Michigan, New Jersey and North Carolina, reported a substantial decreases in recipients over the same period.

TABLE: Recipients of Aid to Families with Dependent Children (AFDC)
DATE: 1992
SOURCE: U.S. Administration for Children and Families, *Quarterly Public Assistance Statistics*, annual

DESCRIPTION: Number of recipients of AFDC. Includes the children and one or both parents, or one caretaker.

Rank		1980 recipients (thousands)	1992 recipients (thousands)
	United States	10,923	13,834
1	California	1,498	2,395
2	New York	1,110	1,171
3	Texas	320	784
4	Ohio	572	721
5	Florida	279	704
6	Michigan	753	684
7	Illinois	691	682
8	Pennsylvania	637	601
9	Georgia	234	400
10	New Jersey	469	347
11	Massachusetts	348	335
12	North Carolina	202	335
13	Tennessee	174	316
14	Washington	173	283
15	Louisiana	219	269
16	Missouri	216	260
17	Wisconsin	232	233
18	Kentucky	175	229
19	Maryland	220	222
20	Indiana	170	199
21	Arizona	60	194
22	Virginia	176	194
23	Minnesota	146	186
24	Mississippi	176	172
25	Connecticut	140	159
26	South Carolina	156	147
27	Oklahoma	92	142
28	Alabama	178	141
29	Colorado	81	125
30	West Virginia	80	119
31	Oregon	94	116
32	Iowa	111	101
33	New Mexico	56	94
34	Kansas	72	86
35	Arkansas	85	73
36	Maine	58	67
37	Washington, DC	82	63
38	Rhode Island	54	61
39	Hawaii	61	54
40	Utah	44	53
41	Nebraska	38	48
42	Nevada	14	35
43	Alaska	16	35
44	Montana	20	34
45	Vermont	24	29
46	New Hampshire	24	29
47	Delaware	34	28
48	Idaho	20	21
49	South Dakota	19	20
50	North Dakota	13	19
51	Wyoming	7	18

AVERAGE MONTHLY AID TO FAMILIES WITH DEPENDENT CHILDREN (AFDC)

Average AFDC payments reflect both an assessment of need prevailing in each state and the amount of federal cash support. Recipients' cash needs vary to some extent according to cost of living, but this is not the only factor. The table shows that differences are even more striking. Alaska provides five times as much assistance per family as Mississippi. The very low levels of support provided by states in the South is the most remarkable feature of this table. The highest levels of support are observed in three West Coast states, the high-price states of Alaska and Hawaii, and states in the Northeast and Upper Midwest.

The differences of magnitude in welfare benefits between states is one of many factors that have fueled debates about welfare. It is unclear how the enactment of a 1996 welfare bill, which assigns each state a fixed sum of money to provide aid for families, will affect the differences seen in this table.

TABLE: Average monthly Aid to Families with Dependent Children (AFDC)
DATE: 1992
SOURCE: U.S. Administration for Children and Families, *Quarterly Public Assistance Statistics*, annual
DESCRIPTION: Average monthly AFDC payments per family 1992.

Rank		1992 average monthly payment ($)
	United States	385
1	California	5,875
2	New York	2,633
3	Michigan	1,167
4	Ohio	979
5	Pennsylvania	922
6	Illinois	891
7	Florida	787
8	Massachusetts	750
9	Washington	572
10	Texas	524
11	New Jersey	518
12	Wisconsin	450
13	Georgia	427
14	Minnesota	388
15	Connecticut	379
16	North Carolina	343
17	Maryland	335
18	Missouri	286
19	Arizona	252
20	Virginia	228

Rank		1992 average monthly payment ($)
21	Indiana	221
22	Kentucky	214
23	Tennessee	210
24	Oregon	200
25	Louisiana	184
26	Oklahoma	173
27	Iowa	164
28	Colorado	163
29	Rhode Island	130
30	Hawaii	130
31	West Virginia	121
32	Kansas	121
33	South Carolina	119
34	Maine	118
35	New Mexico	109
36	Washington, DC	101
37	Alaska	100
38	Mississippi	89
39	Alabama	88
40	Utah	76
41	Vermont	70
42	Nebraska	66
43	Arkansas	60
44	New Hampshire	55
45	Montana	46
46	Nevada	41
47	Delaware	38
48	North Dakota	28
49	Wyoming	27
50	South Dakota	25
51	Idaho	24

RECIPIENTS OF SUPPLEMENTAL SECURITY INCOME (SSI)

The SSI program provides a minimum income for the aged, blind and disabled. It also establishes uniform national basic eligibility requirements and payment standards. It is a federal program, but many states operate parallel programs to supplement federal payments. In many respects the figures ranked here parallel those that rank the states according to the number of AFDC recipients (see Recipients of AFDC, table on page 46).

TABLE: Recipients of Supplemental Security Income (SSI)
DATE: 1992
SOURCE: U.S. Social Security Administration, *Social Security Bulletin*, quarterly and *Annual Statistical Supplement to the Social Security Bulletin*
DESCRIPTION: Total SSI recipients for 1980 and 1992.

Rank		1980 recipients (thousands)	1992 recipients (thousands)
	United States total	4,142	5,566
1	California	718	957
2	New York	366	491
3	Texas	262**	345**
4	Florida	174	267
5	Illinois	124*	220*
6	Pennsylvania	163	220
7	Ohio	119	190
8	Georgia	155	177
9	Michigan	114	171
10	North Carolina	141*	166*
11	Tennessee	131	159
12	Louisiana	137	157
13	Alabama	134*	147*
14	Massachusetts	124	138
15	Kentucky	94*	134*
16	Mississippi	112	126
17	New Jersey	86	124
18	Virginia	81*	110*
19	South Carolina	83*	99*
20	Wisconsin	68	98
21	Missouri	84*	98*
22	Arkansas	78	86
23	Indiana	41*	75*
24	Washington	45	75
25	Maryland	48	69
26	Oklahoma	67*	67*
27	Arizona	30*	57*
28	West Virginia	41**	55**
29	Minnesota	32*	49*
30	Colorado	31*	47*
31	Oregon	22*	39*
32	Iowa	26	37
33	Connecticut	23*	37*
34	New Mexico	25*	37*
35	Kansas	20	30
36	Maine	22	26
37	Rhode Island	15	20
38	Washington, DC	15	18
39	Nebraska	14*	18*
40	Utah	8	16*
41	Hawaii	10	16
42	Nevada	7	15
43	Idaho	8*	13*
44	South Dakota	8	12
45	Montana	7	12
46	Vermont	9	12
47	Delaware	7	9
48	New Hampshire	5*	8*
49	North Dakota	6*	8*
50	Alaska	3*	5*
51	Wyoming	2*	5*

*Data for persons with federal SSI payments only; state has state-administered supplementation.
** Data for persons with federal SSI payments only; state supplementary payments not made.

THE FEDERAL FOOD STAMP PROGRAM

In 1993, 27 million individuals—11.3% of all the households in the nation—received benefits from the Food Stamp Program. Under the program, households meeting nationwide standards for income and assets may receive coupons redeemable for food at most retail food stores. The monthly amount of coupons a household receives is determined by household size and income. A household is defined here as: a person living alone, or a group of related or unrelated persons sharing the same living quarters, a house, an apartment, or other group of rooms. Households without income receive the determined monthly cost of a nutritionally adequate diet for their size household. This amount is updated to account for food price increases. Households with income receive the difference between the amount of a nutritionally adequate diet and 30% of their income, after certain allowable deductions.

TABLE: The Federal Food Stamp Program
DATE: 1993
SOURCES: U.S. Department of Agriculture, Food and Nutrition Service, "Annual Historical Review of FNS Programs" and unpublished data
DESCRIPTION: Number and percent of all households in state participating in the Federal Food Stamp Program.

Rank		Households participating (thousands)	Percent of households participating
	United States	10,782	11.3
1	Mississippi	200	21.4
2	Louisiana	282	18.4
3	West Virginia	124	17.7
4	Washington, DC	41	17.1
5	Tennessee	317	16.4
6	Texas	975	15.2
7	New Mexico	85	14.7
8	New York	943	14.1
9	Kentucky	200	14.1
10	Alabama	216	13.8
11	Maine	61	12.9
12	Ohio	535	12.8
13	Georgia	315	12.4
14	Arizona	178	12.1
15	Michigan	419	12.0
16	Oklahoma	146	11.9
17	Missouri	236*	11.8
18	Hawaii	44	11.6
19	Arkansas	106	11.6
20	Vermont	25	11.5
21	Illinois	493*	11.5

Rank		Households participating (thousands)	Percent of households participating
22	Pennsylvania	518	11.4
23	Florida	606	11.3
24	South Carolina	146	11.1
25	Rhode Island	40	10.6
26	Oregon	123	10.5
27	California	1075	10.0
28	North Carolina	253	9.6
29	Washington	191	9.5
30	Virginia	225	9.3
31	Maryland	159	8.7
32	Indiana	184	8.6
33	Montana	27	8.4
34	Massachusetts	189	8.4
35	Utah	47	8.1
36	Delaware	21	8.0
37	North Dakota	19	7.9
38	Nevada	42	7.8
39	Colorado	108	7.8
40	Minnesota	131	7.7
41	New Jersey	218	7.7
42	South Dakota	20	7.6
43	Kansas	73	7.6
44	Connecticut	93	7.6
45	Wyoming	13	7.5
46	Idaho	29	7.4
47	Nebraska	45	7.4
48	Iowa	78*	7.3
49	Alaska	14	6.8
50	Wisconsin	125	6.7
51	New Hampshire	26	6.2

*Includes disaster relief.

COST OF THE FEDERAL FOOD STAMP PROGRAM

Nationally, the Food Stamp Program cost $7.8 billion in 1980 and $22 billion in 1993. In the two top-ranking states, Texas and California, program costs quadrupled during the 13-year period. Food Stamp funding is highest in the most populous states, followed by the southern states, all of which rank in the top 26. These figures do not appear to parallel the data ranking the number of *households* participating in the Food Stamp Program (see Federal Food Stamp Program table on page 48). This maybe attributable to the variation in size and income of families receiving food stamps.

TABLE: Cost of the Federal Food Stamp Program
DATE: 1993

SOURCES: U.S. Department of Agriculture, Food and Nutrition Service, "Annual Historical Review of FNS Programs" and unpublished data.
DESCRIPTION: Cost of the Federal Food Stamp Program by state for 1980 and 1993.

Rank		1980 cost ($ millions)	1993 cost ($ millions)
	United States	7,859	21,972
1	Texas	514	2,239
2	California	530	2,079
3	New York	726	1,796
4	Florida	421	1,334
5	Ohio	382	1,101
6	Illinois	394	1,060
7	Pennsylvania	373	961
8	Michigan	263	837
9	Georgia	264	657
10	Louisiana	243	653
11	Tennessee	282	611
12	North Carolina	234	480
13	Missouri	142	478
14	New Jersey	226	469
15	Alabama	246	457
16	Virginia	158	432
17	Kentucky	211	422
18	Mississippi	199	416
19	Indiana	154	406
20	Arizona	97	393
21	Washington	90	369
22	Maryland	140	336
23	Massachusetts	171	326
24	South Carolina	181	306
25	Oklahoma	73	294
26	West Virginia	87	261
27	Oregon	80	235
28	Minnesota	62	229
29	Colorado	71	226
30	Wisconsin	68	221
31	Arkansas	122	209
32	New Mexico	81	194
33	Iowa	54	147
34	Connecticut	59	143
35	Kansas	38	141
36	Hawaii	60	132
37	Maine	60	112
38	Utah	22	97
39	Nevada	15	86
40	Nebraska	25	81
41	Washington, DC	41	81
42	Rhode Island	31	73
43	Idaho	29	57
44	Montana	18	54
45	New Hampshire	22	46
46	Delaware	21	46
47	Alaska	27	45
48	South Dakota	18	43
49	Vermont	18	38

Rank		1980 cost ($ millions)	1993 cost ($ millions)
50	North Dakota	9	36
51	Wyoming	6	26

National School Lunch Program

In 1993, 24.8 million children participated in the National School Lunch Program—1.6 million fewer than in 1980. Just under half of all pupils in grades K through 12 received some benefits from the program in 1993. Participation rates are tied to eligibility. Students qualify to participate on the basis of family income. Children from families with incomes below the poverty level qualify for free lunches if they attend a school that participates in the program. Children from families with incomes above the poverty level are also eligible for lunches at a reduced cost under specific federal guidelines.

TABLE: National School Lunch Program
DATE: 1993
SOURCES: U.S. Department of Agriculture, Food and Nutrition Service, "Annual Historical Review of FNS Programs" and unpublished data
DESCRIPTION: Number of individuals participating in the National School Lunch Program for 1980 and 1993.

Rank		1980 participants (thousands)	1993 participants (thousands)
	United States	26,384	24,770
1	California	2,006	2,292
2	Texas	1,835	2,119
3	New York	1,593	1,617
4	Florida	1,055	1,174
5	Pennsylvania	1,331	985
6	Illinois	1,129	959
7	Georgia	894	948
8	Ohio	1,156	943
9	North Carolina	887	751
10	Michigan	866	747
11	Louisiana	767	691
12	Indiana	717	602
13	Tennessee	648	601
14	Virginia	717	586
15	Alabama	607	565
16	Missouri	664	562
17	Kentucky	567	521
18	Minnesota	558	510
19	New Jersey	679	505
20	Wisconsin	533	487
21	South Carolina	489	459

Rank		1980 participants (thousands)	1993 participants (thousands)
22	Massachusetts	703	441
23	Mississippi	430	423
24	Washington	354	406
25	Iowa	439	383
26	Oklahoma	408	370
27	Arizona	291	365
28	Maryland	434	352
29	Kansas	308	316
30	Arkansas	356	310
31	Colorado	299	295
32	Oregon	277	250
33	Utah	233	249
34	Connecticut	288	226
35	Nebraska	203	203
36	West Virginia	245	199
37	New Mexico	174	183
38	Hawaii	162	150
39	Idaho	120	140
40	South Dakota	101	108
41	Maine	146	106
42	North Dakota	93	92
43	Nevada	80	89
44	New Hampshire	101	87
45	Montana	104	87
46	Delaware	68	61
47	Wyoming	51	58
48	Rhode Island	69	56
49	Vermont	59	49
50	Washington, DC	57	47
51	Alaska	33	45

Cost of the National School Lunch Program

This table shows the distribution of $4 billion of federal funds to the states for the National School Lunch Program. The rankings are determined both by the number of pupils in participating schools and on the percentage of pupils who qualified for support because of family income. The most populous states rank near the top of the list.

TABLE: Cost of the National School Lunch Program
DATE: 1993
SOURCES: U.S. Department of Agriculture, Food and Nutrition Service, "Annual Historical Review of FNS Program" and unpublished data

DESCRIPTION: Total cost of the National School Lunch Program for 1980 and 1993.

Rank		1980 cost ($ millions)	1993 cost ($ millions)
	United States	2,200	3,960
1	California	210	522
2	Texas	166	393
3	New York	171	290
4	Florida	102	227
5	Illinois	91	161
6	Georgia	80	140
7	Pennsylvania	93	130
8	Ohio	79	130
9	Louisiana	67	121
10	North Carolina	90	113
11	Michigan	69	105
12	Alabama	62	89
13	New Jersey	58	88
14	Mississippi	50	86
15	Tennessee	55	83
16	Virginia	51	78
17	South Carolina	51	76
18	Kentucky	48	75
19	Missouri	47	72
20	Indiana	39	67
21	Arizona	23	67
22	Washington	26	61
23	Oklahoma	30	58
24	Massachusetts	49	57
25	Wisconsin	32	56
26	Minnesota	33	53
27	Maryland	36	52
28	Arkansas	31	51
29	Colorado	21	40
30	Iowa	24	38
31	New Mexico	19	37
32	Kansas	19	36
33	Oregon	18	35
34	Connecticut	23	31
35	West Virginia	20	31
36	Utah	14	31
37	Nebraska	11	22
38	Idaho	7	18
39	Maine	13	15
40	Hawaii	9	15
41	South Dakota	7	14
42	Nevada	5	13
43	Washington, DC	8	12
44	Montana	6	12
45	Alaska	4	11
46	Rhode Island	7	10
47	North Dakota	5	10
48	New Hampshire	7	9
49	Delaware	5	8
50	Wyoming	3	7
51	Vermont	5	6

HOMELESS PERSONS

The table below does not represent a complete count of the homeless population, but rather an enumeration of the total number of homeless persons in emergency shelters, persons visible in the street and shelters designated exclusively for women. Of the total number of homeless people counted, 74% were located in shelters; 21% were visible in the street; and 5% resided in shelters for women.

TABLE: Homeless Persons
DATE: 1990
SOURCE: U.S. Bureau of the Census, *1990 Census of the Population*
DESCRIPTION: Total number of homeless persons in emergency shelters, persons visible in the street and in shelters designated for women.

Rank		Total homeless
	United States	241,746
1	California	50,144
2	New York	43,960
3	Florida	10,900
4	Texas	10,307
5	Pennsylvania	10,152
6	Illinois	9,772
7	New Jersey	9,364
8	Massachusetts	7,150
9	Washington	5,634
10	Ohio	4,961
11	Arizona	4,911
12	Washington, DC	4,862
13	Georgia	4,572
14	Connecticut	4,570
15	Michigan	4,552
16	Oregon	4,069
17	Maryland	3,229
18	North Carolina	3,211
19	Virginia	3,161
20	Colorado	3,114
21	Indiana	2,798
22	Kansas	2,750
23	Oklahoma	2,675
24	Minnesota	2,621
25	Missouri	2,608
26	Tennessee	2,451
27	Alabama	2,021
28	Hawaii	1,998
29	Louisiana	1,987
30	Wisconsin	1,884
31	Kentucky	1,592
32	Nevada	1,498
33	Iowa	1,301
34	Utah	1,250
35	South Carolina	1,162
36	New Mexico	939
37	Nebraska	825

Rank	State	Total homeless
38	Alaska	683
39	Arkansas	656
40	West Virginia	612
41	Mississippi	591
42	Idaho	558
43	Rhode Island	546
44	South Dakota	528

Rank	State	Total homeless
45	Montana	511
46	Maine	469
47	New Hampshire	412
48	Delaware	368
49	North Dakota	345
50	Vermont	271
51	Wyoming	241

GOVERNMENT REVENUES

This section presents data on revenues of federal, state and local governments. The U.S. Bureau of the Census compiles nationwide statistics relating to state and local governments. The other sources of data are the Department of the Treasury's *United States Government Annual Report* and the Office of Management and Budget. Detailed aggregate data on tax returns and collections are published annually by the Internal Revenue Service (IRS).

The United States' federal organization has resulted in a wide variety of governmental structures: the federal government and the states, thousands of local governments—counties, municipalities, townships, school districts and a variety of "special districts." The Census defined governmental units to include all agencies meeting three criteria: an organized existence, a governmental character and substantial autonomy. In 1992, 86,743 local governments satisfied these criteria. Local governments generate revenue via several mechanisms, including taxes. Some "special districts" cannot impose taxes and, therefore, are financed via rentals, charges for services, benefit assessments, grants from other governments, toll charges and other nontax sources. These special districts cover a range of entities; they include independent public housing authorities, the New York Port Authority and power districts.

Federal, state and local governments raise revenue primarily via taxes. The data reported in this section reveals the widely varying tax systems found in the 50 states. The chapter opens with an overview of revenues generated from federal, state and local governments. Next, it presents reports on the general sources of state and local government revenue and tables detailing the largest revenue-generating areas, income taxes, sales taxes, taxes on gasoline and cigarettes. The chapter concludes with an overview of federal income tax. The final table reports revenue from parimutuel, lotteries and amusement taxes.

STATE GENERAL REVENUE

The sum of all state revenue was over $605 billion in 1992. General revenue includes revenue from the federal government and state taxes, local governments, and charges and miscellaneous revenue. The industrialized and populous states rank at the top of the table.

Per capita revenue is the total amount of general revenue per person. Per capita revenue in the United States averaged $2,379 in 1992. Alaska, first in per capita revenue at $9,101, is more than double second place Hawaii, with per capita revenues of $3,938.

TABLE: State General Revenue
DATE: 1992
SOURCE: U.S. Bureau of the Census, *State Government Finances*
DESCRIPTION: Total general revenue and revenue per capita. Table ranked by total revenue.

Rank		Total revenue ($ millions)	Per capita revenue ($)	Per capita rank
	United States	605,334	2,379	
1	California	79,399	2,572	17
2	New York	60,412	3,334	5
3	Texas	31,346	1,775	49
4	Pennsylvania	29,859	2,486	19
5	Florida	23,652	1,754	50
6	New Jersey	23,400	3,004	8
7	Illinois	23,103	1,986	44
8	Ohio	22,990	2,087	37
9	Michigan	22,079	2,340	24
10	Massachusetts	18,234	3,040	7
11	North Carolina	14,981	2,189	30
12	Washington	13,434	2,616	15
13	Virginia	13,087	2,052	40
14	Georgia	12,379	1,833	48
15	Minnesota	12,347	2,756	13
16	Indiana	12,265	2,166	32
17	Wisconsin	12,107	2,418	22
18	Maryland	11,320	2,306	26
19	Louisiana	10,362	2,417	23
20	Connecticut	10,137	3,090	6
21	Missouri	9,872	1,901	47
22	Tennessee	9,624	1,916	46

Rank		Total revenue ($ millions)	Per capita revenue ($)	Per capita rank
23	Kentucky	9,222	2,456	20
24	Alabama	8,910	2,154	35
25	Arizona	7,975	2,081	38
26	South Carolina	7,862	2,182	31
27	Oregon	7,297	2,451	21
28	Colorado	7,016	2,022	43
29	Oklahoma	6,941	2,161	34
30	Iowa	6,519	2,318	25
31	Alaska	5,343	9,101	1
32	Mississippi	5,290	2,024	42
33	Arkansas	5,190	2,164	33
34	Kansas	4,968	1,969	45
35	New Mexico	4,743	3,000	9
36	Hawaii	4,568	3,938	2
37	West Virginia	4,559	2,516	18
38	Utah	4,060	2,239	28
39	Nebraska	3,526	2,195	29
40	Maine	3,312	2,682	14
41	Rhode Island	2,849	2,835	12
42	Nevada	2,715	2,046	41
43	Delaware	2,456	3,565	4
44	Idaho	2,447	2,294	27
45	New Hampshire	2,303	2,073	39
46	Montana	2,121	2,574	16
47	North Dakota	1,810	2,845	11
48	Wyoming	1,723	3,697	3
49	Vermont	1,701	2,985	10
50	South Dakota	1,518	2,136	36

STATE REVENUE FROM FEDERAL AND LOCAL GOVERNMENTS

During the past 12 years, the amount of federal and local money going to the states has increased over 100%. Local contributions have risen more than federal contributions, reflecting the political climate that moved away from big federal government during that period. In 1970 the federal government gave $12 billion to the states compared with $62 billion in 1980 and $159 billion in 1992, an increase of over 120%. In 1970 local governments contributed $985 million to the general revenue of the states, compared with $2.4 billion in 1980 and $11 billion in 1992, an increase of over 140%.

The table below also shows the balance between federal and local contributions within a state. For example, New York State, ranked second in revenue from the federal government and first in revenue from local government, receives over 20% of its revenue from local sources, while Texas, ranked third in revenues from the federal government and 20th in revenue from local government, receives less than 1% of its revenues from local sources.

TABLE: State Revenue from Federal and Local Governments
DATE: 1992
SOURCE: U.S. Bureau of the Census, *State Government Finances*
DESCRIPTION: General revenue from the federal government and from local governments to the states. Table ranked by federal revenue.

Rank		Revenue from federal government ($ millions)	Revenue from local governments ($ millions)	Local government revenue rank
	United States total	159,041	10,861	
1	California	21,562	1,867	2
2	New York	17,347	4,795	1
3	Texas	8,505	73	20
4	Pennsylvania	7,725	292	6
5	Ohio	6,268	201	11
6	Michigan	5,903	231	8
7	Illinois	5,559	181	12
8	Florida	5,407	305	5
9	New Jersey	5,130	208	10
10	Massachusetts	4,226	401	3
11	Georgia	3,724	47	25
12	North Carolina	3,695	322	4
13	Louisiana	3,676	19	37
14	Tennessee	3,385	42	29
15	Indiana	3,098	105	14
16	Missouri	2,945	11	44
17	Washington	2,930	65	24
18	Wisconsin	2,921	94	16
19	Alabama	2,707	30	30
20	Minnesota	2,687	223	9
21	Kentucky	2,594	16	39
22	Maryland	2,588	74	19
23	Virginia	2,563	163	13
24	South Carolina	2,347	97	15
25	Connecticut	2,270	5	46
26	Oregon	2,036	27	32
27	Mississippi	2,011	66	23
28	Arizona	1,852	258	7
29	Colorado	1,843	75	18
30	Oklahoma	1,736	43	28
31	Arkansas	1,630	6	45
32	Iowa	1,579	72	21
33	West Virginia	1,476	14	42
34	Kansas	1,341	18	38
35	New Mexico	1,116	87	17
36	Utah	1,106	45	27
37	Rhode Island	943	45	26
38	Maine	928	3	50
39	Nebraska	877	20	35
40	Hawaii	845	3	49
41	Alaska	762	11	43
42	New Hampshire	733	67	22
43	Montana	670	15	41
44	Wyoming	646	20	36

Rank		Revenue from federal government ($ millions)	Revenue from local governments ($ millions)	Local government revenue rank
45	Idaho	616	28	31
46	North Dakota	558	23	34
47	South Dakota	545	4	48

Rank		Revenue from federal government ($ millions)	Revenue from local governments ($ millions)	Local government revenue rank
48	Nevada	524	24	33
49	Vermont	504	5	47
50	Delaware	397	15	40

LOCAL GOVERNMENT REVENUE

Local government includes counties, municipalities, townships and school districts. Funding for these governments is supplied by both the federal and state governments; however, local governments generate the bulk of their revenue from their own sources. Nationally, local governments supplied 62% of their funding from their own sources, 34% from their state and 4% from the federal government.

New Mexico, where local governments provide 44% of their own funding, is the only state where local governments provide less than half their own funding. New Hampshire, Hawaii and South Dakota rank highest in generating funding from local sources.

The states that provide the highest percentage of state revenue to their local governments are West Virginia, Delaware, California and Arkansas. Hawaii, Montana, Oregon and Nevada rank highest in percentage of funding from the federal government

TABLE: Local Government Revenue
DATE: 1992
SOURCES: U.S. Bureau of the Census, *1982 Census of Governments, Historical Statistics on Governmental Finances and Employment,* and *Government Finances*
DESCRIPTION: Total local government general revenue and percentage of revenue from the federal government, state governments and the local governments. Percents may not add to 100% due to rounding. Table ranked by total revenue.

Rank		Total revenue in ($ millions)	Percent of revenue from federal government	Percent of revenue from state government	Percent of local government revenue
	United States	572,274	4	34	62
1	California	90,382	3	44	53
2	New York	70,750	3	33	65
3	Texas	35,085	2	27	70
4	Florida	31,384	3	28	69
5	Illinois	24,779	5	28	67
6	Pennsylvania	23,993	4	33	63
7	Ohio	21,808	4	33	63
8	New Jersey	20,615	1	36	63
9	Michigan	19,334	2	32	66
10	Georgia	13,823	4	27	69
11	Minnesota	12,279	4	39	57
12	Virginia	11,902	3	30	67
13	North Carolina	11,857	4	41	55
14	Massachusetts	11,775	5	33	61
15	Wisconsin	11,584	3	43	55
16	Washington	11,361	4	40	56
17	Indiana	9,887	2	36	61
18	Maryland	9,710	4	26	70
19	Missouri	8,133	3	31	66
20	Arizona	8,116	4	37	59

Rank		Total revenue in ($ millions)	Percent of revenue from federal government	Percent of revenue from state government	Percent of local government revenue
21	Colorado	8,061	3	28	69
22	Tennessee	7,744	4	28	68
23	Louisiana	7,719	4	32	63
24	Connecticut	6,924	3	29	68
25	Oregon	6,449	6	26	68
26	Alabama	6,078	4	35	61
27	Iowa	5,599	3	34	63
28	South Carolina	5,520	3	34	62
29	Kentucky	5,271	4	43	54
30	Oklahoma	4,985	3	37	59
31	Kansas	4,852	2	27	71
32	Washington, DC	4,712	38	NA	62
33	Mississippi	4,163	4	40	56
34	Nevada	3,298	6	38	56
35	Nebraska	3,106	4	27	70
36	Arkansas	3,061	3	44	53
37	Utah	3,037	3	36	61
38	New Mexico	2,806	4	52	44
39	West Virginia	2,601	2	46	52
40	Alaska	2,201	4	36	60
41	Maine	2,052	3	33	64
42	New Hampshire	2,049	2	12	85
43	Idaho	1,716	3	41	56
44	Rhode Island	1,550	5	26	70
45	Montana	1,487	7	31	62
46	Wyoming	1,379	2	40	58
47	Hawaii	1,239	8	11	81
48	North Dakota	1,056	4	37	58
49	Delaware	1,054	4	45	51
50	South Dakota	1,019	5	23	72
51	Vermont	927	1	30	69

NA Not applicable.

REVENUE FROM LOCAL TAXES

Local taxes supply the majority of revenue for local government in only seven states and the District of Columbia.

Several states at the top of the list are in New England, which has a history of strong local government.

Taxes represent only one way for local governments to generate revenue. Other means of generating funds include: charges for services, benefits from assessments, toll charges and rentals.

TABLE: Revenue from Local Taxes
SOURCES: U.S. Bureau of the Census, *1982 Census of Governments, Historical Statistics on Government Finances and Employment,* and *Government Finances*
DESCRIPTION: Local government revenue and percentage of total revenue from local taxes.

Rank		Revenue from local taxes ($ millions)	Percent of total revenue
	United States	226,696	40
1	New Hampshire	1,510	74
2	Rhode Island	938	61
3	Vermont	540	58
4	Connecticut	3,976	57
5	Hawaii	683	55
6	South Dakota	543	53
7	Maryland	4,965	51
8	Washington, DC	2,407	51
9	Illinois	12,146	49
10	New Jersey	10,080	49
11	Maine	995	48
12	New York	33,880	48
13	Virginia	5,659	48
14	Massachusetts	5,406	46
15	Oregon	2,916	45
16	Michigan	8,718	45
17	Texas	15,808	45

Rank		Revenue from local taxes ($ millions)	Percent of total revenue
18	Kansas	2,138	44
19	Colorado	3,493	43
20	Nebraska	1,345	43
21	Missouri	3,515	43
22	Ohio	9,222	42
23	Pennsylvania	9,998	42
24	Montana	561	38
25	Iowa	2,093	37
26	Tennessee	2,868	37
27	Georgia	5,102	37
28	Indiana	3,631	37
29	Louisiana	2,826	37
30	Wisconsin	4,220	36
31	Florida	11,377	36
32	Arizona	2,921	36
33	Utah	1,093	36
34	North Dakota	363	34
35	South Carolina	1,771	32
36	Wyoming	440	32
37	Washington	3,467	31
38	Alaska	665	30
39	Oklahoma	1,475	30
40	Minnesota	3,631	30
41	Arkansas	887	29
42	Idaho	496	29
43	California	25,946	29
44	Kentucky	1,508	29
45	North Carolina	3,387	29
46	Alabama	1,720	28
47	Nevada	889	27
48	Delaware	277	26
49	West Virginia	651	25
50	Mississippi	964	23
51	New Mexico	586	21

STATE TAX COLLECTIONS

In 1992 state tax collections totaled over $328 billion. The populous states obviously rank highest. The size of total revenue collected ranged from $46,128 billion in California to $565 million (South Dakota). The government included Washington, DC, in these figures, although it is not a state.

The figures below are a total of taxes and fees on: sales and gross receipts, individual income, net income of corporations, motor fuels, motor vehicle and operator licenses, alcoholic beverages, and tobacco products and other miscellaneous items. The tables that follow detail these taxes and fees.

TABLE: State Tax Collections
DATE: 1992

SOURCE: U.S. Bureau of the Census, *State Government Tax Collections*
DESCRIPTION: Total state government tax collections.

Rank	State	Total ($ millions)
	United States*	328,370
1	California	46,128
2	New York	30,113
3	Texas	17,031
4	Pennsylvania	16,270
5	Florida	14,504
6	Illinois	13,463
7	New Jersey	12,803
8	Ohio	12,115
9	Michigan	11,279
10	Massachusetts	9,903
11	North Carolina	9,010
12	Washington	8,477
13	Minnesota	7,450
14	Wisconsin	7,389
15	Georgia	7,267
16	Virginia	7,025
17	Maryland	6,502
18	Indiana	6,476
19	Connecticut	6,060
20	Missouri	5,131
21	Kentucky	5,081
22	Arizona	4,827
23	Tennessee	4,526
24	Louisiana	4,250
25	Alabama	4,218
26	South Carolina	3,936
27	Oklahoma	3,765
28	Iowa	3,602
29	Colorado	3,521
30	Oregon	3,313
31	Kansas	2,802
32	Arkansas	2,746
33	Hawaii	2,710
34	Mississippi	2,494
35	Washington, DC	2,440
36	West Virginia	2,352
37	New Mexico	2,243
38	Utah	1,989
39	Nebraska	1,890
40	Nevada	1,823
41	Maine	1,664
42	Alaska	1,590
43	Idaho	1,402
44	Delaware	1,341
45	Rhode Island	1,307
46	Montana	1,025
47	New Hampshire	829
48	Vermont	763
49	North Dakota	755
50	Wyoming	646
51	South Dakota	565

*Washington, DC, excluded from total.

STATE SALES TAX

Taxes on sales and gross receipts at the state level represent the largest percentage (33%) of total taxes collected. The sales tax is considered nonprogressive, meaning that the amount of tax on a sales transaction is the same whether paid by a high-income or a low-income consumer. Five states have no sales tax: Alaska, Delaware, Montana, New Hampshire and Oregon. In the five highest-ranked states—Washington, Florida, Tennessee, South Dakota and Texas—sales tax accounts for 50% or more of all taxes collected.

TABLE: State Sales Tax
DATE: 1992
SOURCE: U.S. Bureau of the Census, *State Government Tax Collections*
DESCRIPTION: Tax revenue and percentage of total tax revenue from general sales and gross receipts.

Rank		Total ($ millions)	Percent of total tax collections
	United States*	107,757	33
1	Washington	5,032	59
2	Florida	8,326	57
3	Tennessee	2,515	56
4	South Dakota	289	51
5	Texas	8,576	50
6	Nevada	893	49
7	Hawaii	1,295	48
8	Mississippi	1,182	47
9	New Mexico	983	44
10	Arizona	2,088	43
11	Indiana	2,779	43
12	Utah	802	40
13	Arkansas	1,033	38
14	Missouri	1,917	37
15	Georgia	2,687	37
16	South Carolina	1,452	37
17	Nebraska	663	35
18	Connecticut	2,090	34
19	Maine	573	34
20	Kansas	958	34
21	North Dakota	257	34
22	West Virginia	797	34
23	Michigan	3,666	33
24	California	14,925	32
25	New Jersey	4,049	32
26	Illinois	4,242	32
27	Idaho	439	31
28	Ohio	3,752	31
29	Louisiana	1,269	30
30	Rhode Island	389	30
31	Minnesota	2,191	29
32	Wisconsin	2,127	29
33	Wyoming	183	28
34	Iowa	1,010	28
35	Pennsylvania	4,500	28
36	Kentucky	1,367	27
37	Alabama	1,116	26
38	Colorado	914	26
39	Oklahoma	971	26
40	Maryland	1,580	24
41	North Carolina	2,171	24
42	Virginia	1,571	22
43	Vermont	157	21
44	Massachusetts	1,979	20
45	New York	6,006	20
46	Washington, DC*	442	18
47	Alaska	NA	NA
48	Delaware	NA	NA
49	Montana	NA	NA
50	New Hampshire	NA	NA
51	Oregon	NA	NA

NA Not applicable.
*Washington, DC, excluded from total.

STATE INCOME TAX

Taxes on personal income are the second most important source of revenue for states. They constitute 32% of total state tax revenue, only 1% less than sales tax revenue.

Personal income tax is the single largest source of state revenue in Oregon, Massachusetts and New York. Seven states have no income tax: Alaska, Florida, Nevada, South Dakota, Texas, Washington and Wyoming. Except for Alaska and Wyoming, all of these states rank among the top six states receiving the highest percentage of their revenue from sales tax. Generally, states with high revenue from income taxes have low revenues from sales taxes. States that rely on income rather than sales taxes are considered progressive, meaning higher-income individuals generally spend a larger fraction of their total earnings on taxes than low-income individuals.

TABLE: State Income Tax
DATE: 1992
SOURCE: U.S. Bureau of the Census, *State Government Tax Collections*
DESCRIPTION: Tax revenue and percentage of total tax revenue from individual income tax.

Rank		Total ($ millions)	Percent of total tax collections
	United States*	104,609	32
1	Oregon	2,221	67
2	Massachusetts	5,337	54
3	New York	14,913	50

Rank		Total ($ millions)	Percent of total tax collections
4	Virginia	3,321	47
5	Colorado	1,612	46
6	Maryland	2,907	45
7	Wisconsin	3,142	43
8	Georgia	3,082	42
9	Minnesota	2,999	40
10	North Carolina	3,583	40
11	Utah	781	39
12	Iowa	1,411	39
13	Idaho	535	38
14	Delaware	498	37
15	California	17,030	37
16	Rhode Island	478	37
17	Ohio	4,407	36
18	Missouri	1,844	36
19	South Carolina	1,411	36
20	Vermont	271	36
21	Maine	591	36
22	Nebraska	653	35
23	Illinois	4,582	34
24	Indiana	2,202	34
25	Hawaii	907	33
26	Kentucky	1,679	33
27	Oklahoma	1,218	32
28	New Jersey	4,102	32
29	Montana	322	31
30	Arkansas	850	31
31	Connecticut	1,866	31
32	Kansas	834	30
33	Alabama	1,234	29
34	Pennsylvania	4,689	29
35	Michigan	3,242	29
36	West Virginia	613	26
37	Washington, DC*	628	26
38	Arizona	1,240	26
39	Louisiana	867	20
40	New Mexico	445	20
41	Mississippi	440	28
42	North Dakota	119	16
43	New Hampshire	35	4
44	Tennessee	93	2
45	Alaska	NA	NA
46	Florida	NA	NA
47	Nevada	NA	NA
48	South Dakota	NA	NA
49	Texas	NA	NA
50	Washington	NA	NA
51	Wyoming	NA	NA

NA Not applicable.
*Washington, DC, excluded from total.

STATE CORPORATE INCOME TAX

Corporate income tax revenue represents 7% of total taxes collected nationally, $21.5 billion for 1992. Nevada, Texas, Washington and Wyoming do not have corporate income tax. However, they derive income from business enterprises through severance taxes or, in the case of Nevada, through taxes on gambling and amusements.

TABLE: State Corporate Income tax
DATE: 1992
SOURCE: U.S. Bureau of the Census, *State Government Tax Collections*
DESCRIPTION: Tax revenue and percentage of total tax revenue from corporate income.

Rank		Total ($ millions)	Percent of total collections
	United States*	21,566	7
1	Michigan	1,730	15
2	Alaska	200	13
3	New Hampshire	96	12
4	Pennsylvania	1,624	10
5	Connecticut	594	10
6	California	4,518	10
7	Delaware	129	10
8	New York	2,519	8
9	West Virginia	182	8
10	Massachusetts	757	8
11	Illinois	971	7
12	North Carolina	644	7
13	Kansas	199	7
14	New Jersey	846	7
15	Tennessee	295	7
16	South Dakota	35	6
17	Indiana	386	6
18	Wisconsin	438	6
19	Mississippi	145	6
20	Minnesota	423	6
21	Montana	58	6
22	Nebraska	104	6
23	Louisiana	232	5
24	Iowa	193	5
25	Kentucky	271	5
26	Ohio	642	5
27	Georgia	376	5
28	North Dakota	39	5
29	Washington, DC*	121	5
30	Idaho	68	5
31	Florida	695	5
32	Arkansas	126	5
33	Oregon	152	5
34	Missouri	230	4
35	Arizona	211	4

Rank		Total ($ millions)	Percent of total collections
36	Maine	70	4
37	Vermont	31	4
38	Oklahoma	149	4
39	Alabama	165	4
40	Virginia	273	4
41	Utah	76	4
42	Rhode Island	49	4
43	South Carolina	142	4
44	Colorado	123	3
45	New Mexico	78	3
46	Maryland	217	3
47	Hawaii	68	3
48	Nevada	NA	NA
49	Texas	NA	NA
50	Washington	NA	NA
51	Wyoming	NA	NA

NA Not applicable.

*Washington, DC, excluded from total.

STATE TAXES ON ALCOHOLIC BEVERAGES AND TOBACCO PRODUCTS

Taxes from the sale of alcoholic beverages and tobacco products account for 3% of all state taxes collected. This tax is a significant source of revenue for states such as Florida, New Hampshire and Texas, which have no income tax.

TABLE: State Taxes on Alcoholic Beverages and Tobacco Products

DATE: 1992

SOURCE: U.S. Bureau of the Census, *State Government Tax Collections*

DESCRIPTION: Tax revenue and percent of total tax revenue from the sale of alcoholic beverages and tobacco.

Rank	State	Total ($ millions)	Percent of total tax collections
	United States*	9,717	3
1	Florida	962	7
2	New Hampshire	49	6
3	Texas	970	6
4	Maine	89	5
5	Alabama	178	4
6	South Dakota	23	4
7	Kansas	110	4
8	Vermont	28	4
9	Rhode Island	46	4
10	South Carolina	138	4
11	Louisiana	149	4
12	Nevada	63	3

Rank	State	Total ($ millions)	Percent of total tax collections
13	Mississippi	86	3
14	Arkansas	93	3
15	Oklahoma	126	3
16	Michigan	368	3
17	Tennessee	143	3
18	Washington	267	3
19	Iowa	110	3
20	Oregon	98	3
21	Pennsylvania	481	3
22	Minnesota	218	3
23	Nebraska	54	3
24	New York	829	3
25	Illinois	370	3
26	Georgia	199	3
27	New Jersey	350	3
28	Montana	28	3
29	Connecticut	162	3
30	Wisconsin	193	3
31	Idaho	36	3
32	Hawaii	69	3
33	North Dakota	19	3
34	Ohio	288	2
35	Colorado	83	2
36	Delaware	31	2
37	Indiana	144	2
38	California	1,014	2
39	North Carolina	196	2
40	Utah	43	2
41	Massachusetts	206	2
42	Missouri	103	2
43	Arizona	94	2
44	Alaska	29	2
45	Maryland	117	2
46	West Virginia	41	2
47	Virginia	113	2
48	New Mexico	36	2
49	Kentucky	68	1
50	Wyoming	7	1
51	Washington, DC	23	1

*Washington, DC, excluded from total.

STATE SALES TAX RATES

The table below ranks states by rate of sales tax. It is important to note that in some areas, local sales tax can add significantly to the total tax on sales. The table indicates whether food and prescription drugs are exempt from tax. This exemption is important in analyzing the impact of sales taxes because, nationally, food purchases account for approximately one-quarter of all consumer purchases.

TABLE: State Sales Tax Rates

DATE: 1992

SOURCE: U.S. Bureau of the Census, *State Government Tax Collections*

DESCRIPTION: Sales tax rate.

Rank	State	Sales tax (%)	Notes
1	Mississippi	7.00	D
2	Rhode Island	7.00	F&D
3	California	6.50	F&D*
4	Nevada	6.50	F&D*
5	Washington	6.50	F&D
6	Illinois	6.25	***
7	Connecticut	6.00	F&D
8	Washington, DC	6.00	F&D
9	Kentucky	6.00	F&D
10	Maine	6.00	F&D
11	Minnesota	6.00	F&D*
12	New Jersey	6.00	F&D
13	Pennsylvania	6.00	F&D
14	Tennessee	6.00	D*
15	Texas	6.00	D*
16	West Virginia	6.00	D
17	Arizona	5.00	F&D**
18	Florida	5.00 7.0%	F&D*
19	Idaho	5.00	D
20	Indiana	5.00	F&D
21	Iowa	5.00	F&D
22	Maryland	5.00	F&D
23	Massachusetts	5.00	F&D
24	Nebraska	5.00	F&D*
25	New Mexico	5.00	*
26	North Dakota	5.00	F&D
27	Ohio	5.00 2010 6.75%	F&D*
28	South Carolina	5.00	D
29	Utah	5.00	D*
30	Vermont	5.00	F&D
31	Wisconsin	5.00	F&D*
32	Kansas	4.90	D*
33	Arkansas	4.50	D*
34	Oklahoma	4.50	D*
35	Missouri	4.23	D*
36	Alabama	4.00	D*
37	Georgia	4.00	D*
38	Hawaii	4.00	D
39	Louisiana	4.00	D***
40	Michigan	4.00	F&D
41	New York	4.00	F&D*
42	North Carolina	4.00	D*
43	South Dakota	4.00	D*
44	Virginia	3.50	D*
45	Colorado	3.00	F&D*
46	Wyoming	3.00	D*
47	Alaska	X	X
48	Delaware	X	X
49	Montana	X	X
50	New Hampshire	X	X
51	Oregon	X	X

F Food exempt from sales tax.
D Prescription drugs exempt from sales tax.

*Local sales tax rates are additional.
**Food and prescription drugs are subject to a 1% state tax. In addition, these items may be subject to a 1% local tax.
***Food products subject to a 2 percent state tax.
X No sales tax

GASOLINE TAX RATES

Between 1982 and 1992 gasoline tax rates increased significantly; the median in 1982 was 10 cents a gallon, while in 1992 it was 18 cents a gallon. Compare Connecticut, ranked first in 1992 with a tax rate of 26 cents a gallon with New Hampshire, ranked first in 1982, at 14 cents a gallon. Only Florida lowered gasoline tax rates (from 8 cents in 1982 to 4 cents in 1992). In Georgia, New York and Alaska gasoline tax rates remained unchanged between 1982 and 1992.

TABLE: Gasoline Tax Rates
DATE: 1992
SOURCE: U.S. Bureau of the Census, *State Government Tax Collections*
DESCRIPTION: Gasoline excise tax rates in cents per gallon.

Rank	State	Cents per gallon
1	Connecticut	26
2	Nebraska	23.7
3	Maryland	23.5
4	Rhode Island	23
5	Washington	23
6	North Carolina	22.3
7	Wisconsin	22.2
8	Colorado	22
9	Oregon	22
10	Idaho	21
11	Massachusetts	21
12	Ohio	21
13	Iowa	20
14	Louisiana	20
15	Minnesota	20
16	Montana	20
17	Tennessee	20
18	Texas	20
19	Delaware	19
20	Illinois	19
21	Maine	19
22	Utah	19
23	Nevada	18.75
24	Arkansas	18.5
25	Arizona	18
26	Washington, DC	18
27	Kansas	18
28	Mississippi	18
29	New Hampshire	18
30	South Dakota	18
31	Virginia	17.5
32	North Dakota	17

Rank	State	Cents per gallon
33	Oklahoma	17
34	Hawaii	16*
35	Alabama	16
36	California	16
37	New Mexico	16
38	South Carolina	16
39	West Virginia	15.5
40	Indiana	15
41	Kentucky	15
42	Michigan	15
43	Vermont	15
44	Missouri	13
45	Pennsylvania	12
46	New Jersey	10.5
47	Wyoming	9
48	Alaska	8
49	New York	8
50	Georgia	7.5**
51	Florida	4

*Combined state and county rates are: Hawaii 24.8 cents; Honolulu 32.5 cents; Kauai 26 cents; and Maui 25 cents.
**An additional tax is levied at the rate of 3 percent of the retail sales price, less than the current 7.5 cents per gallon tax.

CIGARETTE TAX RATES

Taxes on cigarettes rose substantially from 1982 to 1992, perhaps because of the increased desire to discourage smoking. Washington, DC's 50 cent tax is the highest in the nation. The top tobacco producing states, North Carolina, Kentucky, and Virginia, rank at the bottom.

TABLE: Cigarette Tax Rates
DATE: 1992
SOURCE: U.S. Bureau of the Census, *State Government Tax Collections*
DESCRIPTION: Cigarette excise tax rate in cents per package.

Rank	State	Cents per package
1	Washington, DC	50
2	Minnesota	48
3	Connecticut	45
4	Texas	41
5	New Jersey	40
6	New York	39
7	Wisconsin	38
8	Maine	37
9	Rhode Island	37
10	Iowa	36
11	Maryland	36
12	California	35
13	Nevada	35
14	Washington	34
15	Florida	33.9
16	Pennsylvania	31
17	Illinois	30

Rank	State	Cents per package
18	Alaska	29
19	North Dakota	29
20	Oregon	28
21	Nebraska	27
22	Massachusetts	26
23	Michigan	25
24	New Hampshire	25
25	Delaware	24
26	Kansas	24
27	Oklahoma	23
28	South Dakota	23
29	Utah	23
30	Arkansas	22
31	Colorado	20
32	Louisiana	20
33	Montana	19.25
34	Arizona	18
35	Idaho	18
36	Mississippi	18
37	Ohio	18
38	Vermont	18
39	West Virginia	17
40	Alabama	16.5
41	Indiana	15.5
42	New Mexico	15
43	Missouri	13
44	Tennessee	13
45	Georgia	12
46	Wyoming	12
47	South Carolina	7
48	North Carolina	5
49	Kentucky	3
50	Virginia	2.5
51	Hawaii	*

*Tax is 40 percent of wholesale price.

FEDERAL INCOME TAX RETURNS

This table ranks states according to per capita income tax dollars paid to the federal government. In 1992 the median per capita income tax paid by a family of four was $1,687. States in the Northeast and Mid-Atlantic areas rank highest in this table. Southern and western states rank at the bottom. Rankings in this table are closely connected to income figures found on Per Capita Personal Income and Median Household Income table (pages 41 and 42).

TABLE: Federal Income Tax Returns
DATE: 1991
SOURCE: U.S. Internal Revenue Service, *Statistics of Income Bulletin*
DESCRIPTION: Number of tax returns, state's total adjusted gross income, total income tax collection and per capita income tax. Table ranked by per capita income tax dollars.

Rank		Number of returns (millions)	Total adjusted gross income ($ millions)	Total income tax ($ millions)	Average per capita income tax ($)
	United States	115,767	3,453,028	473,533	1,878
1	Connecticut	1,610	63,499	10,037	3,050
2	New Jersey	3,827	140,841	20,650	2,661
3	Washington, DC	311	9,942	1,500	2,509
4	Alaska	339	9,315	1,427	2,504
5	Nevada	643	20,138	3,016	2,349
6	Massachusetts	2,836	95,333	13,698	2,285
7	Maryland	2,321	81,110	11,044	2,273
8	New York	8,119	279,687	40,339	2,234
9	Illinois	5,391	172,970	25,118	2,176
10	Washington	2,378	75,255	10,898	2,172
11	Delaware	331	10,748	1,451	2,134
12	Hawaii	567	17,779	2,416	2,129
13	New Hampshire	534	16,883	2,345	2,123
14	California	13,790	448,325	61,650	2,029
15	Virginia	2,908	93,151	12,516	1,991
16	Colorado	1,627	48,145	6,657	1,972
17	Florida	6,250	177,889	25,504	1,921
18	Minnesota	2,048	62,289	8,255	1,863
19	Pennsylvania	5,502	161,105	22,062	1,845
20	Wyoming	211	5,858	835	1,816
21	Rhode Island	458	13,676	1,821	1,814
22	Michigan	4,181	126,862	16,974	1,812
23	Texas	7,607	211,909	30,739	1,772
24	Kansas	1,128	31,923	4,321	1,732
25	Ohio	5,129	142,204	18,692	1,709
26	Wisconsin	2,287	64,917	8,355	1,687
27	Indiana	2,544	71,240	9,384	1,673
28	Georgia	2,947	84,162	10,933	1,651
29	Missouri	2,295	63,471	8,473	1,643
30	Oregon	1,339	37,305	4,801	1,643
31	Vermont	266	7,095	903	1,593
32	Nebraska	745	19,315	2,536	1,592
33	Tennessee	2,208	57,976	7,784	1,572
34	Iowa	1,281	33,209	4,294	1,537
35	Arizona	1,654	44,520	5,680	1,515
36	North Carolina	3,094	82,315	10,191	1,513
37	South Dakota	319	7,469	1,016	1,446
38	North Dakota	284	6,860	911	1,435
39	Maine	556	14,428	1,766	1,430
40	Alabama	1,747	45,109	5,682	1,390
41	Oklahoma	1,347	34,025	4,382	1,381
42	Louisiana	1,723	43,423	5,743	1,351
43	Idaho	445	11,225	1,402	1,350
44	Kentucky	1,538	39,331	4,933	1,329
45	Montana	368	8,489	1,073	1,328
46	Utah	711	19,447	2,340	1,322
47	South Carolina	1,567	39,605	4,703	1,321
48	New Mexico	680	16,303	1,994	1,289
49	West Virginia	700	17,540	2,166	1,203
50	Arkansas	984	22,981	2,791	1,177
51	Mississippi	1,036	22,783	2,645	1,020

STATE EXPENDITURES AND DEBT

This section reviews data on state and local government expenditures. The U.S. Bureau of the Census compiles nationwide statistics relating to state and local governments as well as those on the states' expenditure of federal funds. The statistics have been classified and reported in terms of uniform concepts and categories, rather than according to the highly diverse organization and financing structures used by individual governments.

The first two tables report the distribution of federal funds. The following detail federal aid to state and local governments and itemize state government expenditures. The chapter closes with a table, documenting outstanding total and per capita state debt.

FEDERAL FUNDS TO STATES

It is important to understand the difference between fund monies and trust fund monies in order to evaluate this table. Derived principally from taxes and borrowing, federal fund monies are not restricted by law to any specific government purpose. Federal fund monies are distinct from trust fund monies, which are collected via specific taxes and other receipts for a specific purpose or program in accordance with the terms of the trust agreement or statute. Unemployment insurance and Social Security are financed through trust funds. In total the federal government distributed $1,225 billion nationally, $4,814 per person.

TABLE: Federal Funds to States
DATE: 1993
SOURCE: U.S. Bureau of the Census, *Federal Expenses by State for Fiscal Year 1993*, annual
DESCRIPTION: Total and per capita federal funds to states. Table ranked by per capita funds. Not all federal funds are included in this total (see text).

Rank		Total ($ millions)	Per capita ($)
	United States	1,224,689	4,814
1	Washington, DC	20,250	35,034
2	Alaska	4,611	7,697
3	New Mexico	11,197	6,929
4	Virginia	44,295	6,824
5	Maryland	33,775	6,803
6	Hawaii	7,052	6,017
7	North Dakota	3,642	5,735
8	Massachusetts	34,300	5,705
9	Missouri	29,278	5,594
10	Maine	6,664	5,379
11	Rhode Island	5,287	5,287
12	Montana	4,376	5,216
13	Colorado	18,159	5,092
14	South Dakota	3,627	5,073
15	Alabama	21,180	5,058
16	Connecticut	16,447	5,017
17	Florida	68,523	5,009
18	Mississippi	13,080	4,949
19	West Virginia	8,928	4,906
20	New York	87,442	4,802
21	Pennsylvania	57,742	4,792
22	Nebraska	7,613	4,737
23	Washington	24,832	4,726
24	California	147,364	4,720
25	Wyoming	2,217	4,717
26	Kansas	11,886	4,696
27	Louisiana	20,204	4,685
28	Arizona	18,376	4,669
29	Tennessee	23,778	4,663
30	Oklahoma	14,799	4,580
31	New Jersey	35,885	4,555
32	South Carolina	16,367	4,493
33	Arkansas	10,843	4,473
34	Kentucky	16,797	4,433
35	Idaho	4,825	4,391
36	Georgia	30,139	4,357
37	Iowa	12,131	4,311
38	Texas	75,268	4,174
39	Nevada	5,766	4,151
40	Ohio	45,985	4,146

Rank		Total ($ millions)	Per capita ($)
41	Oregon	12,379	4,083
42	Illinois	47,559	4,066
43	Delaware	2,833	4,047
44	Vermont	2,320	4,029
45	Utah	7,461	4,011
46	Minnesota	18,017	3,989
47	North Carolina	27,210	3,918
48	Michigan	36,830	3,886
49	Indiana	22,111	3,870
50	Wisconsin	18,911	3,754
51	New Hampshire	4,128	3,669

DEFENSE SPENDING IN STATES

In 1993 a total of $1,225 billion in federal funds were available to states, $213 million of which were spent by defense entities in the states. These funds support the country's national defense activities.

The percentage of federal funds spent on defense ranged from 42% in Virginia and Hawaii to 4% in West Virginia, with a median of 15% overall.

TABLE: Defense Spending in States
DATE: 1993
SOURCE: U.S. Bureau of the Census, *Federal Expenses by State for Fiscal Year*, annual
DESCRIPTION: Federal money spent by defense entities in the state and percentage of total federal money spent in states.
UNITED STATES TOTAL: $213,122

Rank	State	Federal funds ($ millions)	Percent of federal funds spent by defense entities
1	Virginia	18,622	42
2	Hawaii	2,928	42
3	Alaska	1,724	37
4	Georgia	8,201	27
5	Colorado	4,824	27
6	Maine	1,728	26
7	California	36,910	25
8	Missouri	6,923	24
9	Arizona	4,211	23
10	Texas	16,081	21
11	Connecticut	3,503	21
12	Maryland	7,157	21
13	Washington	5,205	21
14	Mississippi	2,723	21
15	Utah	1,540	21
16	Massachusetts	7,067	21
17	South Carolina	3,263	20
18	North Carolina	5,254	19

Rank	State	Federal funds ($ millions)	Percent of federal funds spent by defense entities
19	Alabama	4,030	19
20	Florida	12,770	19
21	Oklahoma	2,618	18
22	New Mexico	1,888	17
23	Kentucky	2,630	16
24	Rhode Island	819	15
25	Kansas	1,832	15
26	New Hampshire	626	15
27	Delaware	413	15
28	Louisiana	2,891	14
29	Nevada	823	14
30	North Dakota	513	14
31	Washington, DC	2,828	14
32	Indiana	2,867	13
33	Ohio	5,664	12
34	Nebraska	929	12
35	New Jersey	4,198	12
36	Wyoming	244	11
37	Minnesota	1,921	11
38	South Dakota	357	10
39	Pennsylvania	5,592	10
40	Arkansas	1,016	9
41	Idaho	401	8
42	Tennessee	1,951	8
43	Montana	333	8
44	New York	6,506	7
45	Illinois	3,214	7
46	Wisconsin	1,277	7
47	Michigan	2,373	6
48	Vermont	146	6
49	Oregon	633	5
50	Iowa	594	5
51	West Virginia	361	4

FEDERAL AID TO STATE AND LOCAL GOVERNMENTS

The data presented in this table tabulate money available to states for Medicaid, the administration of programs for families and children, highways, lower-income housing assistance, compensatory education, employment and job training, community development and waste treatment facility construction.

Per capita aid to state and local governments averages $746 nationally. The District of Columbia ranks first because it receives federal aid in lieu of state aid. This table gives a broad view of total federal aid to states. The following nine tables detail the monies and percentage of federal aid apportioned to states for significant programs.

TABLE: Federal Aid to State and Local Governments
SOURCE: U.S. Bureau of the Census, *Federal Expenditures by State for Fiscal Year 1993*
DESCRIPTION: Total and per capita federal aid to state and local governments.

Rank		Total aid ($ millions)	Per capita aid ($)
	United States	195,201	746
1	Washington, DC	1,961	3,392
2	Alaska	948	1,583
3	Wyoming	645	1,372
4	New York	21,166	1,163
5	Louisiana	4,817	1,122
6	Rhode Island	1,107	1,107
7	West Virginia	1,884	1,035
8	North Dakota	640	1,008
9	Montana	831	990
10	Vermont	557	967
11	New Mexico	1,534	949
12	Maine	1,166	941
13	Massachusetts	5,520	918
14	South Dakota	654	915
15	Mississippi	2,285	864
16	Hawaii	984	840
17	Connecticut	2,691	821
18	Kentucky	3,041	802
19	New Jersey	6,189	786
20	Tennessee	3,925	770
21	Arkansas	1,855	765
22	Alabama	3,081	736
23	Minnesota	3,297	730
24	Washington	3,722	708
25	Pennsylvania	8,517	707
26	Michigan	6,654	702
27	Ohio	7,716	696
28	California	21,635	693
29	Oregon	2,099	692
30	South Carolina	2,521	692
31	Nebraska	1,108	690
32	Missouri	3,566	681
33	Wisconsin	3,397	674
34	Arizona	2,640	671
35	Illinois	7,845	671
36	Maryland	3,310	667
37	Indiana	3,732	653
38	Oklahoma	2,111	653
39	Delaware	455	650
40	Idaho	712	648
41	North Carolina	4,498	648
42	Georgia	4,408	637
43	Kansas	1,608	635
44	Utah	1,173	631
45	Iowa	1,737	617
46	Texas	11,035	612
47	Colorado	2,109	592
48	New Hampshire	652	579
49	Florida	7,579	554

Rank		Total aid ($ millions)	Per capita aid ($)
50	Nevada	767	552
51	Virginia	2,945	454

FEDERAL AID FOR MEDICAID

Medicaid, a health insurance program available to individuals who qualify on the basis of income, constitutes the largest portion of federal aid to state and local governments. A joint federal and state program, Medicaid is funded primarily by the federal government. It represented 39% of all federal aid to the states in 1993.

TABLE: Federal Aid for Medicaid
DATE: 1993
SOURCE: U.S. Bureau of the Census, *Federal Expenses by State for Fiscal Year 1993*, annual
DESCRIPTION: Federal aid to states and local governments for Medicaid.

Rank		Total ($ millions)	Percent of total federal aid to state
	United States	75,774	39
1	Louisiana	2,820	59
2	West Virginia	917	49
3	New York	10,228	48
4	Indiana	1,797	48
5	South Carolina	1,210	48
6	Tennessee	1,859	47
7	New Jersey	2,820	46
8	Maine	525	45
9	Rhode Island	480	43
10	Texas	4,736	43
11	North Carolina	1,926	43
12	Kentucky	1,298	43
13	Arkansas	782	42
14	Ohio	3,230	42
15	Kansas	667	41
16	Connecticut	1,103	41
17	Mississippi	933	41
18	Georgia	1,762	40
19	Missouri	1,404	39
20	Alabama	1,204	39
21	Pennsylvania	3,321	39
22	Minnesota	1,276	39
23	Wisconsin	1,304	38
24	Michigan	2,547	38
25	Oklahoma	797	38
26	Florida	2,857	38
27	Arizona	976	37
28	Washington	1,372	37
29	Massachusetts	2,017	37
30	Iowa	617	36

Rank		Total ($ millions)	Percent of total federal aid to state
31	Colorado	728	35
32	California	7,414	34
33	Maryland	1,093	33
34	Nebraska	362	33
35	Illinois	2,545	32
36	New Hampshire	210	32
37	Virginia	922	31
38	Idaho	221	31
39	North Dakota	197	31
40	Oregon	642	31
41	Utah	357	30
42	Vermont	167	30
43	South Dakota	194	30
44	Delaware	132	29
45	New Mexico	438	29
46	Nevada	217	28
47	Montana	232	28
48	Hawaii	221	22
49	Alaska	168	18
50	Washington, DC	345	18
51	Wyoming	103	16

FEDERAL AID FOR THE ADMINISTRATION OF PROGRAMS FOR FAMILIES AND CHILDREN

The data in this table document aid to states for the administration of programs that include support payments for Aid to Families with Dependent Children (AFDC), social service block grants, children and family services, foster care and adoption assistance, low-income home energy assistance, community service block grants, refugee assistance and assistance to legalized aliens.

Funding for these programs constituted 15% of all federal aid to the state and local governments in 1993. Twenty-four percent of California's federal funding is used for the administration of AFDC. Louisiana uses only 8% of federal funding for this purpose. The average for all states is 13%.

TABLE: Federal Aid for the Adminstration of Programs for Families and Children
DATE: 1993
SOURCE: U.S. Bureau of the Census, *Federal Expenses by State for Fiscal Year 1993*, annual
DESCRIPTION: Federal aid to states for the administration of programs for children and families and

percentage of total federal aid to state from these programs.

Rank		Total ($ millions)	Percent of total federal aid to state
	United States	28,347	15
1	California	5,189	24
2	Michigan	1,343	20
3	Washington	669	18
4	Wisconsin	579	17
5	Ohio	1,257	16
6	New York	3,434	16
7	Minnesota	514	16
8	Vermont	86	15
9	Illinois	1,174	15
10	Pennsylvania	1,258	15
11	Arizona	388	15
12	Iowa	255	15
13	Kansas	234	15
14	Oklahoma	307	15
15	Oregon	303	14
16	Massachusetts	757	14
17	Nebraska	149	13
18	Maryland	445	13
19	Utah	157	13
20	Virginia	391	13
21	Florida	1,004	13
22	Maine	152	13
23	North Carolina	586	13
24	Georgia	572	13
25	Delaware	59	13
26	Missouri	454	13
27	New Hampshire	83	13
28	Kentucky	386	13
29	Connecticut	341	13
30	Colorado	265	13
31	New Jersey	775	13
32	Hawaii	123	13
33	Rhode Island	137	12
34	Alaska	117	12
35	Montana	101	12
36	New Mexico	177	12
37	North Dakota	71	11
38	Idaho	76	11
39	Washington, DC	207	11
40	West Virginia	195	10
41	Mississippi	233	10
42	Indiana	378	10
43	Nevada	77	10
44	South Dakota	65	10
45	Texas	1,083	10
46	Tennessee	374	10
47	South Carolina	227	9
48	Alabama	271	9
49	Arkansas	150	8
50	Wyoming	51	8
51	Louisiana	368	8

FEDERAL AID FOR HIGHWAYS

Federal highway aid accounted for 8% of all federal non-defense aid to states and local governments in 1993. The median percentage aid for highways among states and local governments is 10%. The rural, sparsely populated and geographically remote states rank highest in federal highway aid. Highway aid accounted for 24% of total federal aid to Alaska. At the other end of the spectrum, New York received only 4% of its federal aid specifically for highways.

TABLE: Federal Aid for Highways
DATE: 1993
SOURCE: U.S. Bureau of the Census, *Federal Expenses by State for Fiscal Year 1993*, annual
DESCRIPTION: Federal aid to states for highways from the highway trust fund and percentage of total federal aid to states from that program.

Rank		Total ($ millions)	Percent of total federal aid to state
	United States	16,152	8
1	Alaska	223	24
2	Vermont	116	21
3	Hawaii	193	20
4	Montana	161	19
5	South Dakota	121	19
6	Wyoming	119	18
7	North Dakota	109	17
8	New Hampshire	98	15
9	Idaho	104	15
10	New Mexico	218	14
11	Massachusetts	773	14
12	Utah	154	13
13	Nevada	100	13
14	Delaware	57	13
15	Iowa	216	12
16	Nebraska	137	12
17	Connecticut	329	12
18	Rhode Island	132	12
19	Colorado	246	12
20	Arkansas	204	11
21	Indiana	383	10
22	Wisconsin	348	10
23	Kansas	162	10
24	Alabama	307	10
25	Washington	367	10
26	Texas	1,061	10
27	Minnesota	317	10
28	Missouri	339	10
29	North Carolina	425	9
30	Georgia	410	9
31	Arizona	245	9
32	South Carolina	214	8
33	Mississippi	190	8

Rank		Total ($ millions)	Percent of total federal aid to state
34	Florida	630	8
35	Oregon	170	8
36	Maryland	258	8
37	Pennsylvania	659	8
38	Virginia	226	8
39	Oklahoma	159	8
40	West Virginia	141	7
41	Maine	87	7
42	New Jersey	440	7
43	Kentucky	215	7
44	Illinois	544	7
45	Ohio	529	7
46	Michigan	437	7
47	California	1,380	6
48	Tennessee	244	6
49	Louisiana	292	6
50	New York	855	4
51	Washington, DC	52	3

FEDERAL AID FOR LOWER-INCOME HOUSING ASSISTANCE

Lower-income housing assistance includes public housing, housing payments to public agencies and college housing. Federal aid for lower-income housing comprised 6% of all federal aid funding to states and local governments in 1993. The New England states—Rhode Island, Massachusetts, Connecticut and New Hampshire—along with Illinois rank highest in percentage of lower-income housing assistance.

TABLE: Federal Aid to for Lower-Income Housing Assistance
DATE: 1993
SOURCE: U.S. Bureau of the Census, *Federal Expenses by State for Fiscal Year 1993*, annual
DESCRIPTION: Federal aid to states for lower-income housing assistance and percentage of total federal aid to the states from that program.

Rank		Total ($ millions)	Percent of total federal aid to state
	United States	12,457	6
1	Rhode Island	116	10
2	Massachusetts	542	10
3	Illinois	734	9
4	Connecticut	251	9
5	New Hampshire	58	9
6	Hawaii	82	8
7	New Jersey	513	8
8	Virginia	241	8
9	Delaware	37	8

Rank		Total ($ millions)	Percent of total federal aid to state
10	New York	1,701	8
11	Maryland	260	8
12	Maine	85	7
13	Minnesota	237	7
14	Nevada	52	7
15	Ohio	521	7
16	South Dakota	44	7
17	Colorado	141	7
18	Pennsylvania	545	6
19	California	1,384	6
20	Oklahoma	135	6
21	Kentucky	188	6
22	North Dakota	37	6
23	Nebraska	64	6
24	Georgia	252	6
25	Missouri	202	6
26	Arizona	148	6
27	Alaska	53	6
28	Oregon	115	5
29	Florida	405	5
30	Wisconsin	179	5
31	North Carolina	237	5
32	Vermont	29	5
33	Michigan	343	5
34	Washington	190	5
35	Idaho	36	5
36	Alabama	155	5
37	Arkansas	93	5
38	Texas	552	5
39	Iowa	86	5
40	Tennessee	193	5
41	Indiana	183	5
42	Mississippi	108	5
43	Montana	39	5
44	South Carolina	117	5
45	New Mexico	70	5
46	West Virginia	80	4
47	Kansas	66	4
48	Washington, DC	71	4
49	Utah	41	3
50	Louisiana	160	3
51	Wyoming	15	2

FEDERAL AID FOR EMPLOYMENT AND JOB TRAINING

Funding for employment and job training programs was made available to states and localities via the Job Training Partnership Act. In 1993 these programs made up 3% of all federal aid to states and local governments. Aid ranged from 5% in Idaho, Michigan, Nevada and Alaska to 2% in New York, Louisiana and the District of Columbia.

TABLE: Federal Aid for Employment and Job Training
DATE: 1993
SOURCE: U.S. Bureau of the Census, *Federal Expenses by State for Fiscal Year 1993*, annual
DESCRIPTION: Federal aid to states for employment and job training and percentage of total federal aid to states from that program.

Rank		Total ($ millions)	Percent of total federal aid to state
	United States	6,811	3
1	Idaho	36	5
2	Michigan	326	5
3	Nevada	37	5
4	Alaska	44	5
5	Oregon	94	4
6	Illinois	330	4
7	Delaware	19	4
8	California	898	4
9	Washington	153	4
10	Pennsylvania	347	4
11	Utah	47	4
12	Connecticut	105	4
13	Virginia	111	4
14	Wisconsin	128	4
15	Alabama	115	4
16	Ohio	288	4
17	Indiana	139	4
18	Iowa	63	4
19	North Dakota	23	4
20	Arizona	94	4
21	New Hampshire	23	4
22	New Jersey	214	3
23	Arkansas	64	3
24	Missouri	122	3
25	Vermont	19	3
26	Maine	39	3
27	Colorado	70	3
28	Montana	27	3
29	North Carolina	146	3
30	South Dakota	21	3
31	South Carolina	80	3
32	Rhode Island	35	3
33	Kentucky	96	3
34	Hawaii	31	3
35	Oklahoma	66	3
36	Massachusetts	172	3
37	Florida	234	3
38	Nebraska	34	3
39	Maryland	101	3
40	Minnesota	100	3
41	Tennessee	117	3
42	Wyoming	19	3
43	Texas	322	3
44	Mississippi	66	3
45	Georgia	124	3
46	Kansas	44	3
47	West Virginia	50	3

Rank		Total ($ millions)	Percent of total federal aid to state
48	New Mexico	40	3
49	New York	504	2
50	Louisiana	99	2
51	Washington, DC	36	2

State Government General Expenditures

State government expenditures have risen significantly over the past 20 years. In 1970 they totaled $78 billion; the per capita dollar amount was $383. In 1980 expenditures totaled $228 billion, or $1,010 per capita. In 1992 expenditures totaled $612 billion or $2,405 per capita.

The total includes the following functions: education, public welfare, highways, health and hospitals and corrections and other items not shown separately.

TABLE: State Government General Expenditures
DATE: 1992
SOURCE: U.S. Bureau of the Census, *State Government Finances*, annual
DESCRIPTION: General government expenditures and per capita expenditures.

Rank		General expenditures ($ millions)	Per capita expenditures ($)
	United States	611,922	2,405
1	Alaska	4,788	8,157
2	Hawaii	4,903	4,226
3	Wyoming	1,725	3,703
4	New York	60,869	3,359
5	Rhode Island	3,331	3,315
6	Delaware	2,241	3,253
7	New Jersey	24,109	3,095
8	Connecticut	9,957	3,035
9	Massachusetts	17,812	2,970
10	Vermont	1,690	2,966
11	New Mexico	4,594	2,905
12	North Dakota	1,834	2,883
13	Washington	14,724	2,867
14	Minnesota	12,322	2,750
15	California	83,360	2,701
16	Maine	3,232	2,617
17	Montana	2,108	2,558
18	Pennsylvania	30,338	2,526
19	Louisiana	10,683	2,492
20	Kentucky	9,235	2,459
21	Wisconsin	12,258	2,448
22	West Virginia	4,396	2,426
23	Iowa	6,711	2,387
24	Michigan	21,840	2,314
25	Oregon	6,842	2,298

Rank		General expenditures ($ millions)	Per capita expenditures ($)
26	Maryland	11,012	2,244
27	Utah	4,057	2,238
28	Nevada	2,953	2,225
29	South Carolina	7,969	2,212
30	New Hampshire	2,453	2,208
31	Nebraska	3,535	2,201
32	Oklahoma	7,063	2,199
33	Ohio	24,106	2,188
34	Idaho	2,316	2,170
35	Arizona	8,236	2,149
36	North Carolina	14,671	2,144
37	Alabama	8,788	2,125
38	Arkansas	5,062	2,110
39	South Dakota	1,490	2,095
40	Indiana	11,691	2,065
41	Illinois	23,639	2,032
42	Kansas	5,052	2,002
43	Mississippi	5,217	1,996
44	Virginia	12,694	1,991
45	Tennessee	9,633	1,917
46	Georgia	12,781	1,893
47	Colorado	6,494	1,871
48	Florida	24,851	1,842
49	Missouri	9,513	1,832
50	Texas	30,744	1,741

State Spending on Education

Nationally, education constituted the largest portion of state government expenditures in 1992. However, states vary widely in the proportion of funding they commit. Funding education ranged from 48% of all state expenditures in Utah to 18% in Massachusetts. Nebraska and Arizona represented median expenditures at 36%. Comparisons between states can be deceptive. States fund education through a variety of formulas that combine state and local revenue sources. In some states this formula relies primarily on state funding, while in other states it relies on local funding.

TABLE: State Spending on Education
DATE: 1992
SOURCE: U.S. Bureau of the Census, *State Government Finances*, annual
DESCRIPTION: General state government expenditures on education and percent of total state expenditures on education.

Rank		Spending ($ millions)	Percent of total state expenditures
	United States	211,570	35
1	Utah	1,951	48
2	Kansas	2,198	44

Rank		Spending ($ millions)	Percent of total state expenditures
3	Texas	13,283	43
4	North Carolina	6,313	43
5	Oklahoma	3,026	43
6	Idaho	987	43
7	Washington	6,224	42
8	Arkansas	2,123	42
9	New Mexico	1,919	42
10	Colorado	2,709	42
11	Alabama	3,571	41
12	Georgia	5,184	41
13	West Virginia	1,753	40
14	Indiana	4,653	40
15	Iowa	2,649	39
16	Virginia	4,931	39
17	Kentucky	3,572	39
18	South Carolina	3,071	39
19	Mississippi	1,993	38
20	Nevada	1,113	38
21	North Dakota	685	37
22	Missouri	3,529	37
23	Minnesota	4,556	37
24	Montana	771	37
25	Nebraska	1,259	36
26	Arizona	2,930	36
27	Florida	8,814	35
28	Ohio	8,489	35
29	Delaware	789	35
30	Louisiana	3,687	35
31	Wyoming	595	34
32	Wisconsin	4,191	34
33	Michigan	7,416	34
34	California	28,285	34
35	Vermont	563	33
36	Pennsylvania	9,973	33
37	Tennessee	3,101	32
38	Maryland	3,449	31
39	Maine	1,010	31
40	Illinois	7,295	31
41	New York	17,972	30
42	New Jersey	7,018	29
43	South Dakota	430	29
44	Oregon	1,935	28
45	Hawaii	1,344	27
46	Connecticut	2,506	25
47	Alaska	1,201	25
48	Rhode Island	813	24
49	New Hampshire	468	19
50	Massachusetts	3,271	18

STATE SPENDING ON PUBLIC WELFARE

Nationally, state government expenditures on public welfare represented 26% of total state government expendi-

tures in 1992. States historically have had to meet minimum federal mandates with regard to public welfare; however, beyond these federal minimum standards, states are free to set welfare policy as they wish. The expenditures on public welfare range between 38% in New Hampshire and 11% in Wyoming and Alaska. The median percentage is 23%.

TABLE: State Spending on Public Welfare
DATE: 1992
SOURCE: U.S. Bureau of the Census, *State Government Finances*, annual
DESCRIPTION: General state government expenditures on public welfare and percent of total state expenditures on public welfare.

Rank	State	Spending ($ millions)	Percent of total state expenditures
	United States	156,364	26
1	New Hampshire	937	38
2	New York	20,307	33
3	Pennsylvania	9,600	32
4	Maine	1,003	31
5	California	25,248	30
6	Massachusetts	5,303	30
7	Tennessee	2,817	29
8	Ohio	6,494	27
9	Illinois	6,261	26
10	Missouri	2,516	26
11	Georgia	3,313	26
12	Kentucky	2,383	26
13	Michigan	5,575	26
14	New Jersey	6,048	25
15	West Virginia	1,094	25
16	Minnesota	3,022	25
17	Connecticut	2,434	24
18	Maryland	2,677	24
19	Texas	7,410	24
20	Louisiana	2,545	24
21	Arkansas	1,177	23
22	Mississippi	1,210	23
23	Rhode Island	771	23
24	Wisconsin	2,809	23
25	Vermont	381	23
26	Indiana	2,621	22
27	Colorado	1,438	22
28	Arizona	1,812	22
29	Oklahoma	1,540	22
30	Florida	5,334	21
31	Alabama	1,853	21
32	South Carolina	1,618	20
33	North Carolina	2,949	20
34	Nebraska	706	20
35	South Dakota	290	19
36	Iowa	1,306	19
37	Oregon	1,327	19
38	Washington	2,809	19
39	North Dakota	338	18

Rank	State	Spending ($ millions)	Percent of total state expenditures
40	Kansas	891	18
41	Virginia	2,094	16
42	Utah	668	16
43	Montana	334	16
44	New Mexico	710	15
45	Nevada	449	15
46	Idaho	352	15
47	Delaware	292	13
48	Hawaii	598	12
49	Wyoming	191	11
50	Alaska	508	11

STATE SPENDING ON HIGHWAYS

In 1992 state government expenditures on highways constituted 8% of total state government expenditures. The Plains states rank highest in highway expenditures, between 19% and 12%, while New York ranks last (4%). Median highway expenditures are 10%.

TABLE: State Spending on Highways
DATE: 1992
SOURCE: U.S. Bureau of the Census, *State Government Finances*, annual
DESCRIPTION: General state government expenditures on public welfare and percent of total state expenditures on public welfare.

Rank		Total ($ millions)	Percent of total state expenditures
	United States	48,747	8
1	Wyoming	326	19
2	South Dakota	211	14
3	Iowa	949	14
4	Montana	283	13
5	Kansas	649	13
6	Idaho	291	13
7	Nebraska	443	13
8	North Dakota	228	12
9	Virginia	1,521	12
10	Tennessee	1,134	12
11	West Virginia	510	12
12	Arizona	954	12
13	Oklahoma	816	12
14	Alaska	547	11
15	Arkansas	577	11
16	Delaware	234	10
17	Illinois	2,462	10
18	Vermont	176	10
19	Mississippi	539	10
20	Kentucky	934	10
21	Missouri	958	10

Rank		Total ($ millions)	Percent of total state expenditures
22	Colorado	652	10
23	Nevada	295	10
24	North Carolina	1,448	10
25	Oregon	672	10
26	Ohio	2,287	9
27	Indiana	1,078	9
28	Maryland	972	9
29	Florida	2,175	9
30	Minnesota	1,043	8
31	Maine	273	8
32	New Mexico	384	8
33	Connecticut	823	8
34	Louisiana	880	8
35	Texas	2,473	8
36	Utah	324	8
37	Alabama	695	8
38	New Hampshire	193	8
39	Washington	1,154	8
40	New Jersey	1,835	8
41	Hawaii	359	7
42	Pennsylvania	2,191	7
43	Wisconsin	854	7
44	Georgia	875	7
45	Michigan	1,482	7
46	South Carolina	530	7
47	Massachusetts	1,021	6
48	Rhode Island	181	5
49	California	4,375	5
50	New York	2,478	4

STATE SPENDING ON HEALTH AND HOSPITALS

States spent 8% of all their expenditures on health and hospitals in 1992. Alabama ranked highest and West Virginia, Alaska, Idaho, Vermont and Nevada lowest. In some states the federal government also contributes significantly to hospitals through the Medicaid program.

TABLE: State Spending on Health and Hospitals
DATE: 1992
SOURCE: U.S. Bureau of the Census, *State Government Finances*, annual
DESCRIPTION: General state government expenditures on health and hospitals and percent of total state expenditures on health and hospitals.

Rank		Spending ($ millions)	Percent of total state expenditures
	United States	48,123	8
1	Alabama	1,175	13
2	South Carolina	967	12

Rank		Spending ($ millions)	Percent of total state expenditures
3	Virginia	1,424	11
4	Michigan	2,447	11
5	Nebraska	379	11
6	Connecticut	1,058	11
7	Louisiana	1,072	10
8	Oregon	673	10
9	New Mexico	415	9
10	Massachusetts	1,574	9
11	New York	5,356	9
12	Iowa	590	9
13	Kansas	439	9
14	Washington	1,262	9
15	Utah	342	8
16	Oklahoma	595	8
17	Hawaii	411	8
18	Maryland	908	8
19	Texas	2,476	8
20	Georgia	1,025	8
21	Pennsylvania	2,400	8
22	North Carolina	1,154	8
23	Ohio	1,881	8
24	Florida	1,924	8
25	Tennessee	736	8
26	Mississippi	397	8
27	Minnesota	936	8
28	Missouri	721	8
29	Rhode Island	251	8
30	Delaware	164	7
31	Indiana	853	7
32	Arkansas	360	7
33	Illinois	1,604	7
34	Wisconsin	831	7
35	California	5,259	6
36	South Dakota	87	6
37	Montana	123	6
38	New Jersey	1,396	6
39	Colorado	373	6
40	New Hampshire	138	6
41	Kentucky	494	5
42	Wyoming	91	5
43	Arizona	431	5
44	North Dakota	95	5
45	Maine	167	5
46	West Virginia	197	4
47	Alaska	205	4
48	Idaho	94	4
49	Vermont	65	4
50	Nevada	106	4

STATE SPENDING ON CORRECTIONS

Expenditures on corrections is the money used to fund prisons. This money averaged 3% of state government expenditures in 1992. Maryland, Delaware, Georgia and Virginia rank highest in this table. Wyoming, North Dakota and West Virginia rank lowest

TABLE: State Spending on Corrections
DATE: 1992
SOURCE: U.S. Bureau of the Census, *State Government Finances*, annual
DESCRIPTION: General state government expenditures on corrections and percent of total state expenditures on corrections.

Rank		Spending ($ millions)	Percent of total state expenditures
	United States	20,120	3
1	Maryland	556	5
2	Delaware	109	5
3	Georgia	601	5
4	Virginia	580	5
5	Texas	1,336	4
6	Nevada	128	4
7	Connecticut	421	4
8	Arizona	344	4
9	Florida	1,037	4
10	Colorado	265	4
11	Tennessee	380	4
12	Michigan	855	4
13	California	3,226	4
14	North Carolina	551	4
15	Kansas	189	4
16	South Carolina	297	4
17	Washington	545	4
18	Massachusetts	645	4
19	New York	2,008	3
20	Oregon	209	3
21	Rhode Island	101	3
22	Ohio	691	3
23	Oklahoma	201	3
24	Alaska	136	3
25	New Mexico	128	3
26	Wisconsin	338	3
27	Indiana	321	3
28	New Jersey	659	3
29	Illinois	625	3
30	Louisiana	276	3
31	Idaho	58	3
32	Iowa	167	2
33	Utah	97	2
34	Kentucky	210	2
35	Hawaii	105	2
36	Missouri	202	2
37	Arkansas	106	2
38	Alabama	183	2
39	Maine	67	2
40	Nebraska	73	2
41	South Dakota	30	2

Rank		Spending ($ millions)	Percent of total state expenditures
42	Vermont	34	2
43	Pennsylvania	588	2
44	New Hampshire	46	2
45	Montana	37	2
46	Mississippi	87	2
47	Minnesota	194	2
48	Wyoming	24	1
49	North Dakota	16	1
50	West Virginia	36	1

TOTAL AND PER CAPITA STATE GOVERNMENT DEBT OUTSTANDING

Total debt increased $330 million between 1970 and 1992. Debt outstanding per capita averaged $207 in 1970, $540 in 1980 and $1,461 in 1992. Alaska ranks first in per capita debt, exceeding the national average by more than five times. Iowa, Utah, North Carolina and Texas rank lowest in per capita debt, all reporting less than half the national average of $1,461.

TABLE: Total and Per Capita State Government Debt Outstanding

DATE: 1992

SOURCE: U.S. Bureau of the Census, *State Government Finances*, annual

DESCRIPTION: Total outstanding state government debt and per capita outstanding state debt.

Rank		Total ($ millions)	Per capita debt ($)
	United States	371,901	1,461
1	Alaska	4,942	8,418
2	Delaware	3,542	5,141
3	Rhode Island	5,151	5,125
4	Hawaii	4,687	4,040
5	New Hampshire	4,314	3,883
6	Connecticut	11,957	3,644

Rank		Total ($ millions)	Per capita debt ($)
7	New York	55,868	3,083
8	Vermont	1,543	2,706
9	South Dakota	1,889	2,657
10	New Jersey	19,786	2,540
11	Louisiana	9,994	2,331
12	Montana	1,868	2,267
13	Maine	2,637	2,135
14	Oregon	6,295	2,115
15	Massachusetts	24,008	2,003
16	Wyoming	695	1,920
17	Kentucky	6,618	1,763
18	Maryland	8,335	1,698
19	North Dakota	1,027	1,615
20	Illinois	18,742	1,611
21	Nevada	1,934	1,458
22	Wisconsin	7,299	1,458
23	West Virginia	2,594	1,432
24	Washington	7,299	1,400
25	South Carolina	4,785	1,300
26	California	37,824	1,225
27	Missouri	6,301	1,213
28	Idaho	1,292	1,211
29	Utah	2,153	1,188
30	Virginia	7,403	1,161
31	Oklahoma	3,657	1,138
32	Ohio	12,182	1,107
33	Michigan	10,357	1,097
34	Nebraska	1,754	1,092
35	Pennsylvania	12,962	1,079
36	New Mexico	1,605	1,015
37	Alabama	4,129	998
38	Minnesota	4,143	925
39	Indiana	5,172	913
40	Florida	12,295	912
41	Colorado	2,977	858
42	Arkansas	1,942	810
43	Arizona	2,849	743
44	Iowa	1,884	670
45	Georgia	4,471	662
46	Mississippi	1,626	622
47	Tennessee	2,806	559
48	North Carolina	3,619	558
49	Texas	8,001	453
50	Kansas	486	193

HEALTH

This section presents mortality statistics on cause of death, death rates, infant mortality and AIDS. The annual death rate has been cut in half since 1900. Diseases such as typhoid and diphtheria, which once killed thousands every year, have been all but eradicated. However, excitement about the health progress made in the second half of the 20th century has been tempered by the emergence of such new diseases as AIDS and the return of old ones such as tuberculosis.

Statistics in this section are compiled nationwide by the National Center for Health Statistics (NCHS) in its annual report *Vital Statistics of the United States*, and by the Centers for Disease Control and Prevention (CDC).

The annual collection of national death statistics began in 1900 with a national death registration area of 10 states and the District of Columbia. Starting in 1933 additional states began annual collection of death statistics. By 1960 all states were registering all deaths annually. National statistics on fetal deaths have been compiled annually since 1922.

The survey of health statistics in this section begins with reviews of death rates and major causes of death among Americans. Death rates reveal the relative seriousness of specific types of illness and disease in the population. A table on infant mortality follows. Next is a table reporting the number of AIDS cases reported.

When comparing data, it is important to note that Washington, DC, is the center of a large metropolitan area where people from neighboring states may come when they need medical care. This concentration skews the District's statistics.

DEATH RATES 1980 AND 1992

Approximately 2.2 million deaths were recorded nationwide in 1992, or about 8.5 deaths for every 1,000 persons in the population. Between 1980 and 1992 death rates remained comparatively constant. The District of Columbia ranks first in deaths per 1,000 persons for 1992. High death rates are found in states with significant elderly populations

and in a number of states with no recent net inflow of younger migrants. Low death rates are documented in a number of western states, where high birth rates and in-migration have resulted in younger populations. This table provides a useful baseline for evaluating rates of deaths attributed to specific causes recorded in the tables that follow.

TABLE: Death Rates 1980 and 1992
DATE: 1992
SOURCES: U.S. National Center for Health Statistics, *Vital Statistics of the United States*, annual, and *Monthly Vital Statistics Report*
DESCRIPTION: Death rate per 1,000 population for 1980 and 1992. Excludes deaths of nonresidents of the U.S.

Rank		1980 rate per 1,000	1992 rate per 1,000
	United States	8.8	8.5
1	Washington, DC	11.1	11.2
2	West Virginia	9.9	11.1
3	Arkansas	9.9	10.5
4	Florida	10.7	10.4
5	Pennsylvania	10.4	10.3
6	Missouri	10.1	9.7
7	South Dakota	9.5	9.7
8	Mississippi	9.4	9.7
9	Iowa	9.3	9.6
10	Alabama	9.1	9.6
11	Oklahoma	9.3	9.5
12	Rhode Island	9.8	9.4
13	Kentucky	9.2	9.4
14	Tennessee	8.9	9.4
15	Nebraska	9.2	9.2
16	Massachusetts	9.6	9.1
17	New York	9.8	9.1
18	New Jersey	9.4	9.1
19	North Dakota	8.6	9.1
20	Ohio	9.1	9.0
21	Indiana	8.6	8.9
22	Maine	9.6	8.8
23	Kansas	9.3	8.8

Rank		1980 rate per 1,000	1992 rate per 1,000
24	Illinois	9.0	8.7
25	North Carolina	8.2	8.7
26	Louisiana	8.5	8.7
27	Montana	8.5	8.7
28	Oregon	8.3	8.7
29	Connecticut	8.8	8.6
30	Delaware	8.5	8.6
31	South Carolina	8.1	8.5
32	Michigan	8.1	8.4
33	Vermont	9.0	8.3
34	Wisconsin	8.7	8.3
35	Arizona	7.9	8.0
36	Georgia	8.1	7.9
37	Minnesota	8.2	7.8
38	Virginia	8.0	7.8
39	New Hampshire	8.3	7.7
40	Maryland	8.1	7.7
41	Idaho	7.2	7.6
42	Nevada	7.4	7.6
43	Texas	7.6	7.4
44	New Mexico	7.0	7.3
45	Washington	7.7	7.3
46	Wyoming	6.9	7.2
47	California	7.9	7.0
48	Colorado	6.6	6.5
49	Hawaii	5.2	6.0
50	Utah	5.6	5.5
51	Alaska	4.3	3.8

TOTAL DEATH RATES

The United States death rate reached 860.3 per 100,000 persons in 1991. The District of Columbia, West Virginia and Arkansas rank highest; Alaska, Utah and Hawaii lowest. Several factors influence death rates in states, among them, age, population, birth rates and migration.

TABLE: Total Death Rates
DATE: 1991
SOURCES: U.S. National Center for Health Statistics, *Monthly Vital Statistics Report* and unpublished data
DESCRIPTION: Deaths per 100,000 resident population. Total includes other causes not shown separately on the tables that follow.

Rank	State	Total death rates per 100,000 population
	United States	860.3
1	Washington, DC	1,183.1
2	West Virginia	1,108.5
3	Arkansas	1,056.0
4	Florida	1,026.5
5	Pennsylvania	1,025.5
6	Mississippi	990.1

Rank	State	Total death rates per 100,000 population
7	Missouri	986.5
8	Alabama	979.8
9	Iowa	978.6
10	Oklahoma	953.5
11	Kentucky	952.0
12	South Dakota	945.1
13	Rhode Island	936.1
14	Tennessee	935.0
15	New York	927.8
16	Nebraska	924.4
17	Ohio	915.9
18	Maine	909.0
19	New Jersey	908.4
20	Illinois	902.0
21	Kansas	902.0
22	Louisiana	900.4
23	Indiana	893.9
24	Massachusetts	885.2
25	North Dakota	878.1
26	North Carolina	874.0
27	Delaware	871.8
28	Wisconsin	870.6
29	Montana	868.1
30	Oregon	856.1
31	Michigan	853.8
32	Connecticut	851.7
33	South Carolina	841.7
34	Vermont	804.8
35	Georgia	797.3
36	Minnesota	796.7
37	Maryland	790.7
38	Arizona	787.9
39	Virginia	781.6
40	Nevada	775.9
41	New Hampshire	761.4
42	Idaho	742.9
43	Washington	738.8
44	Texas	730.8
45	New Mexico	728.0
46	California	708.6
47	Wyoming	686.7
48	Colorado	668.9
49	Hawaii	600.0
50	Utah	545.3
51	Alaska	386.0

HEART DISEASE DEATH RATES

Except for combat wounds during World War I and World War II, heart disease has been the leading cause of death among Americans in the 20th century. Heart disease takes many forms, including: heart attacks, rheumatic fever and hypertensive heart disease. With the decline in infant deaths and deaths due to specific illnesses in recent years, the leading position of heart disease as a cause of death, especially among older persons, has been strengthened.

Nationwide, approximately 38% of deaths in 1987 were caused by heart disease. In 1991 that had fallen to 33%. The highest rates of heart disease death appeared in West Virginia and Mississippi and lowest in Utah and Alaska. The highest percentages of death due to heart disease occurred in New York, Mississippi and Oklahoma; the lowest in Alaska, the District of Columbia and Colorado.

TABLE: Heart Disease Death Rates
DATE: 1991
SOURCE: U.S. National Center for Health Statistics, *Monthly Vital Statistics Report* and unpublished data
DESCRIPTION: Deaths from heart disease per 100,000 resident population and percent of total deaths due to heart disease.

Rank		Heart disease per (100,000 population)	Percent of total deaths due to heart disease
	United States	285.9	33
1	New York	353.1	38
2	Mississippi	371.6	38
3	Oklahoma	340.4	36
4	West Virginia	392.8	35
5	Pennsylvania	363.3	35
6	Iowa	345.7	35
7	South Dakota	331.2	35
8	Missouri	344.8	35
9	Ohio	319.9	35
10	Nebraska	322.4	35
11	Rhode Island	323.4	35
12	Michigan	294.7	35
13	Illinois	309.0	34
14	Connecticut	290.6	34
15	Florida	348.2	34
16	Kentucky	321.6	34
17	Indiana	299.4	33
18	Tennessee	312.8	33
19	Kansas	301.3	33
20	Wisconsin	289.5	33
21	New Jersey	301.1	33
22	Maine	299.8	33
23	Alabama	322.2	33
24	Arkansas	346.0	33
25	North Dakota	285.5	33
26	Louisiana	292.6	32
27	Delaware	283.2	32
28	New Hampshire	246.4	32
29	Massachusetts	285.4	32
30	North Carolina	281.4	32
31	Nevada	249.8	32
32	Vermont	258.7	32
33	Virginia	250.0	32
34	South Carolina	267.6	32

Rank		Heart disease per (100,000 population)	Percent of total deaths due to heart disease
35	California	222.0	31
36	Georgia	249.4	31
37	Texas	226.7	31
38	Maryland	241.5	31
39	Idaho	225.0	30
40	Minnesota	241.0	30
41	Washington	223.1	30
42	Hawaii	180.4	30
43	Arizona	234.4	30
44	Utah	157.2	29
45	Wyoming	197.8	29
46	Oregon	246.4	29
47	Montana	240.5	28
48	New Mexico	199.9	27
49	Colorado	181.7	27
50	Washington, DC	311.9	26
51	Alaska	82.5	21

CANCER DEATH RATES

Cancer deaths accounted for approximately 21% of all deaths in 1978 and 24% in 1991. Cancer was the number two cause of death among all age groups and the number one cause of death in people ages 45 to 64 years old. The highest percentage of total deaths from cancer occurred in New Hampshire; the lowest in Utah. The proportion of cancer deaths exceeded the overall death rate in several states. For example, Maine, which ranked 18th in total death rates per 100,000 population, ranked second in cancer deaths. Similarly, New Jersey ranked 19th and Massachussetts 24th in total death rates, but ranked 4th and 3rd, respectively, in cancer deaths. Cancer deaths in Alaska surpassed deaths from heart disease by 1% in 1991.

TABLE: Cancer Death Rates
DATE: 1991
SOURCES: U.S. National Center for Health Statistics, *Monthly Vital Statistics Report,* and unpublished data
DESCRIPTION: Deaths from cancer per 100,000 resident population and percent of total deaths due to cancer.

Rank		Deaths (per 100,000)	Percent of total deaths due to cancer
	United States	204.1	24
1	New Hampshire	203.0	27
2	Maine	237.8	26
3	Massachusetts	230.2	26
4	New Jersey	234.3	26
5	Delaware	223.5	26
6	Maryland	200.8	25
7	Florida	260.4	25

Rank		Deaths (per 100,000)	Percent of total deaths due to cancer
8	Rhode Island	236.1	25
9	Connecticut	214.0	25
10	Oregon	212.6	25
11	Washington	183.2	25
12	North Dakota	215.6	25
13	Vermont	197.0	24
14	Pennsylvania	250.8	24
15	Virginia	191.0	24
16	Hawaii	146.2	24
17	Arizona	191.1	24
18	Ohio	221.5	24
19	Kentucky	229.9	24
20	Michigan	205.5	24
21	Nevada	186.1	24
22	Indiana	214.4	24
23	Wisconsin	208.7	24
24	Minnesota	189.3	24
25	Illinois	211.5	23
26	Montana	203.3	23
27	California	165.1	23
28	Iowa	227.5	23
29	Louisiana	208.9	23
30	Missouri	228.8	23
31	West Virginia	256.9	23
32	Colorado	154.2	23
33	New York	213.2	23
34	Texas	167.5	23
35	Kansas	206.2	23
36	Alaska	88.2	23
37	Tennessee	213.4	23
38	South Dakota	215.2	23
39	North Carolina	198.4	23
40	South Carolina	190.2	23
41	Oklahoma	214.8	23
42	Wyoming	153.9	22
43	Arkansas	236.4	22
44	Idaho	164.9	22
45	Alabama	215.5	22
46	Georgia	175.0	22
47	Washington, DC	258.7	22
48	Nebraska	200.0	22
49	Mississippi	213.0	22
50	New Mexico	151.9	21
51	Utah	111.5	20

CEREBROVASCULAR DISEASE DEATH RATES

Cerebrovascular diseases refers to a group of disorders that involve complications in delivery of blood to the brain that characteristically result in strokes. Cerebrovascular disorders make up the third major group of fatal organic diseases, responsible for approximately 9% of all deaths in 1978 and 7% in 1991. Heart disease, cancer and cerebrovascular disease are typically diseases of the elderly and currently are the principal causes of death in the nation. These three account for approximately two-thirds of all deaths.

North Dakota, which ranks 25th in aggregate death rates, ranks fifth in death from cerebrovascular death. Similarly, Tennessee, North Carolina, Nebraska, South Carolina and Wisconsin all rank near the top of the list for cerebrovascular death rates, but lower for overall death rates. The relative age of the population may be a primary factor in the position of these states and the others ranking highest in cerebrovascular death. In other states, ranking high in total death rates, for example, West Virginia, Florida, Pennsylvania and the District of Columbia, heart disease and cancer may cause premature death among people who would otherwise have died of strokes. This is called a "competing cause of mortality" effect. The percentage of total deaths from cerebrovascular disease was reported highest in Arkansas, lowest in Alaska.

TABLE: Cerebrovascular Disease Death Rates
DATE: 1991
SOURCES: U.S. National Center for Health Statistics, *Monthly Vital Statistics Report*, and unpublished data
DESCRIPTION: Deaths from cerebrovascular disease per 100,000 resident population and percent of total deaths from cerebrovascular disease.

Rank		Deaths (per 100,000)	Percent of total deaths due to cerebrovascular disease
	United States	56.9	7
1	Arkansas	89.9	9
2	Hawaii	49.6	8
3	Minnesota	64.4	8
4	South Carolina	67.8	8
5	North Dakota	69.3	8
6	North Carolina	68.3	8
7	Oregon	66.7	8
8	Wisconsin	66.9	8
9	Iowa	74.9	8
10	Washington	56.0	8
11	Nebraska	68.2	7
12	Idaho	54.8	7
13	Tennessee	68.8	7
14	Indiana	64.2	7
15	Montana	62.0	7
16	California	50.6	7
17	Utah	38.6	7
18	Kansas	63.8	7
19	Georgia	56.2	7
20	Alabama	68.7	7
21	South Dakota	65.1	7
22	Mississippi	68.1	7
23	Oklahoma	64.5	7
24	Virginia	52.6	7
25	Missouri	66.3	7
26	Texas	48.6	7

Rank		Deaths (per 100,000)	Percent of total deaths due to cerebrovascular disease
27	Kentucky	63.1	7
28	New Hampshire	50.4	7
29	Illinois	59.5	7
30	Michigan	55.3	6
31	Wyoming	43.9	6
32	Louisiana	57.2	6
33	Florida	64.7	6
34	Connecticut	53.2	6
35	Pennsylvania	63.9	6
36	Massachusetts	54.5	6
37	Ohio	56.2	6
38	Arizona	47.7	6
39	Colorado	40.4	6
40	Rhode Island	56.5	6
41	Delaware	52.2	6
42	West Virginia	65.9	6
43	Maine	53.7	6
44	Vermont	46.7	6
45	Maryland	45.6	6
46	New Jersey	51.8	6
47	New Mexico	41.3	6
48	New York	47.5	5
49	Nevada	37.2	5
50	Washington, DC	56.7	5
51	Alaska	15.4	4

ACCIDENT DEATH RATES

The fifth leading cause of death, accidents accounted for approximately 5.5% of all deaths in 1978, but 4% in 1991. About 35 out of every 100,000 persons in the population died due to accidental cause in 1991. For the population aged one through 44, accidents were the leading cause of death. Approximately half of all accidental deaths were motor vehicle related. The highest rates of accidental death occur in the West and the South. Alaska ranks highest, Massachusetts lowest.

TABLE: Accident Death Rates
DATE: 1991
SOURCES: U.S. National Center for Health Statistics, *Monthly Vital Statistics Report*, and unpublished data
DESCRIPTION: Deaths from accidents per 100,000 resident population and percent of total deaths due to accidents.

Rank		Deaths (per 100,000)	Percent of total deaths due to accidents
	United States	35.4	4
1	Alaska	63.2	16
2	New Mexico	56.3	8
3	Wyoming	46.5	7

Rank		Deaths (per 100,000)	Percent of total deaths due to accidents
4	Idaho	44.3	6
5	Mississippi	56.8	6
6	South Carolina	47.5	6
7	Montana	48.6	6
8	Alabama	53.9	6
9	Utah	29.2	5
10	Colorado	35.4	5
11	Georgia	42.0	5
12	Arizona	40.2	5
13	Texas	35.9	5
14	Arkansas	51.8	5
15	Nevada	37.9	5
16	Kentucky	45.3	5
17	Tennessee	44.4	5
18	North Carolina	41.4	5
19	Oklahoma	44.6	5
20	Louisiana	42.0	5
21	South Dakota	43.4	5
22	West Virginia	49.1	4
23	California	31.3	4
24	Washington	32.5	4
25	Virginia	34.1	4
26	Oregon	37.3	4
27	Kansas	38.8	4
28	Missouri	42.0	4
29	Minnesota	33.2	4
30	Hawaii	25.0	4
31	Indiana	36.9	4
32	Nebraska	38.0	4
33	Iowa	39.5	4
34	Wisconsin	34.7	4
35	Vermont	30.9	4
36	Michigan	32.4	4
37	Delaware	32.9	4
38	North Dakota	32.4	4
39	Illinois	33.1	4
40	Ohio	33.2	4
41	Maine	32.4	4
42	Florida	36.2	4
43	New Hampshire	26.4	3
44	Maryland	27.1	3
45	Pennsylvania	34.1	3
46	New York	28.6	3
47	Rhode Island	28.2	3
48	Connecticut	24.8	3
49	New Jersey	26.4	3
50	Washington, DC	33.4	3
51	Massachusetts	23.4	3

SUICIDE DEATH RATES

Suicide was responsible for approximately 1% of all deaths in 1991. Suicide is the cause of death for approximately 12 out of every 100,000 persons in the population. The total suicide rate is higher among men than among women. For adolescents age 15 to 24 suicide is the third leading cause of death behind accidents and homicide.

Nevada's suicide rate is twice the national average. The other western states of Montana, Wyoming, New Mexico and Arizona also rank high.

TABLE: Suicide Death Rates
DATE: 1991
SOURCES: U.S. National Center for Health Statistics, *Monthly Vital Statistics Report*, and unpublished data
DESCRIPTION: Deaths from suicide per 100,000 resident population.

Rank		Deaths per 100,000
	United States	12.2
1	Nevada	24.8
2	Montana	19.9
3	Wyoming	18.9
4	New Mexico	18.3
5	Arizona	17.7
6	Colorado	16.7
7	Vermont	16.2
8	Utah	16.2
9	Idaho	15.9
10	Florida	15.8
11	Oregon	15.5
12	Maine	14.3
13	Oklahoma	13.9
14	Missouri	13.8
15	Washington	13.8
16	South Dakota	13.5
17	Georgia	13.5
18	Tennessee	13.4
19	West Virginia	13.3
20	Kentucky	13.2
21	Alabama	13.2
22	Louisiana	13.1
23	Texas	13.0
24	Alaska	12.8
25	Virginia	12.6
26	Indiana	12.5
27	North Carolina	12.5
28	Mississippi	12.5
29	Kansas	12.4
30	Michigan	12.2
31	California	12.2
32	Iowa	12.0
33	Nebraska	12.0
34	Arkansas	11.9
35	New Hampshire	11.8
36	South Carolina	11.8
37	Pennsylvania	11.7
38	North Dakota	11.7
39	Wisconsin	11.6
40	Delaware	11.6
41	Minnesota	11.5
42	Ohio	11.3

Rank		Deaths per 100,000
43	Illinois	10.3
44	Connecticut	10.0
45	Hawaii	9.4
46	New York	8.8
47	Maryland	8.8
48	Massachusetts	8.2
49	Rhode Island	8.2
50	New Jersey	6.6
51	Washington, DC	5.7

MOTOR VEHICLE DEATHS

The most populous states rank highest in motor vehicle deaths. The number of deaths dropped nationally by more than 5,000 over the period of time documented in this table. Deaths dropped in every state with the exception of Kentucky, Delaware, South Dakota and Arkansas.

According to the National Center of Health Statistics, death in motor vehicle accidents accounted for 17.3 deaths out of 100,000 population in 1991, placing it just below diabetes (ranking seventh) as a cause of death in all age groups. Men were twice as likely to die in motor vehicle accidents as women, although the rate among women has been increasing.

TABLE: Motor Vehicle Deaths
DATE: 1992; 1995
SOURCES: 1985: National Center for Health Statistics; thereafter, National Safety Council, Itasca, IL, *Accident Facts, 1995*, used by permission copyright.
DESCRIPTION: Includes both traffic and nontraffic motor vehicle deaths.

Rank		1985 deaths	1992 deaths
	United States	45,901	40,300
1	California	5,294	3,816
2	Texas	3,825	3,057
3	Florida	2,968	2,480
4	New York	2,121	1,800
5	Pennsylvania	1,767	1,545
6	Ohio	1,581	1,440
7	Illinois	1,594	1,375
8	Georgia	1,462	1,323
9	Michigan	1,605	1,295
10	North Carolina	1,553	1,262
11	Tennessee	1,219	1,155
12	Alabama	1,005	1,001
13	Missouri	1,005	985
14	Indiana	1,045	902
15	Louisiana	1,011	871
16	Virginia	1,021	839
17	Kentucky	749	819

Rank		1985 deaths	1992 deaths
18	Arizona	942	810
19	South Carolina	943	807
20	New Jersey	986	766
21	Maryland	766	664
22	Washington	786	651
23	Wisconsin	777	644
24	Oklahoma	781	619
25	Mississippi	691	604
26	Arkansas	580	587
27	Minnesota	657	581
28	Colorado	628	519
29	Massachusetts	655	485
30	Oregon	605	464
31	New Mexico	561	461
32	Iowa	478	437
33	West Virginia	461	420
34	Kansas	500	387
35	Connecticut	449	296
36	Nebraska	259	270
37	Utah	335	269
38	Nevada	297	251
39	Idaho	268	243
40	Maine	224	213
41	Montana	233	190
42	South Dakota	142	161
43	Delaware	119	140
44	Hawaii	134	128
45	New Hampshire	198	123
46	Wyoming	145	118
47	Alaska	124	106
48	Vermont	117	96
49	North Dakota	117	88
50	Rhode Island	124	79
51	Washington, DC	96	NA

NA Not available.

INFANT MORTALITY RATES

Nationwide, infant mortality rates fell in every state in the nation between 1980 and 1991. With the noteworthy exception of West Virginia, the southern states, which historically have led the nation in infant mortality, continue to do so. However, the southern states have made strides in reducing infant mortality. Mississippi has reduced the rate by 5.6 deaths per 1,000 live births between 1980 and 1991. The District of Columbia continues to lead the nation with 21 deaths per 1,000 live births. The infant mortality rates reported in two industrialized states, Illinois and Michigan, also exceeded the national rate.

TABLE: Infant Mortality Rates
DATE: 1991

SOURCE: U.S. National Center for Health Statistics, *Vital Statistics of the United States*, annual, and unpublished data
DESCRIPTION: Deaths per 1,000 live births. Represents deaths of infants under one year old, exclusive of fetal deaths. Excludes deaths of nonresidents of the U.S.

Rank		1980 deaths per 1,000 live births	1991 deaths per 1,000 live births
	United States	12.6	8.9
1	Washington, DC	25.0	21.0
2	Delaware	13.9	11.8
3	Georgia	14.5	11.4
4	Mississippi	17.0	11.4
5	South Carolina	15.6	11.3
6	Alabama	15.1	11.2
7	North Carolina	14.5	10.8
8	Illinois	14.8	10.7
9	Louisiana	14.3	10.5
10	Michigan	12.8	10.4
11	Missouri	12.4	10.2
12	Arkansas	12.7	10.2
13	Tennessee	13.5	10.0
14	Virginia	13.6	9.9
15	Oklahoma	12.7	9.6
16	New York	12.5	9.4
17	Ohio	12.8	9.4
18	South Dakota	10.9	9.4
19	Maryland	14.0	9.2
20	Nevada	10.7	9.2
21	Pennsylvania	13.2	9.1
22	Indiana	11.9	9.1
23	Florida	14.6	9.0
24	Kansas	10.4	8.9
25	Kentucky	12.9	8.9
26	Colorado	10.1	8.9
27	Alaska	12.3	8.9
28	New Jersey	12.5	8.7
29	Idaho	10.7	8.7
30	Arizona	12.4	8.6
31	Wisconsin	10.3	8.3
32	West Virginia	11.8	8.2
33	North Dakota	12.1	8.1
34	New Mexico	11.5	8.1
35	Rhode Island	11.0	8.0
36	Iowa	11.8	8.0
37	Wyoming	9.8	7.9
38	Texas	12.2	7.7
39	Nebraska	11.5	7.6
40	California	11.1	7.6
41	Minnesota	10.0	7.5
42	Washington	11.8	7.5
43	Connecticut	11.2	7.4
44	Hawaii	10.3	7.4
45	Oregon	12.2	7.3
46	Montana	12.4	7.0
47	Maine	9.2	6.7

Rank		1980 deaths per 1,000 live births	1991 deaths per 1,000 live births
48	Massachusetts	10.5	6.6
49	New Hampshire	9.9	6.1

Rank		1980 deaths per 1,000 live births	1991 deaths per 1,000 live births
50	Utah	10.4	6.1
51	Vermont	10.7	5.8

AIDS CASES REPORTED

AIDS appears in all states, but is concentrated in a few. The U.S. Centers for Disease Control designates the first 27 states on this table as "Leading States." They account for 94.4% of all AIDS cases. More than half of all AIDS cases were reported in New York, California, Florida, Texas and New Jersey. Historically New York led the nation in AIDS cases, but in 1992 California took the lead.

The number of men with AIDS far exceeds the number of women. However, while the percentage of total AIDS cases declined for men from 93.1% in 1981–84 to 86.1% in 1992, the percentage cases of AIDS among women increased over the same period from 6.9% to 13.9%. The percentage of total AIDS cases among whites declined from 58.9% in 1981–84 to 49.1% in 1992. It increased for blacks over the same period from 26.5% to 34.9%.

In 1991 AIDS was the third leading cause of death in the population 25 to 44 years old, representing 26.5 deaths per 100,000 population.

TABLE: AIDS Cases Reported
DATE: 1992
SOURCE: U.S. Centers for Disease Control and Prevention, Atlanta, GA, unpublished data
DESCRIPTION: AIDS cases reported and percent distribution of AIDS cases. Table ranked by total cases.

Rank		Cases reported 1981–1984	Percent distribution of cases 1981–1984	Cases reported 1992	Percent distribution of cases 1992	Total cases 1981–1992
	United States	7,354		45,472		244,939
1	New York	2,893	39.3	8,398	18.5	50,985
2	California	1,595	21.7	8,539	18.8	46,818
3	Florida	536	7.3	5,101	11.2	24,492
4	Texas	359	4.9	2,920	6.4	17,363
5	New Jersey	481	6.5	2,040	4.5	14,702
6	Illinois	157	2.1	1,912	4.2	8,229
7	Georgia	95	1.3	1,324	2.9	7,044
8	Pennsylvania	145	2.0	1,326	2.9	6,967
9	Maryland	86	1.2	150	2.6	5,307
10	Massachusetts	133	1.8	875	1.9	5,177
11	Washington, DC	113	1.5	706	1.6	4,118
12	Louisiana	73	1.0	710	1.6	3,794
13	Ohio	46	0.6	733	1.6	3,674
14	Virginia	67	0.9	784	1.7	3,525
15	Washington	66	0.9	551	1.2	3,404
16	Michigan	44	0.6	718	1.6	3,343
17	Missouri	35	0.5	708	1.6	3,192
18	Connecticut	85	1.2	646	1.4	3,079
19	North Carolina	23	0.3	584	1.3	2,854
20	Colorado	64	0.9	410	0.9	2,433
21	Arizona	29	0.4	386	0.8	1,943
22	Tennessee	7	0.1	408	0.9	1,864
23	South Carolina	18	0.2	391	0.9	1,785
24	Indiana	29	0.4	402	0.9	1,744
25	Alabama	11	0.1	437	1.0	1,702
26	Oregon	20	0.3	289	0.6	1,565
27	Minnesota	18	0.2	218	0.5	1,264
28	Oklahoma	14	0.2	272	0.6	1,173
29	Nevada	7	0.1	249	0.5	1,141
30	Mississippi	4	0.1	260	0.6	1,115
31	Wisconsin	12	0.2	229	0.5	1,070
32	Hawaii	21	0.3	138	0.3	963
33	Arkansas	1	Z	280	0.6	930

Rank		Cases reported 1981–1984	Percent distribution of cases 1981–1984	Cases reported 1992	Percent distribution of cases 1992	Total cases 1981–1992
34	Kentucky	14	0.2	213	0.5	885
35	Kansas	5	0.1	191	0.4	735
36	Utah	9	0.1	135	0.3	609
37	Rhode Island	11	0.1	106	0.2	579
38	New Mexico	4	0.1	107	0.2	567
39	Delaware	4	0.1	140	0.3	539
40	Iowa	2	Z	111	0.2	423
41	Maine	-	-	44	0.1	313
42	Nebraska	3	Z	61	0.1	309
43	West Virginia	5	0.1	54	0.1	297
44	New Hampshire	5	0.1	46	0.1	292
45	Idaho	-	-	35	0.1	147
46	Alaska	2	Z	15	Z	132
47	Vermont	2	Z	26	0.1	121
48	Montana	-	-	22	Z	108
49	Wyoming	1	Z	5	Z	58
50	South Dakota	-	-	8	Z	37
51	North Dakota	-	-	5	Z	29

Z Rounds to zero. - Represents zero.

HEALTH COSTS

The cost and delivery of health care has been a central focus of public discussion during the 1990s. While the technology of medicine has drastically advanced in the latter half of the 20th century, there exists substantial variation in the amount and quality of health care received by individuals. In 1992, for example, 34 million Americans were without health insurance. Simultaneously, the cost of health care continued a steady increase. In 1980 health care expenditures totaled $158 billion, and rose to $473 billion in 1991, an increase of more than 30%.

This section presents statistics on health expenditures, insurance coverage and health care professionals. The data includes information on Medicare and Medicaid, hospitals and physicians. The sources for the data reported in this section include: the U.S. Health Care Financing Administration (HCFA), which compiles data on national health expenditures, medical cost and insurance coverage, and the Census Bureau, which also issues data on insurance coverage.

This section surveys the total cost of health care and then breaks the cost into component parts. It also offers an overview of the costs of Medicare and Medicaid. Finally, it reports on Americans without health insurance.

HEALTH CARE EXPENDITURES

The figures reported here include spending for hospital care, physician services and prescription drugs. They comprise approximately 70% of all U.S. health care costs. The remaining 30% includes other professional care, nursing home care, research, construction of medical facilities and administration.

Health care expenditures increased nationally at an average annual rate of 10.5% between 1980 and 1991. The highest increases were in Florida, Georgia and Nevada. The lowest average annual increases were in Illinois and Michigan.

TABLE: Health Care Expenditures
DATE: 1991
SOURCE: U.S. Health Care Financing Administration, Office of the Actuary: Data from the Office of National Health Statistics
DESCRIPTION: Data represents spending for services produced by each state's health care providers, as opposed to those consumed by state residents or supplied by state employers. Table ranked by 1991 dollars.

Rank		1980 ($ millions)	1991 ($ millions)	Average annual percent change 1980–1991
	United States	158,452	473,320	10.5
1	California	19,819	58,141	10.3
2	New York	13,423	38,533	10.1
3	Texas	9,368	30,222	11.2
4	Florida	7,404	27,047	12.5
5	Pennsylvania	8,584	25,178	10.3
6	Illinois	8,899	21,234	8.2
7	Ohio	7,561	20,335	9.4
8	Michigan	7,045	17,383	8.6
9	New Jersey	4,506	14,647	11.3
10	Massachusetts	4,892	14,402	10.3
11	Georgia	3,420	12,476	12.5
12	North Carolina	3,161	10,987	12.0
13	Virginia	3,235	10,825	11.6
14	Missouri	3,678	10,226	9.7
15	Tennessee	3,149	9,948	11.0
16	Indiana	3,332	9,749	10.3
17	Maryland	3,091	9,323	10.6
18	Wisconsin	3,117	8,733	9.8
19	Minnesota	2,897	8,726	10.5
20	Washington	2,510	8,486	11.7
21	Louisiana	2,730	8,335	10.7

Rank		1980 ($ millions)	1991 ($ millions)	Average annual percent change 1980–1991
22	Alabama	2,456	7,494	10.7
23	Connecticut	2,155	6,844	11.1
24	Arizona	1,857	6,420	11.9
25	Kentucky	2,010	6,362	11.0
26	Colorado	1,948	6,100	10.9
27	South Carolina	1,527	5,547	12.4
28	Oklahoma	1,888	4,929	9.1
29	Iowa	1,818	4,631	8.9
30	Oregon	1,646	4,597	9.8
31	Kansas	1,675	4,307	9.0
32	Arkansas	1,271	3,968	10.9
33	Mississippi	1,331	3,732	9.8
34	Washington, DC	1,254	3,400	9.5
35	West Virginia	1,268	3,229	8.9
36	Nebraska	1,035	2,794	9.5
37	Utah	751	2,539	11.7
38	New Mexico	684	2,448	12.3
39	Nevada	632	2,274	12.4
40	Hawaii	655	2,144	11.4
41	Maine	652	1,966	10.6
42	Rhode Island	694	1,924	9.7
43	New Hampshire	481	1,917	13.4
44	Delaware	396	1,379	12.0
45	North Dakota	481	1,322	9.6
46	Idaho	426	1,282	10.5
47	South Dakota	405	1,221	10.6
48	Montana	432	1,164	9.4
49	Alaska	312	1,027	11.4
50	Vermont	256	824	11.2
51	Wyoming	234	598	8.9

HOSPITAL CARE EXPENDITURES

Hospital care expenditures represented 63% of total expenditures for 1980 and 60% for 1991. On average, expenditures increased by 9.9% a year between 1980 and 1991. South Carolina and New Hampshire reported the greatest increase in average annual expenditures, and Illinois and Kansas the lowest.

TABLE: Hospital Care Expenditures
DATE: 1991
SOURCE: U.S. Health Care Financing Administration, Office of the Actuary: Data from the Office of National Health Statistics
DESCRIPTION: Data represents spending for services produced by each state's health care providers, as opposed to those consumed by state residents or supplied by state employers. Table ranked by 1991 figures.

Rank		1980 hospital care ($ millions)	1991 hospital care ($ millions)	Average annual percent change 1980–1991
	United States	101,247	286,053	9.9
1	California	11,584	31,128	9.4
2	New York	9,552	25,345	9.3
3	Texas	5,520	18,086	11.4
4	Pennsylvania	6,008	16,622	9.7
5	Florida	4,366	15,210	12.0
6	Illinois	6,205	13,792	7.5
7	Ohio	4,798	12,628	9.2
8	Michigan	4,473	10,663	8.2
9	Massachusetts	3,630	9,097	8.7
10	New Jersey	2,759	8,829	11.2
11	Georgia	2,139	7,603	12.2
12	North Carolina	1,953	6,795	12.0
13	Missouri	2,520	6,660	9.2
14	Virginia	2,068	6,407	10.8
15	Tennessee	2,015	6,239	10.8
16	Indiana	2,123	6,024	9.9
17	Louisiana	1,737	5,277	10.6
18	Maryland	2,033	5,210	8.9
19	Wisconsin	1,947	4,981	8.9
20	Minnesota	1,738	4,607	9.3
21	Washington	1,390	4,581	11.4
22	Alabama	1,588	4,521	10.0
23	Connecticut	1,392	4,089	10.3
24	Kentucky	1,223	3,908	11.1
25	Arizona	1,087	3,615	11.5
26	Colorado	1,218	3,614	10.4
27	South Carolina	972	3,614	12.7
28	Oklahoma	1,171	3,016	9.0
29	Iowa	1,174	2,933	8.7
30	Washington, DC	985	2,641	9.4
31	Oregon	923	2,562	9.7
32	Kansas	1,084	2,545	8.1
33	Mississippi	863	2,425	9.9
34	Arkansas	743	2,359	11.1
35	West Virginia	825	2,000	8.4
36	Nebraska	678	1,789	9.2
37	New Mexico	448	1,570	12.1
38	Utah	452	1,510	11.6
39	Hawaii	360	1,287	12.3
40	Maine	460	1,257	9.6
41	Rhode Island	480	1,215	8.8
42	Nevada	385	1,195	10.8
43	New Hampshire	313	1,129	12.4
44	Delaware	258	800	10.8
45	South Dakota	271	799	10.3
46	North Dakota	313	796	8.8
47	Montana	264	763	10.1
48	Idaho	242	762	11.0
49	Alaska	200	659	11.4

Rank		1980 hospital care ($ millions)	1991 hospital care ($ millions)	Average annual percent change 1980–1991
50	Vermont	173	502	10.2
51	Wyoming	146	394	9.4

EXPENDITURES FOR PHYSICIAN SERVICES

The cost of physician services represented 28% of total health care expenditures in 1980 and 32% in 1991. They increased an average of 11.6% a year between 1980 and 1991. Services provided by physicians recorded a larger increase than total health care, hospital care or prescription drugs. Between 1980 and 1991, average annual expenditures increased most rapidly in New Hampshire and Nevada. They increased least in Montana and Wyoming.

TABLE: Expenditures for Physician Services
DATE: 1991
SOURCE: U.S. Health Care Financing Administration, Office of the the Actuary: data from the Office of National Health Statistics
DESCRIPTION: Data represents spending for services produced by each state's health care providers, as opposed to those consumed by state residents or supplied by state employers. Table ranked by 1991 costs.

Rank		1980 physician services ($ millions)	1991 physician services ($ millions)	Average annual percent change 1980–1991
	United States	45,156	150,891	11.6
1	California	6,938	23,108	11.6
2	New York	3,051	10,611	12.0
3	Florida	2,502	9,881	13.3
4	Texas	3,000	9,754	11.3
5	Pennsylvania	1,960	6,680	11.8
6	Ohio	2,157	6,094	9.9
7	Illinois	2,133	5,731	9.4
8	Michigan	2,044	5,141	8.7
9	New Jersey	1,367	4,569	11.6
10	Massachusetts	971	4,244	14.3
11	Georgia	987	3,902	13.3
12	Minnesota	968	3,571	12.6
13	Virginia	892	3,464	13.1
14	Washington	908	3,336	12.6
15	Maryland	833	3,284	13.3
16	North Carolina	868	3,200	12.6
17	Wisconsin	952	3,077	11.3
18	Indiana	904	2,890	11.1
19	Tennessee	846	2,865	11.7
20	Missouri	883	2,815	11.1

Rank		1980 physician services ($ millions)	1991 physician services ($ millions)	Average annual percent change 1980–1991
21	Louisiana	738	2,400	11.3
22	Arizona	647	2,321	12.3
23	Alabama	633	2,296	12.4
24	Connecticut	590	2,236	12.9
25	Colorado	603	2,122	12.1
26	Kentucky	561	1,814	11.3
27	Oregon	597	1,738	10.2
28	Oklahoma	542	1,471	9.5
29	South Carolina	402	1,455	12.4
30	Kansas	464	1,404	10.6
31	Iowa	488	1,294	9.3
32	Arkansas	375	1,241	11.5
33	Nevada	210	945	14.7
34	Mississippi	326	923	9.9
35	West Virginia	327	900	9.6
36	Utah	245	822	11.6
37	Nebraska	277	779	9.9
38	Hawaii	251	719	10.0
39	New Mexico	185	699	12.9
40	Washington, DC	237	666	9.8
41	New Hampshire	129	641	15.7
42	Maine	141	547	13.1
43	Rhode Island	165	543	11.4
44	Delaware	113	488	14.2
45	North Dakota	140	442	11.0
46	Idaho	141	397	9.9
47	South Dakota	103	342	11.5
48	Montana	137	314	7.8
49	Alaska	96	312	11.3
50	Vermont	61	243	13.4
51	Wyoming	65	155	8.2

EXPENDITURES FOR PRESCRIPTION DRUGS

Prescription drug expenditures constituted 8% of total health care costs in 1980 and 1991. Between 1980 and 1991 their cost increased an average of 10.6% annually. The largest increase was in Arizona and the smallest in Wyoming.

TABLE: Expenditures for Prescription Drugs
DATE: 1991
SOURCE: U.S. Health Care Financing Administration, Office of the Actuary: data from the Office of National Health Statistics.
DESCRIPTION: Data represents spending for services produced by each state's health care providers, as opposed to those consumed by state residents or supplied

by state employers. Expenditures for retail prescription drugs. Table ranked by 1991 costs.

Rank		1990 prescription drugs ($ millions)	1991 prescription drugs ($ millions)	Average annual percent change 1980–1991
	United States	12,049	36,377	10.6
1	California	1,296	3,904	10.5
2	New York	820	2,577	11.0
3	Texas	848	2,382	9.8
4	Florida	536	1,956	12.5
5	Pennsylvania	616	1,876	10.7
6	Illinois	561	1,711	10.7
7	Ohio	607	1,613	9.3
8	Michigan	527	1,578	10.5
9	New Jersey	381	1,249	11.4
10	Massachusetts	290	1,061	12.5
11	North Carolina	340	992	10.2
12	Georgia	294	971	11.5
13	Virginia	275	955	12.0
14	Tennessee	288	844	10.3
15	Indiana	305	835	9.6
16	Maryland	226	829	12.6
17	Missouri	274	751	9.6
18	Alabama	235	677	10.1
19	Wisconsin	218	675	10.8
20	Louisiana	254	658	9.0
21	Kentucky	225	639	10.0
22	Washington	212	568	9.4
23	Minnesota	191	548	10.0
24	Connecticut	174	520	10.5
25	Arizona	123	483	13.3
26	South Carolina	154	479	10.9
27	Oklahoma	175	442	8.8
28	Iowa	156	404	9.0
29	Mississippi	142	384	9.5
30	Arkansas	153	368	8.3
31	Colorado	127	364	10.0
32	Kansas	128	358	9.8
33	West Virginia	116	329	10.0
34	Oregon	125	297	8.2
35	Nebraska	80	227	9.9
36	Utah	54	207	13.0
37	New Mexico	52	179	12.0
38	Rhode Island	48	166	11.8
39	Maine	51	162	11.0
40	New Hampshire	39	146	12.8
41	Hawaii	44	137	10.9
42	Nevada	36	135	12.6
43	Idaho	44	123	9.8
44	Washington, DC	32	93	10.3
45	Delaware	25	91	12.4
46	Montana	31	87	9.8
47	North Dakota	28	84	10.5
48	South Dakota	30	80	9.3
49	Vermont	22	79	12.4
50	Alaska	16	56	12.0
51	Wyoming	23	49	7.2

MEDICARE ENROLLMENT AND PAYMENTS

Medicare, a federal program established in 1966, provides health care to nearly all people over 65. The federal Medicare program consists of two coordinated plans; the first is a hospital insurance plan that covers hospital and related services; the second is a voluntary supplementary medical insurance plan financed in part by monthly premiums paid by participants. The latter covers part of the cost of physician services and related medical services.

The federal government pays the full costs of providing Medicare services (with the exception of the monthly premiums described above). Medicare's payments represent a substantial portion of the federal budget; therefore the program and specifically its costs are the subject of prominent national political debate.

TABLE: Medicare Enrollment and Payments
DATE: 1992
SOURCE: U.S. Health Care Financing Administration, unpublished data
DESCRIPTION: Medicare enrollment. Payments are for calendar year and represent disbursements from federal hospital and medical insurance trust funds. Table ranked by enrollment.

Rank		Enrollment (thousands)	Payments ($ millions)
	United States*	34,853	128,520
1	California	3,421	15,653
2	New York	2,556	10,269
3	Florida	2,455	10,361
4	Pennsylvania	2,014	8,365
5	Texas	1,923	6,978
6	Ohio	1,598	5,721
7	Illinois	1,574	5,565
8	Michigan	1,282	4,642
9	New Jersey	1,126	4,188
10	North Carolina	944	3,006
11	Massachusetts	895	3,780
12	Missouri	804	2,674
13	Indiana	789	2,455
14	Georgia	771	2,864
15	Virginia	760	2,226
16	Wisconsin	734	2,126
17	Tennessee	722	2,895
18	Washington	645	2,145
19	Minnesota	606	1,943
20	Alabama	606	2,100
21	Maryland	567	2,262
22	Kentucky	554	1,788
23	Louisiana	551	2,318
24	Arizona	538	2,077
25	Connecticut	483	1,953

Rank		Enrollment (thousands)	Payments ($ millions)
26	South Carolina	468	1,244
27	Oklahoma	466	1,471
28	Iowa	465	1,242
29	Oregon	445	1,357
30	Arkansas	404	1,309
31	Colorado	382	1,242
32	Mississippi	378	1,235
33	Kansas	373	1,161
34	West Virginia	317	931
35	Nebraska	242	631
36	New Mexico	192	489
37	Maine	190	514
38	Utah	171	427
39	Rhode Island	163	588
40	Nevada	161	598
41	New Hampshire	145	428
42	Idaho	139	300
43	Hawaii	136	404
44	Montana	123	307
45	South Dakota	113	276
46	North Dakota	101	352
47	Delaware	93	267
48	Washington, DC	78	1,112
49	Vermont	77	200
50	Wyoming	55	98
51	Alaska	28	82

*Includes data for enrollees with residence unknown.

MEDICAID RECIPIENTS AND PAYMENTS

Medicaid provides health services to the poor. All states offer this basic service to the indigent who are pregnant, aged, disabled or blind, and families with dependent children. In most states eligibility for Medicaid is automatic for welfare recipients. Over two-thirds of the states also extend benefits to other needy individuals who meet set criteria.

The populous states rank highest in Medicaid recipients. However, payments reflect individual state contributions to the program. For example, in New York, Pennsylvania and Illinois total payments for Medicaid are comparatively higher than other states with the same number of recipients because these states contribute more to the program. Unlike Medicare, which is solely a federal program, Medicaid is a joint program with the federal and state governments sharing the cost. Within federal guidelines, each state establishes its own Medicaid eligibility requirements and the health services to be provided under Medicaid.

TABLE: Medicaid Recipients and Payments
DATE: 1992
SOURCE: U.S. Health Care Financing Administration, unpublished data
DESCRIPTION: Medicare enrollment. Payments are for calendar year and represent disbursements from federal hospital and medical insurance trust funds. Table ranked by recipients.

Rank		Recipients (thousands)	Payments ($ millions)
	United States*	30,251	91,317
1	California	4,486	8,692
2	New York	2,558	15,281
3	Texas	2,025	4,407
4	Florida	1,538	3,518
5	Pennsylvania	1,398	4,213
6	Illinois	1,313	4,070
7	Ohio	1,299	3,653
8	Michigan	1,129	2,802
9	Georgia	864	2,149
10	North Carolina	785	2,083
11	Tennessee	785	1,735
12	Louisiana	702	2,479
13	New Jersey	697	2,802
14	Massachusetts	686	3,248
15	Kentucky	583	1,543
16	Washington	569	1,347
17	Missouri	554	1,350
18	Virginia	515	1,511
19	Indiana	507	2,225
20	Mississippi	487	881
21	Alabama	467	1,056
22	Wisconsin	440	1,677
23	South Carolina	431	1,151
24	Minnesota	406	1,750
25	Arizona	402	209
26	Maryland	377	1,612
27	Oklahoma	360	1,004
28	Arkansas	321	885
29	Connecticut	316	1,663
30	West Virginia	308	795
31	Oregon	295	748
32	Iowa	279	855
33	Colorado	259	814
34	Kansas	227	620
35	Rhode Island	213	774
36	New Mexico	212	478
37	Maine	162	642
38	Nebraska	151	468
39	Utah	137	365
40	Washington, DC	109	499
41	Hawaii	100	270
42	Idaho	87	275
43	Nevada	78	282
44	Vermont	78	222
45	New Hampshire	71	340
46	South Dakota	64	231
47	Delaware	61	219
48	Montana	60	217
49	Alaska	58	187
50	North Dakota	57	253
51	Wyoming	42	114

*Includes data for enrollees with residence unknown.

PERCENTAGE OF THE POPULATION WITHOUT HEALTH INSURANCE

Nationally, 14.2% of Americans were without health insurance averaged over a three year period, 1990 to 1992. The District of Columbia and the southern, southwestern and some western states reported the highest percentage of uninsured populations. Hawaii, which has an employer-based statewide mandatory insurance program, ranks last.

TABLE: Percentage of the Population Without Health Insurance.
DATE: 1992
SOURCE: U.S. Bureau of the Census, *Current Population Reports*
DESCRIPTION: Three-year average of persons without health insurance in percent.
UNITED STATES AVERAGE: 14.2%

Rank		Percent of population without health insurance
1	Washington, DC	22.0
2	Texas	21.9
3	New Mexico	21.0
4	Louisiana	20.8
5	Oklahoma	19.5
6	Mississippi	19.3
7	Nevada	19.3
8	California	19.0
9	Florida	18.7
10	Arkansas	17.6
11	Alabama	17.3
12	Idaho	16.4
13	Georgia	16.1
14	Arizona	15.8

Rank		Percent of population without health insurance
15	Virginia	15.5
16	South Carolina	15.4
17	West Virginia	15.0
18	Alaska	14.9
19	North Carolina	14.2
20	Kentucky	13.6
21	Tennessee	13.6
22	Oregon	13.3
23	Missouri	13.1
24	Delaware	12.7
25	New York	12.6
26	Colorado	12.4
27	Maryland	12.3
28	South Dakota	12.2
29	Montana	12.0
30	Wyoming	11.9
31	Illinois	11.8
32	Indiana	11.5
33	Utah	11.5
34	New Jersey	11.3
35	Maine	11.1
36	Kansas	11.0
37	New Hampshire	10.9
38	Washington	10.7
39	Vermont	10.6
40	Ohio	10.5
41	Rhode Island	10.2
42	Massachusetts	10.1
43	Michigan	9.4
44	Iowa	9.0
45	Minnesota	8.8
46	Pennsylvania	8.8
47	Nebraska	8.7
48	Wisconsin	7.9
49	Connecticut	7.5
50	North Dakota	7.4
51	Hawaii	6.8

ENERGY COSTS

The tables in this section present data on the cost of energy. The principal sources are the U.S. Department of Energy's Energy Information Administration and the American Gas Association.

Many factors must be considered in comparing data on cost and usage of energy among states. For example, the proximity and availability of sources of fuel may impact both cost and usage. The sector (commercial, residential, industrial, transportation) utilizing the fuel alters demand for fuel, which, of course, impacts prices and production.

Uniformity among various energy sources is achieved by converting from a measure of quantity (such as short tons of coal, cubic feet of natural gas, barrels of petroleum, kilowatt-hours of hydroelectric power) to a thermal equivalent, the British thermal units (Btu). A Btu is the amount of energy required to raise the temperature of one pound of water one degree Fahrenheit (F) at or near 39.2 degrees F. Factors are calculated annually from the latest final annual data available and revised when necessary. A kilowatt is a unit of electrical power, which is equal to 1,000 watts.

Energy expenditures are presented in the first table of this section. The remaining tables present data on the major sources of energy: gas, electricity and petroleum products.

ENERGY EXPENDITURES

The table below summarizes the cost of energy from the four major sources: petroleum products, natural gas, coal and electricity sales. The figures are for sales to residential, commercial, industrial and transportation customers.

In 1970 a total of $83 billion was spent on energy, compared with $467 billion in 1991 (these figures do not account for inflation). State comparisons can be deceptive. Climate, availability of sources (i.e. oil and water power) and industrial production are among the factors influencing cost. Per capita costs are lowest in Florida, New York and California. Alaska ranked highest, despite a 13% decrease in costs between 1990 and 1991. The oil-rich states of Alaska, Texas and Louisiana all rank in the top five for per capita expenditures. Expenditures in many midwestern and Plains states approximate the per capita average. In 1991, $1,716 separated the states with the highest per capita costs from those with the lowest.

TABLE: Energy Expenditures
DATE: 1991
SOURCE: U.S. Energy Information Administration, *State Energy Price and Expenditure Report*, annual
DESCRIPTION: Energy expenditures per capita and percent changes 1990–1991. Ranked in per capita dollars.

Rank		Total ($ millions*)	Per capita ($)	Percent change 1990–1991
	United States	467,132	1,853	-0.5
1	Alaska	1,852	3,249	-12.8
2	Wyoming	1,493	3,245	-1.8
3	Louisiana	13,168	3,095	-2.8
4	North Dakota	1,589	2,502	1.1
5	Texas	42,861	2,471	-0.4
6	Indiana	11,920	2,125	-1.6
7	Montana	1,695	2,096	1.4
8	West Virginia	3,751	2,081	-3.4
9	Kansas	5,143	2,061	-2.3
10	Maine	2,538	2,057	-0.1
11	New Jersey	15,874	2,047	0.0
12	Delaware	1,388	2,040	-2.1
13	Alabama	8,301	2,029	-0.4
14	Arkansas	4,687	1,975	-0.2
15	Nebraska	3,093	1,942	-0.4
16	Kentucky	7,188	1,936	-1.1
17	Vermont	1,094	1,930	3.9
18	Ohio	21,089	1,928	1.0
19	New Mexico	2,985	1,927	0.8
20	South Carolina	6,840	1,921	-0.4
21	Washington, DC	1,130	1,899	4.5
22	Oklahoma	5,996	1,888	-3.2
23	Connecticut	6,201	1,885	1.5
24	Georgia	12,479	1,884	-2.7

Rank		Total ($ millions*)	Per capita ($)	Percent change 1990–1991
25	Mississippi	4,881	1,882	-0.9
26	Nevada	2,405	1,875	-0.5
27	Tennessee	9,274	1,872	-3.9
28	North Carolina	12,601	1,871	0.6
29	Iowa	5,212	1,865	1.7
30	Pennsylvania	22,279	1,863	1.2
31	Illinois	21,500	1,863	-3.4
32	Idaho	1,910	1,837	5.4
33	Missouri	9,393	1,821	0.1
34	South Dakota	1,270	1,804	-5.2
35	Hawaii	2,039	1,793	-4.8
36	Michigan	16,754	1,786	1.1
37	Massachusetts	10,598	1,767	0.8
38	Virginia	11,038	1,758	-1.9
39	Rhode Island	1,756	1,747	9.3
40	New Hampshire	1,906	1,727	-3.0
41	Arizona	6,432	1,716	-1.4
42	Minnesota	7,597	1,714	1.9
43	Washington	8,591	1,714	0.8
44	Oregon	5,008	1,714	0.6
45	Maryland	8,049	1,657	2.3
46	Wisconsin	8,152	1,645	1.4
47	Utah	2,868	1,621	4.7
48	Colorado	5,415	1,603	3.9
49	California	47,460	1,562	-1.9
50	New York	28,006	1,551	2.1
51	Florida	20,343	1,533	-2.6

*Total expenditures are the the sum of purchases for each source (including electricity sales) less electric utility purchases of fuel.

GAS UTILITY INDUSTRY

The overwhelming majority of gas customers were residential (92%) in 1992. However, sales to residential customers represented only 47% of all sales and 58% of gas utility revenues. Nationwide, natural gas (measured by quadrillion Btus consumed) was the fuel of choice in 1990 among residential consumers, outranking electricity and fuel oil. Only in the South did electricity consumption exceed natural gas consumption. Natural gas was also the cheapest form of fuel on average across the country (measured by dollars in millions of Btu). (For a definition of Btu see the introduction to this section.)

TABLE: Gas Utility Industry
DATE: 1992
SOURCE: American Gas Association, *Gas Facts*, annual (copyright)
DESCRIPTION: Covers natural, manufactured, mixed, and liquid petroleum gas. Based on questionnaire mailed to all privately and municipally owned gas utilities in the U.S. except those with annual revenues less than $25,000. Ranked by revenues.

Rank		Residential customers (thousands)	Residential revenues ($ millions)
	United States	51,525	26,702
1	California	8,668	2,839
2	New York	3,952	2,762
3	Illinois	3,321	2,123
4	Ohio	2,818	1,773
5	Pennsylvania	2,350	1,737
6	Michigan	2,640	1,695
7	New Jersey	2,025	1,348
8	Texas	3,296	1,169
9	Massachusetts	1,136	879
10	Indiana	1,372	823
11	Wisconsin	1,179	722
12	Georgia	1,376	673
13	Missouri	1,221	595
14	Minnesota	1,013	557
15	Maryland	789	436
16	Colorado	1,022	435
17	Iowa	726	388
18	Connecticut	431	379
19	Virginia	653	379
20	Kansas	764	340
21	Alabama	698	329
22	Oklahoma	833	327
23	Kentucky	643	308
24	Louisiana	928	307
25	Tennessee	661	279
26	North Carolina	575	274
27	Utah	468	244
28	West Virginia	352	223
29	Washington	523	208
30	Arkansas	505	203
31	Arizona	601	201
32	Nebraska	431	201
33	South Carolina	364	161
34	New Mexico	385	155
35	Rhode Island	197	150
36	Florida	516	143
37	Oregon	352	143
38	Mississippi	380	128
39	Nevada	296	103
40	Washington, DC	133	89
41	Montana	183	83
42	Alaska	74	54
43	South Dakota	110	54
44	Wyoming	114	52
45	Delaware	94	51
46	Idaho	134	49
47	North Dakota	90	48
48	New Hampshire	68	46
49	Vermont	24	19
50	Hawaii	32	10
51	Maine	13	6

COST OF ELECTRICITY

The average price of electricity in 1990 was 6.5 cents per kilowatt-hour. Alaska and a cluster of northeastern states rank highest in price. Hawaii and California also rank in the top 10, followed by Pennsylvania, Illinois and Michigan. Many southern states are in the lowest two-thirds.

TITLE: Cost of Electricity
DATE: 1990
SOURCE: U.S. Energy Information Administration, *Annual Electric Utility Report*
DESCRIPTION: Average price per kilowatt hour in cents.
U.S. AVERAGE: 6.5

Rank		Average revenue (cents)
1	Alaska	9.5
2	New York	9.4
3	Connecticut	9.2
4	New Hampshire	9.1
5	Rhode Island	9.1
6	New Jersey	9.1
7	Hawaii	9.0
8	Massachusetts	8.8
9	California	8.8
10	Vermont	8.3
11	Arizona	7.8
12	Pennsylvania	7.7
13	Maine	7.6
14	Illinois	7.5
15	Michigan	7.1
16	New Mexico	7.1
17	Florida	7.0
18	Arkansas	6.7
19	Kansas	6.6
20	Georgia	6.6
21	Missouri	6.5
22	Delaware	6.5
23	North Carolina	6.4
24	Maryland	6.3
25	South Dakota	6.1
26	Mississippi	6.1
27	Virginia	6.0
28	Louisiana	6.0
29	Ohio	5.9
30	Iowa	5.9
31	Washington, DC	5.9
32	Colorado	5.9
33	Texas	5.8
34	North Dakota	5.7
35	Nebraska	5.6
36	South Carolina	5.6
37	Alabama	5.6
38	Oklahoma	5.5
39	Utah	5.5
40	Indiana	5.4

Rank		Average revenue (cents)
41	Wisconsin	5.4
42	Nevada	5.4
43	Minnesota	5.3
44	Tennessee	5.3
45	West Virginia	4.7
46	Kentucky	4.5
47	Wyoming	4.2
48	Oregon	4.2
49	Montana	4.0
50	Idaho	3.8
51	Washington	3.4

REFINER/RESELLER SALES PRICES OF GASOLINE

While the average price of gasoline was lower in 1993 (75.5 cents a gallon) than 1991 (76.5 cents a gallon), not all states experienced a decrease in price. In California the price of gasoline increased in 1993 by 19.1 cents a gallon over the 1991 price. In 1993 the price of gasoline was highest in Hawaii (108.5 cents). Gasoline is cheapest in Michigan (70.8 cents).

TABLE: Refiner/Reseller Sales Price of Gasoline
DATE: 1993
SOURCE: U.S. Energy Information Administration, *Petroleum Marketing Monthly*
DESCRIPTION: Refiner/reseller sales price in cents per gallon. Represents all refinery and gas plant operators' sales through company-operated retail outlets. Gasoline prices exclude excise taxes.

Rank		1991 (cents per gallon)	1993 (cents per gallon)
	United States	76.5	75.5
1	Hawaii	99.1	108.5
2	Alaska	108.7	107.7
3	New Mexico	77.8	85.9
4	New Jersey	83.4	85.4
5	North Dakota	82.8	85.1
6	Arizona	78.6	84.6
7	California	65.3	84.4
8	Nevada	79.2	83.1
9	Vermont	91.6	82.7
10	Connecticut	83.0	81.6
11	Minnesota	77.6	81.1
12	Maine	90.0	80.9
13	Colorado	73.4	80.4
14	New Hampshire	85.2	80.3
15	Wyoming	79.4	80.2
16	Oregon	75.8	79.9
17	Massachusetts	83.1	79.0

Rank		1991 (cents per gallon)	1993 (cents per gallon)
18	West Virginia	81.1	78.4
19	South Dakota	80.8	78.2
20	Rhode Island	82.9	77.6
21	Florida	78.5	77.2
22	Montana	81.3	77.1
23	Nebraska	80.9	76.8
24	New York	87.0	75.8
25	Maryland	78.8	75.5
26	Virginia	77.2	75.4
27	Louisiana	77.2	75.3
28	Delaware	83.8	74.8
29	Texas	76.1	74.8
30	Utah	66.2	74.8
31	Alabama	78.4	74.5
32	Mississippi	78.9	74.5
33	Illinois	76.1	74.1
34	Wisconsin	76.8	73.5
35	Kansas	76.2	73.1
36	Iowa	80.0	72.9
37	Kentucky	78.6	72.9
38	Arkansas	77.5	72.8
39	Georgia	75.9	72.6
40	Idaho	67.0	72.6
41	Tennessee	74.4	72.5
42	Pennsylvania	82.4	72.3
43	Indiana	77.3	71.6
44	Oklahoma	75.8	71.5
45	Ohio	73.4	71.4
46	North Carolina	76.2	71.2
47	Michigan	74.0	70.8
48	Missouri	75.6	69.8
49	South Carolina	75.6	69.8
50	Washington	72.4	69.6

CRUDE PETROLEUM PRODUCTION

Crude petroleum production declined between 1985 and 1992 by almost 650 billion barrels. Alaska and Texas produced approximately half of the nation's domestic crude oil in 1992. Louisiana recorded a substantial decrease in production. In 1985 the state produced 15% of the nation's crude oil, but by 1992 it produced only .05%. (The data excludes offshore production.)

TABLE: Crude Petroleum Production
DATE: 1992
SOURCES: U.S. Energy Information Administration, *Energy Data Reports, Petroleum Supply Annual*
DESCRIPTION: Crude petroleum production 1985 and 1992. State production does not include state offshore production.

Rank		1985 barrels (billions)	1992 barrels (billions)
	United States*	3,274	2,625
1	Texas	889	651
2	Alaska	666	627
3	California	424	305
4	Louisiana	508	143
5	Oklahoma	163	102
6	Wyoming	129	97
7	New Mexico	79	70
8	Kansas	75	54
9	North Dakota	51	33
10	Colorado	30	30
11	Mississippi	31	25
12	Utah	41	23
13	Alabama	22	19
14	Illinois	30	19
15	Montana	30	18
16	Michigan	27	16
17	Arkansas	19	10
18	Ohio	15	9
19	Florida	11	5
20	Kentucky	8	5
21	Nebraska	7	5
22	Indiana	5	3
23	Pennsylvania	5	2
24	West Virginia	4	2
25	New York	1	Z

Z Less than 500,000 dollars or barrels.
*Includes other states not shown separately.

NATURAL GAS PRODUCTION

U.S. natural gas production increased from 1985 to 1992, although the increase was not uniform, and several states experienced declines. The largest increases occurred in the South and Midwest, although states such as Florida and Nebraska experienced declines.

TABLE: Natural Gas Production
DATE: 1992
SOURCES: U.S. Energy Information Administration, *Energy Data Reports, Natural Gas Annual* and *Natural Gas Monthly*
DESCRIPTION: Natural gas production 1985 and 1992. State production does not include state offshore production.

Rank		1985 quantity (billions cubic feet)	1992 quantity (billions cubic feet)
	United States*	17,270	18,712
1	Texas	6,053	6,146
2	Louisiana	5,014	4,914

Rank		1985 quantity (billions cubic feet)	1992 quantity (billions cubic feet)
3	Oklahoma	1,936	2,017
4	New Mexico	905	1,269
5	Wyoming	417	843
6	Kansas	528	658
7	Alaska	321	444
8	California	491	366
9	Alabama	107	355
10	Colorado	178	323
11	Arkansas	155	202
12	Michigan	132	195
13	West Virginia	145	182
14	Utah	83	171
15	Ohio	182	145

Rank		1985 quantity (billions cubic feet)	1992 quantity (billions cubic feet)
16	Pennsylvania	150	139
17	Mississippi	144	92
18	Kentucky	73	80
19	North Dakota	73	55
20	Montana	52	54
21	New York	32	24
22	Florida	11	7
23	Nebraska	2	1
24	Illinois	1	Z
25	Indiana	Z	Z

Z Less than 500,000 dollars or barrels.
*Includes other states not shown separately.

ENERGY SOURCES AND USAGE

The tables in this section present information on the sources and usage of energy. The United States used 41% of the world's energy in 1960. By 1990 it was using 25%. However, absolute energy consumption did not decline in the United States, but rather increased elsewhere.

The principal sources for these tables are the U.S. Department of Energy's Energy Information Association and the U.S. Bureau of the Census.

The preceding section, "Energy Costs," examines the cost of energy by source of fuel and sector or consumer group. Specifically, the tables in this section show the generation and usage of electricity and the fuels used for home heating. Electricity is produced in power plants that convert other forms or sources of energy into this more transportable form. The basic energy sources used in this process vary among states depending on the availability of the source and the policies of the local utility companies. These sources of energy include coal, nuclear energy, hydroelectric energy, natural gas and petroleum products. Electricity is then sold to three categories of consumer: residential, commercial and industrial. Home heating fuels surveyed here include gas, electric and oil.

The states are ranked according to the total amount of electricity produced from a given energy source. States with high overall electrical production (California, for example) may therefore be ranked high in several tables. Electric energy is measured in kilowatt-hours. A kilowatt is a unit of electrical power, which is equal to 1,000 watts.

Total electric generation is shown in the first table. Following is a series of tables detailing the sources of energy that generate electricity: coal, nuclear energy, hydroelectric energy, natural gas and petroleum products. The remaining tables record the use of various home heating fuels: gas, electric and oil.

ELECTRIC ENERGY GENERATION AND CAPABILITY

This table shows total generation of electrical energy from all sources for 1992. The five major sources used to generate electricity are natural gas, petroleum products, nuclear generation, hydroelectric generation and coal. The table below follows population statistics and industrialization. The populous industrial states are at the top of the list.

TABLE: Electric Energy Generation and Capability
DATE: 1992
SOURCES: U.S. Energy Information Administration *Electric Power Annual* and *Inventory of Power Plants in the United States*, annual
DESCRIPTION: Net generation and net summer capability. Covers utilities for public use. Table ranked by net generation

Rank		Net generation (bil. kwh)	Net summer capability (mil. kwh)
	United States	2,797.2	695.1
1	Texas	240.0	62.7
2	Pennsylvania	166.0	33.4
3	Ohio	136.3	27.1
4	Florida	134.0	33.4
5	Illinois	124.8	32.6
6	California	119.3	43.8
7	New York	112.2	31.1
8	Indiana	97.3	20.8
9	Georgia	91.8	21.4
10	Alabama	90.8	19.9
11	Washington	84.1	24.2
12	North Carolina	83.0	20.1
13	Michigan	82.7	22.4
14	Kentucky	77.4	15.3
15	Tennessee	75.4	16.3
16	West Virginia	72.3	14.4

Rank		Net generation (bil. kwh)	Net summer capability (mil. kwh)
17	South Carolina	71.5	16.3
18	Arizona	70.1	15.0
19	Missouri	56.6	15.4
20	Louisiana	55.2	16.7
21	Virginia	49.0	13.8
22	Wisconsin	46.5	10.5
23	Oklahoma	45.9	12.9
24	Wyoming	41.9	5.8
25	Oregon	41.2	11.2
26	Maryland	39.6	10.9
27	Minnesota	37.8	8.9
28	Arkansas	37.4	9.6
29	Utah	32.9	4.8
30	Massachusetts	32.8	9.5
31	Colorado	31.9	6.6
32	Kansas	31.8	9.7
33	New Jersey	31.2	13.8
34	Iowa	29.4	8.1
35	North Dakota	28.6	4.5
36	New Mexico	27.7	5.1
37	Montana	25.5	4.9
38	Connecticut	25.2	7.0
39	Nebraska	22.4	5.5
40	Nevada	21.0	5.1
41	Mississippi	20.5	7.0
42	New Hampshire	13.5	2.5
43	Maine	8.3	2.4
44	Hawaii	6.9	1.6
45	Delaware	6.3	2.1
46	Idaho	6.3	2.4
47	South Dakota	6.2	2.7
48	Vermont	4.7	1.1
49	Alaska	4.2	1.7
50	Rhode Island	0.1	0.2
51	Washington, DC	0.1	0.8

COAL-GENERATED ELECTRICITY

In 1991 coal (59%) was the leading source for generation of electrical energy. The states generating the most electricity from coal, with the exception of Texas, are the traditional coal-producing states. They are located along the Appalachians and around the Great Lakes, where Appalachian coal can be readily transported by railroad and ship. Among the states ranked, the median percentage of coal-generated electricity was a comparatively high 61.1%. In the top nine states coal represented over 90% of the state's electrical energy generation.

TABLE: Coal-Generated Electricity
DATE: 1991

SOURCE: U.S. Energy Information Administration, *Monthly Plant Report*
DESCRIPTION: Percent of total electricity generation from coal-fired generators and coal-fired net generation of electricity.

Rank		Percent	Total (million kwh)
	United States	58.61	1,559,426
1	West Virginia	99.1	76,636
2	Indiana	98.2	96,013
3	Wyoming	98.2	38,681
4	Utah	97.7	31,519
5	Kentucky	95.5	70,500
6	Colorado	94.5	29,603
7	North Dakota	93.5	25,093
8	Ohio	90.9	115,014
9	New Mexico	90.6	25,827
10	Iowa	85.7	24,880
11	Missouri	82.2	48,502
12	Nevada	78.1	15,053
13	Maryland	74.0	23,299
14	Michigan	73.3	65,296
15	Wisconsin	70.6	32,145
16	Kansas	70.0	23,720
17	Alabama	69.9	53,301
18	Georgia	69.3	67,565
19	Delaware	69.1	4,904
20	Tennessee	67.9	50,187
21	Minnesota	66.4	27,588
22	Pennsylvania	61.6	101,996
23	Nebraska	58.5	12,658
24	North Carolina	58.4	46,631
25	Montana	57.9	14,903
26	Oklahoma	55.9	25,189
27	Arkansas	51.7	19,181
28	Arizona	50.8	31,535
29	Texas	50.6	118,354
30	Florida	47.8	59,073
31	Virginia	44.5	21,000
32	Illinois	42.4	53,866
33	Mississippi	41.2	9,446
34	South Dakota	38.5	2,473
35	South Carolina	33.0	22,875
36	Massachusetts	30.9	11,273
37	Louisiana	30.6	17.800
38	New Hampshire	27.4	2,859
39	New Jersey	19.3	7,058
40	New York	19.1	24,617
41	Connecticut	7.3	2,351
42	Washington	7.3	7,352
43	Alaska	6.9	312
44	Oregon	2.6	1,298

NUCLEAR-GENERATED ELECTRICITY

In 1980 nuclear power was the fourth leading source of electrical energy; in 1991 it was the second leading source of electrical energy after coal. Nuclear power accounted for approximately 20% of all electrical energy. Illinois, with 13 nuclear power plants, generates the most kilowatt-hours, followed by Pennsylvania (9) and South Carolina (7).

TABLE: Nuclear-Generated Electricity
DATE: 1991
SOURCE: U.S. Energy Information Administration, *Monthly Power Plant Report*
DESCRIPTION: Percent of total electricity generation from nuclear-powered sources and net energy generation of electricity from nuclear-powered sources in million kilowatt hours.

Rank		Percent	Net generation (mil. kwh.)
	United States	20.5	576,861
1	Vermont	72.4	3,616
2	New Jersey	65.1	23,770
3	South Carolina	61.9	42,881
4	Connecticut	61.5	19,776
5	Illinois	56.8	71,887
6	Maine	53.6	4,881
7	Virginia	50.5	23,820
8	New Hampshire	37.7	4,081
9	Pennsylvania	34.9	57,787
10	Nebraska	34.7	7,511
11	Arizona	33.1	20,598
12	North Carolina	32.4	25,905
13	Mississippi	32.4	7,422
14	Arkansas	30.4	11,282
15	Minnesota	29.2	12,139
16	California	28.5	32,693
17	Georgia	25.4	24,797
18	Wisconsin	24.6	11,226
19	Louisiana	24.4	14,197
20	Michigan	24.3	21,610
21	Kansas	23.3	7,874
22	Tennessee	18.9	14,003
23	New York	18.4	23,623
24	Florida	17.6	21,750
25	Alabama	15.8	12,062
26	Massachusetts	13.9	5,070
27	Missouri	13.6	7,998
28	Oregon	12.4	6,074
29	Iowa	10.4	3,012
30	Ohio	8.4	10,664
31	Washington	5.7	5,742
32	Maryland	4	1,251
33	Texas	6.8	15,859

HYDROELECTRIC-GENERATED ELECTRICITY

Hydroelectric energy accounted for approximately 10% of all electrical energy. Because of their flat terrain New Jersey, Delaware, Louisiana, Mississippi, Illinois, Kansas, Wyoming and Rhode Island have no hydroelectric plants. The dams of Washington, Oregon and northern California account for over 50% of the nation's hydroelectric energy output. New York is the exception on the East Coast because of Niagara Falls. It generates more hydroelectric energy than California.

TABLE: Hydroelectric-Generated Electricity
DATE: 1991
SOURCE: U.S. Energy Information Administration: *Monthly Power Plant Report*
DESCRIPTION: Percent of total electricity generation from hydroelectric plants and net generation of electricity from hydroelectric plants in million kilowatt hours.

Rank		Percent	Total net generation (mil. kwh.)
	United States	10.0	279,388
1	Idaho	100.0	8,617
2	Washington	86.6	87,022
3	Oregon	83.3	40,962
4	South Dakota	61.2	3,934
5	Montana	41.5	10,672
6	Vermont	24.3	1,214
7	Maine	23.3	2,110
8	Alaska	21.7	975
9	California	20.6	23,795
10	New York	20.0	25,748
11	New Hampshire	13.7	1,477
12	Alabama	13.6	10,387
13	Tennessee	12.9	9,537
14	Arizona	12.3	7,667
15	Arkansas	10.0	3,696
16	Nevada	9.0	1,732
17	North Carolina	8.7	6,957
18	Maryland	7.3	2,299
19	North Dakota	6.4	1,711
20	Oklahoma	6.1	2,750
21	Georgia	6.0	4,887
22	Nebraska	5.3	1,140
23	Kentucky	4.3	3,160
24	Colorado	4.1	1,276
25	Wisconsin	3.9	1,791
26	South Carolina	3.9	2,729
27	Missouri	3.7	2,156
28	Iowa	2.9	857

Rank		Percent	Total net generation (mil. kwh.)
29	Connecticut	1.6	502
30	Minnesota	1.6	658
31	Utah	1.6	645
32	Pennsylvania	1.0	1,703
33	Michigan	0.9	798
34	Virginia	0.9	428
35	Massachusetts	0.8	300
36	Texas	0.8	1,794
37	New Mexico	0.7	205
38	West Virginia	0.6	435
39	Indiana	0.5	441
40	Hawaii	0.3	23
41	Ohio	0.1	173
42	Florida	0.1	175

NATURAL GAS– GENERATED ELECTRICITY

Less than 10% of the nation's electricity is generated by natural gas. Rhode Island and Alaska generate most of their electricity from natural gas. Only six other states generate more than 20% of their electricity from natural gas: Louisiana, Texas, California, Oklahoma, Mississippi and New York.

Texas alone accounts for approximately 37% of the nation's electricity generated from natural gas, and along with Texas, California, Louisiana, New York, Florida and Oklahoma, 78% of the total. Texas and Oklahoma have extensive underground gas fields, while offshore gas is abundant in California, Texas and Louisiana. Gas from the Gulf of Mexico can be shipped to Florida at a relatively low cost.

This table documents the amount and percent of total electricity generated from natural gas in 41 states. (The remaining nine states do not generate electricity from natural gas.)

TABLE: Natural Gas–Generated Electricity
DATE: 1991
SOURCE: U.S. Energy Information Administration, *Monthly Power Plant Report*
DESCRIPTION: Gas-fired net generation of electricity and percent of total electricity generation.

Rank		Percent	Total net generation
	United States	10.8	236,999
1	Rhode Island	73.3	434
2	Alaska	63.9	2,870
3	Louisiana	44.8	26,041
4	Texas	41.8	97,260
5	California	39.5	45,222

Rank		Percent	Total net generation
6	Oklahoma	37.9	17,075
7	Mississippi	23.3	5,351
8	New York	16.5	21,263
9	Massachusetts	14.5	5,280
10	Florida	14.2	17,504
11	Nevada	11.5	2,217
12	New Jersey	10.9	3,978
13	Delaware	10.7	759
14	New Mexico	8.5	2,425
15	Arkansas	7.7	2,839
16	Kansas	6.5	2,196
17	Maryland	4.2	1,320
18	Arizona	3.6	2,272
19	Virginia	1.8	758
20	Oregon	1.6	811
21	Connecticut	1.5	472
22	Nebraska	1.4	308
23	Colorado	1.3	408
24	Vermont	1.3	65
25	South Carolina	1.0	703
26	Iowa	.8	231
27	Minnesota	.8	326
28	Michigan	.7	665
29	Alabama	.6	420
30	Illinois	.6	741
31	Indiana	.6	611
32	Missouri	.5	266
33	Wisconsin	.4	169
34	Georgia	.2	152
35	Montana	.2	41
36	North Carolina	.2	165
37	South Dakota	.2	12
38	Utah	.2	54
39	Ohio	.1	91
40	Pennsylvania	.1	183
41	Tennessee	.1	41

PETROLEUM- GENERATED ELECTRICITY

Approximately 4% of the country's electricity is generated from oil. The District of Columbia generates all its electricity from oil. The next six states ranking highest in percentage of electricity generated from oil are all in the Northeast. Florida, Delaware and Maryland make up the remaining states in the top 10. The rest of the states generate 5% or less of their electricity from oil. This table presents the total amount and percent of electricity generated from petroleum or oil in 39 states in 1991. (The other 12 states generate less than 500,000 kwh.)

TABLE: Petroleum-Generated Electricity
DATE: 1991

SOURCE: U.S. Energy Information Administration: *Monthly Power Plant Report*
DESCRIPTION: Percent of electricity generated from petroleum-fired sources and net generation of electricity from petroleum-fired sources.

Rank		Percent	Total net generation (mil. kwh.)
	United States	4.2	103,111
1	Washington, DC	100.0	361
2	Massachusetts	39.9	14,555
3	Rhode Island	26.7	158
4	Connecticut	26.5	8,632
5	New York	26.0	33,404
6	Maine	23.1	2,093
7	New Hampshire	21.2	2,293
8	Florida	20.3	25,092
9	Delaware	20.2	1,438
10	Maryland	10.6	3,328
11	New Jersey	5.0	1,832
12	Virginia	2.5	1,194
13	Pennsylvania	2.4	4,014
14	Minnesota	1.1	441
15	Michigan	0.8	689
16	Indiana	0.7	674
17	West Virginia	0.4	274
18	Illinois	0.3	423
19	Ohio	0.2	301
20	Iowa	0.2	51
21	Kansas	0.2	66
22	Missouri	0.2	89
23	Georgia	0.2	165
24	North Carolina	0.2	167
25	Kentucky	0.2	110
26	Tennessee	0.2	134
27	Arkansas	0.2	74
28	Louisiana	0.2	130
29	Texas	0.2	481
30	Arizona	0.2	118
31	Wisconsin	0.1	47
32	Nebraska	0.1	13
33	North Dakota	0.1	21
34	South Dakota	0.1	8
35	South Carolina	0.1	72
36	Alabama	0.1	92
37	Oklahoma	0.1	49
38	Colorado	0.1	25
39	Vermont	0.1	3

GAS HEAT

Gas is the fuel most commonly used to heat American homes. However, the portion of homes using gas has decreased since 1980 (59%) and 1990 (41%). States where a high percentage of households heat with gas are scattered across the country, including the colder states with high heating bills, such as Illinois and Michigan, and warmer states where homes require heating less frequently, such as California and New Mexico.

TABLE: Gas Heat
DATE: 1990
SOURCE: U.S. Bureau of the Census, *1990 Census of Population and Housing*
DESCRIPTION: Number and percent of homes using utility gas for heating.

Rank	State	Total	Percent
	United States	46,850,923	43
1	Illinois	3,374,432	75
2	Utah	440,040	74
3	California	7,599,735	68
4	Michigan	2,630,526	68
5	Colorado	987,745	67
6	Nebraska	423,144	64
7	Ohio	2,787,946	64
8	Iowa	698,557	61
9	New Mexico	380,379	60
10	Indiana	1,303,759	58
11	Washington, DC	158,471	57
12	Minnesota	1,036,477	56
13	Oklahoma	776,236	55
14	Wisconsin	1,111,733	54
15	Missouri	1,184,832	53
16	New Jersey	1,607,806	52
17	Wyoming	106,247	52
18	Georgia	1,262,087	48
19	Louisiana	825,667	48
20	Arkansas	470,320	47
21	Montana	166,067	46
22	Pennsylvania	2,226,793	45
23	West Virginia	349,011	45
24	Texas	3,060,161	44
25	Nevada	222,229	43
26	Kentucky	629,310	42
27	New York	3,033,958	42
28	Maryland	754,715	40
29	Alabama	645,054	39
30	South Dakota	111,445	38
31	Mississippi	371,478	37
32	Rhode Island	153,766	37
33	Alaska	80,775	35
34	North Dakota	95,510	35
35	Massachusetts	852,905	34
36	Arizona	541,257	33
37	Kansas	717,469	33
38	Tennessee	556,158	27
39	Virginia	662,150	27
40	Delaware	75,467	26
41	Idaho	101,548	26
42	Connecticut	323,226	24
43	Oregon	272,150	23
44	Washington	420,139	21
45	North Carolina	468,698	17

Rank	State	Total	Percent
46	South Carolina	309,510	17
47	New Hampshire	62,553	12
48	Florida	384,495	6
49	Vermont	16,883	6
50	Hawaii	11,723	3
51	Maine	8,181	1

ELECTRIC HEAT

Nationwide, electric heat is the second most common heating source after gas heat. The use of electric heat increased from 18.4% in 1980 to 21% in 1990. Florida (66%) ranked first. Other states with above average frequencies of use of electric power are found in the South, the Southwest and Hawaii, where year-round air-conditioning is a more important concern than heating. The states of the Pacific Northwest rank high because of the relatively high cost of gas heating in the region and the absence of major oil ports.

TABLE: Electric Heat
DATE: 1990
SOURCE: U.S. Bureau of the Census, *1990 Census of Population and Housing*
DESCRIPTION: Number and percent of homes using electricity for heating.

Rank	State	Total	Percent
	United States	23,696,987	21
1	Florida	4,045,573	66
2	Washington	1,030,798	51
3	Tennessee	936,236	46
4	Arizona	704,206	42
5	Oregon	492,454	41
6	North Carolina	1,057,166	38
7	Virginia	919,790	37
8	Hawaii	135,102	35
9	Idaho	143,503	35
10	Nevada	183,376	35
11	Texas	2,438,294	35
12	Louisiana	542,099	32
13	South Carolina	590,013	32
14	Alabama	521,322	31
15	Mississippi	278,922	28
16	Kentucky	414,015	27
17	Maryland	517,117	27
18	Georgia	643,877	24
19	North Dakota	63,226	23
20	West Virginia	173,879	22
21	Arkansas	202,634	20
22	Delaware	54,071	19
23	California	1,996,897	18
24	Washington, DC	51,221	18
25	Indiana	398,892	18
26	Oklahoma	247,777	18

Rank	State	Total	Percent
27	Missouri	354,778	16
28	Ohio	684,664	16
29	South Dakota	46,177	16
30	Montana	54,856	15
31	Connecticut	185,340	14
32	Wyoming	27,830	14
33	Pennsylvania	664,952	13
34	Massachusetts	303,466	12
35	Nebraska	81,650	12
36	Colorado	165,168	11
37	Alaska	22,326	10
38	Illinois	472,210	10
39	Iowa	111,249	10
40	New Hampshire	51,051	10
41	Maine	54,215	9
42	Minnesota	172,304	9
43	New Jersey	279,851	9
44	Utah	51,047	9
45	New Mexico	49,503	8
46	New York	567,513	8
47	Wisconsin	168,615	8
48	Rhode Island	29,833	7
49	Vermont	19,232	7
50	Kansas	111,066	5
51	Michigan	185,631	5

OIL HEAT

The percentage of homes using oil heat decreased from 1980 (18%) to 1990 (13%). Regional variations are noteworthy. The relatively cold states in the Northeast are the most oil dependent. By comparison, oil heat is almost unknown in states stretching across the southern half of the country from Georgia to California.

TABLE: Oil Heat
DATE: 1990
SOURCE: U.S. Bureau of the Census , *1990 Census of Population and Housing*
DESCRIPTION: Number and percent of homes using fuel oil, kerosene, etc. for heating.

Rank	State	Total	Percent
	United States	11,243,727	12.6
1	Maine	323,332	55
2	Connecticut	669,328	51
3	New Hampshire	229,514	46
4	Rhode Island	177,536	43
5	Vermont	114,348	42
6	Massachusetts	989,299	40
7	New York	2,629,898	36
8	Delaware	95,211	33
9	New Jersey	815,317	27
10	Alaska	60,926	26
11	Pennsylvania	1,252,685	25

Rank		Total	Percent
12	Maryland	385,929	20
13	North Carolina	567,025	20
14	Virginia	463,578	19
15	North Dakota	37,773	14
16	Wisconsin	265,600	13
17	South Dakota	35,304	12
18	District of Columbia	31,122	11
19	Minnesota	195,823	11
20	Oregon	125,648	10
21	South Carolina	165,537	9
22	Washington	185,646	9
23	Idaho	32,394	8
24	Ohio	304,718	7
25	West Virginia	53,597	7
26	Indiana	127,072	6
27	Michigan	236,335	6
28	Iowa	58,278	5
29	Kentucky	66,320	4
30	Montana	12,649	4
31	Florida	210,500	3

Rank		Total	Percent
32	Nevada	17,166	3
33	Tennessee	69,965	3
34	Illinois	75,043	2
35	Nebraska	14,835	2
36	Alabama	17,393	1
37	Georgia	35,493	1
38	Missouri	29,560	1
39	Utah	7,048	1
40	Wyoming	1,150	0.5
41	Mississippi	4,340	0.4
42	Arizona	2,791	0.2
43	California	26,427	0.2
44	Colorado	3,326	0.2
45	Louisiana	4,848	0.2
46	New Mexico	1,391	0.2
47	Arkansas	1,669	0.1
48	Hawaii	607	0.1
49	Kansas	2,706	0.1
50	Texas	8,717	0.1
51	Oklahoma	1,010	0.1

PUBLIC EDUCATION

This section surveys four categories of elementary and secondary public education: funding, enrollment, attainment, and number and salary of teachers. The primary sources of data include the National Education Association, U.S. Department of Health and Human Services, U.S. National Center for Education Statistics and the U.S. Bureau of the Census.

Elementary schools are defined in this section as grades 1 through 8 (unless otherwise noted), high schools grades 9 through 12. All states require that children attend school. In general, states require that formal schooling begin by age 6 and continue to age 16. Data on attainment reflect the highest degree or diploma received.

The overall funding of education in the United States demonstrates the nation's historic commitment to local control of schools. In 1980 federal funding for public schools equaled 9% of total funding, state funding 49% and local funding 42%. In 1993, federal funding equaled 7%, state 47% and local 46%. State and local governments independently determine their own methods and formulas for funding education, and the data reported in this section detail these variations. Nationwide, revenue received per pupil increased between 1980 ($4,373) and 1993 ($5,771) (in constant 1993 dollars). Over the same period expenditures per pupil increased from 1980 ($3,837) to 1993 ($5,171) (reported in current dollars).

Shifts in the school-age population are worth noting when assessing the data reported here. In 1980, 21% of the population ranged in age from 5 to 17, and 87% of 5- to 17-year-olds were enrolled in public school. In 1993, 18% of the population was 5 to 17 years old, and 91% were in public school.

The first three tables in this section survey public school funding and expenditures. The next table reports on enrollment in the Head Start program. The final tables survey non-high school graduates; the dropout rate; and present numbers of classroom teachers and teachers' salaries.

FEDERAL FUNDING FOR PUBLIC ELEMENTARY AND SECONDARY EDUCATION

Federal funding accounted for 7% of public school aid. State and local governments supplied the remainder. The majority of this federal aid funded programs for the educationally or economically deprived. These included programs for handicapped students and Head Start. Lesser amounts of federal aid go to districts affected by the presence of federal facilities such as military bases and for a variety of purposes such as support of planning and evaluation or purchase of library materials or special equipment.

Public education is funded in the United States via state, local and federal governments. Nationwide, state governments contributed 47% of school funding. However each state determines its own formula for funding education. In some states the local school districts and governments provide the bulk of funding, while in other states the reverse is the case. The data in this table and the following table illustrate this. For example, comparing New York and California, New York funded its schools most heavily from local contributions (55%), followed by the state contributions (39%) and federal aid (6%). In California the proportions of contributions were reversed. The state contributed 61% of funding, local governments contributed 31%, and the federal government contributed 8%.

Nationwide, local governments and school districts contributed 46% of school funding. The remaining portion was supplied by state government and federal aid. Some states rely most heavily on local government for school funding. In New Jersey most school funding comes from local governments (54%), from the state (43%) and federal aid (3%). By contrast, state government provides the majority (73%) of Washington state's school funding, local government (22%) and federal aid (6%).

TABLE: Federal Funding for Public Elementary and Secondary Education
DATE: 1993
SOURCE: National Education Association, Washington, DC, *Estimates of School Statistics*, annual (copyright) and unpublished data

DESCRIPTION: Federal funding for public elementary and secondary education. Percents may not add to 100 due to rounding. Table ranked by total funding.

Rank		Total funding ($ millions)	Percent of federal funding ($ millions)	Percent of state funding ($ millions)	Percent of local funding ($ millions)
	United States	246,200	7	47	46
1	California	27,146	8	61	31
2	New York	22,504	6	39	55
3	Texas	18,987	7	43	49
4	Pennsylvania	13,771	5	43	52
5	Florida	11,237	8	49	43
6	New Jersey	10,888	3	43	54
7	Michigan	10,733	6	32	62
8	Ohio	10,155	6	40	54
9	Illinois	10,048	9	35	57
10	Massachusetts	5,738	6	34	60
11	Indiana	5,697	5	52	43
12	Virginia	5,565	5	34	61
13	North Carolina	5,471	8	64	28
14	Georgia	5,454	8	48	44
15	Washington	5,422	6	73	22
16	Wisconsin	5,347	4	38	57
17	Maryland	4,840	6	41	53
18	Minnesota	4,695	4	50	45
19	Missouri	4,198	7	38	56
20	Connecticut	4,105	5	38	57
21	Louisiana	3,450	12	54	34
22	Arizona	3,326	9	43	49
23	Tennessee	3,311	11	47	42
24	Colorado	3,136	5	43	52
25	Kentucky	3,093	10	68	22
26	South Carolina	3,020	9	48	43
27	Oregon	2,945	7	38	56
28	Alabama	2,607	13	65	22
29	Oklahoma	2,593	8	63	30
30	Iowa	2,539	6	51	44
31	Kansas	2,366	5	50	45
32	Arkansas	1,880	10	63	28
33	West Virginia	1,861	8	67	25
34	Mississippi	1,812	17	53	30
35	Utah	1,655	7	58	35
36	Nebraska	1,400	6	42	52
37	New Mexico	1,344	13	76	11
38	Maine	1,277	7	51	42
39	Nevada	1,159	5	37	58
40	New Hampshire	1,094	3	8	89
41	Hawaii	1,084	7	91	2
42	Alaska	972	13	64	24
43	Rhode Island	904	5	36	59
44	Idaho	895	8	62	30
45	Montana	827	9	39	52
46	Vermont	677	5	32	62
47	Delaware	655	9	66	25

Rank		Total funding ($ millions)	Percent of federal funding ($ millions)	Percent of state funding ($millions)	Percent of local funding ($ millions)
48	Wyoming	606	6	51	43
49	South Dakota	602	12	27	62
50	Washington, DC	590	13	-	87
51	North Dakota	549	11	45	44

AVERAGE EXPENDITURES PER PUPIL IN PUBLIC ELEMENTARY AND SECONDARY EDUCATION

States and localities possess a high degree of autonomy in per pupil spending in their public schools. Each state and local government independently determines how much of its revenue to devote to education expenditures. This autonomy is evidenced by the range of education spending between states. Top-ranking New Jersey ($9,712) spends $6,000 more than Utah ($3,218). Thirty states fall below the national average of $5,574. In assessing the ranking of states in this table many of the eastern states along with Alaska, Oregon and Wyoming rank in the top third. Many of the southern and western states rank in the lower third.

TABLE: Average Expenditures Per Pupil in Elementary and Secondary Schools
DATE: 1993
SOURCE: National Education Association, Washington, DC, *Estimates of School Statistics*, annual (copyright) and unpublished data
DESCRIPTION: Average expenditure per pupil in average daily attendance in elementary and secondary schools.

Rank		Average expenditure per pupil ($)
	United States	5,574
1	New Jersey	9,712
2	Alaska	9,290
3	New York	8,525
4	Connecticut	8,188
5	Washington, DC	7,998
6	Pennsylvania	7,748
7	Vermont	7,172
8	Rhode Island	6,649

Rank		Average expenditure per pupil ($)
9	Massachusetts	6,505
10	Wisconsin	6,500
11	Maryland	6,447
12	Delaware	6,420
13	Michigan	6,402
14	Oregon	6,240
15	Maine	6,162
16	Ohio	5,963
17	Wyoming	5,932
18	Hawaii	5,806
19	West Virginia	5,689
20	Indiana	5,641
21	New Hampshire	5,619
22	Minnesota	5,572
23	Washington	5,528
24	Virginia	5,517
25	Kansas	5,459
26	Montana	5,348
27	Florida	5,303
28	Iowa	5,297
29	Illinois	5,191
30	Nevada	4,976
31	Colorado	4,969
32	Nebraska	4,950
33	Kentucky	4,942
34	Texas	4,933
35	North Carolina	4,810
36	New Mexico	4,643
37	California	4,608
38	South Carolina	4,573
39	Georgia	4,544
40	Missouri	4,487
41	North Dakota	4,404
42	South Dakota	4,359
43	Louisiana	4,352
44	Arizona	4,140
45	Oklahoma	4,085
46	Tennessee	4,033
47	Idaho	4,025
48	Arkansas	3,838
49	Alabama	3,779
50	Mississippi	3,390
51	Utah	3,218

CAPITAL OUTLAY FOR ELEMENTARY AND SECONDARY SCHOOLS

Capital outlay is revenue used for major expenditures, such as building a new school or major renovations of an existing school. In 1980 capital outlays accounted for 6.8% of total expenditures. In 1993 it was 7.9%. In 1993, $2.8 billion in capital outlays for schools separated first-ranked California and last-ranked Rhode Island. The four most populous states ranked in the top four here. However, population and capital spending often diverge. Washington state ranks fifth in funding for capital outlays, but 15th in population. Similarly, Minnesota ranks ninth in capital outlays, but 20th in population. In comparing capital outlays between states, there are various factors that influence spending beside population: age of population, influx of new populations (see section entitled Population), and the methods a state uses to raise revenue for capital outlays.

TABLE: Capital Outlay for Elementary and Secondary Schools
DATE: 1993
SOURCES: National Education Association, Washington, DC, *Estimates of School Statistics*, annual (copyright) and unpublished data
DESCRIPTION: Capital outlay.

Rank		Capital outlay ($ millions)
	United States	19,896
1	California	2,853
2	Texas	1,949
3	New York	1,561
4	Florida	1,419
5	Washington	963
6	Michigan	847
7	Ohio	718
8	Arizona	678
9	Minnesota	636
10	North Carolina	580
11	Wisconsin	503
12	Indiana	477
13	Illinois	459
14	Georgia	458
15	Virginia	442
16	Colorado	419
17	Missouri	404
18	Oregon	368
19	Oklahoma	356
20	Maryland	297
21	South Carolina	268
22	Kentucky	221
23	Alabama	218
24	Kansas	218

Rank		Capital outlay ($ millions)
25	Nevada	210
26	Arkansas	196
27	Pennsylvania	194
28	Massachusetts	179
29	Louisiana	172
30	Iowa	158
31	Connecticut	156
32	New Mexico	147
33	West Virginia	136
34	New Jersey	131
35	Mississippi	130
36	Nebraska	119
37	Maine	93
38	Idaho	62
39	Montana	61
40	Tennessee	56
41	South Dakota	55
42	Hawaii	52
43	Wyoming	49
44	Utah	41
45	Delaware	37
46	Alaska	36
47	Vermont	34
48	North Dakota	29
49	Washington, DC	21
50	New Hampshire	20
51	Rhode Island	8

HEAD START ENROLLMENT

A federally mandated program, Head Start provides schooling nationwide to preschool children who qualify on the basis of need. Two key factors effect a state's ranking high in Head Start enrollment: large numbers of preschool population (see Resident Population by Age table page 122) and poverty, particularly among preschool children. The populous states rank highest, followed by the southern states, where incomes are low (see the Per Capita Personal Income table on page 41) and poverty rates comparatively high.

TITLE: Head Start Enrollment
DATE: 1991
SOURCE: U.S. Department of Health and Human Services, Office of Development Services
DESCRIPTION: Head Start enrollment. Percents may not add up to 100 because of rounding.
UNITED STATES TOTAL: 583,471

Rank		Enrollment	Percent of total
1	California	49,945	8.56
2	Texas	33,615	5.76
3	New York	32,492	5.57

Rank		Enrollment	Percent of total
4	Ohio	27,794	4.76
5	Illinois	27,184	4.65
6	Michigan	24,914	4.27
7	Mississippi	21,511	3.68
8	Pennsylvania	21,247	3.64
9	Florida	19,034	3.26
10	Georgia	14,978	2.56
11	Louisiana	14,558	2.49
12	North Carolina	13,438	2.30
13	Alabama	12,463	2.13
14	Kentucky	11,772	2.01
15	Tennessee	11,546	1.98
16	Missouri	11,348	1.94
17	New Jersey	11,051	1.89
18	Massachusetts	9,624	1.64
19	Indiana	9,543	1.63
20	Wisconsin	9,161	1.57
21	Oklahoma	8,562	1.47
22	South Carolina	8,544	1.46
23	Virginia	8,345	1.43
24	Arkansas	7,761	1.33
25	Maryland	7,234	1.24
26	Minnesota	6,654	1.14
27	Colorado	6,124	1.05
28	Washington	5,386	0.92
29	Arizona	5,344	0.92
30	Connecticut	5,051	0.87
31	Iowa	4,971	0.85
32	New Mexico	4,647	0.80
33	Kansas	4,332	0.74
34	Oregon	3,634	0.62
35	Utah	3,097	0.53
36	Maine	2,928	0.50
37	Nebraska	2,820	0.48
38	Washington, DC	2,560	0.44
39	Rhode Island	2,197	0.38
40	Hawaii	1,846	0.32
41	Montana	1,786	0.31
42	South Dakota	1,569	0.27
43	Idaho	1,502	0.26
44	North Dakota	1,208	0.21
45	Delaware	1,199	0.21
46	Vermont	1,041	0.18
47	Wyoming	990	0.17
48	Alaska	970	0.17
49	New Hampshire	945	0.16
50	Nevada	911	0.16
51	West Virginia	NA	NA

POPULATION NOT HIGH SCHOOL GRADUATES

This table reports the number and percentage of the population over 25 years of age who are not high school graduates. Ranked here according to the percentage of nonhigh school graduates, the southern states dominate the top of

the list. By contrast, with the exceptions of Vermont and New Hampshire, the states with lowest percentage of non-high school graduates are all west of the Mississippi.

TABLE: Population Not High Schools Graduates
DATE: 1990
SOURCE: U.S. Bureau of the Census, *1990 Census of Population*
DESCRIPTION: Numbers and percent of population not high school graduates. For persons 25 years old and over.

Rank		Population not high school graduates	Percent of population not high school graduates
	United States	39,343,718	24.8
1	Mississippi	549,685	35.7
2	Kentucky	825,857	35.4
3	West Virginia	398,527	34.0
4	Arkansas	503,481	33.7
5	Alabama	843,638	33.1
6	Tennessee	1,033,914	32.9
7	South Carolina	687,260	31.7
8	Louisiana	803,872	31.7
9	North Carolina	1,277,747	30.0
10	Georgia	1,169,815	29.1
11	Rhode Island	184,344	28.0
12	Texas	2,872,559	27.9
13	Washington, DC	109,866	26.9
14	Missouri	858,368	26.1
15	Florida	2,271,074	25.6
16	Oklahoma	506,961	25.4
17	Pennsylvania	1,994,278	25.3
18	New York	2,977,604	25.2
19	New Mexico	229,974	24.9
20	Virginia	987,203	24.8
21	Indiana	850,014	24.4
22	Ohio	1,684,888	24.3
23	California	4,450,528	23.8
24	Illinois	1,735,789	23.8
25	New Jersey	1,205,206	23.3
26	North Dakota	92,427	23.3
27	Michigan	1,356,759	23.2
28	South Dakota	98,720	22.9
29	Delaware	96,472	22.5
30	Maryland	673,932	21.6
31	Wisconsin	662,072	21.4
32	Arizona	491,080	21.3
33	Nevada	167,628	21.2
34	Maine	168,460	21.2
35	Connecticut	457,208	20.8
36	Idaho	121,787	20.3
37	Massachusetts	792,657	20.0
38	Hawaii	141,506	19.9
39	Iowa	353,800	19.9
40	Vermont	68,637	19.2
41	Montana	96,469	19.0

Rank		Population not high school graduates	Percent of population not high school graduates
42	Kansas	293,272	18.7
43	Oregon	343,609	18.5
44	Nebraska	181,072	18.2
45	New Hampshire	127,423	17.8
46	Minnesota	488,765	17.6
47	Wyoming	47,113	17.0
48	Washington	505,783	16.2
49	Colorado	328,056	15.6
50	Utah	133,315	14.9
51	Alaska	43,244	13.4

DROPOUTS

Nationwide the dropout rate is 11.2%. However, in many southern and western states the dropout rate is between 15% and 11.4%. Indiana and Missouri are the only states outside the southern or western regions that exceed the national average.

TABLE: Dropouts
DATE: 1990
SOURCE: U.S. Bureau of the Census, *1990 Census of Population*
DESCRIPTION: Percent of population who are 16 to 19 years old and have dropped out of school. A dropout is a person who is not in regular school and who has not completed the 12th grade or received a general equivalency degree.

Rank		Dropouts
	United States	11.2
1	Nevada	15.2
2	Arizona	14.4
3	Florida	14.3
4	California	14.2
5	Georgia	14.1
6	Washington, DC	13.9
7	Tennessee	13.4
8	Kentucky	13.3
9	Texas	12.9
10	Alabama	12.6
11	Louisiana	12.5
12	North Carolina	12.5
13	Mississippi	11.8
14	Oregon	11.8
15	New Mexico	11.7
16	South Carolina	11.7
17	Arkansas	11.4
18	Indiana	11.4
19	Missouri	11.4
20	Rhode Island	11.1

Rank		Dropouts
21	Alaska	10.9
22	Maryland	10.9
23	West Virginia	10.9
24	Illinois	10.6
25	Washington	10.6
26	Delaware	10.4
27	Idaho	10.4
28	Oklahoma	10.4
29	Michigan	10.0
30	Virginia	10.0
31	New York	9.9
32	Colorado	9.8
33	New Jersey	9.6
34	New Hampshire	9.4
35	Pennsylvania	9.1
36	Connecticut	9.0
37	Ohio	8.9
38	Kansas	8.7
39	Utah	8.7
40	Massachusetts	8.5
41	Maine	8.3
42	Montana	8.1
43	Vermont	8.0
44	South Dakota	7.7
45	Hawaii	7.5
46	Wisconsin	7.1
47	Nebraska	7.0
48	Wyoming	6.9
49	Iowa	6.6
50	Minnesota	6.4
51	North Dakota	4.6

CLASSROOM TEACHERS

In 1980 the school-age population (those between 5 and 17 years old) was 21%, and the number of teachers totaled 2,211,000. In 1993 the school population was 19.3%, and number of teachers totaled 2,464,000. Not surprisingly, the most populous states rank highest here. In 1991 the ratio of students to teachers was 15.5 to 1.

TABLE: Classroom Teachers
DATE: 1993
SOURCE: National Education Association, Washington, DC, *Estimates of School Statistics*, 1992–1993 (copyright)
DESCRIPTION: Total number of public elementary and secondary school classroom teachers. Elementary includes kindergarten.

Rank		Elementary teachers (thousands)	Secondary teachers (thousands)	Total number of teachers (thousands)
	United States	1,490,000	974,000	2,464,000
1	Texas	118.0	101.4	219.3
2	California	159.0	56.7	215.7

Rank		Elementary teachers (thousands)	Secondary teachers (thousands)	Total number of teachers (thousands)
3	New York	92.1	92.2	184.3
4	Illinois	78.8	32.3	111.1
5	Florida	59.0	48.6	107.6
6	Ohio	68.0	34.4	102.4
7	Pennsylvania	51.3	49.6	100.9
8	New Jersey	52.7	30.4	83.0
9	Michigan	57.4	25.0	82.4
10	Georgia	49.1	24.0	73.1
11	Virginia	40.2	27.2	67.4
12	North Carolina	40.3	25.7	66.0
13	Massachusetts	24.6	32.6	57.2
14	Indiana	29.2	25.3	54.5
15	Missouri	28.2	24.8	53.0
16	Wisconsin	34.0	18.9	52.9
17	Tennessee	32.9	13.2	46.1
18	Louisiana	31.5	14.1	45.6
19	Minnesota	23.3	22.0	45.3
20	Washington	26.7	17.7	44.3
21	Maryland	25.3	18.1	43.4
22	Alabama	22.5	19.3	41.7
23	Oklahoma	20.7	17.8	38.5
24	Kentucky	26.3	11.6	37.9
25	South Carolina	24.8	11.7	36.5
26	Arizona	27.0	8.1	35.1
27	Connecticut	23.8	10.6	34.4
28	Colorado	17.0	16.4	33.4
29	Iowa	15.1	16.4	31.5
30	Kansas	17.6	12.1	29.8
31	Mississippi	17.3	10.7	28.0
32	Oregon	17.6	10.3	27.8
33	Arkansas	12.7	13.3	26.0
34	West Virginia	12.2	8.6	20.8
35	Utah	11.0	8.4	19.4
36	Nebraska	10.8	8.2	19.0
37	New Mexico	12.1	5.2	17.3
38	Maine	9.3	5.8	15.1
39	Nevada	7.2	4.8	12.0
40	Idaho	6.2	5.6	11.8
41	New Hampshire	8.1	3.6	11.7
42	Hawaii	5.8	4.5	10.3
43	Montana	6.7	3.4	10.1
44	Rhode Island	5.3	4.5	9.8
45	South Dakota	6.2	2.6	8.8
46	North Dakota	5.1	2.7	7.8
47	Alaska	5.1	2.1	7.2
48	Vermont	3.7	3.5	7.2
49	Washington, DC	4.3	2.5	6.8
50	Wyoming	3.4	3.2	6.6
51	Delaware	3.2	3.0	6.3

TEACHER SALARIES

This table ranks states according to average public school teachers' salaries. Nationwide, in 1980 the average teacher's salary totaled $15,970; in 1993 it rose to $35,000. (These figures are not adjusted for inflation.) Connecticut, ($48,300) one of the wealthiest states (see section entitled Income page 38) ranks first here, followed by the densely populated industrialized states. Alaska is also in the top 10, reflecting its high cost of living. (See the section entitled Income page 38.) The average teacher salary in 32 states falls below the national average ($35,000).

TABLE: Teacher Salaries
DATE: 1993
SOURCE: National Education Association, Washington, DC, *Estimates of School Statistics*, 1992–93 (copyright)
DESCRIPTION: Average salary of elementary and secondary public school classroom teachers.

Rank		Salary ($ thousands)
	United States	35.0
1	Connecticut	48.3
2	Alaska	46.0
3	New York	45.0
4	Michigan	43.6
5	New Jersey	42.7
6	Pennsylvania	41.2
7	California	40.0
8	Maryland	38.8
9	Washington, DC	38.7
10	Illinois	38.6
11	Massachusetts	38.2
12	Rhode Island	37.9
13	Hawaii	36.5
14	Delaware	36.2
15	Wisconsin	35.9
16	Oregon	35.9
17	Washington	35.8
18	Minnesota	35.1
19	Indiana	35.1
20	Vermont	34.8
21	Ohio	34.5
22	Nevada	34.1
23	New Hampshire	33.9
24	Colorado	33.5
25	Kansas	32.9
26	Virginia	32.3
27	Arizona	31.4
28	Florida	31.2
29	Kentucky	31.1
30	West Virginia	30.3
31	Maine	30.3
32	Wyoming	30.1
33	Iowa	30.1
34	Georgia	30.1
35	Texas	29.9
36	Missouri	29.4
37	North Carolina	29.3

Rank		Salary ($ thousands)		Rank		Salary ($ thousands)
38	South Carolina	29.2		45	Idaho	27.0
39	Tennessee	29.0		46	Alabama	27.0
40	Nebraska	28.8		47	New Mexico	26.5
41	Montana	27.6		48	Oklahoma	25.9
42	Louisiana	27.6		49	North Dakota	25.2
43	Arkansas	27.4		50	Mississippi	24.4
44	Utah	27.2		51	South Dakota	24.3

HIGHER EDUCATION

This section covers higher education, specifically the number of institutions, enrollment, and educational attainment. The primary sources are the National Center for Education Statistics and the U.S. Bureau of the Census.

Nationwide in 1960, 8% of the population over 25 years old reported completing four years of college or more (advanced degrees, such as MAs or PhDs or professional degrees). By 1993 persons with a bachelor's degree or more climbed to 22%. In 1993 the western part of the United States reported the highest percentage of population with a bachelor's degree (17%) followed by the Northeast (15%), Midwest and South (both 13%). Enrollment in institutions of higher learning increased 40% between 1970 and 1992. In 1993 average tuition at a public four-year college for an in-state student living on campus was approximately $8,500. At a private college it totaled approximately $17,800.

The tables in this section use the term *college* to include junior or community colleges, regular four-year colleges and universities and graduate or professional schools.

The first three tables survey college enrollment. The final table details educational attainment.

COLLEGE ENROLLMENT

This table shows enrollment at private and public colleges by state. Approximately two-thirds of all students are enrolled in public institutions, where average tuition is significantly less than at private schools.

States with an established and extensive system of public institutions of higher learning ranked highest in public enrollment. California with one of the largest and oldest public university systems ranked first in public enrollment. Eighty-eight percent of all college students enrolled in California were enrolled in public institutions in 1992. New York, which also has a large and established public university system, ranked first in students enrolled in private institutions (43%) and third in public

(57%) enrollees. In Nevada, which reported a total of nine colleges, 98% of students were enrolled in public institutions.

TABLE: College Enrollment
DATE: 1992
SOURCE: U.S. National Center for Education Statistics, *Digest of Education Statistics*, annual
DESCRIPTION: College enrollment in public and private institutions in thousands. Figures based on fall enrollment of resident and extension students attending full-time or part-time. U.S. total includes service schools.

Rank		Public enrollment (thousands)	Private enrollment (thousands)
	United States	11,388	3,104
1	California	1,748	229
2	Texas	832	106
3	New York	611	459
4	Illinois	566	182
5	Florida	511	107
6	Michigan	473	86
7	Ohio	437	136
8	Pennsylvania	363	267
9	North Carolina	316	68
10	Virginia	298	57
11	New Jersey	278	65
12	Wisconsin	257	51
13	Arizona	256	20
14	Washington	239	38
15	Indiana	235	62
16	Georgia	233	61
17	Maryland	228	40
18	Minnesota	212	61
19	Colorado	211	29
20	Alabama	206	24
21	Missouri	199	98
22	Tennessee	192	51
23	Massachusetts	183	240
24	Louisiana	177	27
25	Oklahoma	159	23
26	Kentucky	158	30

Rank		Public enrollment (thousands)	Private enrollment (thousands)
27	Kansas	153	16
28	South Carolina	146	26
29	Oregon	145	23
30	Iowa	128	50
31	Mississippi	110	14
32	Connecticut	108	58
33	Nebraska	103	19
34	Utah	97	36
35	New Mexico	95	4
36	Arkansas	86	12
37	West Virginia	79	11
38	Nevada	63	1
39	Hawaii	50	12
40	Idaho	47	11
41	Rhode Island	43	36
42	Maine	41	17
43	North Dakota	37	4
44	Delaware	35	7
45	New Hampshire	35	29
46	Montana	34	6
47	Wyoming	31	1
48	South Dakota	30	7
49	Alaska	29	2
50	Vermont	21	16
51	Washington, DC	12	70

COLLEGE ENROLLMENT BY GENDER

In every state with the exceptions of Utah, North Dakota and the United States military academies, women outnumbered men. Women represented 55% of all undergraduates and 53% of all graduate students. However, they made up only 39% of the enrollment in professional schools.

TABLE: College Enrollment by Gender
DATE: 1992
SOURCE: U.S. National Center for Education Statistics, *Digest of Education Statistics*, annual
DESCRIPTION: Percentage of college enrollment and enrollment by gender. Figures are for fall enrollment of resident and extension students attending full-time or part-time. U.S. total includes service schools.

Rank		Enrollment (thousands)	Percent of males enrolled	Percent of females enrolled
	United States	14,491	45	55
1	California	1,977	46	54
2	New York	1,070	44	56
3	Texas	939	46	54
4	Illinois	748	45	55
5	Pennsylvania	630	46	54
6	Florida	618	44	56

Rank		Enrollment (thousands)	Percent of males enrolled	Percent of females enrolled
7	Ohio	573	46	54
8	Michigan	560	45	55
9	Massachusetts	423	45	55
10	North Carolina	383	44	56
11	Virginia	354	44	56
12	New Jersey	342	44	56
13	Wisconsin	308	45	55
14	Indiana	297	46	54
15	Missouri	297	45	55
16	Georgia	293	44	56
17	Washington	276	45	55
18	Arizona	276	46	54
19	Minnesota	273	45	55
20	Maryland	268	43	57
21	Tennessee	243	45	55
22	Colorado	240	47	53
23	Alabama	231	45	55
24	Louisiana	204	43	57
25	Kentucky	188	42	58
26	Oklahoma	182	46	54
27	Iowa	178	46	54
28	South Carolina	171	43	57
29	Kansas	169	45	55
30	Oregon	167	47	53
31	Connecticut	166	44	56
32	Utah	133	51	49
33	Mississippi	124	44	56
34	Nebraska	123	46	54
35	New Mexico	99	44	56
36	Arkansas	97	43	57
37	West Virginia	90	45	55
38	Washington, DC	82	46	53
39	Rhode Island	79	45	55
40	New Hampshire	64	44	56
41	Nevada	64	45	55
42	Hawaii	61	45	55
43	Maine	58	42	58
44	Idaho	58	45	55
45	Delaware	43	43	57
46	North Dakota	40	50	50
47	Montana	40	47	53
48	South Dakota	38	44	56
49	Vermont	37	43	57
50	Wyoming	32	43	57
51	Alaska	31	41	59

COLLEGE ENROLLMENT BY RACE AND HISPANIC ORIGIN

Not surprisingly, Hawaii (64%), whose majority native population is non-white, registered the largest percentage of minority students. Other states with large numbers of

Hispanics, California (39%), New Mexico (39%) and Texas (31%), also ranked high in minority college enrollment. Many of the southern states with proportionally larger black populations ranked highest in percentage of black college students enrolled in each state.

TABLE: College Enrollment by Race and Hispanic Origin

DATE: 1992
SOURCE: U.S. National Center for Education Statistics, *Digest of Education Statistics,* annual
DESCRIPTION: Enrollment by race in percentages. Figures are for opening fall enrollment of resident and extension students attending full-time. U.S. totals include service schools.

Rank		Enrollment (thousands)	Percent White* enrollment	Percent minority** enrollment	Percent Black* enrollment	Percent Hispanic enrollment
	United States	14,491	75	22	10	7
1	Alabama	231	75	23	21	1
2	Alaska	31	80	18	4	2
3	Arizona	276	76	22	3	12
4	Arkansas	97	82	17	14	1
5	California	1,977	56	39	7	16
6	Colorado	240	28	15	3	8
7	Connecticut	166	83	14	7	4
8	Delaware	43	82	16	12	1
9	Washington, DC	82	50	39	31	3
10	Florida	618	71	27	12	12
11	Georgia	293	72	26	22	1
12	Hawaii	61	28	64	2	2
13	Idaho	58	92	5	Z	2
14	Illinois	748	73	25	13	7
15	Indiana	297	88	10	6	2
16	Iowa	178	89	6	3	1
17	Kansas	169	86	10	5	2
18	Kentucky	188	90	8	6	1
19	Louisiana	204	68	29	25	2
20	Maine	58	94	4	1	Z
21	Maryland	268	71	26	19	2
22	Massachusetts	423	81	14	5	4
23	Michigan	560	82	15	10	2
24	Minnesota	273	91	7	2	1
25	Mississippi	124	69	29	28	Z
26	Missouri	297	85	12	9	1
27	Montana	40	85	13	Z	Z
28	Nebraska	123	91	7	3	2
29	Nevada	64	80	18	5	6
30	New Hampshire	64	93	5	1	1
31	New Jersey	342	72	24	11	8
32	New Mexico	99	59	39	3	29
33	New York	1,070	70	26	12	8
34	North Carolina	383	76	22	19	1
35	North Dakota	40	89	7	Z	Z
36	Ohio	573	85	12	9	1
37	Oklahoma	182	79	17	7	2
38	Oregon	167	89	10	2	2
39	Pennsylvania	630	85	12	7	2
40	Rhode Island	79	87	10	4	3
41	South Carolina	171	75	23	21	1
42	South Dakota	38	90	7	Z	Z
43	Tennessee	243	81	17	15	1
44	Texas	939	66	31	10	18
45	Utah	133	90	6	1	2

Rank		Enrollment (thousands)	Percent White* enrollment	Percent minority** enrollment	Percent Black* enrollment	Percent Hispanic enrollment
46	Vermont	37	94	4	Z	Z
47	Virginia	354	77	21	15	2
48	Washington	276	83	14	3	3
49	West Virginia	90	93	5	4	0
50	Wisconsin	308	89	8	4	2
51	Wyoming	32	91	7	Z	4

Z-Fewer than 500.
*Non-Hispanic.
**Includes other races not shown separately.

EDUCATIONAL ATTAINMENT

The level of educational attainment increased significantly during the 1980s. In 1980, 16% of the population over 25 years old had completed four or more years of college. By 1990 it increased to more than 20%. National percentages for attainment by race and ethnicity for those over 25 years old who had completed four or more years of college in 1980 were: whites 17%, blacks 8%, Asians and Pacific Islanders (not available) and Hispanics 8%. By 1990 the figures were: whites 22%, blacks 11%, Asians and Pacific Islanders 40% and Hispanics 9%. The data regarding gender over the same period showed that 21% of males and 13% of females over 25 years old had completed four or more years of college in 1980. By 1990, 25% of males and 19% of females had completed college.

In five states the percentage of the population with bachelor's degrees was below 10%: Mississippi, Indiana, Arkansas, Kentucky and West Virginia.

By contrast, in only the District of Columbia and three states, Connecticut, Maryland and Massachusetts, did the percentage of the population with advanced degrees exceed 10%.

TABLE: Educational Attainment
DATE: 1990
SOURCE: U.S. Bureau of the Census, *1990 Census of Population and Housing*
DESCRIPTION: Percent of population with some college, associate's, bachelor's and advanced degrees. For persons 25 years old and over. Figures reflect highest degree received.

Rank		Percent of population with some college, but no degree	Percent of population with associate's degree	Percent of population with a bachelor's degree	Percent of population with an advanced degree
	United States	18.7	6.2	13.1	7.2
1	Alabama	16.8	5.0	10.1	5.5
2	Alaska	27.6	7.2	15.0	8.0
3	Arizona	25.4	6.8	13.3	7.0
4	Arkansas	16.6	3.7	8.9	4.5
5	California	22.6	7.9	15.3	8.1
6	Colorado	24.0	6.9	18.0	9.0
7	Connecticut	15.9	6.6	16.2	11.0
8	Delaware	16.9	6.5	13.7	7.7
9	Washington, DC	15.6	3.1	16.1	17.2
10	Florida	19.4	6.6	12.0	6.3
11	Georgia	17.0	5.0	12.9	6.4
12	Hawaii	20.1	8.3	15.8	7.1
13	Idaho	24.2	7.5	12.4	5.3
14	Illinois	19.4	5.8	13.6	7.5
15	Indiana	16.6	5.3	9.2	6.4
16	Iowa	17.0	7.7	11.7	5.2
17	Kansas	21.9	5.4	14.1	7.0
18	Kentucky	15.2	4.1	8.1	5.5
19	Louisiana	17.2	3.3	10.5	5.6
20	Maine	16.1	6.9	12.7	6.1
21	Maryland	18.6	5.2	15.6	10.9
22	Massachusetts	15.8	7.2	16.6	10.6
23	Michigan	20.4	6.7	10.9	6.4

Rank		Percent of population with some college, but no degree	Percent of population with associate's degree	Percent of population with a bachelor's degree	Percent of population with an advanced degree
24	Minnesota	19.0	8.6	15.6	6.3
25	Mississippi	16.9	5.2	9.7	5.1
26	Missouri	18.4	4.5	11.7	6.1
27	Montana	22.1	5.6	14.1	5.7
28	Nebraska	21.1	7.1	13.1	5.9
29	Nevada	25.8	6.2	10.1	5.2
30	New Hampshire	18.0	8.1	16.4	7.9
31	New Jersey	15.5	5.2	16.0	8.8
32	New Mexico	20.9	5.0	12.1	8.3
33	New York	15.7	6.5	13.2	9.9
34	North Carolina	16.8	6.8	12.0	5.4
35	North Dakota	20.5	10.0	13.5	4.5
36	Ohio	17.0	5.3	11.1	5.9
37	Oklahoma	21.3	5.0	11.8	6.0
38	Oregon	25.0	6.9	13.6	7.0
39	Pennsylvania	12.9	5.2	11.3	6.6
40	Rhode Island	15.0	6.3	13.5	7.8
41	South Carolina	15.8	6.3	11.2	5.4
42	South Dakota	18.8	7.4	12.3	4.9
43	Tennessee	16.9	4.2	10.5	5.4
44	Texas	21.1	5.2	13.9	6.5
45	Utah	27.9	7.8	15.4	6.8
46	Vermont	14.7	7.2	15.4	8.9
47	Virginia	18.5	5.5	15.4	9.1
48	Washington	25.0	7.9	15.9	7.0
49	West Virginia	13.2	3.8	7.5	4.8
50	Wisconsin	16.7	7.1	12.1	5.6
51	Wyoming	24.2	6.9	13.1	5.7

POPULATION

The tables in this section present data on size, growth and density of population. The data reported here are used repeatedly in evaluating the indicators that appear in other sections. The primary source is the U.S. Bureau of the Census, which conducts the census and other periodic surveys of population characteristics.

The United States Constitution provides for a census of the population every 10 years, chiefly to determine the correct apportionment of members to the House of Representatives among the states. The first census took place in 1790, when only 5% of the nation's population lived in towns. Philadelphia was the largest city with 68,000 residents. By contrast, 75% of Americans lived in urban areas in 1990 and 23 of the nation's cities had half a million or more residents. In 1996 the United States ranked behind two other nations in total population, China and India.

This section assesses the nation's population, using several measures. The first three tables survey population, population change and population density. These are followed by two tables examining the metropolitan and non-metropolitan populations of each state. The U.S. Office of Management and Budget, or OMB, defines a metropolitan area as the combination of a core containing a large population nucleus, together with adjoining communities that have a high degree of social and economic integration with that core. The entire country is classified as metropolitan, [inside Metropolitan Statistical Areas (MSAs) or Consolidated Metropolitan Statistical Areas (CMSAs)] or nonmetropolitan (outside MSAs or CMSAs).

The next table shows the percentage of urban and rural population in each state. Urban and rural populations are distinct from metropolitan and nonmetropolitan populations described above. The urban population, as defined by the Census Bureau, comprises all persons living in a place of 2,500 persons or more. An urbanized area comprises one or more places and the adjacent densely settled surrounding territory that together have a minimum population of 50,000 persons. People not residing in these urban areas constitute the rural population.

The populations of the 50 largest metropolitan areas (MSAs and CMSAs) and the population of the 50 largest cities, exclusive of any surrounding metropolitan areas, are detailed in two separate tables. Two tables assess the population by age. The first gives the percentages of population broken down by age; the second shows percentage of population under 18 and over 65 years of age in the largest metropolitan areas.

RESIDENT POPULATION

The top three states—California, New York and Texas—accounted for 26% of the nation's total population. The next five states—Florida, Pennsylvania, Illinois, Ohio and Michigan—made up an additional 22%. None of the remaining 42 states exceeded 3% of the nation's total population.

Several southern and southwestern states reported substantial increases in population. Texas, which ranked sixth in population in 1960, ranked third in 1996. Similarly, Florida went from 10th in 1960 to fourth in 1996. Arizona, Nevada, Washington, Colorado and Hawaii also gained substantial population. Arizona went from 35th in 1960 to 21st in 1996, Nevada from 49th to 39th, Washington from 23rd to 15th, Colorado from 33rd to 25th and Hawaii from 43rd to 35th.

Over the same period states in the Northeast and Midwest lost population. Pennsylvania, Illinois and Ohio dropped two places in rank. Massachusetts and Rhode Island dropped four; Iowa dropped six places.

TABLE: Resident Population
DATE: 1996
SOURCES: U.S. Bureau of the Census, *1990 Census of Population and Housing Unit Counts; Current Population Reports*, Population Estimates Program, 1996 and unpublished data
DESCRIPTION: Resident population for 1960 and 1996.

Rank		1960 (thousands)	1960 rank	1996 (thousands)
	United States	179,323		265,284
1	California	15,717	2	31,878
2	Texas	9,580	6	19,128
3	New York	16,782	1	18,185
4	Florida	4,952	10	14,400
5	Pennsylvania	11,319	3	12,056
6	Illinois	10,081	4	11,846
7	Ohio	9,706	5	11,173
8	Michigan	7,823	7	9,594
9	New Jersey	6,067	8	7,988
10	Georgia	3,943	16	7,353
11	North Carolina	4,556	12	7,323
12	Virginia	3,967	14	6,675
13	Massachusetts	5,149	9	6,092
14	Indiana	4,662	11	5,840
15	Washington	2,853	23	5,533
16	Missouri	4,320	13	5,358
17	Tennessee	3,567	17	5,320
18	Wisconsin	3,952	15	5,160
19	Maryland	3,101	21	5,072
20	Minnesota	3,414	18	4,658
21	Arizona	1,302	35	4,428
22	Louisiana	3,257	20	4,350
23	Alabama	3,267	19	427
24	Kentucky	3,038	22	3,884
25	Colorado	1,754	33	3,823
26	South Carolina	2,383	26	3,699
27	Oklahoma	2,328	27	3,301
28	Connecticut	2,535	25	3,274
29	Oregon	1,769	32	3,204
30	Iowa	2,758	24	2,852
31	Mississippi	2,178	29	2,716
32	Kansas	2,179	28	2,572
33	Arkansas	1,786	31	2,508
34	Utah	891	38	2,000
35	Hawaii	633	43	1,834
36	West Virginia	1,860	30	1,826
37	New Mexico	951	37	1,713
38	Nebraska	1,411	34	1,652
39	Nevada	285	49	1,603
40	Maine	969	36	1,243
41	Idaho	667	42	1,189
42	New Hampshire	607	45	1,162
43	Rhode Island	859	39	990
44	Montana	675	41	879
45	South Dakota	681	40	732
46	Delaware	446	46	725
47	North Dakota	632	44	643
48	Alaska	226	50	607
49	Vermont	390	47	589
50	Washington, DC	764	NA	543
51	Wyoming	330	48	481

NA Not applicable.

POPULATION CHANGE

The western states of Nevada, Idaho, Utah, Colorado, Washington, New Mexico, Texas, Alaska and California recorded the greatest overall increases in population from 1960 to 1993. The southern states of Georgia, Florida, Virginia and North Carolina also reported substantial increases. Between 1960 and 1990 the only eastern states that registered growth above the national averages were Vermont and New Hampshire. No eastern states ranked above the national average between 1990 and 1993. Growth rates in the Midwest and the majority of the East Coast states fell below the national average, particularly from 1970 to 1996.

Idaho, Montana and Wyoming recorded significant increases in population between 1970 and 1980. The population of these three states had been relatively stagnant prior to 1970 and fell below the national average from 1980 to 1990. The growth reported in Idaho, Montana and Wyoming during the 1970s is probably attributable to the exploitation of energy resources that resulted from a change in oil prices. In Montana and Idaho, after a period of comparatively slow growth in the 1980s, the populations of both states increased substantially above the national average from 1990 to 1996.

Some of the population change in a given state occurs because the number of births is greater than the number of deaths among residents; but net migration—the balance between people moving to and from a state—is usually more important in accounting for the change.

TABLE: Population Change
DATE: 1996
SOURCES: U.S. Bureau of the Census, *Census of Population 1970 and 1980; 1990 Census of Population and Housing, Population and Housing Unit Counts; Current Population Reports*, and Population Estimates Program, 1996
DESCRIPTION: Percent change in state population 1960–1996. Table ranked by 1990–1996 figures.

Rank		1960–1970	1970–1980	1980–1990	1990–1996
	United States	13.4	11.4	9.8	6.7
1	Nevada	71.3	63.8	50.1	33.4
2	Arizona	36.3	53.1	34.8	20.8
3	Idaho	6.9	32.4	6.7	18.1
4	Utah	18.9	37.9	17.9	16.1
5	Colorado	26.0	30.8	14.0	16.0
6	Washington	19.6	21.1	17.8	13.7
7	Georgia	16.4	19.1	18.6	13.5
8	New Mexico	6.9	28.1	16.3	13.1
9	Oregon	18.3	25.9	7.9	12.7
10	Texas	16.9	27.1	19.4	12.6
11	Florida	37.2	43.5	32.7	11.3

Rank		1960–1970	1970–1980	1980–1990	1990–1996
12	Alaska	33.8	32.8	36.9	10.4
13	North Carolina	11.6	15.7	12.7	10.4
14	Montana	2.9	13.3	1.6	10.1
15	Tennessee	10.1	16.9	6.2	9.1
16	Delaware	22.8	8.4	12.1	8.8
17	Virginia	17.3	14.9	15.7	7.9
18	California	27.1	18.5	25.7	7.1
19	Arkansas	7.7	18.9	2.8	6.8
20	Hawaii	21.7	25.3	14.9	6.8
21	Minnesota	11.5	7.1	7.3	6.4
22	Maryland	26.5	7.5	13.4	6.1
23	South Carolina	8.7	20.5	11.7	6.1
24	Wyoming	0.7	41.3	-3.4	6.1
25	Alabama	5.4	13.1	3.8	5.8
26	Mississippi	1.8	13.7	2.1	5.5
27	Wisconsin	11.8	6.5	4.0	5.5
28	Indiana	11.4	5.7	1.0	5.3
29	Kentucky	6.0	13.7	0.7	5.3
30	South Dakota	-2.1	3.7	0.8	5.2
31	Oklahoma	9.9	18.2	4.0	4.9
32	New Hampshire	21.5	24.8	20.5	4.8
33	Missouri	8.3	5.1	4.1	4.7
34	Nebraska	5.2	5.7	0.5	4.7
35	Vermont	14.1	15.0	10.0	4.6
36	Kansas	3.2	5.1	4.8	3.8
37	Illinois	10.2	2.8	Z	3.6
38	New Jersey	18.2	2.7	5.0	3.3
39	Michigan	13.5	4.3	0.4	3.2
40	Louisiana	11.9	15.4	0.3	3.1
41	Ohio	9.8	1.3	0.5	3.0
42	Iowa	2.5	3.1	-4.7	2.7
43	West Virginia	-6.2	11.8	-8.0	1.8
44	Pennsylvania	4.3	0.5	0.1	1.5
45	Maine	2.5	13.2	9.2	1.3
46	Massachusetts	10.5	0.8	4.9	1.3
47	New York	8.7	-3.7	2.5	1.1
48	North Dakota	-2.3	5.7	-2.1	0.7
49	Connecticut	19.6	2.5	5.8	-0.4
50	Rhode Island	10.5	-0.3	5.9	-1.3
51	Washington, DC	-1.0	-15.6	-4.9	-10.5

Z Less than 0.5 percent.

POPULATION DENSITY

Massachusetts, Rhode Island, Connecticut, New York, New Jersey, Delaware, Maryland and Washington, DC form a geographical block known as the East Coast Corridor, running along the shore from Boston to Washington, DC. Geographically, this is the densest part of the country. Yet, because New York and Pennsylvania contain large tracts of rural land, they rank 6th and 10th, respectively.

Measures of average density should not be confused with measures of population concentration presented in several other tables. The table below shows the nation's overall pattern of density. Those tables dealing with metropolitan areas and cities compare the amount of density.

TABLE: Population Density
DATE: 1990, 1996
SOURCE: U.S. Bureau of the Census, Census of Population: 1970; U.S. Bureau of the Census, Population Estimates Program, 1996.
DESCRIPTION: Population per square mile of land area.

Rank		Population per square mile 1960	Population per square mile 1996	Land area (square miles)
	United States	50.7	75.0	3,536,338
1	New Jersey	817.8	1,076.7	7,419
2	Rhode Island	822.5	947.3	1,045
3	Massachusetts	656.9	777.2	7,838
4	Connecticut	523.2	675.7	4,845
5	Maryland	317.2	518.9	9,775
6	New York	355.4	385.1	47,224
7	Delaware	228.3	370.8	1,955
8	Hawaii	98.5	285.5	6,423
9	Ohio	237.0	273.0	40,953
10	Pennsylvania	252.6	269.0	44,820
11	Florida	91.7	266.7	53,997
12	Illinois	181.3	213.1	55,593
13	California	100.8	204.3	155,973
14	Michigan	137.7	168.9	56,809
15	Virginia	100.2	168.6	39,598
16	Indiana	130.0	162.8	35,870
17	North Carolina	93.5	150.3	48,718
18	New Hampshire	67.7	129.5	8,969
19	Tennessee	86.5	129.1	41,219
20	Georgia	68.1	126.9	57,919
21	South Carolina	79.1	122.8	30,111
22	Louisiana	74.8	99.8	43,566
23	Kentucky	76.5	97.7	39,732
24	Wisconsin	72.8	95.0	54,314
25	Alabama	64.4	84.2	50,750
26	Washington	42.9	83.1	66,581
27	Missouri	62.7	77.8	68,898
28	West Virginia	77.2	75.8	24,087
29	Texas	36.6	73.0	261,914
30	Vermont	42.2	63.7	9,249
31	Minnesota	42.9	58.5	79,617
32	Mississippi	46.4	57.9	46,914
33	Iowa	49.4	51.0	55,875
34	Arkansas	34.3	48.2	52,075
35	Oklahoma	33.9	48.1	68,679
36	Maine	31.4	40.3	30,865
37	Arizona	11.5	39.0	113,642
38	Colorado	16.9	36.8	103,729
39	Oregon	18.4	33.4	96,002
40	Kansas	26.6	31.4	81,823
41	Utah	10.8	24.3	82,168
42	Nebraska	18.4	21.5	76,878

Rank		Population per square mile 1960	Population per square mile 1996	Land area (square miles)
43	Nevada	2.6	14.6	109,806
44	Idaho	8.1	14.4	82,751
45	New Mexico	7.8	14.1	121,364
46	South Dakota	9.0	9.6	75,896
47	North Dakota	9.2	9.3	68,994
48	Montana	4.6	6.0	145,556
49	Wyoming	3.4	4.9	97,105
50	Alaska	0.4	1.1	570,374
51	Washington, DC	12,440	8902.0	61

METROPOLITAN POPULATION

"Metropolitan areas" as defined by the U.S. Office of Management and Budget (OMB) refers to the 250 Metropolitan Statistical Areas (MSAs) and 18 Consolidated Metropolitan Statistical Areas (CMSAs). According to the OMB, a metropolitan area is a core containing a large population nucleus, together with adjoining communities that have a high degree of social and economic integration with that core. The entire country is classified as metropolitan, (inside MSAs or CMSAs) or nonmetropolitan (outside MSAs or CMSAs).

New Jersey's entire population is classified as metropolitan. The state ranks first in metropolitan population, followed by California, Massachusetts, Connecticut, Rhode Island, Florida and New York. Montana, Wyoming and Idaho ranked lowest in metropolitan population.

Nevada had the largest increase in metropolitan population, over 70% between 1980 and 1992. The neighboring southwestern states, Arizona and New Mexico, rank second and fifth in terms of increase. Wyoming experienced a decrease in an already small metropolitan population, as did West Virginia and the District of Columbia. New Hampshire was the only eastern state where the percentage of metropolitan population increased at a rate above the national average.

TABLE: Metropolitan Population
DATE: 1992
SOURCE: U.S. Bureau of the Census, *1990 Census of Population and Housing* and unpublished data
DESCRIPTION: Metropolitan refers to 250 metropolitan statistical areas and 18 consolidated metropolitan statistical areas as defined by the Office of Management and Budget. Table ranked by percent change.

Rank		1980	1992	Percent change 1980–1992
	United States	78.1	79.7	14.9
1	Nevada	83.2	84.8	70.3
2	Arizona	83.3	84.7	43.3
3	Alaska	43.4	41.8	41.0
4	Florida	92.7	93.0	38.7
5	New Mexico	51.8	56.0	31.3
6	Georgia	64.2	67.7	30.8
7	California	96.8	96.7	30.4
8	Texas	81.1	83.9	28.6
9	Washington	81.5	83.0	26.8
10	Virginia	74.2	77.5	24.9
11	Idaho	27.2	30.0	24.4
12	Utah	77.2	77.5	24.4
13	New Hampshire	58.1	59.4	23.8
14	Colorado	80.5	81.8	21.7
15	North Carolina	63.8	66.3	21.0
16	South Dakota	28.0	32.6	19.1
17	South Carolina	67.8	69.8	18.9
18	Maryland	93.0	92.8	16.4
19	Kansas	50.1	54.6	16.1
20	Vermont	26.0	27.0	15.9
21	Minnesota	65.6	69.3	15.8
22	Oregon	68.3	70.0	15.7
23	Delaware	83.5	82.7	15.1
24	Hawaii	79.0	74.7	13.2
25	North Dakota	35.9	41.6	12.4
26	Mississippi	28.4	30.7	12.1
27	Tennessee	66.3	67.7	11.8
28	Oklahoma	57.0	60.1	11.7
29	Arkansas	42.1	44.7	11.2
30	Nebraska	46.4	50.6	11.1
31	Maine	36.0	35.7	9.0
32	Alabama	65.7	67.4	8.9
33	Wisconsin	67.5	68.1	7.1
34	Missouri	67.4	68.3	6.9
35	New Jersey	100.0	100.0	6.2
36	Rhode Island	93.5	93.6	5.8
37	Connecticut	96.0	95.7	5.2
38	Kentucky	47.4	48.5	4.9
39	Montana	24.0	24.0	4.6
40	Indiana	70.8	71.6	4.3
41	Massachusetts	96.4	96.2	4.2
42	Illinois	82.8	84.0	3.1
43	New York	91.9	91.7	2.9
44	Louisiana	74.3	75.0	2.7
45	Iowa	41.1	43.8	2.5
46	Ohio	81.4	81.3	2.0
47	Michigan	83.3	82.7	1.0
48	Pennsylvania	84.8	84.8	1.0
49	Wyoming	29.9	29.7	-1.8
50	West Virginia	40.8	41.8	-5.0
51	Washington, DC	100.0	100.0	-8.3

CHANGE IN NONMETROPOLITAN POPULATION

Nonmetropolitan areas are those outside the designated 250 Metropolitan Statistical Areas (MSAs) and 18 Consolidated Metropolitan Statistical Areas (CMSAs). Nationally, the nonmetropolitan population increased only 4.5% between 1980 and 1992, where the metropolitan population rose by 14.9%. Nevada's and Alaska's nonmetropolitan populations increased over 50%. Eleven states lost nonmetropolitan population. With the exceptions of Louisiana and West Virginia, all were located in the midwestern and Plains states, extending from Illinois to Wyoming. Montana, Vermont, Wyoming, Idaho, Mississippi and South Dakota reported the highest percentage of rural population.

TABLE: Change in Nonmetropolitan Population
DATE: 1992
SOURCE: U.S. Bureau of the Census, *1990 Census of Population and Housing* and unpublished data
DESCRIPTION: Nonmetropolitan population 1980 and 1992 with percentage change 1980–1992.

Rank		1980 percent	1992 percent	Percent change 1980–1992
	United States	21.9	20.3	4.5
1	Nevada	16.8	15.2	50.5
2	Alaska	56.6	58.2	50.3
3	Hawaii	21.0	25.3	44.8
4	California	3.2	3.3	34.3
5	Florida	7.3	7.0	34.2
6	Arizona	16.7	15.3	29.9
7	Utah	22.8	22.5	22.6
8	Delaware	16.5	17.3	22.3
9	Maryland	7.0	7.2	19.1
10	New Hampshire	41.9	40.6	17.4
11	Washington	18.5	17.0	14.0
12	Colorado	19.5	18.2	12.3
13	Connecticut	4.0	4.3	12.1
14	Georgia	35.8	32.3	11.8
15	Massachusetts	3.6	3.8	11.2
16	New Mexico	48.2	44.0	10.7
17	Maine	64.0	64.3	10.4
18	Vermont	74.0	73.0	10.2
19	Idaho	72.8	70.0	8.6
20	South Carolina	32.2	30.2	8.2
21	North Carolina	36.2	33.7	8.0
22	Oregon	31.7	30.0	6.7
23	Michigan	16.7	17.3	5.9
24	New York	8.1	8.3	5.9
25	Texas	18.9	16.1	5.8
26	Rhode Island	6.5	6.4	5.1

Rank		1980 percent	1992 percent	Percent change 1980–1992
27	Tennessee	33.7	32.3	4.9
28	Montana	76.0	76.0	4.5
29	Virginia	25.8	22.5	4.3
30	Wisconsin	32.5	31.9	4.0
31	Missouri	32.6	31.7	2.8
32	Ohio	18.6	18.7	2.4
33	Pennsylvania	15.2	15.2	1.5
34	Alabama	34.3	32.6	1.1
35	Kentucky	52.6	51.5	0.5
36	Mississippi	71.6	69.3	0.4
37	Wyoming	70.1	70.3	-0.7
38	Louisiana	25.7	25.0	-1.2
39	Oklahoma	43.0	39.9	-1.8
40	Minnesota	34.4	30.7	-2.2
41	Kansas	49.9	45.4	-3.3
42	South Dakota	72.0	67.4	-3.9
43	Illinois	17.2	16.0	-5.6
44	Nebraska	53.6	49.4	-6.0
45	Iowa	58.9	56.2	-8.2
46	West Virginia	59.2	58.2	-8.8
47	North Dakota	64.1	58.4	-11.4
48	Indiana	29.2	28.4	Z
49	Arkansas	57.9	55.3	Z
50	New Jersey	X	X	X
51	Washington, DC	X	X	X

X Not applicable.
Z Less than .05 percent.

URBAN AND RURAL POPULATION

The U.S. Bureau of the Census defines urban population as comprising all persons living in a place of 2,500 or more persons. An urbanized area comprises one or more places and the adjacent densely settled surrounding territory that together have a minimum population of 50,000 persons. The population not classified as urban constitutes the rural population.

The urban/rural classifications used in this table are distinct from the metropolitan/nonmetropolitan classification used in the previous tables. This distinction is manifested in two respects. First, the data presented in this table capture population of small towns that are outside of large metropolitan centers. Second, urban populations are included here that may not be part of larger political units, such as cities and counties.

Nationwide, 75.2% of the population lived in urban places and 24.8% in rural places. In 34 states the rural population exceeded the nation's total percentage of rural population. In 16 states the urban population exceeded the nation's total percentage of urban population. In several states, such as South Dakota, North Carolina, North Dakota, Kentucky and Montana, the urban and rural populations were roughly equal.

TOTAL: Urban and Rural Population
DATE: 1990
SOURCE: U.S. Bureau of the Census, *1990 Census of Population and Housing*
DESCRIPTION: Total population and percent urban and rural.

Rank		Total population (thousands)	Percent urban	Percent rural
	United States	248,710	75.2	24.8
1	California	29,760	92.6	7.4
2	New York	17,990	84.3	15.7
3	Texas	16,987	80.3	19.7
4	Florida	12,938	184.8	15.2
5	Pennsylvania	11,882	68.9	31.1
6	Illinois	11,431	84.6	15.4
7	Ohio	10,847	74.1	25.9
8	Michigan	9,295	70.5	29.5
9	New Jersey	7,730	89.4	10.6
10	North Carolina	6,629	50.4	49.6
11	Georgia	6,478	63.2	36.8
12	Virginia	6,187	69.4	30.6
13	Massachusetts	6,016	84.3	15.7
14	Indiana	5,544	64.9	35.1
15	Missouri	5,117	68.7	31.3
16	Wisconsin	4,892	65.7	34.3
17	Tennessee	4,877	60.9	39.1
18	Washington	4,867	76.4	23.6
19	Maryland	4,781	81.3	18.7
20	Minnesota	4,375	69.9	30.1
21	Louisiana	4,220	68.1	31.9
22	Alabama	4,041	60.4	39.6
23	Kentucky	3,685	51.8	48.2
24	Arizona	3,665	87.5	12.5
25	South Carolina	3,487	54.6	45.4
26	Colorado	3,294	82.4	17.6
27	Connecticut	3,287	79.1	20.9
28	Oklahoma	3,146	67.7	32.3
29	Oregon	2,842	70.5	29.5
30	Iowa	2,777	60.6	39.4
31	Mississippi	2,573	47.1	52.9
32	Kansas	2,478	69.1	30.9
33	Arkansas	2,351	53.5	46.5
34	West Virginia	1,793	36.1	63.9
35	Utah	1,723	87.0	13.0
36	Nebraska	1,578	66.1	33.9
37	New Mexico	1,515	73.0	27.0
38	Maine	1,228	44.6	55.4
39	Nevada	1,202	88.3	11.7
40	New Hampshire	1,109	51.0	49.0
41	Hawaii	1,108	89.0	11.0
42	Idaho	1,007	57.4	42.6
43	Rhode Island	1,003	86.0	14.0
44	Montana	799	52.5	47.5
45	South Dakota	696	50.0	50.0
46	Delaware	666	73.0	27.0
47	North Dakota	639	53.3	46.7
48	Washington, DC	607	100.0	0.0
49	Vermont	563	32.2	67.8
50	Alaska	550	67.5	32.5
51	Wyoming	454	65.0	35.0

POPULATION OF LARGEST METROPOLITAN AREAS

The table below is another indication of the general shift in population from the Northeast and Midwest to the South and Southwest.

The greatest metropolitan population increases between 1980 and 1990 were in Las Vegas, Orlando and in West Palm Beach. The greatest losses in population occurred in Pittsburgh, Buffalo and Detroit.

TABLE: Population of Largest Metropolitan Areas
DATE: 1992
SOURCE: U.S. Bureau of the Census, *1990 Census of Population and Housing*
DESCRIPTION: Population figures for CMSAs and MSAs for 1980 and 1992 with percentage change 1980–1992. Table ranked by percent change.

Rank	Metropolitan area	1980 population (thousands)	1992 population (thousands)	1980–1992 percent change
1	Las Vegas MSA	528	971	84
2	Orlando MSA	805	1,305	62
3	West Palm Beach MSA	577	901	56
4	Austin MSA	585	901	54
5	Phoenix MSA	1,600	2,330	46

Rank	Metropolitan area	1980 population (thousands)	1992 population (thousands)	1980–1992 percent change
6	Sacramento CMSA	1,100	1,563	42
7	Atlanta MSA	2,233	3,143	41
8	San Diego MSA	1,862	2,601	40
9	Dallas CMSA	3,046	4,215	38
10	Raleigh-Durham MSA	665	909	37
11	Jacksonville MSA	722	953	32
12	Los Angeles CMSA	11,498	15,048	31
13	Tampa MSA	1,614	2,107	31
14	Seattle CMSA	2,409	3,131	30
15	Houston CMSA	3,118	3,962	27
16	San Antonio MSA	1,089	1,379	27
17	Miami CMSA	2,644	3,309	25
18	Charlotte MSA	971	1,212	25
19	Norfolk MSA	1,201	1,497	25
20	Salt Lake City CMSA	910	1,128	24
21	Nashville MSA	851	1,023	20
22	Denver CMSA	1,742	2,089	20
23	Portland CMSA	1,584	1,897	20
24	Washington-Baltimore CMSA	5,791	6,920	20
25	San Francisco CMSA	5,368	6,410	19
26	Minneapolis-St. Paul MSA	2,198	2,618	19
27	Columbus MSA	1,214	1,394	15
28	Grand Rapids MSA	841	964	15
29	Oklahoma City MSA	861	984	14
30	Greensboro MSA	951	1,078	13
31	Kansas City MSA	1,449	1,617	12
32	Memphis MSA	939	1,034	10
33	Indianapolis MSA	1,306	1,424	9
34	Cincinnati CMSA	1,726	1,865	8
35	Hartford MSA	1,081	1,156	7
36	Boston CMSA	5,122	5,439	6
37	Philadelphia CMSA	5,649	5,939	5
38	Providence MSA	1,077	1,131	5
39	Rochester MSA	1,031	1,081	5
40	St. Louis MSA	2,414	2,519	4
41	New York CMSA	18,906	19,670	4
42	Milwaukee CMSA	1,570	1,629	4
43	Chicago CMSA	8,115	8,410	4
44	Dayton MSA	942	962	2
45	Louisville MSA	954	968	2
46	New Orleans MSA	1,304	1,303	0
47	Detroit CMSA	5,293	5,246	-1
48	Cleveland CMSA	2,938	2,890	-2
49	Buffalo MSA	1,243	1,194	-4
50	Pittsburgh MSA	2,571	2,406	-6

THE 50 LARGEST CITIES

The 50 largest cities are ranked here based on 1992 population. Data here reflect only the population within the designated city limits.

Only the cities in the South experienced significant growth from 1990 to 1992. Several of the Large cities in the Northeast and Midwest actually lost population. This is yet another indication of movement away from the "Rust Belt."

TABLE: The 50 Largest Cities

DATE: 1992

SOURCE: U.S. Bureau of the Census, Census of Population, 1990 and 1992

DESCRIPTION: Population of the 50 largest cities and percent change 1990–1992.

Rank	City	1992 population (thousands)	Percent change 1990–1992
1	New York, NY	7,312	-0.1
2	Los Angeles, CA	3,490	0.1
3	Chicago, IL	2,768	-0.5
4	Houston, TX	1,690	3.7
5	Philadelphia, PA	1,553	-2.1
6	San Diego, CA	1,149	3.4
7	Dallas, TX	1,022	1.6
8	Phoenix, AZ	1,012	2.9
9	Detroit, MI	1,012	-1.5
10	San Antonio, TX	966	3.3
11	San Jose, CA	801	2.4
12	Indianapolis, IN*	747	2.1
13	San Francisco, CA	729	0.7
14	Baltimore, MD	726	-1.3
15	Jacksonville, FL*	661	4.1
16	Columbus, OH	643	1.6
17	Milwaukee, WI	617	-1.8
18	Memphis, TN	610	-Z
19	Washington, DC	585	-3.6
20	Boston, MA	552	-3.9
21	El Paso, TX	544	5.5
22	Seattle, WA	520	0.6
23	Cleveland, OH	503	-0.6
24	Nashville-Davidson, TN*	495	1.4
25	Austin, TX	492	5.7

Rank	City	1992 population (thousands)	Percent change 1990–1992
26	New Orleans, LA	490	-1.5
27	Denver, CO	484	3.5
28	Fort Worth, TX	454	1.5
29	Oklahoma City, OK	454	2.1
30	Portland, OR	445	1.9
31	Long Beach, CA	439	2.2
32	Kansas City, MO	432	-0.8
33	Virginia Beach, VA	417	6.1
34	Charlotte, NC	416	5.1
35	Tucson, AZ	415	2.4
36	Albuquerque, NM	398	3.6
37	Atlanta, GA	395	0.2
38	St. Louis, MO	384	-3.3
39	Sacramento, CA	383	3.6
40	Fresno, CA	376	6.2
41	Tulsa, OK	375	2.2
42	Oakland, CA	373	0.3
43	Honolulu, HI**	371	1.7
44	Miami, FL	367	2.4
45	Pittsburgh, PA	367	-0.8
46	Cincinnati, OH	364	0.1
47	Minneapolis, MN	363	-1.5
48	Omaha, NE	340	1.2
49	Toledo, OH	329	-1.1
50	Buffalo, NY	323	-1.5

*Represents the portion of a consolidated city that is not within one or more separately incorporated places.
**Includes county of Honolulu.
Z Less than .05 percent.

RESIDENT POPULATION BY AGE

Nationally, the largest segment of the population is aged 5 to 17 years old (18%). Not surprisingly, those over 85 years old made up the smallest percentage (1%). Utah (10%) and Alaska (10%) ranked highest in percentage of population under 5 years old. Four western states also ranked highest in population aged 5 to 17 years old: Utah (26%), Idaho (22%), Alaska (22%) and Wyoming (22%).In the 18-to-24-year old age range Mississippi (12%) ranked first and Florida (8%) last.All other states were comparatively equal in the percentage of population aged 18 to 24, ranging from 9% to 11%. Alaska (20%) ranked first and West Virginia (13%) last in percentage of population aged 25 to 34 years old. Alaska (20%) also ranked first in the percentage of population aged 35 to 44 years old. Several states ranked at the bottom: Mississippi, Arkansas and Utah (all 14%). In the next category, percentage of population aged 45 to 54, Utah (9%) ranked last. In all the other states the range was comparatively narrow, 10% to 12%. The percentage of population aged 55 to 64 years old ranged from 9% to 7% nationwide with the exceptions of Utah (6%) and Alaska (6%). Florida (11%) and Alaska (3%) demonstrated the relatively wide range of percentage of populations aged 65 to 74 years old among the states. Florida (6%) and Alaska (1%) spanned the states in the percentage of population aged 75 to 84 years old. Montana (5%) ranked first in population among persons age 85 and over.

TABLE: Resident Population by Age
DATE: 1993
SOURCE: U.S. Bureau of the Census, Current Population Reports
DESCRIPTION: Percentage of resident population by age. Includes armed forces stationed in area.

Rank		Total (thousands)	% under 5 years	% 5 to 17 years	% 18 to 24 years	% 25 to 34 years	% 35 to 44 years	% 45 to 54 years	% 55 to 64 years	% 65 to 74 years	% 75 to 84 years	% 85 years and over	% 65 years and over
	United States	257,908	8	18	10	16	16	11	8	7	4	1	12.7
1	California	31,211	9	18	10	18	16	11	7	6	3	1	11
2	New York	18,197	8	17	10	17	16	12	9	7	4	1	13
3	Texas	18,031	9	20	11	17	16	10	7	6	3	1	10
4	Florida	13,679	7	16	8	15	15	11	9	11	6	2	19
5	Pennsylvania	12,048	7	17	10	15	16	11	9	9	5	2	16
6	Illinois	11,697	8	18	10	16	16	11	8	7	4	1	13
7	Ohio	11,091	7	19	10	15	16	11	9	8	4	1	13
8	Michigan	9,478	7	19	10	16	16	11	8	7	4	1	12
9	New Jersey	7,879	7	17	9	16	16	12	9	8	4	1	14
10	North Carolina	6,945	7	17	11	16	16	12	9	7	4	1	12
11	Georgia	6,917	8	19	11	17	16	12	8	6	3	1	10
12	Virginia	6,491	7	17	11	17	17	12	8	7	3	1	11
13	Massachusetts	6,012	7	16	10	18	16	11	8	8	5	2	14
14	Indiana	5,713	7	19	11	15	16	11	8	7	4	1	13
15	Washington	5,255	8	19	9	16	17	12	7	7	4	1	12
16	Missouri	5,234	7	19	10	15	15	11	9	8	5	2	14
17	Tennessee	5,099	7	18	10	16	16	12	9	7	4	1	13
18	Wisconsin	5,038	7	20	10	16	16	11	8	7	5	2	13
19	Maryland	4,965	8	17	9	18	17	12	8	7	3	1	11
20	Minnesota	4,517	7	20	9	16	16	11	8	7	4	2	13
21	Louisiana	4,295	8	21	11	16	15	10	8	7	4	1	11
22	Alabama	4,187	7	19	11	15	15	11	9	7	4	1	13
23	Arizona	3,936	8	19	10	16	15	10	8	8	4	1	13
24	Kentucky	3,789	7	19	11	15	16	11	9	7	4	1	13
25	South Carolina	3,643	8	19	11	16	16	11	8	7	4	1	12
26	Colorado	3,566	8	18	10	17	18	12	7	6	3	1	10
27	Connecticut	3,277	7	17	9	16	16	12	9	8	5	2	14
28	Oklahoma	3,231	7	20	10	15	15	11	8	8	5	2	14
29	Oregon	3,032	7	19	9	15	17	12	8	8	5	1	14
30	Iowa	2,814	7	19	10	14	15	11	9	8	5	2	15
31	Mississippi	2,643	8	21	12	15	14	10	8	7	4	1	12
32	Kansas	2,531	7	20	10	15	16	10	8	7	5	2	14
33	Arkansas	2,424	7	19	10	14	14	11	9	8	5	2	15
34	Utah	1,860	10	26	12	15	14	9	6	5	3	1	9
35	West Virginia	1,820	6	18	11	13	16	12	9	9	5	2	15
36	New Mexico	1,616	8	21	10	15	16	11	8	6	4	4	11
37	Nebraska	1,607	7	20	10	15	15	10	8	7	5	2	14
38	Nevada	1,389	8	17	9	18	16	12	8	7	3	3	11
39	Maine	1,239	7	18	10	15	17	11	9	8	5	2	14
40	Hawaii	1,172	8	18	10	17	17	11	8	7	4	3	12
41	New Hampshire	1,125	7	18	10	17	17	12	8	7	4	1	12
42	Idaho	1,099	8	22	10	14	16	11	7	7	4	4	12
43	Rhode Island	1,000	7	16	10	16	16	11	8	9	5	2	15
44	Montana	839	7	21	9	13	17	11	8	7	5	5	13
45	South Dakota	715	8	21	10	14	15	10	8	8	5	2	15
46	Delaware	700	8	17	10	17	16	11	9	8	4	1	12
47	North Dakota	635	7	20	10	15	15	10	8	7	5	2	15
48	Alaska	599	10	22	10	18	20	11	6	3	1	1	4
49	Washington, DC	578	7	13	11	20	16	11	8	7	4	1	13
50	Vermont	576	7	18	11	16	17	12	8	7	4	1	12
51	Wyoming	470	7	22	10	15	17	11	7	6	4	4	11

POPULATION UNDER 18 AND OVER 65 YEARS OF AGE IN THE 50 LARGEST METROPOLITAN AREAS

This table is ranked by population and shows the percentage of population in two age groups, under 18 and over 65 years old. Salt Lake City has the youngest metropolitan area and West Palm Beach has the oldest.

TABLE: Population Under 18 and Over 65 Years of Age in the 50 Largest Metropolitan Areas

DATE: 1990

SOURCE: U.S. Bureau of the Census, *1990 Census of Population and Housing* and unpublished data

DESCRIPTION: Percent of population under 18 and over 65 years in large metropolitan areas. Rank is based on unrounded figures for CMSAs and MSAs only.

Rank	City	Percent under 18 years	Percent 65 years and over
1	New York CMSA	23.0	13.1
2	Los Angeles CMSA	26.6	9.8
3	Chicago CMSA	26.1	11.4
4	Washington-Baltimore CMSA	23.9	9.9
5	San Francisco CMSA	23.1	11.1
6	Philadelphia CMSA	24.4	13.5
7	Boston CMSA	22.7	12.7
8	Detroit CMSA	26.1	11.5
9	Dallas CMSA	27.2	8.3
10	Houston CMSA	28.9	7.3
11	Miami CMSA	22.7	16.6
12	Atlanta MSA	25.9	8.0
13	Seattle CMSA	25.0	10.8
14	Cleveland CMSA	24.9	13.9
15	Minneapolis-St. Paul MSA	26.4	9.8
16	San Diego MSA	24.5	10.9
17	St. Louis MSA	26.3	12.8
18	Pittsburgh MSA	22.0	17.1
19	Phoenix MSA	26.4	12.6
20	Tampa MSA	20.4	21.6
21	Denver CMSA	25.7	9.2
22	Portland CMSA	25.8	12.4
23	Cincinnati CMSA	26.8	11.8
24	Milwaukee CMSA	26.4	12.4
25	Kansas City MSA	26.4	11.6
26	Sacramento CMSA	26.2	10.8
27	Norfolk MSA	26.4	9.2
28	Indianapolis MSA	26.2	11.4
29	Columbus MSA	25.1	10.0
30	San Antonio MSA	29.0	10.3
31	Orlando MSA	23.8	12.9
32	New Orleans MSA	28.1	11.0
33	Charlotte MSA	24.7	10.9
34	Buffalo MSA	23.6	15.2
35	Hartford MSA	22.6	13.2
36	Providence MSA	22.8	15.1
37	Salt Lake City	35.6	8.4
38	Rochester MSA	25.1	12.5
39	Greensboro MSA	22.9	12.4
40	Memphis MSA	27.9	10.4
41	Nashville MSA	25.1	10.6
42	Oklahoma City MSA	26.6	11.0
43	Las Vegas MSA	24.3	11.6
44	Louisville MSA	25.3	12.6
45	Grand Rapids MSA	28.6	11.1
46	Dayton MSA	25.3	12.4
47	Jacksonville MSA	26.0	10.9
48	Raleigh-Durham MSA	22.7	9.5
49	Austin MSA	25.6	7.8
50	West Palm Beach MSA	19.6	24.3

ETHNIC AND RACIAL DIVERSITY

This section presents statistics on the ethnicity, race and language of the United States population. The primary source is the U.S. Bureau of the Census. The U.S. Office of Management and Budget (OMB) provides standards on ethnic and racial categories for statistical reporting that the Census Bureau uses in its surveys. The basic racial categories are American Indian or Alaska Native (Native American), Asian or Pacific Islander, black and white. The standards define Hispanic origin as an ethnicity. The Bureau of the Census employs a method of self-identification, meaning that respondents define their own racial or ethnic identity. This method is not intended to reflect any biological or anthropological definition. The Census Bureau acknowledges that the racial categories in their surveys include both racial, national origin or sociocultural groups. In the 1990 census, the question about race included a write-in option for persons who do not identify with a specific racial group.

The language spoken at home is the subject of the first three tables. Race and ethnicity are surveyed in the remaining tables.

ENGLISH-SPEAKING POPULATION

English is the only language spoken at home by more than 80% of the American population. The highest concentration of English only speakers is in the South; the lowest in the Southwest and the large states with significant immigrant populations. This table can be misleading. It should not be used as an indication of proficiency in English. About 2% of the population reported a lack of English proficiency.

TITLE: English-Speaking Population
DATE: 1990
SOURCE: U.S. Bureau of the Census, *1990 Census of Population and Housing*
DESCRIPTION: Number of people five years and over who speak only English at home.

Rank		Total	Percent speaking only English
	United States	198,600,798	86
1	Kentucky	3,348,473	97
2	West Virginia	1,642,729	97
3	Arkansas	2,125,884	97
4	Mississippi	2,312,289	97
5	Alabama	3,651,936	97
6	Tennessee	4,413,193	97
7	South Carolina	3,118,376	96
8	Missouri	4,570,494	96
9	Iowa	2,483,135	96
10	North Carolina	5,931,435	96
11	Georgia	5,599,642	95
12	Indiana	4,900,334	95
13	Nebraska	1,389,032	95
14	Oklahoma	2,775,957	95
15	Montana	703,198	95
16	Ohio	9,517,064	95
17	Minnesota	3,811,700	94
18	Wyoming	394,904	94
19	Kansas	2,158,011	94
20	Wisconsin	4,267,496	94
21	Vermont	491,112	94
22	Idaho	867,708	94
23	South Dakota	599,232	93
24	Michigan	8,024,930	93
25	Delaware	575,393	93
26	Oregon	2,448,772	93
27	Pennsylvania	10,278,294	93
28	Virginia	5,327,898	93
29	Utah	1,432,947	92
30	North Dakota	543,942	92
31	New Hampshire	935,825	91
32	Maryland	4,030,234	91
33	Washington	4,098,706	91
34	Maine	1,036,681	91
35	Louisiana	3,494,359	90
36	Colorado	2,722,355	89
37	Alaksa	435,260	86
38	Washington, DC	498,936	87
39	Nevada	964,298	87
40	Illinois	9,086,726	86

Rank		Total	Percent speaking only English
41	Massachusetts	4,753,523	85
42	Connecticut	2,593,825	85
43	California	18,764,213	84
44	Rhode Island	776,931	83
45	Florida	9,996,969	83
46	New Jersey	5,794,548	80
47	Arizona	2,674,519	79
48	New York	12,634,328	77
49	Hawaii	771,485	75
50	Texas	11,635,518	75
51	New Mexico	896,049	64

SPANISH-SPEAKING POPULATION

Spanish was the primary language of large segments of the population in four border states, California, Texas, Arizona and New Mexico. The metropolitan areas of New York City, Chicago and Miami also contained large Spanish-speaking communities, which accounts for the high rank of New York, Illinois and Florida here. Many of the residents of these communities traced their origins to Puerto Rico, Mexico or Cuba. Nationwide, 7.5% of the population five years old and over spoke Spanish at home.

TITLE: Spanish-Speaking Population
DATE: 1990
SOURCE: U.S. Bureau of the Census, *1990 Census of Population and Housing*
DESCRIPTION: Number of people five years and over who speak Spanish at home.

Rank		Total	Percent speaking Spanish
	United States	17,345,064	7.5
1	New Mexico	388,186	27.9
2	California	5,478,712	24.5
3	Texas	3,443,106	22.1
4	Arizona	478,234	14.2
5	Florida	1,447,747	12.0
6	New York	1,848,825	11.0
7	New Jersey	621,416	8.6
8	Nevada	85,474	7.7
9	Illinois	728,380	6.9
10	Colorado	203,896	6.7
11	Washington, DC	35,021	6.1
12	Connecticut	167,007	5.5
13	Massachusetts	228,458	4.1
14	Idaho	37,081	4.0
15	Rhode Island	35,492	3.8
16	Utah	51,945	3.3
17	Wyoming	13,790	3.3
18	Washington	143,647	3.2

Rank		Total	Percent speaking Spanish
19	Oregon	83,087	3.1
20	Maryland	122,871	2.8
21	Kansas	62,059	2.7
22	Virginia	152,663	2.7
23	Delaware	15,302	2.5
24	Oklahoma	64,562	2.2
25	Georgia	122,295	2.0
26	Alaska	10,020	2.0
27	Pennsylvania	213,096	1.9
28	Louisiana	72,173	1.9
29	Indiana	90,146	1.8
30	North Carolina	105,963	1.7
31	Nebraska	24,555	1.7
32	Wisconsin	75,931	1.7
33	Michigan	137,490	1.6
34	Ohio	139,194	1.4
35	South Carolina	44,427	1.4
36	Hawaii	13,729	1.3
37	Missouri	59,585	1.3
38	Arkansas	27,351	1.3
39	Iowa	31,620	1.2
40	Alabama	42,653	1.1
41	Tennessee	49,661	1.1
42	Montana	8,083	1.1
43	Mississippi	25,061	1.1
44	Minnesota	42,362	1.0
45	New Hampshire	9,619	0.9
46	Kentucky	31,293	0.9
47	West Virginia	13,337	0.8
48	South Dakota	5,033	0.8
49	North Dakota	4,296	0.7
50	Vermont	3,196	0.6
51	Maine	5,934	0.5

NON-ENGLISH-SPEAKING POPULATION

In the United States, 13.8% of the population spoke a language other than English at home. In order, Spanish, French, German, Italian and Chinese were the leading alternatives to English in 1990. New Mexico, California and Texas ranked highest here, due in large part to their Spanish-speaking populations. One-quarter of Hawaii's population spoke a language other than English at home. Japanese, Tagalog and Chinese were the leading alternatives. California and New York ranked second and fifth respectively here; both reported more than 10,000 speakers in over 20 different languages surveyed.

TITLE: Non-English-Speaking Population
DATE: 1990
SOURCE: U. S. Bureau of the Census, *1990 Census of Population and Housing*

DESCRIPTION: Percent of population who speak languages other than English at home.

Rank		Total speaking languages other than English	Percent
	United States	31,844,979	13.8
1	New Mexico	493,999	35.5
2	California	8,619,334	31.5
3	Texas	3,970,304	25.4
4	Hawaii	254,724	24.8
5	New York	3,908,720	23.3
6	Arizona	700,287	20.8
7	New Jersey	1,406,148	19.5
8	Florida	2,098,315	17.3
9	Rhode Island	159,492	17.0
10	Connecticut	466,175	15.2
11	Massachusetts	852228	15.2
12	Illinois	1,499,112	14.2
13	Nevada	146,152	13.2
14	Washington, DC	71,348	12.5
15	Alaska	60,165	12.1
16	Colorado	320,631	10.5
17	Louisiana	391,994	10.1
18	Maine	105,441	9.2
19	Washington	403,173	9.0
20	Maryland	395,051	8.9
21	New Hampshire	88,796	8.7
22	North Dakota	46,897	7.9
23	Utah	120,404	7.8
24	Oregon	191,710	7.3
25	Pennsylvania	806,876	7.3
26	Virginia	418,521	7.3
27	Delaware	42,327	6.9
28	Michigan	569,807	6.6
29	South Dakota	41,994	6.5
30	Idaho	58,995	6.4
31	Vermont	30,409	5.8
32	Wisconsin	263,638	5.8
33	Kansas	131,604	5.7
34	Wyoming	23,809	5.7
35	Minnesota	227,161	5.6
36	Ohio	5,466,148	5.4
37	Montana	37020	5.0
38	Oklahoma	145,798	5.0
39	Georgia	284,546	4.8
40	Indiana	245,826	4.8
41	Nebraska	69,872	4.8
42	Iowa	100,391	3.9
43	North Carolina	240,866	3.9
44	Missouri	178,210	3.8
45	South Carolina	113,163	3.5
46	Alabama	107,866	2.9
47	Tennessee	131,550	2.9
48	Arkansas	60,781	2.8
49	Mississippi	66,516	2.8
50	West Virginia	44,203	2.6
51	Kentucky	86,482	2.5

BLACK POPULATION

Black Americans constitute the largest racial minority in the country. Asked to indicate the racial group with which they identify themselves, 12.1% of the total population selected "black." The largest group of black Americans reported here are located in the metropolitan areas of the most populous states, but the highest percentages of blacks in state populations reside in the South: Mississippi, South Carolina, Louisiana, Georgia and Alabama.

TABLE: Black Population
DATE: 1990
SOURCE: U.S. Bureau of the Census, *1990 Census of Population and Housing*
DESCRIPTION: Black population and blacks as a percentage of state population.

Rank		Total	Percent of state population
	United States	29,986,060	12.1
1	New York	2,859,055	15.9
2	California	2,208,801	7.4
3	Texas	2,021,632	11.9
4	Florida	1,759,534	13.6
5	Georgia	1,746,565	27.0
6	Illinois	1,694,273	14.8
7	North Carolina	1,456,323	22.0
8	Louisiana	1,299,281	30.8
9	Michigan	1,291,706	13.9
10	Maryland	1,189,899	24.9
11	Virginia	1,162,994	18.8
12	Ohio	1,154,826	10.6
13	Pennnsylvania	1,089,795	9.2
14	South Carolina	1,039,884	29.8
15	New Jersey	1,036,825	13.4
16	Alabama	1,020,705	25.3
17	Mississippi	915,057	35.6
18	Tennessee	778,035	16.0
19	Missouri	548,208	10.7
20	Indiana	432,092	7.8
21	Washington, DC	399,604	65.8
22	Arkansas	373,912	15.9
23	Massachusetts	300,130	5
24	Connecticut	274,269	8.3
25	Kentucky	262,907	7.1
26	Wisconsin	244,539	5
27	Oklahoma	233,801	7.4
28	Washington	149,801	3.1
29	Kansas	143,076	5.8
30	Colorado	133,146	4
31	Delaware	112,460	16.9
32	Arizona	110,524	3
33	Minnesota	94,944	2.2
34	Nevada	78,771	6.6
35	Nebraska	57,404	3.6
36	West Virginia	56,295	3.1

Rank		Total	Percent of state population
37	Iowa	48,090	1.7
38	Oregon	46,178	1.6
39	Rhode Island	38,861	3.9
40	New Mexico	30,210	2
41	Hawaii	27,195	2.5
42	Alaska	22,451	4.1
43	Utah	11,576	0.7
44	New Hampshire	7,198	0.6
45	Maine	5,138	0.4
46	Wyoming	3,606	0.8
47	North Dakota	3,524	0.6
48	Idaho	3,370	0.3
49	South Dakota	3,258	0.5
50	Montana	2,381	0.3
51	Vermont	1,951	0.3

HISPANIC POPULATION

The Hispanic population of the United States is classified as a group according to ethnicity and national origin. In 1990, 9% of the population identified themselves as Hispanic. The state-by-state distribution of Hispanic persons paralleled the distribution of people speaking Spanish at home. The majority of Hispanics reside in the Southwest. Hispanic populations are also concentrated in Florida and metropolitan New York and Chicago. In every state the population of those of Hispanic *origin* is greater than the population using the Spanish *language* at home.

TABLE: Hispanic Population
DATE: 1990
SOURCE: U.S. Bureau of the Census, *1990 Census of Population and Housing*
DESCRIPTION: Hispanic population and Hispanics as a percentage of total state population.

Rank		Total	Percent of population
	United States	22,354,059	9
1	California	7,687,938	25.8
2	Texas	4,339,905	25.5
3	New York	2,214,026	12.3
4	Florida	1,574,143	12.2
5	Illinois	904,446	7.9
6	New Jersey	739,861	9.6
7	Arizona	688,338	18.8
8	New Mexico	579,224	38.2
9	Colorado	424,302	12.9
10	Massachusetts	287,549	4.8
11	Pennsylvania	232,262	2
12	Washington	214,570	4.4
13	Connecticut	213,116	6.5
14	Michigan	201,596	2.2

Rank		Total	Percent of population
15	Virginia	160,288	2.6
16	Ohio	139,696	1.3
17	Maryland	125,102	2.6
18	Nevada	124,419	10.4
19	Oregon	112,707	4
20	Georgia	108,922	1.7
21	Indiana	98,788	1.8
22	Kansas	93,670	1.9
23	Wisconsin	93,194	1.9
24	Louisiana	93,044	2.2
25	Oklahoma	86,160	2.7
26	Utah	84,597	4.9
27	Hawaii	81,390	7.3
28	North Carolina	76,726	1.2
29	Missouri	61,702	1.2
30	Minnesota	53,884	1.2
31	Idaho	52,927	5.3
32	Rhode Island	45,752	4.6
33	Nebraska	36,969	2.3
34	Tennessee	32,741	0.7
35	Washington, DC	32,710	5.4
36	Iowa	32,647	1.2
37	South Carolina	30,551	0.9
38	Wyoming	25,751	5.7
39	Alabama	24,629	0.6
40	Kentucky	21,984	0.6
41	Arkansas	19,876	0.8
42	Alaska	17,803	3.2
43	Mississippi	15,931	0.6
44	Delaware	15,820	2.4
45	Montana	12,174	1.5
46	New Hampshire	11,333	1.0
47	West Virginia	8,489	0.5
48	Maine	6,829	0.6
49	South Dakota	5,252	0.8
50	North Dakota	4,665	0.7
51	Vermont	3,661	0.7

ASIAN/PACIFIC ISLANDER POPULATION

Approximately 3%—7.3 million persons—of the population identified themselves as Asian/Pacific Islanders. China, the Philippines, Japan, India, Korea, Vietnam, Samoa and Guam are the most important places of origin. In 1990 over 60% of the Asian/Pacific population lived in California, New York and Hawaii. The majority of the people in Hawaii are of Asian/Pacific extraction.

TABLE: Asian/Pacific Islander Population
DATE: 1990
SOURCE: U.S. Bureau of the Census, *1990 Census of Population and Housing*

DESCRIPTION: Asian/Pacific Islander population, and Asian/Pacific Islanders as a percentage of total state population.

Rank		Total	Percent of state population
	United States	7,273,662	2.9
1	California	2,845,659	9.6
2	New York	693,760	3.9
3	Hawaii	685,236	61.8
4	Texas	319,459	1.9
5	Illinois	285,311	2.5
6	New Jersey	272,521	3.5
7	Washington	210,958	4.3
8	Virginia	159,053	2.6
9	Florida	154,302	1.2
10	Massachusetts	143,392	2.4
11	Maryland	139,719	2.9
12	Pennsylvania	137,438	1.2
13	Michigan	104,983	1.1
14	Ohio	91,179	0.8
15	Minnesota	77,886	1.8
16	Georgia	75,781	1.2
17	Oregon	69,269	2.4
18	Colorado	59,862	1.8
19	Arizona	55,206	1.5
20	Wisconsin	53,583	1.1
21	North Carolina	52,166	0.8
22	Connecticut	50,698	1.5
23	Missouri	41,277	0.8
24	Louisiana	41,099	1
25	Nevada	38,127	3.2
26	Indiana	37,617	0.7
27	Oklahoma	33,563	1.1
28	Utah	33,371	1.9
29	Tennessee	31,839	0.7
30	Kansas	31,750	1.3
31	Iowa	25,476	0.9
32	South Carolina	22,382	0.6
33	Alabama	21,797	0.5
34	Alaska	19,728	3.6
35	Rhode Island	18,325	1.8
36	Kentucky	17,812	0.5
37	New Mexico	14,124	0.9
38	Mississippi	13,016	0.5
39	Arkansas	12,530	0.5
40	Nebraska	12,422	0.8
41	Washington, DC	11,214	1.8
42	Idaho	9,365	0.9
43	New Hampshire	9,343	0.8
44	Delaware	9,057	1.4
45	West Virginia	7,459	0.4
46	Maine	6,685	0.5
47	Montana	4,259	0.5
48	North Dakota	3,462	0.5
49	Vermont	3,215	0.6
50	South Dakota	3,123	0.4
51	Wyoming	2,806	0.6

NATIVE AMERICAN POPULATION

The Native American population, including Eskimo and Aleuts, constituted less than 1% of the total population of the United States in 1990. The bulk of the Native American population resided in the West and the upper Midwest, with smaller groups in North Carolina and Florida. The Eskimo and Aleuts resided mainly in Alaska. Native Americans exceeded 5% of the state population in Alaska, New Mexico, Oklahoma, South Dakota and Arizona.

TABLE: Native American Population
DATE: 1990
SOURCE: U.S. Bureau of the Census, *1990 Census of Population and Housing*
DESCRIPTION: American Indian, Eskimo and Aleut population and their percentage of total state population.

Rank		Total	Percent of state population
	United States	1,959,234	0.8
1	Oklahoma	252,420	8.0
2	California	242,164	0.8
3	Arizona	203,527	5.6
4	New Mexico	134,355	8.9
5	Alaska	85,698	15.6
6	Washington	81,483	1.7
7	North Carolina	80,155	1.2
8	Texas	65,877	0.4
9	New York	62,651	0.3
10	Michigan	55,638	0.6
11	South Dakota	50,575	7.3
12	Minnesota	49,909	1.1
13	Montana	47,679	6.0
14	Wisconsin	39,387	0.8
15	Oregon	38,496	1.4
16	Florida	36,335	0.3
17	Colorado	27,776	0.8
18	North Dakota	25,917	4.1
19	Utah	24,283	1.4
20	Kansas	21,965	0.9
21	Illinois	21,836	0.2
22	Ohio	20,358	0.2
23	Mississippi	19,835	0.4
24	Nevada	19,637	1.6
25	Louisiana	18,541	0.4
26	Alabama	16,506	0.4
27	Virginia	15,282	0.2
28	New Jersey	14,970	0.2
29	Pennsylvania	14,733	0.1
30	Idaho	13,780	1.4
31	Georgia	13,348	0.2
32	Maryland	12,972	0.3
33	Arkansas	12,773	0.5
34	Indiana	12,720	0.2

Rank		Total	Percent of state population
35	Nebraska	12,410	0.8
36	Massachusetts	12,241	0.2
37	Tennessee	10,039	0.2
38	Wyoming	9,479	2.1
39	Mississippi	8,525	0.3
40	South Carolina	8,246	0.2
41	Iowa	7,349	0.3
42	Connecticut	6,654	0.2
43	Maine	5,998	0.5
44	Kentucky	5,769	0.2
45	Hawaii	5,099	0.5
46	Rhode Island	4,071	0.4
47	West Virginia	2,458	0.1
48	New Hampshire	2,134	0.2
49	Delaware	2,019	0.3
50	Vermont	1,696	0.3
51	Washington, DC	1,466	0.2

WHITE POPULATION

In 1990, 80.3% of the population identified themselves as white compared with 83.2% in 1980. Only five states had a white population of less than 70%: Mississippi, Louisiana, South Carolina, California and Hawaii. In Hawaii, whites constituted only about one-third of the population.

TABLE: White Population
DATE: 1990
SOURCE: U.S. Bureau of the Census, *1990 Census of Population and Housing*
DESCRIPTION: White population and precentage of total state population.

Rank		Total	Percent of state population
	United States	199,868,070	80.3
1	California	20,524,327	69.0
2	New York	13,385,255	74.4
3	Texas	12,774,762	75.2
4	Florida	10,749,285	83.1
5	Pennsylvania	10,520,201	88.5
6	Ohio	9,521,756	87.8
7	Illinois	8,952,978	78.3

Rank		Total	Percent of state population
8	Michigan	7,756,086	83.4
9	New Jersey	6,130,465	79.3
10	Massachusetts	5,405,374	89.8
11	Indiana	5,020,700	90.6
12	North Carolina	5,008,491	75.6
13	Virginia	4,791,739	77.4
14	Georgia	4,600,148	71.0
15	Wisconsin	4,512,523	92.2
16	Missouri	4,486,228	87.7
17	Washington	4,308,937	88.5
18	Minnesota	4,130,395	94.4
19	Tennessee	4,048,068	83.0
20	Maryland	3,393,964	71.0
21	Kentucky	3,391,832	92.0
22	Alabama	2,975,797	73.6
23	Arizona	2,963,186	80.8
24	Colorado	2,905,474	88.2
25	Connecticut	2,859,353	87.0
26	Louisiana	2,839,138	67.3
27	Iowa	2,683,090	96.6
28	Oregon	2,636,787	92.8
29	Oklahoma	2,583,512	82.1
30	South Carolina	2,406,974	69.0
31	Kansas	2,231,986	90.1
32	Arkansas	1,944,744	82.7
33	West Virginia	1,725,523	96.2
34	Mississippi	1,633,461	63.5
35	Utah	1,615,845	93.8
36	Nebraska	1,480,558	93.8
37	Maine	1,208,360	98.4
38	New Mexico	1,146,028	75.6
39	New Hampshire	1,087,433	98.0
40	Nevada	1,012,695	84.3
41	Idaho	950,451	94.4
42	Rhode Island	917,375	91.4
43	Montana	741,111	92.7
44	South Dakota	637,515	91.6
45	North Dakota	604,142	94.6
46	Vermont	555,088	98.6
47	Delaware	535,094	80.3
48	Wyoming	427,061	94.2
49	Alaska	415,492	75.5
50	Hawaii	369,616	33.4
51	Washington, DC	179,667	29.6

RACIAL COMPOSITION OF THE 50 LARGEST METROPOLITAN AREAS

This table shows the percentage of minority groups residing in the nation's major metropolitan areas. The black population was concentrated most heavily in the southern, midwestern and eastern metropolitan areas, such as Memphis, New Orleans, Detroit, Chicago, Philadelphia and New York. The Hispanic population represented about one-third of Los Angeles's and Miami's population.

TABLE: Racial Composition of the 50 Largest Metropolitan Areas

DATE: 1990
SOURCE: U.S. Bureau of the Census, *1990 Census of Population and Housing*
DESCRIPTION: Percent of populations defined by race and inhabitants of Hispanic origin for the 50 largest metropolitian areas.

Metropolitan areas are shown in rank order of total population of consolidated metropolitan statistical areas (CMSAs) and metropolitan statistical areas (MSAs).

Rank	Metropolitan area	Total population	Percent black	Percent American Indian, Eskimo, Aleut	Percent Asian and Pacific Islander	Percent Hispanic origin*
1	New York CMSA	19,549,649	17.7	0.2	4.6	14.6
2	Los Angeles CMSA	14,531,529	8.5	0.6	9.2	32.9
3	Chicago CMSA	8,239,820	19.0	0.2	3.1	10.9
4	Washington-Baltimore CMSA	6,727,050	25.2	0.3	3.7	3.9
5	San Francisco CMSA	6,253,311	8.6	0.7	14.8	15.5
6	Philadelphia CMSA	5,892,937	18.4	0.2	2.0	3.8
7	Boston CSMA	5,455,403	4.8	0.2	2.5	4.4
8	Detroit CMSA	5,187,171	20.5	0.4	1.4	2.0
9	Dallas CMSA	4,037,282	14.0	0.5	2.4	13.0
10	Houston CMSA	3,731,131	17.9	0.3	3.5	20.7
11	Miami CMSA	3,192,582	18.5	0.2	1.4	33.3
12	Seattle CMSA	2,970,328	4.5	1.3	6.1	3.0
13	Atlanta MSA	2,959,950	25.2	0.2	1.8	2.0
14	Cleveland CMSA	2,859,644	15.6	0.2	1.0	1.9
15	Minneapolis-St. Paul MSA	2,538,834	3.5	1.0	2.6	1.5
16	San Diego MSA	2,498,016	6.4	0.8	7.9	20.4
17	St. Louis MSA	2,492,525	17.0	0.2	1.0	1.1
18	Pittsburgh MSA	2,394,811	7.5	0.1	0.7	0.6
19	Phoenix MSA	2,238,480	3.5	2.2	1.6	17.0
20	Tampa MSA	2,067,959	9.0	0.3	1.1	6.7
21	Denver CMSA	1,980,140	5.0	0.7	2.2	12.8
22	Cincinnati CMSA	1,817,571	11.2	0.1	0.8	0.5
23	Portland-Salem CMSA	1,793,476	2.5	1.0	3.2	4.0
24	Milwaukee CMSA	1,607,183	13.3	0.5	1.2	3.8
25	Kansas City MSA	1,582,875	12.7	0.5	1.1	2.9
26	Sacramento CMSA	1,481,102	6.9	1.1	7.7	11.6
27	Norfolk MSA	1,443,244	28.3	0.3	2.4	2.3
28	Indianapolis MSA	1,380,491	13.2	0.2	0.8	0.9
29	Columbus MSA	1,345,450	12.1	0.2	1.6	0.8
30	San Antonio MSA	1,324,749	6.7	0.4	1.2	47.4
31	New Orleans MSA	1,285,270	34.8	0.3	1.7	4.2
32	Orlando MSA	1,224,852	12.0	0.3	1.7	8.2
33	Buffalo MSA	1,189,288	10.3	0.6	0.9	2.0
34	Charlotte MSA	1,162,093	19.9	0.4	1.0	0.9
35	Hartford, CT MSA	1,157,585	8.3	0.2	1.5	6.9
36	Providence MSA	1,134,350	3.3	0.3	1.8	4.2
37	Salt Lake City MSA	1,072,227	1.0	0.8	2.4	5.8
38	Rochester MSA	1,062,470	8.9	0.3	1.3	3.0
39	Greensboro MSA	1,050,304	19.3	0.3	0.7	0.7
40	Memphis MSA	1,007,306	40.7	0.2	0.8	0.8
41	Nashville MSA	985,026	15.5	0.2	1.0	0.8
42	Oklahoma City MSA	958,839	10.5	4.8	1.9	3.6
43	Dayton MSA	951,270	13.3	0.2	1.0	0.8
44	Louisville MSA	948,829	12.9	0.2	0.6	0.6
45	Grand Rapids MSA	937,891	6.9	0.6	0.9	3.1

Rank	Metropolitan area	Total population	Percent black	Percent American Indian, Eskimo, Aleut	Percent Asian and Pacific Islander	Percent Hispanic origin*
46	Jacksonville MSA	906,727	20.0	0.3	1.7	2.5
47	Richmond MSA	865,640	29.2	0.3	1.4	1.1
48	West Palm Beach MSA	863,518	12.5	0.1	1.0	7.7
49	Albany MSA	861,424	4.6	0.2	1.2	1.7
50	Raleigh MSA	855,545	24.2	0.3	1.6	1.3

*Persons of Hispanic origin may be of any race.

IMMIGRATION AND FOREIGN-BORN POPULATIONS

This section presents data on the immigrant and foreign-born populations in the United States. The principal source of immigration data is the *Statistical Yearbook* of the Immigration and Naturalization Service (INS). Data from the U.S. Bureau of the Census were also used.

Immigrants are aliens admitted for legal permanent residence into the United States. The procedure for admission differs depending on whether the alien resides inside or outside the United States at the time of application for permanent residence. Eligible aliens residing in the United States are allowed to change their status from temporary to permanent through the INS. The immigrant category includes persons who may have entered the United States as nonimmigrants or refugees, but who subsequently qualified for permanent resident status. The total number of immigrants at any one time is a function of new immigration from abroad and the rate at which immigrants obtain citizenship. United States immigration law gives preferential immigration status to aliens who are related to U.S. citizens or legal permanent residents, aliens with needed job skills, or aliens who qualify as refugees.

The data presented here do not include illegal immigrants living in the United States.

The first table shows the total number of immigrants admitted to the United States for legal permanent residence in 1992. The tables that follow present the leading countries of origin of 1992 immigrants, the foreign-born population of the United States and the three leading ancestry groups in each state.

IMMIGRANTS

Approximately one million immigrants were admitted to the United States in 1992. Seventy-five percent resided in just six states: California, New York, Texas, Florida, New Jersey and Illinois. The Plains states, the southern states (with the exception of Florida) and the midwestern states (with the exception of Illinois) recorded virtually no immigrants.

California ranked first in the number of new immigrants from seven out of the nine leading countries of origin: Mexico, Vietnam, Philippines, (the former) Soviet Union, and China.

TABLE: Immigrants
DATE: 1992
SOURCE: U.S. Immigration and Naturalization Service, *Statistical Yearbook*, annual
DESCRIPTION: Total number of immigrants admitted to the United States in 1992 and percent of total.

Rank		Total immigrants	Percent of total
	United States	962,642	
1	California	336,663	35.0
2	New York	149,399	16.0
3	Texas	75,533	8.0
4	Florida	61,127	6.0
5	New Jersey	48,314	5.0
6	Illinois	43,532	5.0
7	Massachusetts	22,231	2.0
8	Virginia	17,739	2.0
9	Pennsylvania	16,213	2.0
10	Washington	15,861	2.0
11	Arizona	15,792	2.0
12	Maryland	15,408	2.0
13	Michigan	14,268	1.0
14	Georgia	11,243	1.0
15	Connecticut	10,345	1.0
16	Ohio	10,194	1.0
17	Hawaii	8,199	1.0
18	Minnesota	6,851	1.0
19	Colorado	6,553	1.0
20	North Carolina	6,425	1.0
21	Oregon	6,275	1.0
22	Nevada	5,086	1.0
23	Washington, DC	4,275	0.4
24	Wisconsin	4,261	0.4
25	Missouri	4,250	0.4
26	Louisiana	4,230	0.4
27	New Mexico	3,907	0.4
28	Oklahoma	3,147	0.3

Rank		Total immigrants	Percent of total
29	Indiana	3,115	0.3
30	Tennessee	2,995	0.3
31	Kansas	2,924	0.3
32	Rhode Island	2,920	0.3
33	Utah	2,744	0.3
34	Iowa	2,228	0.2
35	Kentucky	2,119	0.2
36	South Carolina	2,118	0.2
37	Alabama	2,109	0.2
38	Nebraska	1,486	0.2
39	New Hampshire	1,250	0.1
40	Idaho	1,186	0.1
41	Alaska	1,165	0.1
42	Arkansas	1,039	0.1
43	Delaware	1,034	0.1
44	Maine	847	0.1
45	Mississippi	842	0.1
46	West Virginia	723	0.1
47	Vermont	668	0.1
48	South Dakota	522	0.1
49	North Dakota	513	0.1
50	Montana	493	0.1
51	Wyoming	281	Less than 0.1

Mexican Immigrants

Mexico accounted for 22% of all the nation's immigrants in 1992. Ninety percent of them resided in California, Texas, Arizona and Illinois. Mexican emigrés accounted for over half of all 1992 emigrés to Arizona, New Mexico and Texas. Interestingly, Mexican immigrants accounted for less than 1% of Massachusetts's immigrant population, the lowest in the nation, although nationwide, Massachusetts ranked seventh in the number of immigrants.

TABLE: Mexican Immigrants
DATE: 1992
SOURCE: U.S. Immigration and Naturalization Service, *Statistical Yearbook*, annual
DESCRIPTION: Total number of immigrants admitted to the United States from Mexico and percentage of state's total immigrants from Mexico.

Rank		Total	Percent
	United States	213,381	22
1	California	132,138	39
2	Texas	39,301	52
3	Arizona	10,779	68
4	Illinois	9,861	23
5	New Mexico	2,543	65
6	Florida	2,389	4
7	Nevada	2,128	42
8	New York	1,809	1
9	Colorado	1,447	22

Rank		Total	Percent
10	Georgia	1,343	12
11	Washington	1,239	8
12	Oregon	846	13
13	North Carolina	583	9
14	Oklahoma	537	17
15	New Jersey	537	1
16	Kansas	452	15
17	Utah	425	15
18	Michigan	423	3
19	Wisconsin	402	9
20	Indiana	385	12
21	Idaho	380	32
22	Virginia	334	2
23	Nebraska	316	21
24	Pennsylvania	259	2
25	Maryland	237	2
26	Iowa	234	11
27	Minnesota	195	3
28	Ohio	187	2
29	Missouri	171	4
30	Arkansas	168	16
31	Tennessee	155	5
32	South Carolina	141	7
33	Connecticut	121	1
34	Louisiana	118	3
35	Massachusetts	101	0.5
36	Hawaii	99	1
37	Alabama	94	4
38	Delaware	82	8
39	Kentucky	75	4
40	Alaska	64	5
41	Wyoming	61	22
42	Mississippi	46	5
43	Montana	42	9
44	Washington, DC	41	1
45	West Virginia	18	2
46	Rhode Island	17	1
47	Maine	15	2
48	New Hampshire	15	1
49	South Dakota	13	2
50	North Dakota	11	2
51	Vermont	4	1

Vietnamese Immigrants

Vietnam accounted for 8% of all immigrants and ranked second in number of emigrés to the United States in 1992. Sixty-one percent of Vietnamese immigrants resided in California, Texas, Washington, New York and Virginia in 1992. Although their numbers are small, Vietnamese immigrants constitute approximately one-third of all immigrants residing in Iowa, Louisiana, Nebraska, Vermont and North Dakota.

TABLE: Vietnamese Immigrants
DATE: 1992
SOURCE: U.S. Immigration and Naturalization Service, *Statistical Yearbook*, annual
DESCRIPTION: Total number of immigrants admitted to the United States from Vietnam and percentage of state's total immigrants from Vietnam.

Rank		Total	Percent
	United States	77,663	8
1	California	33,477	10
2	Texas	6,669	9
3	Washington	3,179	20
4	New York	2,810	2
5	Virginia	2,339	13
6	Pennsylvania	2,196	14
7	Massachusetts	2,102	9
8	Florida	1,844	3
9	Georgia	1,796	16
10	Louisiana	1,321	31
11	Oregon	1,216	19
12	Maryland	1,194	8
13	Minnesota	1,189	17
14	New Jersey	1,180	2
15	Illinois	1,174	3
16	Missouri	1,057	25
17	North Carolina	929	14
18	Colorado	909	14
19	Michigan	902	6
20	Arizona	892	6
21	Washington, DC	751	18
22	Iowa	738	33
23	Kansas	733	25
24	Oklahoma	726	23
25	Hawaii	692	8
26	Tennessee	628	21
27	Ohio	554	5
28	Connecticut	515	5
29	Utah	491	18
30	Nebraska	466	31
31	Kentucky	397	19
32	Alabama	347	16
33	New Mexico	299	8
34	Mississippi	192	23
35	Wisconsin	188	4
36	Vermont	186	28
37	Nevada	172	3
38	Indiana	161	5
39	Arkansas	157	15
40	North Dakota	142	28
41	South Carolina	110	5
42	Maine	103	12
43	Alaska	100	9
44	New Hampshire	97	8
45	South Dakota	83	16
46	Delaware	69	7
47	Rhode Island	65	2
48	Idaho	55	5

Rank		Total	Percent
49	West Virginia	54	7
50	Montana	15	3
51	Wyoming	2	1

PHILIPPINE IMMIGRANTS

The Philippines accounted for 6% of total immigrants in 1992 and was the third leading country of origin. Over half of all Philippine immigrants, from 1992, resided in either New York or California. While California ranked first in the number of immigrants from the Philippines, Filipinos accounted for only 6% of the state's total 1992 immigrants. Philippine immigration exceeded 13% in only two states: Hawaii and Alaska.

TABLE: Philippine Immigrants
DATE: 1992
SOURCE: U.S. Immigration and Naturalization Service, *Statistical Yearbook*, annual
DESCRIPTION: Total number of immigrants admitted to the United States from the Philippines and percentage of state's total immigrants from the Philippines.

Rank		Total	Percent
	United States	58,926	6
1	California	26,846	8
2	New York	5,484	4
3	New Jersey	4,077	8
4	Hawaii	4,001	49
5	Illinois	2,467	6
6	Texas	2,117	3
7	Florida	1,799	3
8	Washington	1,624	10
9	Virginia	1,441	8
10	Maryland	892	6
11	Nevada	686	13
12	Michigan	555	4
13	Pennsylvania	510	3
14	Ohio	475	5
15	Arizona	420	3
16	Massachusetts	417	2
17	Connecticut	407	4
18	Georgia	381	3
19	Alaska	368	32
20	Oregon	307	5
21	North Carolina	279	4
22	Colorado	261	4
23	Missouri	257	6
24	Minnesota	218	3
25	South Carolina	209	10
26	Louisiana	194	5
27	Indiana	189	6
28	Washington, DC	171	4

Rank		Total	Percent
29	Wisconsin	165	4
30	Tennessee	154	5
31	Oklahoma	150	5
32	Kentucky	124	6
33	New Mexico	121	3
34	Iowa	112	5
35	Kansas	106	4
36	Utah	103	4
37	Alabama	99	5
38	Mississippi	89	11
39	Nebraska	82	6
40	Rhode Island	76	3
41	Maine	65	8
42	Arkansas	64	6
43	Idaho	57	5
44	Delaware	51	5
45	Montana	50	10
46	West Virginia	49	7
47	North Dakota	41	8
48	New Hampshire	38	3
49	South Dakota	37	7
50	Wyoming	27	10
51	Vermont	14	2

FORMER SOVIET UNION IMMIGRANTS

Ranking sixth in number of immigrants in 1992, the former Soviet Union accounted for 5% of total immigration. Fifty-four percent of the Soviet emigrés resided in California and New York. Another 16% settled in either Illinois, Pennsylvania or Washington state. With the exception of the Great Lakes region, virtually no Soviet emigrés settled in areas other than the East and West coasts.

TABLE: Former Soviet Union Immigrants
DATE: 1992
SOURCE: U.S. Immigration and Naturalization Service, *Statistical Yearbook*, annual
DESCRIPTION: Total number of immigrants admitted from the former Soviet Union and the percentage of state's total immigrants.

Rank		Total	Percent
	United States	43,606	5
1	California	12,655	4
2	New York	11,392	8
3	Illinois	2,379	5
4	Pennsylvania	2,350	14
5	Washington	2,076	13
6	Ohio	1,771	17
7	Massachusetts	1,637	7
8	Maryland	1,401	9
9	New Jersey	1,273	3

Rank		Total	Percent
10	Oregon	932	15
11	Connecticut	618	6
12	Texas	480	1
13	Michigan	477	3
14	Florida	447	1
15	Minnesota	436	6
16	Colorado	425	6
17	Georgia	386	3
18	Virginia	316	2
19	Rhode Island	224	8
20	Missouri	206	5
21	Kentucky	166	8
22	Arizona	141	1
23	Tennessee	137	5
24	Kansas	126	4
25	Indiana	121	4
26	North Carolina	114	2
27	Utah	105	4
28	Wisconsin	103	2
29	South Dakota	80	15
30	Maine	71	8
31	Idaho	53	4
32	Montana	50	10
33	Iowa	50	2
34	Oklahoma	42	1
35	Alaska	38	3
36	Alabama	38	2
37	New Hampshire	36	3
38	Louisiana	35	1
39	New Mexico	31	1
40	Nebraska	30	2
41	South Carolina	29	1
42	Washington, DC	28	1
43	Nevada	26	1
44	Vermont	20	3
45	Delaware	19	2
46	Hawaii	14	0.2
47	Mississippi	7	1
48	North Dakota	6	1
49	Wyoming	4	1
50	West Virginia	3	0.4
51	Arkansas	2	0.2

DOMINICAN REPUBLIC IMMIGRANTS

Emigration from the Dominican Republic accounted for 4% of total immigration to the United States in 1992. Seventy percent of Dominican immigrants in 1992 settled in New York state, primarily in New York City. Dominican immigrants residing in New Jersey, Florida and Massachusetts accounted for virtually the rest of this group. California, a leader in most other immigrant groups, ranked tenth in Dominican immigrants. Dominicans made up less than 1% percent of the state's total immigrant population in 1992.

TABLE: Dominican Republic Immigrants
DATE: 1992
SOURCE: U.S. Immigration and Naturalization Service, *Statistical Yearbook*, annual
DESCRIPTION: Total number of immigrants admitted to the United States from the Dominican Republic and the percentage of the state's total immigrants.

Rank		Total	Percent
	United States total	36,576	4
1	New York	25,631	17.0
2	New Jersey	4,761	10.0
3	Florida	2,077	3.0
4	Massachusetts	2,076	9.0
5	Rhode Island	528	18.0
6	Connecticut	247	2.0
7	Pennsylvania	200	1.0
8	Maryland	164	1.0
9	Washington, DC	113	3.0
10	California	108	0.0
11	Texas	107	0.1
12	Illinois	91	0.2
13	Virginia	68	0.4
14	New Hampshire	52	4.2
15	Michigan	51	0.4
16	Georgia	44	0.4
17	Ohio	36	0.4
18	Alaska	30	3.0
19	Louisiana	29	1.0
20	North Carolina	27	0.4
21	Arizona	16	0.1
22	Delaware	14	1.0
23	Missouri	11	0.3
24	South Carolina	10	0.5
25	Minnesota	10	0.1
26	Colorado	9	0.1
27	Washington	9	0.1
28	Tennessee	7	0.2
29	Nevada	7	0.1
30	Oregon	7	0.1
31	Indiana	6	0.2
32	Oklahoma	6	0.2
33	Utah	4	0.1
34	Vermont	3	0.4
35	West Virginia	3	0.4
36	Kansas	3	0.1
37	North Dakota	2	0.4
38	Maine	2	0.2
39	Iowa	2	0.1
40	Wisconsin	2	0.0
41	Mississippi	1	0.1
42	Idaho	1	0.1
43	Alabama	1	0.0
44	Arkansas	0	0.0
45	Hawaii	0	0.0
46	Kentucky	0	0.0
47	Montana	0	0.0
48	Nebraska	0	0.0

Rank		Total	Percent
49	New Mexico	0	0.0
50	South Dakota	0	0.0
51	Wyoming	0	0.0

CHINESE IMMIGRANTS

Immigrants from mainland China constituted 4% of total immigration to the United States in 1992. The majority of immigrants have settled in California and New York, followed by Texas, Massachusetts, New Jersey and Illinois. Chinese immigration has been comparatively even across the states.

TABLE: Chinese Immigrants
DATE: 1992
SOURCE: U.S. Immigration and Naturalization Service, *Statistical Yearbook*, annual
DESCRIPTION: Total number of immigrants admitted to the United States from Mainland China and the percentage of the state's total immigrants.

Rank		Total	Percent
	United States	38,759	4
1	California	11,684	3
2	New York	10,986	7
3	Texas	1,818	2
4	Massachusetts	1,440	6
5	New Jersey	1,376	3
6	Illinois	1,220	3
7	Pennsylvania	1,003	6
8	Maryland	736	5
9	Virginia	730	4
10	Michigan	618	4
11	Florida	587	1
12	Washington	587	4
13	Hawaii	528	6
14	Ohio	484	5
15	Georgia	416	4
16	Connecticut	390	4
17	Oregon	355	6
18	Colorado	302	5
19	Arizona	290	2
20	Minnesota	282	4
21	Missouri	241	6
22	North Carolina	228	4
23	Wisconsin	199	5
24	Utah	197	7
25	Washington, DC	192	4
26	Indiana	175	6
27	Louisiana	161	4
28	Nevada	147	3
29	Oklahoma	127	4
30	Kansas	112	4

Rank		Total	Percent
31	New Mexico	102	3
32	Alabama	99	5
33	Tennessee	94	3
34	Nebraska	80	5
35	South Carolina	80	4
36	Kentucky	78	4
37	Rhode Island	69	2
38	Delaware	63	6
39	West Virginia	59	8
40	Idaho	58	5
41	Iowa	54	2
42	New Hampshire	54	4
43	Maine	48	6
44	Mississippi	42	5
45	North Dakota	31	6
46	Arkansas	30	3
47	Wyoming	29	10
48	Montana	27	5
49	Vermont	25	4
50	Alaska	13	1
51	South Dakota	13	2

EL SALVADORAN IMMIGRANTS

Ranking eighth in immigration, El Salvador made up 3% of total immigration to the United States in 1992. Ninety percent of El Salvadoran immigration occurred in five states and the District of Columbia. California ranked first, with the vast majority of immigrants, followed by Texas, New York, Virginia, Maryland and the District of Columbia. With the exception of Nevada, in the remaining 44 states El Salvadorans constituted 1% or less of the 1992 immigrant populations. In the District of Columbia El Salvadorans accounted for 15% of the 1992 immigrant population. In no state did the El Salvadoran population of 1992 immigrants exceed 7%.

TABLE: El Salvadoran Immigrants
DATE: 1992
SOURCE: U.S. Immigration and Naturalization Service, *Statistical Yearbook*, annual
DESCRIPTION: Total number of immigrants admitted to the United States from El Salvador and percentage of state's total immigrants.

Rank		Total	Percent
	United States	26,166	3.0
1	California	15,051	4.0
2	Texas	3,586	5.0
3	New York	2,014	1.0
4	Virginia	1,300	7.0
5	Maryland	947	6.0

Rank		Total	Percent
6	Washington, DC	640	15.0
7	New Jersey	635	1.0
8	Florida	461	1.0
9	Illinois	263	1.0
10	Massachusetts	248	1.0
11	Nevada	190	4.0
12	Arizona	123	1.0
13	Georgia	121	1.0
14	Connecticut	70	1.0
15	Washington	56	0.4
16	Pennsylvania	48	0.3
17	North Carolina	45	1.0
18	Oregon	39	1.0
19	Rhode Island	32	1.0
20	Colorado	30	0.5
21	Utah	29	1.0
22	Louisiana	27	1.0
23	Wisconsin	21	0.5
24	Tennessee	17	1.0
25	Minnesota	16	0.2
26	Arkansas	15	1.0
27	Michigan	15	0.1
28	Alabama	12	1.0
29	New Mexico	12	0.3
30	Missouri	12	0.3
31	Alaska	10	1.0
32	Iowa	10	0.4
33	Ohio	10	0.1
34	South Carolina	9	0.4
35	Kansas	9	0.3
36	Oklahoma	9	0.3
37	Idaho	7	1.0
38	Nebraska	5	0.3
39	Indiana	5	0.2
40	Hawaii	5	0.1
41	West Virginia	3	0.4
42	Kentucky	3	0.1
43	Vermont	2	0.3
44	Delaware	2	0.2
45	Montana	1	0.2
46	New Hampshire	1	0.1
47	Maine	0	0.0
48	Mississippi	0	0.0
49	North Dakota	0	0.0
50	South Dakota	0	0.0
51	Wyoming	0	0.0

POLISH IMMIGRANTS

Polish immigrants accounted for 4% of total immigration to the United States in 1992. Five states accounted for 85% of Polish immigrants: Illinois, New York, New Jersey, Connecticut and California. Poles constituted 22% of Illinois's immigrant population exceeded only by Mexicans, who made up 23% of the state's 1992 immigrants.

TABLE: Polish Immigrants

DATE: 1992

SOURCE: U.S. Immigration and Naturalization Service, *Statistical Yearbook*, annual

DESCRIPTION: Total number of immigrants admitted to the United States from Poland and percentage of state's total immigrants.

Rank		Total	Percent
	United States	25,498	3.0
1	Illinois	9,756	22.0
2	New York	5,565	4.0
3	New Jersey	4,339	9.0
4	Connecticut	1,180	11.0
5	California	767	0.2
6	Massachusetts	543	2.0
7	Pennsylvania	517	3.0
8	Michigan	454	3.0
9	Florida	348	1.0
10	Washington	260	2.0
11	Texas	214	0.3
12	Ohio	208	1.0
13	Maryland	157	1.0
14	Wisconsin	133	3.0
15	Virginia	112	1.0
16	Indiana	101	3.0
17	Colorado	92	1.0
18	Rhode Island	78	3.0
19	North Carolina	73	1.0
20	Arizona	61	0.4
21	Georgia	57	1.0
22	Minnesota	57	1.0
23	Alaska	45	4.0
24	Missouri	44	1.0
25	Utah	29	1.0
26	Tennessee	28	1.0
27	South Carolina	27	1.0
28	Nebraska	23	2.0
29	Washington, DC	22	1.0
30	Oregon	22	0.4
31	Nevada	21	0.4
32	New Hampshire	19	2.0
33	Louisiana	17	0.4
34	Iowa	15	1.0
35	Idaho	14	1.0
36	Kansas	14	0.5
37	Oklahoma	12	0.4
38	Maine	11	1.0
39	Alabama	10	0.5
40	New Mexico	10	0.3
41	Delaware	8	1.0
42	Kentucky	8	0.4
43	Wyoming	7	2.0
44	West Virginia	6	1.0
45	Vermont	5	1.0
46	Hawaii	4	0.0
47	Montana	2	0.4
48	Arkansas	1	0.1

Rank		Total	Percent
49	North Dakota	1	0.2
50	South Dakota	1	0.2
51	Mississippi	0	0.0

FOREIGN-BORN POPULATIONS

The native population is defined by the U.S. Census Bureau as those born in the United States, Puerto Rico or an outlying area of the United States. It also includes those born at sea or in a foreign country who have at least one American parent. All others are classified as "foreign-born." Foreign-born populations exceeded 10% in only five states and were 5% or less in approximately two-thirds of the states.

Comparing data in this table with that in "Immigrants" on page 133 reveals that the ranking of states by immigrant population does not directly parallel the ranking of foreign-born populations as a percentage of the whole population. However, the ranking of foreign-born populations entering the country between 1980 and 1990 is more closely aligned with immigrant populations recorded for 1992.

TABLE: Foreign-Born Populations

DATE: 1990

SOURCE: U.S. Bureau of the Census, *1990 Census of Population and Housing*

DESCRIPTION: Foreign-born populations. Table ranked by percent of total population.

Rank		Number (thousands)	Percent of total population	Number entering between 1980–1990 (thousands)
	United States	19,767	7.9	8,664
1	California	6,459	21.7	3,256
2	New York	2,852	15.9	1,190
3	Hawaii	163	14.7	67
4	Florida	1,663	12.9	660
5	New Jersey	967	12.5	385
6	Washington, DC	59	9.7	34
7	Massachusetts	574	9.5	223
8	Rhode Island	95	9.5	35
9	Texas	1,524	9.0	718
10	Nevada	105	8.7	48
11	Connecticut	279	8.5	90
12	Illinois	952	8.3	371
13	Arizona	278	7.6	117
14	Washington	322	6.6	129
15	Maryland	313	6.6	148
16	New Mexico	81	5.3	31
17	Virginia	312	5.0	159
18	Oregon	139	4.9	61

Rank		Number (thousands)	Percent of total population	Number entering between 1980–1990 (thousands)
19	Alaska	25	4.5	11
20	Colorado	142	4.3	57
21	Michigan	355	3.8	94
22	New Hampshire	41	3.7	10
23	Utah	59	3.4	26
24	Delaware	22	3.3	7
25	Vermont	18	3.1	3
26	Pennsylvania	369	3.1	116
27	Maine	36	3.0	7
28	Idaho	29	2.9	13
29	Georgia	173	2.7	90
30	Minnesota	113	2.6	51
31	Kansas	63	2.5	31
32	Wisconsin	122	2.5	41
33	Ohio	260	2.4	71
34	Oklahoma	65	2.1	30
35	Louisiana	87	2.1	35

Rank		Number (thousands)	Percent of total population	Number entering between 1980–1990 (thousands)
36	Nebraska	28	1.8	10
37	North Carolina	115	1.7	52
38	Montana	14	1.7	3
39	Indiana	94	1.7	31
40	Wyoming	8	1.7	2
41	Missouri	84	1.6	30
42	Iowa	43	1.6	19
43	North Dakota	9	1.5	3
44	South Carolina	50	1.4	18
45	Tennessee	59	1.2	26
46	South Dakota	8	1.1	2
47	Alabama	44	1.1	18
48	Arkansas	25	1.1	10
49	Kentucky	34	0.9	14
50	West Virginia	16	0.9	4
51	Mississippi	20	0.8	8

THREE LEADING ANCESTRY GROUPS

This table shows by state the three leading ethnic or racial ancestry groups identified by responses to the U.S. Census Bureau Survey. The states are ranked by the number of Americans claiming the largest ancestry group. Nationally, German (22%), Irish (15%) and English (13%) were the three leading ancestry groups.

TABLE: Three Leading Ancestry Groups
DATE: 1990
SOURCE: U.S. Bureau of the Census, *1990 Census of Population*
DESCRIPTION: Three leading ancestry groups ranked by leading ancestry group.

Rank		Leading ancestry group		Second ancestry group		Third ancestry group	
		Group	Number (thousands)	Group	Number (thousands)	Group	Number (thousands)
	United States	German	57,947	Irish	38,736	English	32,652
1	California	Mexican	5,322	German	4,935	English	3,646
2	Pennsylvania	German	4,315	Irish	2,256	Italian	1,373
3	Ohio	German	4,068	Irish	1,896	English	1,449
4	Texas	Mexican	3,403	German	2,950	Irish	2,369
5	Illinois	German	3,326	Irish	1,861	Afro-American	1,426
6	New York	German	2,899	Italian	2,838	Irish	2,800
7	Michigan	German	2,666	Irish	1,320	English	1,315
8	Wisconsin	German	2,631	Irish	612	Polish	506
9	Florida	German	2,410	Irish	1,899	English	1,846
10	Indiana	German	2,085	Irish	965	English	767
11	Minnesota	German	2,021	Norwegian	757	Irish	574
12	Missouri	German	1,843	Irish	1,038	English	743
13	Massachusetts	Irish	1,571	English	921	Italian	844
14	New Jersey	Italian	1,457	Irish	1,415	German	1,408
15	Georgia	Afro-American	1,421	Irish	971	English	890
16	Iowa	German	1,395	Irish	527	English	389
17	Washington	German	1,390	English	897	Irish	768
18	North Carolina	Afro-American	1,228	German	1,111	English	987
19	Maryland	German	1,218	Afro-American	966	Irish	769
20	Virginia	German	1,186	English	1,051	Afro-American	970
21	Louisiana	Afro-American	1,097	French	550	Irish	518

Rank		Leading ancestry group		Second ancestry group		Third ancestry group	
		Group	Number (thousands)	Group	Number (thousands)	Group	Number (thousands)
22	Colorado	German	1,064	English	582	Irish	538
23	Kansas	German	968	Irish	436	English	406
24	Oregon	German	879	English	575	Irish	467
25	Arizona	German	878	English	586	Irish	530
26	Tennessee	Irish	875	German	724	English	692
27	South Carolina	Afro-American	870	German	500	Irish	486
28	Alabama	Afro-American	839	American	687	Irish	617
29	Kentucky	German	798	Irish	696	American	586
30	Nebraska	German	795	Irish	272	English	209
31	Mississippi	Afro-American	775	Irish	393	American	317
32	Utah	English	750	German	299	Danish	163
33	Oklahoma	German	714	Irish	642	American Indian	469
34	Connecticut	Italian	628	Irish	614	English	463
35	West Virginia	German	469	Irish	348	English	270
36	Arkansas	Irish	464	German	400	Afro-American	307
37	Maine	English	372	French	224	Irish	217
38	South Dakota	German	355	Norwegian	106	Irish	88
39	North Dakota	German	325	Norwegian	189	Irish	54
40	Washington, DC	Afro-American	315	German	39	Irish	34
41	Idaho	English	291	German	279	Irish	142
42	Montana	German	285	Irish	139	English	137
43	Nevada	German	280	English	207	Irish	200
44	New Hampshire	English	266	Irish	232	French	205
45	Hawaii	Japanese	262	Filipino	176	Hawaiian	157
46	New Mexico	German	234	Mexican	216	Spanish	191
47	Rhode Island	Irish	214	Italian	199	English	161
48	Wyoming	German	158	English	101	Irish	73
49	Vermont	English	147	French	133	Irish	101
50	Delaware	Irish	139	German	138	English	123
51	Alaska	German	127	English	77	Irish	74

FAMILY

This section presents data on marriage, divorce, families, households, and birth. The primary sources are the National Center for Health Statistics (NCHS) and the U.S. Bureau of the Census.

The registration of vital events such as marriage, divorce and birth is primarily a state and local function. The civil laws of every state provide for a birth (and death) registration system. The birth-and-death registration system began in 1915 in 10 states and the District of Columbia, and grew to include the entire United States.

Marriage and divorce statistics were first compiled in 1887–88. Currently 42 states and the District of Columbia report statistics on marriage to the National Office of Vital Statistics. Thirty-one states report statistics on divorce to that office as well. Total figures for the states reporting to the National Office of Vital Statistics and for the nonreporting states are gathered by collecting already summarized data on marriages and divorces reported by state offices of vital statistics and by county offices of registration. A married couple, as defined here by the Census Bureau, means a husband and wife living together in the same household with or without children.

MARRIAGES

Marriages nationwide declined over the 12-year period covered. In 1992 the matrimonial rate was 9.3 per 1,000, down from 10.6 in 1980. State rates of marriage ranged from 15.6 in Arkansas to 7.0 in both Massachusetts and North Carolina. Nevada, with its active wedding industry, was an anomaly with a rate of 86.1 per 1,000. Rates were highest in the South and West and lower in the East and Midwest.

The term *household* used in the tables in this section is defined by the Census Bureau as comprising all persons who occupy a housing unit, such as a house, an apartment, or other groups of rooms, or a single room that constitutes separate living quarters. A household includes the related family members and all unrelated persons, such as lodgers, foster children, wards, or employees who share a housing unit. A person living alone or a group of unrelated persons sharing the same housing unit is also counted as a household. The "householder" is the first adult household member listed on the census survey. The instructions call for listing first the person (or one of the persons) in whose name the home is owned or rented.

According to the Census Bureau the term *family* refers to a group of two or more persons related by birth, marriage or adoption residing together in a household.

Data presented by race for births came from the National Center for Health Statistics (NCHS) and were based on information contained in the certificates of registration of birth.

The first tables report on marriage and divorce. The tables that follow report data on families, married couples, children, single parent families, households and births.

TABLE: Marriages
DATE: 1992
SOURCE: U.S. National Center for Health Statistics, *Vital Statistics Reports of the United States,* annual; and *Monthly Vital Statistics Reports*
DESCRIPTION: Number and rate of marriages for 1980 and 1992 based on place of occurrence.

Rank		1980 number (thousands)	1980 marriages (per 1,000)	1992 number (thousands)	1992 marriages (per 1,000)
	United States	2,390.3	10.6	2362***	9.3
1	Nevada	114.3	142.8	114.2	86.1
2	Arkansas	26.5	11.6	37.3	15.6
3	Hawaii	11.9	12.3	17.6	15.2
4	South Carolina	53.9	17.3	53.3	14.8

Rank		1980 number (thousands)	1980 marriages (per 1,000)	1992 number (thousands)	1992 marriages (per 1,000)
5	Tennessee	59.2	12.9	70.9	14.1
6	Idaho	13.4	14.2	14.5	13.5
7	Kentucky	32.7*	8.9	49.9*	13.3
8	Utah	17.0	11.6	19.9	11.0
9	Virginia	60.2	11.3	69.7	10.9
10	South Dakota	8.8	12.7	7.6	10.6
11	Wyoming	6.9	14.6	4.9	10.5
12	Vermont	5.2	10.2	5.9	10.4
13	Texas	181.8	12.8	183.0	10.4
14	Florida	108.3	11.1	138.1	10.2
15	Oklahoma	46.5	15.4	31.8	9.9
16	Alaska	5.4	13.3	5.7	9.8
17	Alabama	49.0	12.6	40.5	9.8
18	Colorado	34.9	12.1	33.7	9.7
19	Arizona	30.2	11.1	36.4	9.5
20	Georgia	70.6	12.9	63.4	9.4
21	Maine	12.0	10.7	11.2	9.1
22	Maryland	46.3	11.0	44.1	9.0
23	Indiana	57.9	10.5	50.4	8.9
24	Washington	47.7	11.6	45.1	8.8
25	Montana	8.3	10.6	7.2	8.8
26	Connecticut	26.0	8.4	28.9	8.8
27	Missouri	54.6	11.1	45.4	8.7
28	Mississippi	27.9	11.1	22.8	8.7
29	New York	144.5	8.2	156.3	8.6
30	Kansas	24.8	10.5	21.7	8.6
31	Ohio	99.8	9.2*	92.2	8.4
32	Louisiana	43.5	10.3	35.4	8.3
33	Oregon	23.0	8.7	24.3	8.2
34	New Mexico	16.6	12.8**	13.0	8.2
35	Illinois	109.8	9.6	93.5	8.0
36	Nebraska	14.2	9.1	12.8	8.0
37	New Hampshire	9.3	10.0	8.8	7.9
38	Iowa	27.5	9.4	22.1	7.9
39	North Dakota	6.1	9.3	4.8	7.6
40	Michigan	86.9	9.4	70.7	7.5
41	Wisconsin	41.1	8.7	37.1	7.4
42	Delaware	4.4	7.5	5.1	7.3
43	Rhode Island	7.5	7.9	7.3	7.3
44	Minnesota	37.6	9.2	32.3	7.2
45	New Jersey	55.8	7.6	55.2	7.1
46	Massachusetts	46.3	8.1	42.2	7.0
47	North Carolina	46.7	7.9	48.2	7.0
48	West Virginia	17.4	8.9	12.3	6.8
49	Washington, DC	5.2	8.1	4.0	6.7
50	Pennsylvania	93.7	7.9	80.4	6.7
51	California****	210.9	8.9	NA	NA

NA Not Available
*Data are incomplete.
** Premarital health forms issued.
***Estimate for U.S. is based on monthly reports adjusted for observed differences from final monthly figures. State figures are not adjusted
**** Marriage data include nonlicensed marriages registered.

DIVORCE

Divorce rates declined from 5.2 per 1,000 population in 1980 to 4.8 per 1,000 population in 1992. In 1990 the rate ranged from a high in Nevada of 11.4 to a low of 3.0 in New Jersey. A regional comparison reveals higher rates in the South and West and lower rates in the East and Midwest.

TABLE: Divorce
DATE: 1992
SOURCE: U.S. National Center for Health Statistics, *Vital Statistics Reports of the United States*, annual; and *Monthly Vital Statistics Reports*
DESCRIPTION: Number and rate of divorces for 1980 and 1992 by place of occurrence. Includes annulments.

Rank		1980 number (thousands)	1980 divorces (per 1,000)	1992 number (thousands)	1992 divorces (per 1,000)
	United States	1,189.0	5.2	1,215.0	4.8
1	Arkansas	15.9*	6.9*	18.4*	7.7
2	Oklahoma	24.2	8.0	23.4	7.3
3	Wyoming	4.0	8.5	3.2	6.9
4	Tennessee	30.2	6.6	33.9	6.8
5	Arizona	19.9	7.3	25.6	6.7
6	Alabama	26.7	6.9	27.0	6.5
7	Kentucky	16.7	4.6	24.2*	6.4
8	Idaho	6.6	7.0	6.7	6.3
9	Alaska	3.5	8.8	3.7	6.3
10	Florida	71.6	7.3	84.1	6.2
11	New Mexico	10.4DP	8.0	9.7	6.2
12	Georgia	34.7	6.4	39.6	5.9
13	Washington	28.6	6.9	29.4	5.7
14	Mississippi	13.8*	5.5*	14.6	5.6
15	Texas	96.8	6.8	99.0	5.6
16	Colorado	18.6	6.4	19.5	5.6
17	West Virginia	10.3	5.3	9.9	5.4
18	Oregon	17.8	6.7	15.9	5.3
19	North Carolina	28.1	4.8	36.2	5.3
20	Utah	7.8	5.3	9.7	5.3
21	Montana	4.9	6.3	4.3	5.2
22	Kansas	13.4	5.7	13.2	5.2
23	Vermont	2.6	5.1	3.0	5.2
24	New Hampshire	5.3	5.7	5.5	5.0
25	Missouri	27.6	5.6	25.7	4.9
26	Ohio	58.8*	5.4*	53.5	4.9
27	Delaware	2.3	3.9	3.4	4.9
28	Maine	6.2	5.5	5.9	4.8
29	Virginia	23.6	4.4	29.7	4.7
30	Washington, DC	4.7	7.3	2.7	4.5
31	South Carolina	13.6	4.4	15.9	4.4
32	Hawaii	4.4	4.6	5.0	4.3
33	Michigan	45.0	4.9	39.4	4.2
34	Nebraska	6.4	4.1	6.6	4.1
35	South Dakota	2.8	4.1	2.9	4.1
36	Iowa	11.9	4.1	11.0	3.9
37	Illinois	51.0	4.5	43.6	3.7
38	Wisconsin	17.5	3.7	18.3	3.7
39	Rhode Island	3.6	3.8	3.6	3.6
40	North Dakota	2.1	3.3	2.3	3.6
41	Minnesota	15.4	3.8	16.3	3.6
42	Maryland	17.5	4.1	17.6	3.6
43	Pennsylvania	34.9	2.9	39.9	3.3
44	New Jersey	27.8	3.8	25.4	3.3
45	Connecticut	13.5	4.3	10.1	3.1
46	New York	62.0	3.5	57.0	3.1

Rank		1980 number (thousands)	1980 divorces (per 1,000)	1992 number (thousands)	1992 divorces (per 1,000)
47	Massachusetts	17.9	3.1	16.7	2.8
48	California	133.5S	5.6	NA	NA
49	Indiana	40**	7.3**	NA**	NA
50	Louisiana	18.1***	4.3	NA*	NA
51	Nevada	13.8	17.3	NA	NA

* Data are incomplete.
**Includes divorce petitions filed for some counties.
***Excludes figures for States shown below as not available.
DP Divorce petitions filed.
S Data include legal separations.
NA Not available.

NUMBER OF SINGLE PARENT FAMILIES

Single parent families were headed by either a male or female householder where either no wife or husband was present. Nationwide, these families represented approximately 20% of all families in 1990. In actual numbers the South (23 million) ranked first in single parent families, followed by the Midwest (16 million), and the Northeast and West (both with approximately 13 million). California, ranked first, was just above the national average.

TABLE: Number of Single Parent Families
DATE: 1990
SOURCE: Census Bureau, *U.S. Summary of Population & Housing Characteristics*
DESCRIPTION: Number and percentage of single parent families.
U.S. AVERAGE: 263,083

Rank		Total	Percentage
1	Washington, DC	58,979	48
2	Louisiana	286,600	26
3	New York	1,173,467	26
4	Mississippi	176,138	26
5	California	1,669,872	23
6	Georgia	406,316	23
7	Maryland	297,251	23
8	Alabama	245,508	22
9	Illinois	652,918	22
10	Massachusetts	344,471	22
11	Michigan	556,028	22
12	Nevada	67,827	22
13	New Mexico	87,698	22
14	Delaware	37,884	21
15	New Jersey	442,644	21
16	North Carolina	387,847	21
17	Rhode Island	56,603	21
18	Tennessee	288,450	21
19	Alaska	26,758	20
20	Arizona	192,300	20

Rank		Total	Percentage
21	Connecticut	179,833	20
22	Florida	720,091	20
23	Hawaii	52,988	20
24	Ohio	601,112	20
25	Pennsylvania	653,917	20
26	Texas	908,338	20
27	Virginia	327,271	20
28	Arkansas	124,197	19
29	Colorado	163,922	19
30	Kentucky	199,266	19
31	Missouri	263,611	19
32	Indiana	278,331	18
33	Oklahoma	159,360	18
34	Oregon	137,547	18
35	South Carolina	176,204	18
36	Washington	235,667	18
37	West Virginia	94,154	18
38	Maine	58,120	17
39	Vermont	25,990	17
40	Wisconsin	227,162	17
41	Kansas	106,105	16
42	Minnesota	188,159	16
43	Montana	35,140	16
44	New Hampshire	47,294	16
45	Nebraska	64,913	15
46	South Dakota	27,787	15
47	Utah	62,833	15
48	Wyoming	19,025	15
49	Idaho	38,996	14
50	Iowa	110,926	14
51	North Dakota	23,896	14

SINGLE PARENT FAMILIES HEADED BY WOMEN

This table shows the percentage of single families that were headed by women with no husband present in 1990. These families accounted for 71% of all single family households.

Seven of the top ranked states (along with Washington, DC) were located in the South.

TABLE: Single Parent Families Headed by Women
DATE: 1990
SOURCE: United States Bureau of the Census, *U.S. Summary of Population & Housing Characteristics*
DESCRIPTION: Percentage of single parent families headed by women.

Rank		Percentage
	United States	71
1	Alabama	82
2	Washington, DC	82
3	Louisiana	82
4	Mississippi	82
5	Georgia	81
6	South Carolina	81
7	Tennessee	81
8	Alaska	80
9	Kentucky	80
10	Michigan	80
11	North Carolina	80
12	Ohio	80
13	Massachusetts	79
14	Missouri	79
15	Oklahoma	79
16	Connecticut	78
17	Indiana	78
18	Maryland	78
19	New York	78
20	Pennsylvania	78

Rank		Percentage
21	Rhode Island	78
22	Utah	78
23	Virginia	78
24	West Virginia	78
25	Delaware	77
26	Illinois	77
27	Iowa	77
28	Kansas	77
29	Nebraska	77
30	Texas	77
31	Wisconsin	77
32	Colorado	76
33	Florida	76
34	Maine	76
35	New Jersey	76
36	Minnesota	75
37	Montana	75
38	South Dakota	75
39	Arizona	74
40	Idaho	74
41	New Hampshire	74
42	New Mexico	74
43	Oregon	74
44	Vermont	74
45	Washington	74
46	Wyoming	74
47	North Dakota	73
48	California	71
49	Hawaii	71
50	Nevada	70
51	Alaska	68

HOUSEHOLDS

The number of households increased by about half between 1970 (63 million) and 1993 (95 million). However, nationwide the rate of growth slowed between 1970–1980 (26.7%) compared to the period 1980–1990 (14.4%). Between 1970 and 1990 all the states reported an increase in the number of households. Only the District of Columbia registered a decrease for all three periods, -3.6% from 1970 to 1980, -1.4 from 1980 to 1990 and -3.7 from 1990 to 1993.

From 1970 to 1980 increases in the number of households by more than 50% were recorded in Nevada (90%), Arizona (77.5%), Colorado (53.6%), Utah (50.6%), New Mexico (52.6%), Wyoming (58%), Alaska (66.3%) and Florida (63.9). By comparison, the rate between 1980 and 1990 exceeded 50% only in Nevada (53.2) and exceeded 30% in only Alaska (43.7%) and Arizona (43%).

TABLE: Households
DATE: 1993
SOURCE: U.S. Bureau of the Census, *Census of Population: 1970, 1980 and 1990*; and *Current Population Reports*
DESCRIPTION: Number of households and percent change. A household includes the related family members and all unrelated persons who share the same housing unit. Table ranked by 1993 households.

Rank		1970 households (thousands)	1980 households (thousands)	1990 households (thousands)	1993 households (thousands)	1970–1980 percent change	1980–1990 percent change	1990–1993 percent change
	United States	63,450	80,390	91,947	95,133	26.7	14.4	3.5
1	California	6,574	8,630	10,381	10,779	31.3	20.3	3.8
2	New York	5,914	6,340	6,639	6,691	7.2	4.7	0.8
3	Texas	3,434	4,929	6,071	6,420	43.5	23.2	5.8

Rank		1970 households (thousands)	1980 households (thousands)	1990 households (thousands)	1993 households (thousands)	1970–1980 percent change	1980–1990 percent change	1990–1993 percent change
4	Florida	2,285	3,744	5,135	5,381	63.9	37.1	4.8
5	Pennsylvania	3,705	4,220	4,496	4,556	13.9	6.5	1.3
6	Illinois	3,502	4,045	4,202	4,290	15.5	3.9	2.1
7	Ohio	3,289	3,834	4,088	4,185	16.5	6.6	2.4
8	Michigan	2,653	3,195	3,419	3,497	20.4	7.0	2.3
9	New Jersey	2,218	2,549	2,795	2,849	14.9	9.7	1.9
10	North Carolina	1,510	2,043	2,517	2,637	35.4	23.2	4.8
11	Georgia	1,369	1,872	2,367	2,535	36.7	26.4	7.1
12	Virginia	1,391	1,863	2,292	2,418	34.0	23.0	5.5
13	Massachusetts	1,760	2,033	2,247	2,258	15.5	10.5	0.5
14	Indiana	1,609	1,927	2,065	2,139	19.7	7.2	3.6
15	Washington	1,106	1,541	1,872	2,009	39.3	21.5	7.3
16	Missouri	1,521	1,793	1,961	1,996	17.9	9.4	1.8
17	Tennessee	1,213	1,619	1,854	1,938	33.4	14.5	4.5
18	Wisconsin	1,329	1,652	1,822	1,875	24.3	10.3	2.9
19	Maryland	1,175	1,461	1,749	1,822	24.3	19.7	4.2
20	Minnesota	1,154	1,445	1,648	1,697	25.2	14.0	3.0
21	Alabama	1,034	1,342	1,507	1,565	29.8	12.3	3.9
22	Louisiana	1,052	1,412	1,499	1,529	34.2	6.2	2.0
23	Arizona	539	957	1,369	1,467	77.5	43.0	7.2
24	Kentucky	984	1,263	1,380	1,420	28.4	9.2	2.9
25	Colorado	691	1,061	1,282	1,385	53.6	20.8	8.0
26	South Carolina	734	1,030	1,258	1,321	40.3	22.1	5.0
27	Connecticut	933	1,094	1,230	1,231	17.2	12.5	0
28	Oklahoma	851	1,119	1,206	1,227	31.5	7.8	1.7
29	Oregon	692	992	1,103	1,170	43.4	11.3	6.0
30	Iowa	896	1,053	1,064	1,074	17.5	1.1	0.9
31	Kansas	727	872	945	961	19.9	8.3	1.7
32	Mississippi	637	827	911	934	29.9	10.2	2.5
33	Arkansas	615	816	891	916	32.6	9.2	2.8
34	West Virginia	547	686	689	699	25.4	0.3	1.5
35	Nebraska	474	571	602	610	20.6	5.4	1.2
36	Utah	298	449	537	582	50.6	19.8	8.3
37	New Mexico	289	441	543	577	52.6	22.9	6.3
38	Nevada	160	304	466	537	90.1	53.2	15.1
39	Maine	303	395	465	472	30.5	17.7	1.5
40	New Hampshire	225	323	411	420	43.5	27.1	2.0
41	Idaho	219	324	361	392	48.0	11.3	8.7
42	Hawaii	203	294	356	379	44.8	21.2	6.4
43	Rhode Island	292	339	378	376	16.0	11.6	-0.6
44	Montana	217	284	306	320	30.6	7.9	4.4
45	South Dakota	201	243	259	263	20.8	6.8	1.5
46	Delaware	165	207	247	261	25.7	19.5	5.4
47	Washington, D.C.	263	253	250	240	-3.6	-1.4	-3.7
48	North Dakota	182	228	241	240	25.4	5.8	-0.2
49	Vermont	132	178	211	217	35.0	18.1	2.9
50	Alaska	79	131	189	206	66.3	43.7	9.1
51	Wyoming	105	166	169	173	58.3	1.9	2.7

PERSONS PER HOUSEHOLD

The average size of households decreased by about a tenth of a percent between 1980 and 1993. Households decreased on average in every state in the nation between 1980 and 1993 with the exception of California. Several southern states recorded the greatest decline over the period covered (South Carolina, West Virginia, North Carolina, Alabama, Kentucky and Mississippi). Utah was the only state where the average household exceeded three people in 1993.

Household size has been declining. In 1975 the average household size slipped below three persons per household. This long-term trend is the result of several factors, including: declining birth rates; affluence, which enables people to afford their own housing; rates of divorce; and marital separation. High average household size tends to be associated with high birthrates and low median ages.

TABLE: Persons Per Household
DATE: 1993
SOURCES: U.S. Bureau of the Census, *1990 Census of Population* and *Current Population Reports*
DESCRIPTION: Persons per household.

Rank		1980	1993
	United States	2.75	2.64
1	Utah	3.20	3.15
2	Hawaii	3.15	2.99
3	California	2.68	2.82
4	Alaska	2.93	2.81
5	Idaho	2.85	2.75
6	Mississippi	2.97	2.75
7	New Mexico	2.90	2.75
8	Texas	2.82	2.75
9	Louisiana	2.91	2.74
10	New Jersey	2.84	2.71
11	South Carolina	2.93	2.67
12	Georgia	2.84	2.66
13	Illinois	2.76	2.66
14	Maryland	2.82	2.66
15	Michigan	2.84	2.65
16	Wyoming	2.78	2.65
17	New York	2.70	2.64
18	Arizona	2.79	2.63
19	Alabama	2.84	2.62
20	South Dakota	2.74	2.62
21	Wisconsin	2.77	2.62
22	Delaware	2.79	2.61
23	New Hampshire	2.75	2.61
24	Kentucky	2.82	2.60
25	Virginia	2.77	2.60
26	Indiana	2.77	2.59
27	Minnesota	2.74	2.59
28	Ohio	2.76	2.59
29	Arkansas	2.74	2.58
30	Connecticut	2.76	2.58
31	Massachusetts	2.72	2.57
32	Pennsylvania	2.74	2.57
33	Tennessee	2.77	2.57
34	Nebraska	2.66	2.56
35	Oklahoma	2.62	2.56
36	Rhode Island	2.70	2.56
37	Vermont	2.75	2.56
38	Washington	2.61	2.56
39	Kansas	2.62	2.55
40	Maine	2.75	2.55
41	Missouri	2.67	2.55
42	Montana	2.70	2.55
43	North Carolina	2.78	2.55
44	West Virginia	2.79	2.55
45	Nevada	2.59	2.54
46	North Dakota	2.75	2.54
47	Oregon	2.60	2.54
48	Iowa	2.68	2.53
49	Colorado	2.65	2.52
50	Florida	2.55	2.49
51	Washington, DC	2.40	2.24

CHILDREN PER HOUSEHOLD

The average household with children had 1.89 children per household in 1990. All the states in the top 12 were west of the Mississippi. Similarly, all the states in the bottom third were east of the Mississippi.

TABLE: Children Per Household
DATE: 1990
SOURCE: United States Bureau of the Census, *U.S. Summary of Population & Housing Characteristics*
DESCRIPTION: Average number of persons under 18 in households with persons under 18.

Rank		Average
	United States	1.89
1	Utah	2.46
2	Idaho	2.13
3	South Dakota	2.05
4	Arizona	2.01
5	North Dakota	1.99
6	Alaska	1.98
7	Nebraska	1.98
8	Wyoming	1.98
9	California	1.97
10	New Mexico	1.97
11	Montana	1.96
12	Minnesota	1.95
13	Mississippi	1.95
14	Wisconsin	1.95
15	Hawaii	1.94
16	Louisiana	1.94
17	Texas	1.94
18	Illinois	1.93
19	Iowa	1.93
20	Kansas	1.93
21	Michigan	1.91
22	Oregon	1.90
23	Washington	1.89

Rank		Average
24	Indiana	1.87
25	Missouri	1.87
26	Nevada	1.87
27	New York	1.87
28	Ohio	1.87
29	Colorado	1.86
30	Oklahoma	1.86
31	Arkansas	1.85
32	Pennsylvania	1.85
33	Massachusetts	1.84
34	South Carolina	1.83
35	Vermont	1.83
36	Alabama	1.82
37	Florida	1.82
38	Georgia	1.82
39	New Jersey	1.82
40	Connecticut	1.81
41	Delaware	1.81
42	New Hampshire	1.81
43	Rhode Island	1.81
44	Washington, DC	1.80
45	Maine	1.80
46	Maryland	1.78
47	Kentucky	1.77
48	Virginia	1.76
49	Tennessee	1.75
50	West Virginia	1.75
51	North Carolina	1.74

MEDIAN AGE OF HOUSEHOLD

In 1820 the median age was 16.7 years. By 1940 it was 29 years and in 1992, 33 years. A primary factor in the increase in the median age is the declining birthrates coupled with increasing life expectancy. The median age of the population fluctuated within a range of 1.5 years between 1940 and 1980. However, as the "baby boom" generation born after World War II passes into middle age, the median age will continue to increase.

TABLE: Median Age of Household
DATE: 1990
SOURCE: U. S. Bureau of the Census, *U.S. Summary of Population & Housing Characteristics*
DESCRIPTION: Median age of persons in U.S. households.

Rank		1980 median age	1990 median age
	United States	30.0	33.0
1	Florida	34.7	36.4
2	West Virginia	30.4	35.4
3	Pennsylvania	32.1	35.0
4	New Jersey	32.0	34.5
5	Oregon	30.2	34.5
6	Connecticut	32.0	34.4
7	Iowa	30.0	34.0
8	Rhode Island	31.8	34.0
9	Maine	30.4	33.9
10	New York	31.9	33.9
11	Arkansas	30.6	33.8
12	Montana	29.0	33.8
13	Massachusetts	31.2	33.6
14	Tennessee	30.1	33.6
15	Missouri	30.9	33.5
16	Nevada	30.3	33.3
17	Ohio	29.9	33.3
18	Oklahoma	30.1	33.2
19	North Carolina	29.6	33.1
20	Washington	29.8	33.1
21	Alabama	29.3	33.0
22	Kentucky	29.1	33.0
23	Maryland	30.3	33.0
24	Nebraska	29.7	33.0
25	Vermont	29.4	33.0
26	Delaware	29.7	32.9
27	Kansas	30.1	32.9
28	Wisconsin	29.4	32.9
29	Illinois	29.9	32.8
30	Indiana	29.2	32.8
31	New Hampshire	30.1	32.8
32	Hawaii	28.4	32.6
33	Michigan	28.8	32.6
34	Virginia	29.8	32.6
35	Colorado	28.6	32.5
36	Minnesota	29.2	32.5
37	South Dakota	28.9	32.5
38	North Dakota	28.3	32.4
39	Arizona	29.2	32.2
40	South Carolina	28.2	32.0
41	Wyoming	27.1	32.0
42	Georgia	28.7	31.6
43	California	29.9	31.5
44	Idaho	27.6	31.5
45	New Mexico	27.4	31.3
46	Mississippi	27.7	31.2
47	Louisiana	27.4	31.0
48	Texas	28.2	30.8
49	Alaska	26.1	29.4
50	Utah	24.2	26.2

HOUSEHOLDS WITH PERSONS 65 AND OLDER

With its large retirement population, it is not surprising that Florida leads the ranking. States in the Northeast are also high on the list. The ranking is a result not only of the movement of the elderly, but also of younger Americans' migration from older cities to new areas in the West.

TABLE: Households with Persons 65 and Older
DATE: 1990
SOURCE: United States Bureau of the Census, *U.S. Summary of Population & Housing Characteristics*
DESCRIPTION: Households with persons 65 and over.

Rank		Households with one or more persons over 65	Percent of total households
	United States	22,154,422	24
1	Florida	1,636,887	31
2	Pennsylvania	1,289,885	28
3	West Virginia	197,789	28
4	Iowa	288,213	27
5	Arkansas	247,961	27
6	Rhode Island	105,366	27
7	New Jersey	738,247	26
8	South Dakota	69,819	26
9	New York	1,708,908	25
10	Massachusetts	575,808	25
11	Missouri	503,164	25
12	Alabama	382,345	25
13	Connecticut	310,839	25
14	Mississippi	236,810	25
15	Nebraska	152,186	25
16	North Dakota	61,805	25
17	Illinois	1,021,268	24
18	Ohio	996,307	24
19	Wisconsin	446,890	24
20	Kentucky	338,113	24
21	Arizona	333,837	24
22	Oklahoma	299,390	24
23	Oregon	272,297	24
24	Kansas	234,849	24
25	Maine	114,341	24
26	Hawaii	87,831	24
27	Montana	74,004	24
28	Michigan	788,901	23
29	Indiana	489,101	23
30	Tennessee	444,871	23
31	South Carolina	289,404	23
32	Idaho	83,623	23
33	Washington, DC	57,903	23
34	Delaware	57,105	23
35	North Carolina	577,813	22
36	Minnesota	372,603	22
37	Louisiana	340,645	22
38	California	2,241,643	21
39	Washington	401,440	21
40	Maryland	371,615	21
41	New Mexico	117,238	21
42	New Hampshire	86,810	21
43	Vermont	46,308	21
44	Texas	1,227,974	20

Rank		Households with one or more persons over 65	Percent of total households
45	Virginia	476,716	20
46	Georgia	476,557	20
47	Nevada	93,342	20
48	Utah	104,236	19
49	Wyoming	33,558	19
50	Colorado	233,048	18
51	Alaska	16,809	8

HOUSEHOLDS WITH PARENTS 65 AND OLDER LIVING WITH CHILDREN

Hawaii ranks first in this table. Almost 4% of all Hawaiian households included a person 65 years old or older living with a son or daughter.

TABLE: Households with Parents 65 and Older Living with Children
DATE: 1990
SOURCE: United States Bureau of the Census, *U.S. Summary of Population & Housing Characteristics*
DESCRIPTION: Number of households with one or more parents 65 and over living with a son or daughter.

Rank		Households	Percentage of total households
	United States	1,748,559	2.00
1	Hawaii	13,926	3.90
2	New Jersey	84,172	3.01
3	California	303,150	2.92
4	New York	187,308	2.82
5	Florida	121,765	2.37
6	Rhode Island	8,792	2.32
7	Connecticut	27,936	2.27
8	Maryland	38,958	2.22
9	Nevada	10,362	2.22
10	Massachusetts	46,571	2.07
11	Illinois	83,278	1.98
12	Georgia	44,005	1.85
13	Pennsylvania	81,965	1.82
14	Washington, DC	4,540	1.81
15	Virginia	41,208	1.80
16	South Carolina	22,393	1.78
17	Delaware	4,336	1.75
18	Texas	106,030	1.74
19	Arizona	23,473	1.71
20	Alabama	24,682	1.63
21	North Carolina	41,152	1.63
22	Tennessee	29,888	1.61
23	New Hampshire	6,487	1.57

Rank		Households	Percentage of total households
24	Louisiana	23,459	1.56
25	Michigan	51,094	1.49
26	Ohio	58,222	1.42
27	New Mexico	7,666	1.41
28	Maine	6,473	1.39
29	Arkansas	12,156	1.36
30	West Virginia	9,286	1.35
31	Wisconsin	21,090	1.26
32	Alaska	2,320	1.22
33	Indiana	25,195	1.22
34	Oregon	13,511	1.22
35	Washington	22,944	1.22
36	Vermont	2,566	1.21
37	Colorado	14,917	1.16

Rank		Households	Percentage of total households
38	Utah	6,119	1.13
39	Oklahoma	13,448	1.11
40	Idaho	3,201	.88
41	Kansas	8,379	.88
42	Minnesota	14,075	.85
43	Montana	2,629	.85
44	Wyoming	1,386	.82
45	South Dakota	1,910	.73
46	Iowa	7,720	.72
47	Nebraska	4,280	.71
48	North Dakota	1,602	.66
49	Mississippi	14,876	.16
50	Kentucky	17,913	.13
51	Missouri	23,745	.12

BIRTHS BY RACE AND HISPANIC ORIGIN

This table records the total number of births and the number of white, black and Hispanic origin births in 1990 by state. White and black births as percentage of births are also shown.

Data presented by race for births came from the National Center for Health Statistics (NCHS) and were based on information contained in the certificates of registration of birth.

Nationwide 79% of all births were classified as white and 17% as black. Births of Hispanic origin may be of any race and therefore could be classified under either black or white. The origin of the mother determines whether the birth is classified as Hispanic. Hispanic births represent a substantial portion of all births in California, Texas and Arizona. A subset of Hispanic births—those to mothers of Mexican origin—were particularly high in comparison to total births in California, Texas and Arizona.

TABLE: Births by Race and Hispanic Origin
DATE: 1991
SOURCE: U.S. National Center for Health Statistics, *Vital Statistics of the United States*, annual, and *Monthly Vital Statistics Report*
DESCRIPTION: Live births by race (of child) and Hispanic origin. Excludes births to nonresidents of the U.S. Percentage of white and black births will not add to 100% because total births include other races. Table ranked by "all races."

Rank		All Races* (thousands)	White births (thousands)	Black births (thousands)	Births of Hispanic origin ** (thousands)	Percent of White births	Percent of Black births
	United States	4,110.9	3,241.3	682.6	632.1	79	17
1	California	610.1	500.7	47.7	214.3	82	8
2	Texas	317.7	267.3	43.1	121.3	84	14
3	New York	292.6	216.7	62.2	53.7	74	21
4	Florida	194.0	145.2	45.7	28.2	75	24
5	Illinois	194.2	145.5	43.2	25.7	75	22
6	Pennsylvania	168.9	139.9	25.8	6	83	15
7	Ohio	165.8	137.7	26.4	2.6	83	16
8	Michigan	150.2	116	31.6	4.4	77	21
9	New Jersey	121.4	92.8	23.7	17.5	76	20
10	Georgia	110.3	68.3	40.3	2.6	62	37
11	North Carolina	102.4	69.3	30.4	1.8	68	30
12	Virginia	97.4	70.3	23.8	3.7	72	24
13	Massachusetts	88.2	76	8.7	8.5	86	10
14	Indiana	85.7	75.4	9.5	1.8	88	11
15	Maryland	79.2	51.1	25	2.5	65	32
16	Missouri	78.7	63.9	13.7	1.1	81	17

Rank		All Races* (thousands)	White births (thousands)	Black births (thousands)	Births of Hispanic origin **	Percent of White births (thousands)	Percent of Black births
17	Washington	79.7	70.6	3.1	6.5	89	4
18	Louisiana	72.2	40.6	30.4	0.9	56	42
19	Tennessee	74.5	56	17.8	0.5	75	24
20	Wisconsin	72.1	62.3	7.2	2	86	10
21	Arizona	68.1	58.5	2.5	20.6	86	4
22	Minnesota	67.1	60.6	2.8	1.3	90	4
23	Alabama	62.8	40.7	21.7	0.4	65	34
24	South Carolina	57.6	34.6	22.5	0.6	60	39
25	Kentucky	54.3	48.7	5.3	0.2	90	10
26	Colorado	53.8	49.1	2.9	9.8	91	5
27	Connecticut	48.6	41.1	6.3	5.2	85	13
28	Oklahoma	47.8	37.5	5.2	1.9	79	11
29	Mississippi	43.2	21.9	20.8	0.1	51	48
30	Oregon	42.5	39.5	1	3.3	93	2
31	Kansas	37.8	33.7	3.2	2.1	89	8
32	Iowa	39.0	37.1	1.2	0.7	95	3
33	Utah	36.0	34.2	0.2	2.2	95	0
34	Arkansas	35.5	26.8	8.3	0.4	75	23
35	New Mexico	27.8	23	0.6	12.6	83	2
36	Nebraska	24.0	22	1.3	1	92	6
37	Nevada	22.0	18.7	2.1	3.7	85	9
38	West Virginia	22.5	21.6	0.8	0.1	96	4
39	Hawaii	19.9	5.9	0.6	2.2	30	3
40	Idaho	16.8	16.3	0.1	1.5	97	0
41	Maine	16.8	16.4	0.1	0.1	98	0
42	New Hampshire	16.3	16.1	0.1	NA	99	0
43	Rhode Island	14.7	12.9	1.1	1.4	88	8
44	Montana	11.5	10	Z	0.3	87	Z
45	Alaska	11.7	7.9	0.5	0.4	67	4
46	Delaware	11.2	8.1	2.9	0.4	73	25
47	South Dakota	10.9	9.1	0.1	0.1	83	1
48	Washington, DC	11.8	1.6	9.2	0.9	14	78
49	North Dakota	8.9	7.9	0.1	0.1	89	1
50	Vermont	8.0	7.9	Z	Z	99	Z
51	Wyoming	6.7	6.3	0.1	0.5	94	1

NA Not available.
Z Less than 50.
* Includes other races not shown separately.
** Persons of Hispanic origin may be of any race. Births by Hispanic origin of mother.

LOW BIRTH-WEIGHT BABIES

This table shows the percentage of low birth-weight babies by state in 1980 and 1991. A low birth-weight baby weighs less than 5 pounds 8 ounces (2,5000 grams). Low birth weight is a potentially preventable cause of morbidity and mortality in newborn children. The percentage of low birth-weight babies increased nationally between 1980 and 1991. The District of Columbia and eight southern states ranked highest.

TABLE: Low Birth-Weight Babies
DATE: 1991

SOURCES: U.S. National Center for Health Statistics, *Vital Statistics of the United States,* annual; and *Monthly Vital Statistics Report*

DESCRIPTION: Percent of low birth-wieght babies. Less than 2,500 grams (5 pounds-8 ounces). Represents registered births. Based on 100% of births in all states. Excludes births to nonresidents of the United States.

Rank		1980	1991
	United States	6.8	7.1
1	Washington, DC	12.8	15.4
2	Mississippi	8.7	9.7
3	Louisiana	8.6	9.4

Rank		1980	1991
4	South Carolina	8.6	9.2
5	Tennessee	8.0	8.8
6	Alabama	7.9	8.7
7	Georgia	8.6	8.6
8	North Carolina	7.9	8.4
9	Arkansas	7.6	8.2
10	Colorado	8.2	8.2
11	Maryland	8.2	8.1
12	New York	7.4	7.9
13	Delaware	7.7	7.9
14	Illinois	7.2	7.8
15	Michigan	6.9	7.8
16	Ohio	6.8	7.5
17	Missouri	6.6	7.5
18	New Jersey	7.2	7.4
19	Florida	7.6	7.4
20	Pennsylvania	6.5	7.3
21	Virginia	7.5	7.2
22	Kentucky	6.8	7.2
23	Nevada	6.6	7.2
24	Texas	6.9	7.1
25	New Mexico	7.6	7.1
26	Wyoming	7.3	7.0
27	Connecticut	6.7	6.9
28	West Virginia	6.7	6.8
29	Hawaii	7.1	6.8
30	Indiana	6.3	6.7
31	Oklahoma	6.8	6.6
32	Arizona	6.2	6.4
33	Kansas	5.8	6.2
34	Wisconsin	5.4	6.1
35	Rhode Island	6.3	6.0
36	Utah	5.2	6.0
37	Massachusetts	6.1	5.9
38	Idaho	5.3	5.8
39	California	5.9	5.8
40	Vermont	5.9	5.7
41	Iowa	5.0	5.7
42	Nebraska	5.6	5.6
43	Montana	5.6	5.6
44	Maine	6.5	5.4
45	South Dakota	5.1	5.4
46	Minnesota	5.1	5.3
47	Washington	5.1	5.1
48	New Hampshire	5.4	4.9
49	Oregon	4.9	4.9
50	North Dakota	4.9	4.8
51	Alaska	5.4	4.7

BIRTHS TO TEENAGE MOTHERS

Nationwide, of all babies born in 1980, 16.5% were born to teenage mothers, compared with 12.9% in 1991. The top 10 states were all located in the South, with the excep-tion of Oklahoma. Three southwestern states, New Mexico, Texas and Arizona, followed close behind.

TABLE: Births to Teenage Mothers
DATE: 1991
SOURCE: U.S. National Center for Health Statistics, *Vital Statistics of the United States*, annual; and *Monthly Vital Statistics Report*
DESCRIPTION: Births to teenage mothers as a percent of total births. Based on 100% of births in all states. Represents registered births. Excludes births to nonresidents of the United States.

Rank		1980	1991
	United States	15.6	12.9
1	Mississippi	23.2	21.7
2	Arkansas	21.6	19.9
3	Alabama	20.6	18.5
4	Tennessee	19.9	17.7
5	West Virginia	20.1	17.6
6	Louisiana	20.1	17.6
7	Washington, DC	20.7	17.4
8	Kentucky	21.1	17.4
9	Oklahoma	19.6	17.2
10	South Carolina	19.8	17.0
11	Georgia	20.7	16.7
12	New Mexico	18.2	16.5
13	North Carolina	19.2	16.2
14	Texas	18.3	16.0
15	Arizona	16.5	14.8
16	Indiana	17.3	14.4
17	Missouri	16.9	14.4
18	Ohio	15.7	14.0
19	Wyoming	15.5	14.0
20	Florida	18.2	13.9
21	Idaho	13.1	13.3
22	Michigan	14.0	13.2
23	Illinois	15.7	13.0
24	Nevada	15.4	12.9
25	Oregon	13.3	12.3
26	Kansas	15.0	12.2
27	Delaware	16.7	12.2
28	Colorado	13.3	11.8
29	California	13.9	11.8
30	Virginia	15.5	11.5
31	Montana	12.4	11.5
32	South Dakota	13.5	11.0
33	Maine	15.3	10.9
34	Pennsylvania	13.9	10.8
35	Utah	11.0	10.8
36	Washington	12.5	10.8
37	Hawaii	11.5	10.6
38	Iowa	12.5	10.5
39	Alaska	11.8	10.5
40	Maryland	14.8	10.4
41	Wisconsin	12.3	10.3
42	Rhode Island	12.3	9.8

Rank		1980	1991
43	Nebraska	12.1	9.8
44	Vermont	13.0	9.3
45	New York	11.8	9.2
46	North Dakota	10.9	8.7
47	New Jersey	12.3	8.4
48	Connecticut	11.4	8.2
49	Minnesota	10.4	8.1
50	Massachusetts	10.7	8.0
51	New Hampshire	10.7	7.1

BIRTHS TO UNMARRIED WOMEN

Babies born to unmarried women represented 18.4% of all births in 1980 and 29.2% of all births in 1991. Similar to the ranking of teenage births, the southern and southwestern states ranked highest. However, New York, California, Illinois and Florida were also at the top of the list.

TABLE: Births to Unmarried Women
DATE: 1991
SOURCE: U.S. National Center for Health Statistics, *Vital Statistics of the United States*, annual; and *Monthly Vital Statistics Report*
DESCRIPTION: Births to unmarried women as a percent of total births. Based on 100% of births in all states. Represents registered births. Excludes births to nonresidents of the United States.

Rank		1980	1991
	United States	18.4	29.2
1	Washington, DC	56.5	65.9
2	Mississippi	28.0	42.0
3	Louisiana	23.4	38.4
4	New Mexico	16.1	38.1
5	Arizona	18.7	34.6
6	South Carolina	23.0	34.1
7	Georgia	23.2	33.8
8	New York*	23.8	33.5

Rank		1980	1991
9	California*	21.4	33.3
10	Nevada*	13.5	32.5
11	Illinois	22.5	32.3
12	Florida	23.0	32.2
13	Tennessee	19.9	32.1
14	Delaware	24.2	32.0
15	Alabama	22.2	31.5
16	North Carolina	19.0	30.9
17	Ohio*	17.8	30.5
18	Maryland*	25.2	30.3
19	Missouri	17.6	29.9
20	Pennsylvania	17.7	29.9
21	Arkansas	20.5	29.1
22	Indiana	15.5	28.2
23	Virginia	19.2	27.3
24	Oklahoma	14.0	27.2
25	Connecticut*	17.9	27.1
26	Rhode Island	15.7	26.8
27	West Virginia	13.1	26.7
28	Michigan*	16.2	26.6
29	Alaska	15.1	26.4
30	Oregon	14.8	26.4
31	New Jersey	21.1	26.1
32	Kentucky	15.1	25.4
33	Hawaii	17.6	25.4
34	Washington	13.6	25.1
35	Wisconsin	13.9	25.0
36	Montana*	12.5	25.0
37	South Dakota	13.4	24.7
38	Massachusetts	15.7	24.7
39	Maine	13.9	24.1
40	Colorado	13.0	23.7
41	Vermont	13.7	22.7
42	Kansas	12.3	22.4
43	Wyoming	8.2	22.1
44	Minnesota	11.4	22.0
45	Iowa	10.3	22.0
46	Nebraska	11.6	21.3
47	North Dakota	9.2	21.1
48	Texas*	13.3	17.9
49	Idaho	7.9	17.8
50	New Hampshire	11.0	17.1
51	Utah	6.2	14.3

*Marital status of mother is inferred.

HOUSING

This section presents information on the number and type of housing units, the value and price of housing and data on construction. The primary source of these data is the U.S. Census Bureau and the National Association of RE-ALTORS.

The Census Bureau defines a housing unit as a group of rooms or a single room occupied or intended for occupancy as separate living quarters. Housing units include single family homes, attached homes and apartments. Transient accommodations, such as barracks for workers, dormitories and other institution quarters are not counted as housing units.

The first two tables in this section detail occupied housing units. These are followed by tables on the value of housing, rent, vacancy, and characteristics of housing units.

HOUSING UNITS AND OWNER OCCUPIED UNITS

In 1983, 64.5% of the population owned their own homes. In 1990, 64.2% of the population lived in housing they owned. The states with the lowest percentage of owner-occupied housing were clustered in the Northeast: New York, Massachusetts, Rhode Island and Washington, DC. The rest were in the West: Oregon, Washington, Colorado, Texas, California and Nevada. Alaska and Hawaii also ranked at the bottom of the list. One factor affecting home ownership is the value of housing.

TABLE: Housing Units and Owner Occupied Units
DATE: 1990
SOURCE: U.S. Bureau of the Census, *1990 Census of Housing*, and Census of Population and Housing, 1990 Summary Tape File
DESCRIPTION: Total number of housing units and percentage of owner-occupied housing units in total occupied units.

Rank		Occupied housing units (thousands)	Percent owner occupied
	United States	91,947.4	64.2
1	West Virginia	688.6	74.1
2	Minnesota	1,647.9	71.8
3	Mississippi	911.4	71.5
4	Michigan	3,419.3	71.0
5	Pennsylvania	4,496.0	70.7
6	Alabama	1,506.8	70.5
7	Maine	465.3	70.5
8	Delaware	247.5	70.3
9	Indiana	2,065.4	70.2
10	Idaho	360.7	70.1
11	Iowa	1,064.3	70.0
12	South Carolina	1,258.0	69.9
13	Kentucky	1,379.8	69.6
14	Arkansas	891.2	69.6
15	Vermont	210.7	69.0
16	Missouri	1,961.2	68.8
17	New Hampshire	411.2	68.2
18	Utah	537.3	68.1
19	Oklahoma	1,206.1	68.1
20	Tennessee	1,853.7	68.0
21	North Carolina	2,517.0	68.0
22	Kansas	944.7	67.9
23	Wyoming	168.8	67.8
24	Ohio	4,087.5	67.5
25	New Mexico	542.7	67.4
26	Montana	306.2	67.3
27	Florida	5,134.9	67.2
28	Wisconsin	1,822.1	66.7
29	Nebraska	602.4	66.5
30	Virginia	2,291.8	66.3
31	South Dakota	259.0	66.1
32	Louisiana	1,499.3	65.9
33	Connecticut	1,230.5	65.6
34	North Dakota	240.9	65.6
35	Maryland	1,749.0	65.0
36	Georgia	2,366.6	64.9
37	New Jersey	2,794.7	64.9
38	Illinois	4,202.2	64.2
39	Arizona	1,368.8	64.2

Rank		Occupied housing units (thousands)	Percent owner occupied
40	Oregon	1,103.3	63.1
41	Washington	1,872.4	62.6
42	Colorado	1,282.5	62.3
43	Texas	6,070.9	60.9
44	Rhode Island	378.0	59.5
45	Massachusetts	2,247.1	59.3
46	Alaska	188.9	56.1
47	California	10,381.2	55.6
48	Nevada	466.3	54.8
49	Hawaii	356.3	53.9
50	New York	6,639.3	52.2
51	Washington, DC	249.6	38.9

CONDOMINIUMS

A condominium is individually owned housing that is part of a larger structure, such as an apartment building or connected town house. While condominiums are individually owned, the owner is not necessarily the occupant.

Condominiums constituted 4.4% of occupied housing in 1990. Some of the states that ranked at bottom in percentage of owner-occupied housing ranked at the top here: Hawaii, Washington, DC, California, Colorado, Nevada and Massachusetts. The southern and Plains states had the lowest proportion of occupied condominiums.

TABLE: Condominiums
DATE: 1990
SOURCE: U.S. Bureau of the Census, *1990 Census of Housing,* and Census of Population and Housing, 1990 Summary Tape File
DESCRIPTION: Total occupied housing units and condominiums as a percent of occupied housing units.

Rank		Occupied housing units (thousands)	Percent condominium
	United States	91,947.4	4.4
1	Hawaii	356.3	18.4
2	Florida	5,134.9	12.9
3	Washington, DC	249.6	10.4
4	Connecticut	1,230.5	8.7
5	California	10,381.2	7.4
6	Colorado	1,282.5	7.3
7	Nevada	466.3	6.7
8	New Jersey	2,794.7	6.7
9	Massachusetts	2,247.1	6.1
10	Arizona	1,368.8	6.0
11	New Hampshire	411.2	5.8
12	Maryland	1,749.0	5.5
13	Illinois	4,202.2	5.4
14	Alaska	188.9	5.3
15	Virginia	2,291.8	4.8
16	Utah	537.3	4.6

Rank		Occupied housing units (thousands)	Percent condominium
17	New York	6,639.3	4.6
18	Vermont	210.7	3.1
19	Minnesota	1,647.9	3.1
20	Washington	1,872.4	3.0
21	Rhode Island	378.0	2.8
22	Texas	6,070.9	2.7
23	Michigan	3,419.3	2.7
24	Georgia	2,366.6	2.6
25	Delaware	247.5	2.6
26	Ohio	4,087.5	2.5
27	North Carolina	2,517.0	2.5
28	South Carolina	1,258.0	2.3
29	North Dakota	240.9	2.3
30	Pennsylvania	4,496.0	2.0
31	Tennessee	1,853.7	2.0
32	Missouri	1,961.2	2.0
33	Kansas	944.7	1.7
34	Oregon	1,103.3	1.7
35	Wisconsin	1,822.1	1.6
36	Maine	465.3	1.6
37	Louisiana	1,499.3	1.6
38	Oklahoma	1,206.1	1.5
39	New Mexico	542.7	1.5
40	Indiana	2,065.4	1.4
41	Kentucky	1,379.8	1.3
42	Wyoming	168.8	1.2
43	Idaho	360.7	1.2
44	Nebraska	602.4	1.2
45	Montana	306.2	1.2
46	Iowa	1,064.3	1.1
47	Alabama	1,506.8	1.1
48	South Dakota	259.0	0.8
49	Arkansas	891.2	0.7
50	West Virginia	688.6	0.6
51	Mississippi	911.4	0.6

MEDIAN HOME VALUE

In 1980 the median value of a unit of housing was $45,000. That increased to $69,700 in 1990. The value of owner-occupied housing was generally highest in the West and lowest in the South. In Hawaii, where the rate of home ownership was relatively low, the value of housing ranked highest in the nation in both 1980 and 1990. The affluent suburbs of New York City, Boston and Washington, DC, accounted for the high average value of housing in Connecticut, Massachusetts, New Jersey, Rhode Island, New York, Maryland and Virginia. The New England states, in general, documented particularly high increases in housing values between 1980 and 1990.

TABLE: Median Home Value
DATE: 1990

SOURCE: U.S. Bureau of the Census, *Summary of Population and Housing Characteristics*

DESCRIPTION: Median value in dollars of owner-occupied homes, and percentage change from 1980 to 1990. The table is ranked by median value.

Rank		1990 Median ($)	Percent change 1980–1990
	United States	69,700	68
1	Hawaii	245,300	107
2	California	195,500	131
3	Connecticut	177,800	171
4	Massachusetts	162,800	236
5	New Jersey	162,300	170
6	Rhode Island	133,500	185
7	New York	131,600	188
8	New Hampshire	129,400	174
9	Washington, DC	123,900	NA
10	Maryland	116,500	100
11	Delaware	100,100	125
12	Nevada	95,700	39
13	Vermont	95,500	126
14	Alaska	94,400	24
15	Washington	93,400	56
16	Virginia	91,000	90
17	Maine	87,400	130
18	Colorado	82,700	29
19	Illinois	80,900	52
20	Arizona	80,100	46
21	Florida	77,100	71
22	Minnesota	74,000	39

Rank		1990 Median ($)	Percentage change 1980–1990
23	Georgia	71,300	93
24	New Mexico	70,100	55
25	Pennsylvania	69,700	78
26	Utah	68,900	20
27	Oregon	67,100	18
28	North Carolina	65,800	83
29	Ohio	63,500	41
30	Wisconsin	62,500	29
31	Wyoming	61,600	4
32	South Carolina	61,100	74
33	Michigan	60,600	55
34	Missouri	59,800	63
35	Texas	59,600	52
36	Louisiana	58,500	36
37	Tennessee	58,400	64
38	Idaho	58,200	28
39	Montana	56,600	22
40	Indiana	53,900	45
41	Alabama	53,700	58
42	Kansas	52,200	38
43	North Dakota	50,800	16
44	Kentucky	50,500	48
45	Nebraska	50,400	33
46	Oklahoma	48,100	35
47	West Virginia	47,900	24
48	Arkansas	46,300	49
49	Iowa	45,900	13
50	Mississippi	45,600	45
51	South Dakota	45,200	23

NEW HOUSING

This table shows the number and value of new housing units for 1987 and 1993. Ranked according to the number of housing units per state, these data provide some general parameters regarding the total number of units being built in each state and their total value. Nationwide, the total number of new units built decreased between 1987 (1.5 million) and 1993 (1.2 million). However, the total value of housing increased $9 million between 1987 ($98 billion) and 1993 ($107 billion).

TABLE: New Housing

DATE: 1993

SOURCE: U.S. Bureau of the Census, *Current Construction Reports*, annual

DESCRIPTION: Number and valuation of new privately owned housing units. Based on about 17,000 places in the United States having building permit systems.

Rank		1987 new units (thousands)	1987 valuation ($ millions)	1993 new units (thousands)	1993 valuation ($ millions)
	United States	1,534.8	98,346	1,199.1	106,801
1	Florida	178.8	9,210	115.1	9,658
2	California	251.8	19,560	84.3	10,195
3	Texas	50.5	3,570	77.8	6,896
4	Georgia	64.2	3,723	53.9	4,302
5	North Carolina	54.3	3,104	53.3	4,431
6	Virginia	66.7	3,697	45.0	3,700
7	Illinois	50.4	3,807	44.7	4,487
8	Ohio	45.2	2,999	44.2	4,319
9	Washington	38.3	2,224	41.3	3,629
10	Pennsylvania	54.8	3,588	40.1	3,547

Rank		1987 new units (thousands)	1987 valuation ($ millions)	1993 new units (thousands)	1993 valuation ($ millions)
11	Michigan	46.6	2,626	39.8	3,390
12	Arizona	40.2	2,775	38.7	3,778
13	Wisconsin	24.1	1,330	32.1	2,624
14	Indiana	27.3	1,756	30.8	2,896
15	Maryland	41.1	2,485	30.0	2,309
16	Colorado	18.0	1,235	29.9	3,096
17	New York	62.2	4,417	28.6	2,621
18	Minnesota	33.4	2,422	27.3	2,672
19	Tennessee	29.9	1,765	27.0	2,171
20	New Jersey	51.5	3,575	25.2	2,087
21	Nevada	16.3	786	23.3	1,637
22	Missouri	29.1	1,643	21.7	1,750
23	South Carolina	23.5	1,405	21.1	1,694
24	Oregon	12.2	753	20.5	1,956
25	Massachusetts	40.4	3,084	17.5	1,891
26	Utah	7.7	509	17.3	1,508
27	Alabama	14.5	648	16.1	1,147
28	Kentucky	13.2	740	15.9	1,173
29	Idaho	3.2	201	11.6	929
30	Louisiana	8.5	450	11.2	859
31	Kansas	11.8	802	11.0	1,028
32	Iowa	5.8	314	10.6	882
33	Arkansas	6.5	320	10.0	644
34	Connecticut	26.8	1,806	9.2	930
35	New Mexico	9.3	549	8.9	775
36	Oklahoma	6.2	363	8.7	809
37	Mississippi	6.6	324	8.1	495
38	Nebraska	4.9	242	7.8	551
39	Hawaii	6.9	470	6.6	679
40	Delaware	7.1	319	4.9	313
41	New Hampshire	14.6	1,017	4.2	381
42	Maine	9.8	584	3.8	309
43	South Dakota	1.9	85	3.7	242
44	North Dakota	2.0	93	2.9	190
45	Montana	0.8	48	2.9	212
46	Rhode Island	7.2	396	2.6	235
47	West Virginia	1.9	88	2.6	185
48	Vermont	4.6	299	2.3	202
49	Alaska	0.7	63	1.7	228
50	Wyoming	0.6	37	1.2	136
51	Washington, DC	1.2	43	0.3	21

MEDIAN SALES PRICE OF HOMES

Total metropolitan median sales price increased between 1985 ($75,500) and 1993 ($106,700). All the metro areas ranked reported some increase between the years covered. The increase was highest in the San Francisco ($105,000) metropolitan area and lowest in the Dallas metropolitan area ($500).

TABLE: Median Sales Price of Homes
DATE: 1993
SOURCE: National Association of REALTORS, Washington, DC, *Home Sales*, monthly, and *Home Sales Yearbook: 1990* (copyright)
DESCRIPTION: Median sales price of exsisting one-family homes in selected metropolitan areas. Table ranked by 1993 sale price.

Rank		Population (thousands)	1985 sale price ($ thousands)	1993 sale price ($ thousands)	Amount of increase ($ thousands)
	United States	248,710	75.5	106.7	31.2
1	Honolulu, HI	836	162.1	358.5	196.4
2	San Francisco-Oakland-San Jose, CA CMSA	6,253	145.1	250.2	105.1
3	Anaheim-Santa Ana, CA PMSA	2,411	134.7	220.7	86.0
4	Los Angeles, CA PSMA	8,863	125.2	197.9	72.7
5	San Diego, CA	2,498	107.4	177.4	70.0
6	New York, NY-NJ-CT CMSA	18,087	134.0	173.2	39.2
7	Boston, MA PMSA	2,871	134.2	173.2	39.0
8	Washington, DC-MD-VA	3,924	97.1	158.3	61.2
9	Chicago, IL PMSA	8,066	81.1	142.0	60.9
10	Riverside/San Bernardino, CA PSMA	2,589	85.0	134.5	49.5
11	Sacramento, CA	1,481	77.9	129.4	51.5
12	Philadelphia, PA-NJ PMSA	4,857	74.0	118.0	44.0
13	Baltimore, MD	2,382	72.6	115.7	43.1
14	West Palm Beach-Boca Raton-Delray Beach, FL	864	88.3	114.6	26.3
15	Albany-Schenectady-Troy, NY	874	60.3	112.3	52.0
16	Charlotte, NC	1,162	69.4	106.1	36.7
17	Portland, OR PMSA	1,240	61.5	106.0	44.5
18	Denver, CO PMSA	1,623	84.3	104.7	20.4
19	Milwaukee, WI PMSA	1,432	67.5	104.1	36.6
20	Ft. Lauderdale-Hollywood, FL PMSA	1,255	74.6	103.1	28.5
21	Miami-Hialeah, FL PMSA	1,937	80.5	98.8	18.3
22	Minneapolis-St. Paul, MN-WI	2,464	75.2	98.2	23.0
23	Birmingham, AL	908	64.5	96.5	32.0
24	Cleveland, OH PMSA	1,831	64.4	95.0	30.6
25	Dallas, TX PMSA	2,553	94.0	94.5	0.5
26	Richmond, VA	866	NA	94.1	NA
27	Columbus, OH	1,377	62.2	91.8	29.6
28	Cincinnati, OH-KY-IN PMSA	1,453	60.2	91.4	31.2
29	Nashville, TN	985	66.1	90.4	24.3
30	Orlando, FL	1,073	70.3	90.1	19.8
31	Phoenix, AZ	2,122	74.8	89.1	14.3
32	Memphis, TN-AR-MS	982	64.6	87.0	22.4
33	Indianapolis, IN	1,250	55.0	86.6	31.6
34	Detroit, MI PMSA	4,382	51.7	86.0	34.3
35	Salt Lake City-Ogden, UT	1,072	66.7	84.9	18.2
36	St. Louis, MO-IL	2,444	65.7	84.8	19.1
37	Rochester, NY	1,002	64.2	84.8	20.6
38	Kansas City, MO-KS	1,566	61.4	83.6	22.2
39	Buffalo-Niagara Falls, NY CMSA	1,189	46.7	83.5	36.8
40	Ft. Worth, TX PMSA	1,332	NA	82.9	NA
41	Pittsburgh, PA PMSA	2,057	NA	82.2	NA
42	Dayton-Springfield, OH	951	NA	82.1	NA
43	Houston, TX PMSA	3,302	78.6	80.9	2.3
44	Jacksonville, FL	907	58.4	77.1	18.7
45	San Antonio, TX	1,302	67.7	77.0	9.3
46	New Orleans, LA	1,239	NA	76.8	NA
47	Tampa-St. Petersburg-Clearwater, FL	2,068	58.4	75.0	16.6
48	Louisville, KY-IN	953	50.6	74.5	23.9
49	Oklahoma City, OK	959	64.7	64.9	0.2
50	Seattle-Tacoma, WA CMSA	2,559	NA	63.6	NA

MSA's metropolitan statistical areas. except as indicated.
NA Not available.
CMSA consolidated statistical metropolitan areas
PMSA primary metropolitan statistical areas

AVERAGE MONTHLY RENT

Rent averaged $442 nationwide; however average rent was higher in only 18 states. This indicates a clustering of expensive housing in a few states such as Hawaii, California and Connecticut. This figure contibutes to the high cost of living in these areas. The ranking of states roughly parallels that showing the median value of owner-occupied housing.

TABLE: Average Monthly Rent
DATE: 1990
SOURCE: U.S. Bureau of the Census, *Summary of Population and Housing.*
DESCRIPTION: Average monthly rent.

Rank		Rent ($)
	United States	442
1	Hawaii	650
2	California	620
3	Connecticut	598
4	New Jersey	592
5	Massachusetts	580
6	Alaska	559
7	New Hampshire	549
8	Maryland	548
9	Nevada	509
10	Delaware	495
11	Virginia	495
12	Rhode Island	489
13	New York	486
14	Florida	481
15	Washington, DC	479
16	Vermont	446
17	Illinois	445
18	Washington	445
19	Arizona	438
20	Georgia	433
21	Michigan	423
22	Minnesota	422
23	Maine	419
24	Colorado	418
25	Oregon	408
26	Pennsylvania	404
27	Wisconsin	399
28	Texas	395
29	North Carolina	382
30	Ohio	379
31	South Carolina	376
32	Indiana	374
33	Kansas	372
34	New Mexico	372
35	Utah	369
36	Missouri	368
37	Tennessee	357
38	Louisiana	352

Rank		Rent ($)
39	Nebraska	348
40	Oklahoma	340
41	Iowa	336
42	Wyoming	333
43	Idaho	330
44	Arkansas	328
45	Alabama	325
46	Kentucky	319
47	North Dakota	313
48	Montana	311
49	Mississippi	309
50	South Dakota	306
51	West Virginia	303

RENTALS

This table ranks states according to rental units as a percentage of total housing units. It also shows the total number of rental units in each state. Rental units include houses, apartments or a room or combination of rooms intended for occupancy as a separate living quarters. Nationwide in 1990, 30% of all housing units were rentals. The highest percentages of rental units were located in the Northeast—the District of Columbia, New York and Massachusetts—and the West—California and Nevada.

TABLE: Rentals
DATE: 1990
SOURCE: U.S. Bureau of the Census, *Summary of Population and Housing*
DESCRIPTION: Total occupied housing units and rental units as a percentage of occupied housing units.

Rank		Occupied housing units	Percent rental
	United States	32,268,035	30
1	Washington, DC	152,069	55
2	New York	3,150,574	44
3	Hawaii	162,820	42
4	California	4,553,387	41
5	Nevada	209,175	40
6	Massachusetts	910,047	37
7	Rhode Island	152,032	37
8	Arkansas	358,065	36
9	Alaska	81,927	35
10	Washington	687,032	34
11	Illinois	1,470,362	33
12	Oregon	394,927	33
13	Texas	2,332,892	33
14	Colorado	472,590	32
15	Connecticut	418,520	32
16	Maryland	598,309	32
17	New Jersey	973,650	32
18	Georgia	808,365	31
19	Ohio	1,293,380	30

Rank		Occupied housing units	Percent rental
20	Virginia	746,163	30
21	Arizona	485,781	29
22	Louisiana	501,319	29
23	Nebraska	186,632	28
24	North Carolina	777,929	28
25	North Dakota	78,484	28
26	South Dakota	81,179	28
27	Tennessee	568,875	28
28	Utah	169,793	28
29	Wisconsin	582,371	28
30	Florida	1,669,618	27
31	Missouri	585,022	27
32	New Mexico	173,081	27
33	Alabama	426,024	26
34	Indiana	589,881	26
35	Kentucky	392,285	26
36	Montana	93,906	26
37	Oklahoma	370,654	26
38	Pennsylvania	1,287,662	26
39	Delaware	72,176	25
40	Idaho	102,432	25
41	Iowa	285,742	25
42	Michigan	966,241	25
43	New Hampshire	127,782	25
44	Wyoming	51,450	25
45	Minnesota	445,865	24
46	Mississippi	247,496	24
47	Maine	133,275	23
48	Vermont	61,841	23
49	West Virginia	168,341	22
50	South Carolina	368,861	20
51	Kansas	289,751	13

HOUSING VACANCY RATES

In 1990 the vacancy rate averaged 11%. Generally, the low rates of vacancy in a state indicate tight housing markets, and higher rates indicate slack housing markets.

TABLE: Housing Vacancy Rates
DATE: 1990
SOURCE: U.S. Bureau of the Census, *Summary of Population and Housing Characteristics*
DESCRIPTION: Unoccupied housing units as a percentage of total housing units.

Rank		Percentage
	United States	11
1	Vermont	22
2	Maine	21
3	Alaska	19
4	Arizona	18
5	New Hampshire	18

Rank		Percentage
6	Wyoming	17
7	Florida	16
8	Delaware	15
9	Montana	15
10	New Mexico	14
11	Oklahoma	14
12	Colorado	13
13	Idaho	13
14	Louisiana	13
15	North Dakota	13
16	Texas	13
17	South Carolina	12
18	West Virginia	12
19	Arkansas	11
20	Michigan	11
21	Minnesota	11
22	Missouri	11
23	North Carolina	11
24	South Dakota	11
25	Wisconsin	11
26	Alabama	10
27	Washington, DC	10
28	Georgia	10
29	Kansas	10
30	Michigan	10
31	Nevada	10
32	Utah	10
33	Hawaii	9
34	Massachusetts	9
35	Nebraska	9
36	New Jersey	9
37	Pennsylvania	9
38	Rhode Island	9
39	Tennessee	9
40	Indiana	8
41	Kentucky	8
42	Maryland	8
43	New York	8
44	Oregon	8
45	Virginia	8
46	Washington	8
47	California	7
48	Connecticut	7
49	Illinois	7
50	Iowa	7
51	Ohio	7

HOUSING UNITS

Nationwide, 22% of housing was built between 1970 and 1979, 21% between 1980 and 1990 and 18% in 1939 or earlier. Therefore, the remaining 39% was built between 1940 and 1969, equaling the percentage of housing built between 1970 and 1990. Several high-growth southern and southwestern states ranked highest in housing built between 1980 and 1990: Nevada, Arizona, Florida, Georgia, Texas, North Carolina and New Mexico. Thirty-eight percent of Alaska's housing was built between 1980 and 1990; however the state had virtually no housing before 1939.

TABLE: Housing Units
DATE: 1990

SOURCE: U.S. Bureau of the Census, *1990 Census of Housing*, and Census of Population and Housing, 1990 Summary Tape File.

DESCRIPTION: Percent of housing units built in the stated time period and median year housing built. Table ranked by median year. Percentges will not add to 100%, because not all years are shown.

Rank		Total housing units (thousands)	1939 or earlier (percent)	1970–1979 (percent)	1980–1990 (percent)	Median year built
	United States	102,263.7	18.4	21.8	20.7	1965
1	Nevada	518.9	2.9	30.5	40.1	1977
2	Arizona	1,659.4	3.2	30.7	37.8	1976
3	Alaska	232.6	3.0	32.7	38.0	1976
4	Florida	6,100.3	3.7	29.3	35.0	1975
5	Georgia	2,638.4	8.1	24.5	32.1	1973
6	Texas	7,009.0	7.1	25.9	29.7	1972
7	South Carolina	1,424.2	8.5	26.3	29.0	1972
8	New Mexico	632.1	8.1	26.5	27.5	1972
9	North Carolina	2,818.2	9.9	24.3	28.6	1971
10	Colorado	1,477.3	13.0	28.9	24.7	1971
11	Mississippi	1,010.4	8.6	27.5	24.1	1971
12	Arkansas	1,000.7	9.4	27.8	24.2	1971
13	Utah	598.4	13.5	28.1	24.4	1971
14	Wyoming	203.4	15.6	31.1	21.4	1971
15	Virginia	2,496.3	11.0	23.6	26.3	1970
16	Tennessee	2,026.1	10.2	24.8	24.2	1970
17	Alabama	1,670.4	9.3	25.5	23.5	1970
18	Idaho	413.3	15.9	32.4	18.0	1970
19	Hawaii	389.8	6.7	30.5	20.8	1970
20	Washington	2,032.4	15.7	24.6	23.1	1969
21	Louisiana	1,716.2	10.6	25.3	22.1	1969
22	Oklahoma	1,406.5	12.4	25.4	22.1	1969
23	New Hampshire	503.9	27.1	20.5	27.7	1968
24	California	11,182.9	10.7	21.7	22.9	1967
25	Kentucky	1,506.8	15.9	25.0	20.0	1967
26	Oregon	1,193.6	16.8	28.7	16.6	1967
27	Delaware	289.9	14.3	20.2	24.3	1967
28	Montana	361.2	21.8	26.6	17.5	1966
29	Maryland	1,891.9	15.5	19.6	21.6	1965
30	North Dakota	276.3	24.7	26.6	16.6	1965
31	Missouri	2,199.1	20.4	21.5	18.3	1964
32	Minnesota	1,848.4	24.5	22.1	18.5	1963
33	Vermont	271.2	36.5	19.6	22.4	1963
34	West Virginia	781.3	23.7	22.8	17.7	1962
35	Indiana	2,246.0	24.2	20.2	14.5	1961
36	Kansas	1,044.1	24.5	20.3	16.9	1961
37	South Dakota	292.4	30.4	24.6	14.8	1961
38	Michigan	3,847.9	20.8	20.4	13.6	1960
39	Wisconsin	2,055.8	28.5	21.1	14.5	1960
40	Nebraska	660.6	30.7	22.1	12.9	1960
41	Maine	587.0	34.9	19.8	20.7	1960
42	Ohio	4,371.9	25.8	18.6	12.2	1959
43	New Jersey	3,075.3	24.6	14.9	14.8	1959
44	Connecticut	1,320.9	25.5	15.7	15.7	1959
45	Illinois	4,506.3	27.1	18.4	11.7	1958
46	Iowa	1,143.7	35.0	20.2	10.0	1956
47	Rhode Island	414.6	34.0	14.7	15.1	1955

Rank		Total housing units (thousands)	1939 or earlier (percent)	1970–1979 (percent)	1980–1990 (percent)	Median year built
48	Pennsylvania	4,938.1	35.1	15.8	12.4	1954
49	Massachusetts	2,472.7	38.9	14.1	13.8	1953
50	New York	7,226.9	35.7	11.9	9.4	1952
51	Washington, DC	278.5	37.7	8.4	5.5	1947

INCOMPLETE PLUMBING

The components of a complete plumbing system are defined by the U.S. Census Bureau as hot and cold running water, a flush toilet and a bathtub or shower. Approximately 99% of all housing units in the nation contain all of these facilities, an increase of 1% over 1980 figures. The highest proportions of incomplete plumbing were found in predominantly rural states such as Alaska and in the poorer states of the South.

TABLE: Incomplete Plumbing
DATE: 1990
SOURCE: U.S. Bureau of the Census, *1990 Census of Housing*, and Census of Population and Housing, 1990 Summary Tape File.
DESCRIPTION: Total housing units that lack plumbing and percent of total housing lacking plumbing.

Rank		Total housing units lacking plumbing (thousands)	Percent of total housing units lacking plumbing
	United States	1,101.7	1.1
1	Alaska	29.0	12.5
2	Maine	20.8	3.5
3	West Virginia	25.1	3.2
4	New Mexico	20.0	3.2
5	Kentucky	44.2	2.9
6	Vermont	6.1	2.3
7	Mississippi	21.9	2.2
8	South Dakota	5.9	2.0
9	North Dakota	5.6	2.0
10	Montana	7.0	1.9
11	Arizona	31.5	1.9
12	Virginia	46.1	1.8
13	Arkansas	18.4	1.8
14	Alabama	27.5	1.6
15	Tennessee	32.4	1.6
16	Wyoming	3.2	1.6
17	North Carolina	43.0	1.5
18	Idaho	6.0	1.5
19	Wisconsin	29.8	1.4
20	South Carolina	20.2	1.4
21	Minnesota	24.4	1.3
22	Louisiana	21.9	1.3
23	Missouri	26.8	1.2
24	Texas	85.1	1.2
25	New Hampshire	5.9	1.2
26	Hawaii	4.3	1.1
27	Georgia	28.5	1.1
28	Utah	5.9	1.0
29	Oklahoma	13.8	1.0
30	Pennsylvania	47.1	1.0
31	New York	67.3	0.9
32	Washington	18.6	0.9
33	Oregon	10.4	0.9
34	Iowa	9.8	0.9
35	Michigan	32.5	0.8
36	Washington, DC	2.3	0.8
37	Colorado	11.8	0.8
38	Nebraska	5.2	0.8
39	Ohio	32.9	0.8
40	Kansas	7.9	0.8
41	Indiana	16.2	0.7
42	Maryland	12.7	0.7
43	Illinois	29.3	0.7
44	California	69.4	0.6
45	Delaware	1.7	0.6
46	Rhode Island	2.3	0.5
47	Nevada	2.7	0.5
48	New Jersey	15.6	0.5
49	Massachusetts	12.4	0.5
50	Florida	28.0	0.5
51	Connecticut	5.7	0.4

RELIGION

This section presents data on the major Christian churches and Judaism. The sources are *Churches and Church Membership* and *Christian Church Adherents* published by the Glenmary Research Center and the *American Jewish Yearbook, 1992* published by the American Jewish Committee.

The figures on Christian church adherents were based on reports of 133 church groupings. Church adherents were defined as "all members, including full members, their children and the estimated number of other regular participants who were not considered as communicant, confirmed or full members."

CHRISTIAN CHURCH ADHERENTS

In 1980, 49.3% of the the nation's population were identified as church members. In 1990, the percentage increased to 52.7%. Participation was highest in the South and Northeast, followed by the Midwest and the West. Utah ranked first in percentage of church adherents. The Church of Latter-day Saints (Mormons) was the dominant church among Utah's church adherents. Twenty-eight states and the District of Columbia exceeded the national average.

TABLE: Christian Church Adherents
DATE: 1990

Data on the Jewish population included Jews who defined themselves as Jewish by religion and Jewish in cultural terms. These data were compiled according to estimates made by local Jewish federations across the country. In addition, most large Jewish communities have conducted Jewish demographic surveys from which the Jewish population can be determined.

The first table in this section is a survey of Christian church adherents in each state. This is followed by individual tables documenting the percentage of Roman Catholics, Methodists, Baptists, Presbyterians, Lutherans, Mormons, Seventh-day Adventists and Jews in each state.

SOURCE: B. Quinn, H. Anderson, M. Bradley, P. Goetting, and P. Shriver, *Churches and Church Membership in the United States 1980*, Glenmary Research Center (copyright)
M. Bradley, N. Green, Jr., D. Jones, M. Lynn, and L. McNeil, *Churches and Church Membership in the United States 1990*, Glenmary Research Center (copyright)
DESCRIPTION: Numbers of Christian Church adherents and percent of adherents in state populations. "Adherents" are defined as "all members, including full members, their children and the estimated number of other regular church participants."

Rank		1980 (thousands)	1980 percent of population*	1990 (thousands)	1990 percent of population*
	United States	111,736	49.3	131,084	52.7
1	Utah	1,097	75.1	1,371	79.6
2	North Dakota	482	73.8	484	75.8
3	Rhode Island	710	75.0	754	75.1
4	Alabama	2,230	57.3	2,858	70.7
5	Louisiana	2,404	57.2	2,959	70.1
6	Mississippi	1,385	54.9	1,804	70.1
7	South Dakota	462	66.9	474	68.1
8	Oklahoma	1,751	57.9	2,097	66.7
9	Minnesota	2,644	64.9	2,807	64.2
10	Wisconsin	3,029	64.4	3,125	63.9

Rank		1980 (thousands)	1980 percent of population*	1990 (thousands)	1990 percent of population*
11	Texas	7,752	54.5	10,787	63.5
12	Nebraska	990	63.1	1,000	63.4
13	South Carolina	1,603	51.3	2,149	61.6
14	Massachusetts	3,669	64.0	3,666	60.9
15	Tennessee	2,485	54.1	2,966	60.8
16	Arkansas	1,282	56.1	1,423	60.5
17	Iowa	1,781	61.1	1,675	60.3
18	Kentucky	1,979	54.1	2,216	60.1
19	North Carolina	3,169	53.9	3,962	59.8
20	Connecticut	1,890	60.8	1,935	58.9
21	Pennsylvania	7,177	60.5	6,961	58.6
22	New Mexico	767	58.9	883	58.3
23	Illinois	6,251	54.7	6,591	57.7
24	Washington, DC	304	47.6	349	57.5
25	Georgia	2,560	46.9	3,659	56.5
26	Missouri	2,613	53.1	2,883	56.3
27	New Jersey	3,923	53.3	4,305	55.7
28	New York	8,548	48.7	9,970	55.4
29	Kansas	1,262	53.4	1,341	54.1
30	Idaho	472	50.0	507	50.4
31	Michigan	3,932	42.5	4,580	49.3
32	Ohio	5,306	49.1	5,307	48.9
33	Wyoming	207	44.0	216	47.6
34	Indiana	2,451	44.6	2,617	47.2
35	Virginia	2,221	41.5	2,898	46.8
36	Delaware	238	40.1	297	44.6
37	Maryland	1,673	39.7	2,101	43.9
38	Montana	348	44.2	341	42.7
39	West Virginia	772	39.6	740	41.3
40	Vermont	244	47.7	232	41.2
41	Arizona	1,065	39.2	1,505	41.1
42	Florida	3,707	38.0	5,106	39.5
43	California	8,082	34.1	11,665	39.2
44	New Hampshire	407	44.2	431	38.9
45	Colorado	1,052	36.4	1,244	37.8
46	Maine	461	41.0	439	35.8
47	Hawaii	319	33.1	384	34.6
48	Washington	1,275	30.9	1,580	32.5
49	Alaska	123	30.6	175	31.8
50	Oregon	946	35.9	903	31.8
51	Nevada	233	29.1	366	30.5

* For 1980 and 1990, based on U.S. Bureau of the Census data for resident population.

ROMAN CATHOLICS

Roman Catholics made up 21.5% of the population of the United States, and 42% of all church adherents in 1990. The Catholic populations documented here reflect the settlement patterns of earlier generations of immigrants. Wisconsin and Illinois, states that had a large number of German Catholic immigrants in the nineteenth century, currently have a comparatively high percentage of Catholics in the population. In California Catholics accounted for 24% of the state's population. Because registered church adherents comprised only 39.2% of

California's population, Catholics accounted for the majority of the church-affiliated population in the state in 1990. In Texas Baptists (24.1%) and Catholics (21%) are represented in equal proportions within the population.

TABLE: Roman Catholics
DATE: 1990
SOURCE: B. Quinn, H. Anderson, M. Bradley, P. Goetting, and P. Shriver, *Churches and Church Membership in the United States 1980*, Glenmary Research Center (copyright)

M. Bradley, N. Green, Jr., D. Jones, M. Lynn, and L. McNeil, *Churches and Church Membership in the United States 1990*, Glenmary Research Center (copyright)
DESCRIPTION: Percent of Roman Catholics in the total state population.

Rank		1980 percent	1990 percent
	United States	21.0	21.5
1	Rhode Island	63.7	63.1
2	Massachusetts	53.0	49.2
3	Connecticut	44.7	41.8
4	New Jersey	40.2	41.3
5	New York	35.6	40.5
6	Louisiana	31.0	32.4
7	Wisconsin	32.8	31.8
8	Illinois	31.5	31.6
9	Pennsylvania	32.7	30.9
10	New Mexico	33.5	30.8
11	North Dakota	26.7	27.1
12	New Hampshire	31.0	26.8
13	Vermont	30.6	25.6
14	Minnesota	25.6	25.4
15	Michigan	22.1	25.2
16	California	20.1	24.0
17	Maine	24.5	21.5
18	Nebraska	21.2	21.2
19	Hawaii	21.8	21.0
20	Texas	16.4	21.0
21	South Dakota	20.1	20.7
22	Ohio	22.5	19.7
23	Iowa	18.5	18.7
24	Arizona	17.8	17.9
25	Delaware	17.3	17.5
26	Maryland	17.5	17.4
27	Missouri	16.3	15.7
28	Montana	17.8	15.7
29	Kansas	14.3	14.9
30	Colorado	14.0	14.7
31	Nevada	13.8	13.1
32	Wyoming	13.2	13.1
33	Washington, DC	NA	12.8
34	Indiana	13.2	12.6
35	Florida	13.9	12.4
36	Washington	9.2	10.8
37	Kentucky	10.0	9.9
38	Oregon	12.2	9.8
39	Alaska	9.9	8.2
40	Idaho	7.5	7.3
41	Virginia	5.3	6.2
42	West Virginia	5.4	6.1
43	Oklahoma	3.5	4.6
44	Utah	4.1	3.8
45	Mississippi	3.8	3.7
46	Alabama	2.7	3.4
47	Georgia	2.6	3.2
48	Arkansas	2.5	3.1

Rank		1980 percent	1990 percent
49	Tennessee	2.5	2.8
50	North Carolina	1.6	2.3
51	South Carolina	1.9	2.3

NA Not available

METHODISTS

Methodists represented 4.5% of the total population and 8.5% of all church adherents in 1990. Methodists were concentrated in a broad band of states stretching from Delaware, Maryland and Virginia to Nebraska, Kansas and Oklahoma, and throughout the South.

TABLE: Methodists
DATE: 1990
SOURCE: B. Quinn, H. Anderson, M. Bradley, P. Goetting, and P. Shriver, *Churches and Church Membership in the United States 1980*, Glenmary Research Center (copyright)
M. Bradley, N. Green, Jr., D. Jones, M. Lynn, and L. McNeil, *Churches and Church Membership in the United States 1990*, Glenmary Research Center (copyright)
DESCRIPTION: Percent of Methodists in the total state population.

Rank		1980 percent	1990 percent
	United States	5.1	4.5
1	Oklahoma	10.4	10.4
2	West Virginia	11.3	10.2
3	Iowa	10.9	9.8
4	Kansas	11.1	9.6
5	Mississippi	9.9	9.3
6	Delaware	10.2	9.2
7	Nebraska	10.0	9.2
8	North Carolina	10.1	9.1
9	South Carolina	9.5	8.9
10	Arkansas	9.4	8.4
11	Alabama	8.9	8.2
12	Georgia	8.9	8.2
13	Tennessee	9.0	8.1
14	Virginia	9.4	7.9
15	Maryland	7.6	6.5
16	Indiana	7.0	6.2
17	Kentucky	6.4	6.2
18	South Dakota	6.7	6.2
19	Pennsylvania	6.6	6.1
20	Ohio	6.9	6.0
21	Texas	6.6	5.9
22	Missouri	5.5	5.0
23	Vermont	5.2	4.4
24	Louisiana	4.0	4.1
25	Illinois	4.4	3.9
26	North Dakota	4.1	3.7

Rank		1980 percent	1990 percent
27	Florida	4.4	3.6
28	New Mexico	4.1	3.6
29	Minnesota	3.6	3.3
30	Wisconsin	3.5	3.1
31	Washington, DC	NA	3.0
32	Maine	3.4	2.9
33	Wyoming	3.2	2.9
34	Colorado	3.4	2.8
35	Michigan	3.1	2.7
36	New York	2.9	2.6
37	Montana	3.1	2.4
38	New Jersey	2.5	2.2
39	Idaho	2.4	2.1
40	Washington	2.4	1.8
41	Connecticut	2.0	1.7
42	New Hampshire	2.2	1.7
43	Arizona	1.9	1.6
44	Oregon	1.9	1.5
45	Massachusetts	1.3	1.2
46	Alaska	1.1	0.9
47	Rhode Island	0.9	0.9
48	California	1.2	0.9
49	Hawaii	0.7	0.8
50	Nevada	0.9	0.7
51	Utah	0.4	0.4

NA Not available.

BAPTISTS

In 1990 Baptists represented the largest non-Catholic religious group in the country. Baptists accounted for 11.7% of the total population and 22% of all church adherents and were highly concentrated in the southern states and in smaller numbers in Missouri, Oklahoma, Texas and New Mexico. Two specific denominations are enumerated in the table below—the Southern Baptist Convention and the American Baptist Churches in the U.S.A.—and estimated for two large denominations of black churches—the National Baptist Convention U.S.A. and the National Baptist Convention of America.

TABLE: Baptists
DATE: 1990
SOURCE: B. Quinn, H. Anderson, M. Bradley, P. Goetting, and P. Shriver, *Churches and Church Membership in the United States 1980*, Glenmary Research Center (copyright)
M. Bradley, N. Green, Jr., D. Jones, M. Lynn, and L. McNeil, *Churches and Church Membership in the United States 1990*, Glenmary Research Center (copyright)
DESCRIPTION: Percent of Baptists in the total state population.

Rank		1980 percent	1990 percent
	United States	8.0	11.7
1	Mississippi	30.2	46.4
2	Alabama	30.4	42.5
3	South Carolina	25.7	35.6
4	Georgia	25.4	34.5
5	Oklahoma	26.5	33.5
6	Tennessee	26.3	32.7
7	Arkansas	22.9	31.5
8	North Carolina	23.0	29.2
9	Kentucky	24.3	28.5
10	Louisiana	15.5	27.2
11	Washington, DC	NA	25.5
12	Texas	18.9	24.1
13	Virginia	13.6	18.8
14	Missouri	14.5	18.7
15	Florida	9.7	13.3
16	New Mexico	10.1	11.1
17	West Virginia	9.5	10.8
18	Maryland	3.8	9.1
19	Kansas	6.2	8.5
20	Delaware	1.3	7.4
21	Indiana	4.4	7.0
22	Illinois	3.2	6.9
23	Alaska	4.6	6.6
24	Ohio	2.6	6.5
25	Wyoming	3.8	5.7
26	Arizona	4.5	5.5
27	Michigan	1.4	5.4
28	Nevada	2.5	4.6
29	Colorado	3.3	4.5
30	California	2.5	4.3
31	New York	1.3	4.2
32	New Jersey	1.1	4.1
33	Connecticut	1.5	3.8
34	Rhode Island	2.7	3.3
35	Nebraska	1.8	3.0
36	Pennsylvania	1.2	3.0
37	Maine	3.5	2.9
38	Washington	2.0	2.7
39	Idaho	2.1	2.6
40	Hawaii	1.5	2.5
41	Massachusetts	1.3	2.5
42	South Dakota	2.0	2.3
43	Iowa	1.6	2.2
44	Wisconsin	0.6	2.2
45	Montana	1.7	2.1
46	New Hampshire	2.1	2.1
47	Oregon	1.7	2.0
48	Vermont	2.2	1.8
49	North Dakota	0.9	1.2
50	Utah	0.9	1.2
51	Minnesota	0.5	1.1

NA Not available.

PRESBYTERIANS

In 1990, 1.5% of the total population and 2.8% of all church adherents belonged to two major Presbyterian denominations: the United Presbyterian Church U.S.A. and the Presbyterian Church in America. Members of the latter denomination resided only in the South and the bordering states of Kansas and Missouri, while members of the former denomination were scattered throughout the country. Presbyterians were located along a broad band stretching from Pennsylvania through Ohio and into the Midwest. The southern denomination of Presbyterians were focused in North Carolina and South Carolina, Virginia and West Virginia.

TABLE: Presbyterians
DATE: 1990
SOURCE: B. Quinn, H. Anderson, M. Bradley, P. Goetting, and P. Shriver, *Churches and Church Membership in the United States 1980*, Glenmary Research Center (copyright)
M. Bradley, N. Green, Jr., D. Jones, M. Lynn, and L. McNeil, *Churches and Church Membership in the United States 1990*, Glenmary Research Center (copyright)
DESCRIPTION: Percent of Presbyterians in the total state population.

Rank		1980 percent	1990 percent
	United States	1.8	1.5
1	Pennsylvania	4.0	3.4
2	North Carolina	3.5	3.3
3	South Carolina	3.0	3.3
4	Iowa	3.6	3.1
5	Nebraska	3.7	3.1
6	Delaware	2.8	2.7
7	Kansas	3.3	2.6
8	South Dakota	2.7	2.4
9	Virginia	2.7	2.4
10	West Virginia	2.4	2.2
11	North Dakota	2.2	1.9
12	Ohio	2.4	1.9
13	Wyoming	2.2	1.9
14	Georgia	1.7	1.8
15	New Jersey	2.4	1.8
16	Tennessee	1.8	1.8
17	Missouri	1.9	1.7
18	Colorado	2.0	1.6
19	Washington, DC	NA	1.6
20	Florida	1.6	1.6
21	Indiana	2.0	1.6
22	Minnesota	1.9	1.5
23	Mississippi	1.1	1.5
24	Washington	1.7	1.5
25	Alabama	1.1	1.4
26	Illinois	1.7	1.4
27	Michigan	1.7	1.4

Rank		1980 percent	1990 percent
28	Montana	1.7	1.4
29	Oklahoma	1.6	1.3
30	Oregon	1.6	1.3
31	Arkansas	1.3	1.2
32	Kentucky	1.4	1.2
33	Maryland	1.3	1.2
34	Texas	1.4	1.2
35	Alaska	1.4	1.1
36	Idaho	1.3	1.1
37	New York	1.4	1.1
38	Arizona	1.2	1
39	New Mexico	1.3	1
40	Wisconsin	1.2	1
41	California	1.1	0.9
42	Louisiana	0.8	0.7
43	Nevada	0.6	0.5
44	Utah	0.5	0.4
45	Connecticut	0.3	0.3
46	Rhode Island	0.3	0.3
47	Hawaii	0.1	0.2
48	New Hampshire	0.2	0.2
49	Vermont	0.2	0.2
50	Maine	0.1	0.1
51	Massachusetts	0.1	0.1

NA Not available.

LUTHERANS

Lutherans made up 4.1% of the population nationwide and 7.7% of all church adherents in 1990. Strong denominational divisions among Lutherans reflected both theological differences and ethnic groupings, such as, German, Swedish or Norwegian. Data for the two largest groups, the Evangelical Lutheran Church in America and the Lutheran Church–Missouri Synod, were combined in this table. The upper Midwest, where many German and Scandinavian populations settled, represented the largest concentration of Lutherans.

TABLE: Lutherans
DATE: 1990
SOURCE: B. Quinn, H. Anderson, M. Bradley, P. Goetting, and P. Shriver, *Churches and Church Membership in the United States 1980*, Glenmary Research Center (copyright)
M. Bradley, N. Green, Jr., D. Jones, M. Lynn, and L. McNeil, *Churches and Church Membership in the United States 1990*, Glenmary Research Center (copyright)
DESCRIPTION: Percent of Lutherans in the total state population.

Rank		1980 percent	1990 percent
	United States	3.6	4.1
1	North Dakota	31.9	32.1
2	Minnesota	26.0	23.7

Rank		1980 percent	1990 percent
3	South Dakota	23.4	21.2
4	Nebraska	15.9	15.5
5	Wisconsin	20.0	14.5
6	Iowa	14.2	14.1
7	Montana	9.0	8.1
8	Pennsylvania	6.7	5.9
9	Illinois	5.5	5.2
10	Michigan	5.1	4.5
11	Wyoming	3.9	4.5
12	Kansas	4.4	4.3
13	Ohio	4.0	3.8
14	Washington	4.3	3.6
15	Indiana	3.5	3.4
16	Missouri	3.3	3.4
17	Colorado	3.6	3.3
18	Maryland	3.6	2.9
19	Idaho	2.8	2.6
20	Oregon	3.0	2.6
21	Alaska	2.4	2.4
22	Arizona	2.4	2.1
23	South Carolina	1.9	1.9
24	Texas	1.8	1.7
25	Connecticut	1.7	1.6
26	North Carolina	1.5	1.6
27	New York	1.7	1.5
28	New Jersey	1.7	1.4
29	Delaware	1.7	1.3
30	Virginia	1.4	1.3
31	Florida	1.4	1.2
32	Nevada	1.2	1.2
33	New Mexico	1.1	1.2
34	Oklahoma	0.9	1.2
35	California	1.4	1.1
36	Washington, DC	NA	0.9
37	Arkansas	0.7	0.8
38	West Virginia	0.8	0.8
39	Georgia	0.6	0.6
40	Hawaii	0.4	0.6
41	Louisiana	0.7	0.6
42	Massachusetts	0.5	0.6
43	Rhode Island	0.7	0.6
44	Tennessee	0.5	0.6
45	Utah	0.6	0.6
46	Kentucky	0.4	0.5
47	New Hampshire	0.4	0.5
48	Alabama	0.4	0.4
49	Vermont	0.3	0.4
50	Maine	0.1	0.3
51	Mississippi	0.3	0.3

NA Not available.

MORMONS

In 1990 Mormons comprised 1.4% of the total population and 2.6% of all church adherents. The Church is dominant in Utah, where 71.8% of the population were identified as adherents. Mormons accounted for smaller groups in other western states: Idaho, Wyoming, Nevada and Arizona. Mormons remain the most geographically concentrated major religious group in the country. However, they resided in varying numbers in all 50 states.

TABLE: Mormons
DATE: 1990
SOURCE: B. Quinn, H. Anderson, M. Bradley, P. Goetting, and P. Shriver, *Churches and Church Membership in the United States 1980*, Glenmary Research Center (copyright)
M. Bradley, N. Green, Jr., D. Jones, M. Lynn, and L. McNeil, *Churches and Church Membership in the United States 1990*, Glenmary Research Center (copyright)
DESCRIPTION: Percent of Mormons in the total state population.

Rank		1980 percent	1990 percent
	United States	1.2	1.4
1	Utah	67.4	71.8
2	Idaho	25.5	26.6
3	Wyoming	8.6	10.1
4	Nevada	6.9	7.4
5	Arizona	5.1	5.5
6	Montana	3.3	3.6
7	Hawaii	2.9	3.5
8	Oregon	2.8	3.2
9	Washington	2.5	3.1
10	Alaska	2.2	2.9
11	New Mexico	2.2	2.6
12	Colorado	1.8	2.1
13	California	1.7	1.8
14	Kansas	0.4	0.7
15	Nebraska	0.4	0.7
16	South Dakota	0.4	0.7
17	Texas	0.5	0.7
18	Virginia	0.5	0.7
19	Oklahoma	0.5	0.6
20	Florida	0.4	0.5
21	Georgia	0.4	0.5
22	Maine	0.4	0.5
23	Missouri	0.4	0.5
24	North Carolina	0.4	0.5
25	South Carolina	0.4	0.5
26	Vermont	0.3	0.5
27	West Virginia	0.4	0.5
28	Alabama	0.3	0.4
29	Arkansas	0.3	0.4
30	Delaware	0.2	0.4
31	Indiana	0.3	0.4
32	Iowa	0.3	0.4
33	Kentucky	0.3	0.4
34	Louisiana	0.3	0.4
35	Maryland	0.3	0.4
36	Mississippi	0.3	0.4
37	New Hampshire	0.3	0.4

Rank		1980 percent	1990 percent
38	North Dakota	0.2	0.4
39	Illinois	0.2	0.3
40	Michigan	0.2	0.3
41	Minnesota	0.2	0.3
42	Ohio	0.2	0.3
43	Tennessee	0.2	0.3
44	Connecticut	0.2	0.2
45	Massachusetts	0.1	0.2
46	New Jersey	0.1	0.2
47	New York	0.1	0.2
48	Pennsylvania	0.2	0.2
49	Wisconsin	0.2	0.2
50	Washington, DC	NA	0.1
51	Rhode Island	0.1	0.1

NA Not available.

SEVENTH-DAY ADVENTISTS

In 1990 Seventh-Day Adventists accounted for .4% of the population. Seventh-Day Adventists were included in this chapter to represent the typical geographical distribution of fundamentalists and Pentecostals. Seventh-Day Adventists report a strong following in the West and South.

TABLE: Seventh-Day Adventists
DATE: 1990
SOURCE: B. Quinn, H. Anderson, M. Bradley, P. Goetting, and P. Shriver, *Churches and Church Membership in the United States 1980*, Glenmary Research Center (copyright)
M. Bradley, N. Green, Jr., D. Jones, M. Lynn, and L. McNeil, *Churches and Church Membership in the United States 1990*, Glenmary Research Center (copyright)
DESCRIPTION: Percent of Seventh-Day Adventists in the total state population.

Rank		1980 percent	1990 percent
	United States	0.3	0.4
1	Oregon	1.2	1.2
2	Washington, DC	NA	0.9
3	Idaho	0.7	0.8
4	Washington	0.8	0.8
5	California	0.6	0.7
6	Tennessee	0.5	0.6
7	Alabama	0.3	0.5
8	Alaska	0.4	0.5
9	Colorado	0.5	0.5
10	Hawaii	0.5	0.5
11	Maryland	0.4	0.5
12	Montana	0.5	0.5
13	Nebraska	0.5	0.5
14	North Dakota	0.6	0.5

Rank		1980 percent	1990 percent
15	Florida	0.3	0.4
16	Georgia	0.3	0.4
17	Michigan	0.4	0.4
18	Wyoming	0.5	0.4
19	Arizona	0.3	0.3
20	Arkansas	0.2	0.3
21	Delaware	0.2	0.3
22	Kansas	0.2	0.3
23	Maine	0.2	0.3
24	Mississippi	0.2	0.3
25	New Mexico	0.3	0.3
26	New York	0.2	0.3
27	North Carolina	0.3	0.3
28	Oklahoma	0.3	0.3
29	South Dakota	0.4	0.3
30	Illinois	0.2	0.2
31	Indiana	0.2	0.2
32	Iowa	0.2	0.2
33	Kentucky	0.1	0.2
34	Louisiana	0.2	0.2
35	Massachusetts	0.1	0.2
36	Minnesota	0.2	0.2
37	Missouri	0.2	0.2
38	Nevada	0.2	0.2
39	New Jersey	0.2	0.2
40	Ohio	0.2	0.2
41	Pennsylvania	0.1	0.2
42	South Carolina	0.2	0.2
43	Texas	0.2	0.2
44	Virginia	0.2	0.2
45	West Virginia	0.2	0.2
46	Wisconsin	0.2	0.2
47	Connecticut	0.1	0.1
48	New Hampshire	0.1	0.1
49	Rhode Island	0.1	0.1
50	Utah	0.1	0.1
51	Vermont	0.1	0.1

NA Not available.

JEWISH POPULATION

In 1991 the Jewish population accounted for 2.3% of the total population. New York City, historically a principal port of entry for Jews from Central and Eastern Europe, remained the nucleus of a large portion of the population. Many Jews and their descendants have settled in New York state and neighboring New Jersey and Connecticut. States with major metropolitan areas also reported comparatively high percentages of Jews in their population.

TABLE: Jewish Population
DATE: 1991
SOURCE: American Jewish Committee, *1992 American Jewish Year Book*, 1992, American Jewish Committee and Jewish Publication Society (copyright)

DESCRIPTION: Percent of Jews in total state population.

Rank		1981 percent	1991 percent
	United States	2.6	2.3
1	New York	12.2	9.1
2	New Jersey	5.9	5.5
3	Florida	4.8	4.6
4	Massachusetts	4.2	4.6
5	Maryland	4.4	4.4
6	Washington, DC	NA	4.2
7	Connecticut	3.3	3.2
8	California	3.2	3.1
9	Pennsylvania	3.5	2.8
10	Illinois	2.3	2.2
11	Arizona	1.7	2.0
12	Nevada	1.8	1.7
13	Rhode Island	2.3	1.6
14	Colorado	1.1	1.5
15	Delaware	1.6	1.4
16	Michigan	1.0	1.2
17	Missouri	1.5	1.2
18	Ohio	1.3	1.2
19	Georgia	0.7	1.1
20	Virginia	1.1	1.1
21	Vermont	0.5	0.8
22	Maine	0.6	0.7
23	Minnesota	0.9	0.7
24	Washington	0.5	0.7

Rank		1981 percent	1991 percent
25	Wisconsin	0.6	0.7
26	Hawaii	0.6	0.6
27	Kansas	0.5	0.6
28	New Hampshire	0.5	0.6
29	Texas	0.5	0.6
30	Nebraska	0.5	0.5
31	Oregon	0.4	0.5
32	Alaska	0.2	0.4
33	Louisiana	0.4	0.4
34	New Mexico	0.6	0.4
35	Tennessee	0.4	0.4
36	Indiana	0.4	0.3
37	Kentucky	0.3	0.3
38	Alabama	0.2	0.2
39	Iowa	0.3	0.2
40	North Carolina	0.2	0.2
41	Oklahoma	0.2	0.2
42	South Carolina	0.3	0.2
43	Utah	0.2	0.2
44	Arkansas	0.1	0.1
45	Mississippi	0.1	0.1
46	Montana	0.1	0.1
47	North Dakota	0.2	0.1
48	South Dakota	0.1	0.1
49	West Virginia	0.4	0.1
50	Idaho	0.1	0
51	Wyoming	0.1	0

NA Not available.

AGRICULTURE

This section presents statistics on farms, the value of farm real estate and farm income. The primary sources are the U.S. Census Bureau, and the National Agricultural Statistical Service and the Economic Research Service, both of the U.S. Department of Agriculture. The Census Bureau defined a farm as any place where $1,000 or more of agricultural products were produced or sold or normally would have been sold during the year. Farmland, according to the Census Bureau, refers to all land under the control of a farm operator, including land not actually under cultivation or not used for pasture or grazing. The first three tables in this section detail the number and acreage of farms. These are followed by tables on the value of farm real estate and farm income.

NUMBER OF FARMS

The United States experienced a decline in the number of farms from 1980 (2.4 million) to 1993 (2.1 million). With the exceptions of Massachusetts and Montana, the number of farms either remained the same or fell in all states. This was a result of the continuing decline in the family farm, the consolidation of large amounts of farmland by agribusiness, and the loss of farms to suburban development. Between 1980 and 1993 the greatest declines were in North Carolina, where farms decreased by 34,000, and in Illinois, where farms decreased by 27,000. In 1993, 27% of all the nation's farms were located in five states: Texas, Missouri, Iowa, Kentucky and Minnesota. The table below includes all farms regardless of type of ownership. Any place meeting the definition of farm (see below), whether owned or managed, leased or rented, is included here.

TABLE: Number of Farms
DATE: 1993
SOURCE: U.S. Dept. of Agriculture, *National Agricultural Statistics Service, Farm Numbers, 1975–80; Farm and Land in Farms, Final Estimates by States, 1979–1987; Farm and Land in Farms, 1993.*

DESCRIPTION: Number of farms in 1980 and 1993 with change from 1980 to 1993. A farm is defined as any place where $1,000 or more of agricultural products have been sold during a year. Table ranked by 1993 number.

Rank		1980 number of farms (thousands)	1993 number of farms (thousands)	*Change in the number of farms 1980 to 1993
	United States	2,440	2,068	372
1	Texas	196	185	11
2	Missouri	120	106	14
3	Iowa	119	100	19
4	Kentucky	102	91	11
5	Minnesota	104	87	17
6	Tennessee	96	86	10
7	Illinois	107	80	27
8	Wisconsin	93	79	14
9	California	81	76	5
10	Ohio	95	76	19
11	Oklahoma	72	71	1
12	Kansas	75	65	10
13	Indiana	87	63	24
14	North Carolina	93	59	34
15	Nebraska	65	55	10
16	Michigan	65	52	13
17	Pennsylvania	62	51	11
18	Alabama	59	47	12
19	Arkansas	59	46	13
20	Georgia	59	45	14
21	Virginia	58	43	15
22	Florida	39	39	0
23	Mississippi	55	39	16
24	New York	47	38	9
25	Oregon	35	37	(2)
26	Washington	38	36	2
27	South Dakota	39	35	5
28	North Dakota	40	33	7
29	Louisiana	37	29	8
30	Colorado	27	26	2
31	Montana	24	25	(1)
32	South Carolina	34	24	10

172

Rank		1980 number of farms (thousands)	1993 number of farms (thousands)	*Change in the number of farms 1980 to 1993
33	Idaho	24	21	4
34	West Virginia	22	20	2
35	Maryland	18	15	3
36	New Mexico	14	14	1
37	Utah	14	13	1
38	Wyoming	9	9	0
39	New Jersey	9	8	1
40	Arizona	8	8	0
41	Maine	8	7	1
42	Vermont	8	7	1
43	Massachusetts	6	7	(1)
44	Hawaii	4	4	0
45	Connecticut	4	4	0
46	New Hampshire	3	3	0
47	Delaware	4	3	1
48	Nevada	3	2	1
49	Rhode Island	1	1	0
50	Alaska	Z	1	Z

*Numbers in parentheses indicate an increase in the number of farms.
Z Fewer than 500 farms or less than 500,000 acres.

FARMLAND

Approximately half of the nation's total land area (exclusive of Alaska) was designated farmland. This included land used for pasture and grazing as well as for crops. A broad band of states running from Montana and North Dakota in the North through Wyoming, South Dakota, Nebraska, Kansas, Colorado, Iowa and Oklahoma and down through the Southwest to Texas, New Mexico and Arizona ranked highest in farm acreage. Nationwide, the United States experienced a decline in farmland from 1980 to 1983. Acreage in farms either remained the same or declined in all states.

TABLE: Farmland
DATE: 1993
SOURCE: U.S. Dept. of Agriculture, National Agricultural Statistics Service, *Farm Numbers, 1975–80*; *Farm and Land in Farms, Final Estimates by States, 1979–1987*; *Farm and Land in Farms, 1993*
DESCRIPTION: Farmland 1980 and 1993 with percent decline. Farmland is defined as all land under the control of a farm operator, including land not actually under cultivation or not used for pasture or grazing.

Rank		1980 farmland (million acres)	1993 farmland (million acres)	Percent decline 1987 to 1993
	United States	1,039	978	5.87
1	Texas	138	130	6.15
2	Montana	62	60	3.22
3	Kansas	48	48	0.00
4	Nebraska	48	47	3.54
5	New Mexico	47	44	6.38
6	South Dakota	45	44	2.22
7	North Dakota	42	40	4.76
8	Arizona	38	36	5.26
9	Wyoming	35	35	0.00
10	Oklahoma	35	34	2.94
11	Iowa	34	33	2.94
12	Colorado	36	33	8.33
13	Missouri	31	30	3.33
14	California	34	30	13.33
15	Minnesota	30	30	0.00
16	Illinois	29	28	3.44
17	Oregon	18	18	0.00
18	Wisconsin	19	17	10.50
19	Indiana	17	16	5.88
20	Washington	16	16	0.00
21	Arkansas	17	15	11.76
22	Ohio	16	15	6.25
23	Kentucky	15	14	6.66
24	Idaho	15	14	6.66
25	Mississippi	15	13	13.33
26	Tennessee	14	12	14.28
27	Georgia	15	12	20.00
28	Utah	12	11	8.33
29	Michigan	11	11	0.00
30	Florida	13	10	23.07
31	Alabama	12	10	16.66
32	North Carolina	12	9	25.00
33	Nevada	9	9	0.00
34	Louisiana	10	9	10.00
35	Virginia	10	9	10.00
36	New York	9	8	11.11
37	Pennsylvania	9	8	11.11
38	South Carolina	6	5	16.66
39	West Virginia	4	4	0.00
40	Maryland	3	2	33.30
41	Hawaii	2	2	0.00
42	Vermont	2	2	0.00
43	Maine	2	1	50.00
44	Alaska	2	0.9	55.00
45	New Jersey	1	0.9	10.00
46	Massachusetts	1	0.7	30.00
47	Delaware	1	0.6	40.00
48	New Hampshire	1	0.5	50.00
49	Connecticut	Z	0.4	NA
50	Rhode Island	Z	0.06	NA

Z Fewer than 500 farms or less than 500,000 acres.
NA Not Available

ACREAGE PER FARM

The number of farms declined in the United States, but the average size of farms increased, reflecting the trend toward consolidation and away from the family farm. The states with large tracts of rangeland used for grazing ranked highest in this table. The states ranked in the middle portion contained farms that cultivated grain and orchards producing citrus fruits. Smaller farms, located primarily in the Great Lakes region, the South and the Northeast, specialized in dairy, poultry, fruit and vegetable production.

TABLE: Acreage Per Farm
DATE: 1993
SOURCE: U.S. Dept. of Agriculture, *National Agricultural Statistics Service, Farm Numbers, 1975–80; Farm and Land in Farms, Final Estimates by States, 1979–1987; Farm and Land in Farms, 1993*
DESCRIPTION: Average farm acreage 1980 and 1993 with percent change 1980–1993. Table ranked by 1993 figures.

Rank		1980 acreage per farm	1993 acreage per farm	Percent change 1980–1993
	United States	426	473	11.01
1	Arizona	5,080	4,557	-10.29
2	Wyoming	3,846	3,742	-2.71
3	Nevada	3,100	3,708	19.62
4	New Mexico	3,467	3,274	-5.57
5	Montana	2,601	2,445	-6.00
6	Alaska	3,378	1,759	-4.48
7	Colorado	1,358	1,286	-5.28
8	South Dakota	1,169	1,281	9.60
9	North Dakota	1,043	1,224	17.37
10	Utah	919	862	-6.25
11	Nebraska	734	856	16.67
12	Kansas	644	735	14.19
13	Texas	705	703	-3.26
14	Idaho	623	659	5.70
15	Oklahoma	481	479	-0.44
16	Oregon	517	473	-8.51
17	Washington	429	444	0.36
18	California	417	391	-6.29
19	Hawaii	458	389	-15.15
20	Illinois	269	354	31.51
21	Minnesota	291	341	17.31
22	Arkansas	280	335	19.56
23	Mississippi	265	333	25.79
24	Iowa	284	333	17.25
25	Louisiana	273	297	8.62
26	Missouri	261	285	9.16
27	Georgia	254	269	5.86
28	Florida	344	264	-23.22
29	Indiana	193	254	31.60
30	Delaware	186	220	18.28
31	Vermont	226	219	-3.17

Rank		1980 acreage per farm	1993 acreage per farm	Percent change 1980–1993
32	Wisconsin	200	216	8.23
33	New York	200	216	7.90
34	Alabama	207	213	27.85
35	South Carolina	188	212	12.73
36	Michigan	175	206	17.58
37	Maine	195	200	2.56
38	Ohio	171	200	16.96
39	Virginia	169	200	18.34
40	West Virginia	191	185	-3.14
41	New Hampshire	160	174	8.80
42	North Carolina	126	159	26.44
43	Kentucky	143	155	8.35
44	Pennsylvania	145	155	6.83
45	Maryland	157	147	-6.58
46	Tennessee	142	144	1.53
47	New Jersey	109	104	-4.98
48	Connecticut	117	103	-12.39
49	Massachusetts	116	98	-15.10
50	Rhode Island	87	90	3.45

AVERAGE VALUE OF LAND AND BUILDINGS

The value of farm real estate depends on the productivity of the land and its scarcity in a given area. The table below skews the value in favor of small farms because the value of farm buildings and facilities are included in the figures. The five states at the top of the list all border large metropolitan areas where continued urban expansion has caused land to become more valuable. The states with large tracts of grazing land ranked at the bottom of the list. The data showing the change in the value of farm real estate between 1980 and 1993 documents the increasing value of land in the states ranked highest. Nationwide, the value of farm real estate per acre declined in the 1980s, reflecting a recession in agriculture. It began rising again in the early 1990s as the economy improved.

TABLE: Average Value of Land and Buildings
DATE: 1993
SOURCE: U.S. Dept. of Agriculture, Economic Research Service, *1980 Farm Real Estate Market Developments*, annual; beginning 1985 *Agricultural Resources, Agricultural Land Values and Markets, Situation and Outlook Report*, annual
DESCRIPTION: Average value of farmland per acre. Total value of land and buildings is estimated by multiplying the number of acres of farmland by the average value per acre of land and buildings. Excludes Alaska and Hawaii. Table ranked by 1993 figures.

Rank		1980 ($)	1990 ($)	1993 ($)
	United States	737	668	700
1	Rhode Island	2,523	5,028	4,894
2	New Jersey	2,947	4,634	4,536
3	Connecticut	2,387	4,417	4,299
4	Massachusetts	1,608	3,763	3,662
5	Maryland	2,238	2,420	2,521
6	Delaware	1,798	2,259	2,362
7	New Hampshire	1,004	2,237	2,178
8	Florida	1,381	2,085	2,074
9	Pennsylvania	1,464	1,807	1,747
10	California	1,424	1,704	1,722
11	Illinois	2,041	1,389	1,503
12	Indiana	1,863	1,244	1,366
13	North Carolina	1,219	1,263	1,319
14	Virginia	1,028	1,516	1,295
15	Ohio	1,730	1,204	1,267
16	Iowa	1,840	1,102	1,245
17	Vermont	721	1,190	1,158
18	Michigan	1,111	1,005	1,130
19	New York	720	974	1,119
20	Kentucky	976	981	1,084
21	Tennessee	976	996	1,049
22	Maine	594	1,019	992
23	Georgia	896	1,012	964
24	Louisiana	1,256	915	945
25	Wisconsin	1,004	803	932
26	Minnesota	1,086	805	896
27	South Carolina	900	909	871
28	Alabama	780	839	863
29	Washington	736	779	782
30	Arkansas	918	750	759
31	Mississippi	819	728	757
32	Missouri	902	679	715
33	West Virginia	669	613	696
34	Idaho	698	661	691
35	Oregon	587	571	657
36	Nebraska	635	550	580
37	Oklahoma	614	497	512
38	Kansas	587	462	494
39	Texas	436	495	471
40	Utah	530	389	464
41	North Dakota	405	340	388
42	Colorado	387	358	383
43	South Dakota	292	328	370
44	Arizona	267	263	305
45	Montana	235	238	270
46	New Mexico	185	196	225
47	Nevada	248	194	215
48	Wyoming	161	149	149

GROSS FARM INCOME

The table below presents gross farm income, income before deducting taxes, losses and charges. This figure rose significantly in several western states, notably North Dakota and Washington. However, several states actually experienced a loss in gross that was accompanied by a decline in their profits (see Net Farm Income table on page 176).

TABLE: Gross Farm Income
DATE: 1992
SOURCE: U.S. Department of Agriculture, Economic Research Service, *Economic Indicators of the Farm Sector: State Financial Summary, 1992,* and unpublished data
DESCRIPTION: Gross farm income 1988 and 1992 with percent change 1988–1992. Table ranked by percent change.

Rank		1988 gross farm income ($ millions)	1992 gross farm income ($ millions)	Percent change 1988–1992
	United States	175,808	197,741	12.48
1	North Dakota	2,635	3,809	44.59
2	Washington	3,818	5,007	31.14
3	Kentucky	3,026	3,821	26.28
4	Illinois	7,591	9,268	22.09
5	South Dakota	3,269	3,953	20.92
6	Montana	1,737	2,085	20.03
7	Indiana	4,593	5,469	19.07
8	Michigan	3,213	3,787	17.86
9	North Carolina	5,181	6,088	17.52
10	Connecticut	451	527	16.88
11	Massachusetts	477	556	16.51
12	Maine	472	550	16.49
13	Vermont	455	529	16.35
14	Arkansas	4,691	5,398	15.05
15	Oregon	2,635	3,019	14.56
16	Iowa	10,584	12,111	14.43
17	New Mexico	1,465	1,674	14.26
18	Ohio	4,469	5,096	14.02
19	Missouri	4,512	5,127	13.65
20	Alabama	2,968	3,369	13.52
21	New York	2,811	3,174	12.91
22	Georgia	4,192	4,716	12.49
23	Pennsylvania	3,568	4,009	12.36
24	Texas	12,671	14,236	12.36
25	West Virginia	392	440	12.30
26	Idaho	2,708	3,025	11.71
27	Wyoming	829	922	11.19
28	Minnesota	7,176	7,976	11.14
29	Maryland	1,441	1,596	10.79
30	Mississippi	2,913	3,211	10.26
31	Wisconsin	5,460	5,971	9.36
32	California	17,875	19,539	9.31
33	Virginia	2,295	2,495	8.71
34	Kansas	7,748	8,384	8.20
35	Utah	827	893	8.08
36	New Jersey	728	770	5.71
37	Oklahoma	4,119	4,350	5.61
38	Florida	6,034	6,372	5.59
39	Louisiana	2,150	2,259	5.09
40	New Hampshire	175	184	5.09

Rank		1988 gross farm income ($ millions)	1992 gross farm income ($ millions)	Percent change 1988–1992
41	Nebraska	9,540	9,970	4.51
42	South Carolina	1,307	1,362	4.23
43	Tennessee	2,501	2,606	4.20
44	Nevada	261	268	2.69
45	Delaware	681	696	2.19

Rank		1988 gross farm income ($ millions)	1992 gross farm income ($ millions)	Percent change 1988–1992
46	Colorado	4,342	4,426	1.94
47	Hawaii	601	581	-3.31
48	Arizona	2,095	1,954	-6.73
49	Rhode Island	90	80	-10.57
50	Alaska	37	33	-11.14

NET FARM INCOME

Net income is the farm's profit. It represents the income remaining after the deduction of all taxes, charges, outlays and losses have been paid. Nationwide, farmers' profit rose slightly between 1988 and 1992. However, a number of states showed a decline, reflecting the impact of local conditions and the market for the major commodities produced in the states.

TABLE: Net Farm Income
DATE: 1992
SOURCE: U.S. Dept. of Agriculture, Economic Research Service, *Economic Indicators of the Farm Sector: State Financial Summary, 1992* and unpublished data
DESCRIPTION: Net farm income 1988 and 1992.

Rank		1988 Net farm income ($ millions)	Percent profit	1992 Net farm income ($ millions)	Percent profit
	United States	38,781	22	48,647	25
1	California	5,814	33	4,756	24
2	Texas	2,075	16	3,464	24
3	Iowa	1,758	17	2,465	20
4	Nebraska	2,163	23	2,692	27
5	Illinois	792	10	1,699	18
6	Kansas	1,357	18	1,723	21
7	Minnesota	1,461	20	1,481	19
8	Florida	2,702	45	2,777	44
9	North Carolina	1,715	33	2,453	40
10	Wisconsin	943	17	811	14
11	Indiana	303	7	729	13
12	Arkansas	1,210	26	1,405	26
13	Missouri	700	16	875	17
14	Ohio	898	20	1,214	24
15	Washington	901	24	1,337	27
16	Georgia	1,148	27	1,681	36
17	Colorado	714	16	947	21
18	Oklahoma	819	20	1,083	25
19	Pennsylvania	719	20	832	21
20	South Dakota	787	24	1,395	35
21	Kentucky	743	25	1,307	34
22	North Dakota	189	7	1,091	29
23	Michigan	466	14	581	15
24	Alabama	807	27	1,141	34
25	Mississippi	747	26	674	21
26	New York	533	19	622	20
27	Idaho	642	24	939	31
28	Oregon	731	28	696	23
29	Tennessee	454	18	608	23
30	Virginia	501	22	627	25
31	Louisiana	568	26	491	22
32	Montana	187	11	463	22
33	Arizona	729	35	595	30
34	New Mexico	278	19	491	29
35	Maryland	353	24	388	24
36	South Carolina	323	25	338	25

Rank		1988 Net farm income ($ millions)	Percent profit	1992 Net farm income ($ millions)	Percent profit
37	Wyoming	97	12	239	26
38	Utah	209	25	281	32
39	New Jersey	230	32	213	28
40	Delaware	173	25	135	19
41	Hawaii	117	19	27	5
42	Massachusetts	161	34	200	36
43	Maine	104	22	138	25
44	Vermont	105	23	133	25
45	Connecticut	152	34	190	36
46	West Virginia	42	11	79	18
47	Nevada	59	23	56	21
48	New Hampshire	50	28	45	24
49	Rhode Island	48	54	36	45
50	Alaska	11	30	6	18

GOVERNMENT PAYMENTS TO FARMERS

The federal government has played an important role in the economics of farming since the New Deal through farm subsidies and payments to farmers. During the 1980s and 1990s much of that program was under attack by critics who opposed big government and supported a move to a free-market economy in agriculture. The impact of this move is shown in the table below. Nationally, federal payments to farmers decreased $2 million between 1989 and 1992. Yet, not all states experienced a decline. The Northwest and Mountain states, some states in New England, and Florida all received higher payments in 1992 than in 1989.

TABLE: Government Payments to Farmers
DATE: 1992
SOURCE: U.S. Dept. of Agriculture, Economic Research Service, *Economic Indicators of the Farm Sector: State Financial Summary, 1992*
DESCRIPTION: Farm income from government payments 1989 and 1992.

Rank		1989 government payments ($ millions)	1992 government payments ($ millions)	Change 1989–1992 ($ millions)
	United States	10,887	9,168	-1719.00
1	Texas	1,248.71	1,162.04	-86.67
2	Iowa	981.21	662.28	-318.93
3	Kansas	588.45	592.15	3.70
4	Illinois	725.94	480.65	-245.29
5	Nebraska	542.31	478.73	-63.58
6	North Dakota	474.85	443.16	-31.69
7	California	372.09	430.38	58.29
8	Minnesota	599.85	422.02	-177.83
9	Arkansas	439.68	410.03	-29.65
10	Montana	289.38	298.77	9.39
11	Missouri	356.39	293.65	-62.75
12	Mississippi	325.16	279.90	-45.26
13	South Dakota	340.26	271.90	-68.36
14	Louisiana	249.76	270.84	21.08
15	Oklahoma	234.82	248.32	13.51
16	Indiana	333.69	232.52	-101.17
17	Colorado	83.44	203.23	19.79
18	Washington	131.13	188.74	57.61
19	Georgia	173.06	182.30	9.24
20	Ohio	274.00	166.12	-107.88
21	Wisconsin	522.33	166.03	-356.31
22	Michigan	61.97	142.51	-119.46
23	Idaho	99.09	137.40	38.31
24	Alabama	20.86	119.13	-1.73
25	Tennessee	141.05	115.87	-25.18
26	Oregon	60.38	87.47	27.09
27	Arizona	85.11	75.58	-9.53
28	North Carolina	93.92	74.81	-19.11
29	South Carolina	72.70	72.59	-0.11
30	Kentucky	118.42	72.13	-46.30
31	New Mexico	64.68	60.00	-4.68
32	Florida	38.32	53.09	14.76
33	Pennsylvania	68.40	48.77	-19.63
34	New York	76.03	47.87	-28.15
35	Wyoming	34.14	36.66	2.52
36	Utah	34.54	35.97	1.44
37	Virginia	38.60	29.07	-9.53
38	Maryland	23.74	16.07	-7.67
39	Nevada	6.30	11.24	4.94
40	New Jersey	21.48	10.70	-10.79
41	Maine	7.14	10.25	3.11
42	West Virginia	11.60	6.86	-4.74
43	Vermont	7.06	5.55	-1.51
44	Massachusetts	3.86	4.76	0.90
45	Delaware	4.82	2.98	-1.84
46	Connecticut	2.20	2.22	0.02
47	Hawaii	Z	1.82	NA

Rank		1989 government payments ($ millions)	1992 government payments ($ millions)	Change 1989–1992 ($ millions)
48	Alaska	1.14	1.69	0.55
49	New Hampshire	2.30	1.55	-0.75
50	Rhode Island	Z	Z	

Z Less than $500,000.
NA Not Applicable.

Farm Marketing Income

The table below breaks out farm marketing income— income from marketing crops and livestock—from total farm income, which includes government payments. It also shows the relationship between gross and marketing income. This offers a general indication of the significance of government payments to farmers. Marketing is a larger percentage of total income in truck farming and dairy farming states of the Northeast and West. It represents a lower portion of total income in the Midwest and South.

TABLE: Farm Marketing Income
DATE: 1992
SOURCE: U.S. Dept. of Agriculture, *Economic Indicators of the Farm Sector: State Financial Summary, 1992*
DESCRIPTION: Total farm income and marketing income as a percentage of total income. Table ranked by marketing income as a percentage of gross income.

Rank		Gross income ($ millions)	Marketing income ($ millions)	Marketing income as percent of gross income
	United States	197,741	171,168	86.56
1	Nevada	268	273	101.94
2	Hawaii	581	564	97.13
3	Florida	6,372	6,145	96.43
4	Arizona	1,954	1,835	93.92
5	California	19,539	18,234	93.32
6	Maine	550	513	93.26
7	Idaho	3,025	2,816	93.07
8	New York	3,174	2,946	92.81

Rank		Gross income ($ millions)	Marketing income ($ millions)	Marketing income as percent of gross income
9	Connecticut	527	489	92.74
10	Wisconsin	5,971	5,499	92.09
11	New Mexico	1,674	1,530	91.41
12	Delaware	696	636	91.36
13	Colorado	4,426	4,038	91.24
14	Pennsylvania	4,009	3,618	90.26
15	Rhode Island	80	72	89.82
16	Washington	5,007	4,454	88.97
17	Minnesota	7,976	7,082	88.80
18	Massachusetts	556	491	88.35
19	Nebraska	9,970	8,783	88.09
20	Maryland	1,596	1,391	87.14
21	Michigan	3,787	3,286	86.78
22	South Carolina	1,362	1,177	86.41
23	Georgia	4,716	4,073	86.37
24	Virginia	2,495	2,134	85.55
25	Vermont	529	452	85.46
26	New Jersey	770	657	85.33
27	Iowa	12,111	10,330	85.29
28	Arkansas	5,398	4,602	85.26
29	North Carolina	6,088	5,181	85.10
30	Kentucky	3,821	3,221	84.30
31	Alabama	3,369	2,830	84.01
32	Wyoming	922	773	83.86
33	Montana	2,085	1,742	83.56
34	Oklahoma	4,350	3,635	83.56
35	Kansas	8,384	7,000	83.50
36	Utah	893	738	82.67
37	Oregon	3,019	2,490	82.49
38	Indiana	5,469	4,505	82.38
39	Illinois	9,268	7,634	82.37
40	Ohio	5,096	4,167	81.78
41	Louisiana	2,259	1,846	81.72
42	South Dakota	3,953	3,229	81.70
43	Texas	14,236	11,620	81.62
44	North Dakota	3,809	3,094	81.21
45	Mississippi	3,211	2,602	81.03
46	Tennessee	2,606	2,103	80.72
47	Missouri	5,127	4,123	80.42
48	New Hampshire	184	144	78.38
49	Alaska	33	25	77.91
50	West Virginia	440	343	77.85

CRIME

This section presents data on crimes, law enforcement, corrections, and the death penalty. The primary sources are the Federal Bureau of Investigation (FBI), Bureau of the Census, The Department of Justice and the Law Enforcement Assistance Administration.

The data reported in the tables in this section are based on crime statistics collected by the FBI from sheriffs and state and local police around the country. The FBI groups crime figures into two general categories: violent and property crimes. Violent crimes include: murder (including nonnegligent homicide), forcible rapes (which includes forcible rapes and attempts), robbery (stealing or taking anything by force or threat of force including attempted robbery) and aggravated assault (including assault with attempt to kill). Property crimes include: burglary (unlawful entry to commit a felony or theft, including attempted burglary), larceny-theft (including theft of property without use of force or fraud) and motor vehicle theft (including all cases where vehicles were driven away and abandoned).

The Bureau of Justice Statistics compiles annual data on prisons and jails. A prison is a confinement facility having custodial authority over adults sentenced for more than one year. A jail is a facility, usually operated by a local law enforcement agency, holding persons sentenced for a year or less or awaiting trial or other legal proceedings.

The first eight tables in this section detail crime statistics. They are followed by three tables reporting on police and corrections enforcement, five tables on incarceration and one table on the death penalty.

TOTAL CRIME RATE

The crimes enumerated here include violent crimes identified as murder, forcible rape, robbery and aggravated assault, and property crimes identified as burglary, larceny-theft and motor vehicle theft. The figures were based on crimes known to the police; unreported crimes can raise the total significantly, particularly in categories such as rape, where reporting is traditionally low.

Crime rose nationally between 1985 and 1992 by 9%. Some states in the South experienced a significant rise, while Mountain states and states in the Northwest actually experienced a decline.

TABLE: Total Crime Rate
DATE: 1992
SOURCE: U.S. Federal Bureau of Investigation, *Crime in the United States*, annual
DESCRIPTION: Total crime rate. Table ranked by 1992 rate.

Rank		1985 Crime rate per 100,000 population	1992 Crime rate per 100,000 population	Percentage of change in the rate 1985 – 1992
	United States*	5,207	5,660	9
1	Florida	7,574	8,358	10
2	Texas	6,569	7,058	7
3	Arizona	7,116	7,029	-1
4	California	6,518	6,679	2
5	Louisiana	5,564	6,546	18
6	New Mexico	6,486	6,434	-1
7	Georgia	5,110	6,405	25
8	Maryland	5,373	6,225	16
9	Nevada	6,575	6,204	-6
10	Washington	6,529	6,173	-5
11	Hawaii	5,201	6,112	18
12	Colorado	6,919	5,959	-14
13	South Carolina	4,841	5,893	22
14	New York	5,589	5,858	5
15	Oregon	6,730	5,821	-14
16	North Carolina	4,121	5,802	41
17	Illinois	5,384	5,765	7
18	Utah	5,317	5,659	6
19	Michigan	6,366	5,611	-12
20	Alaska	5,877	5,570	-5
21	Oklahoma	5,425	5,432	0
22	Kansas	4,375	5,320	22
23	Alabama	3,942	5,268	34
24	Tennessee	4,167	5,136	23
25	Missouri	4,366	5,097	17
26	New Jersey	5,094	5,064	-1

Rank		1985 Crime rate per 100,000 population	1992 Crime rate per 100,000 population	Percentage of change in the rate 1985 – 1992
27	Connecticut	4,705	5,053	7
28	Massachusetts	4,758	5,003	5
29	Delaware	4,961	4,848	-2
30	Arkansas	3,585	4,762	33
31	Indiana	3,914	4,687	20
32	Ohio	4,187	4,666	11
33	Montana	4,549	4,596	1
34	Minnesota	4,134	4,591	11
35	Rhode Island	4,723	4,578	-3
36	Wyoming	4,015	4,575	14
37	Nebraska	3,695	4,324	17
38	Wisconsin	4,017	4,319	8
39	Virginia	3,779	4,299	14
40	Mississippi	3,266	4,282	31
41	Idaho	3,908	3,996	2
42	Iowa	3,943	3,957	0
43	Maine	3,672	3,524	-4
44	Vermont	3,888	3,410	-12
45	Pennsylvania	3,037	3,393	12
46	Kentucky	2,947	3,324	13
47	New Hampshire	3,252	3,081	-5
48	South Dakota	2,641	2,999	14
49	North Dakota	2,679	2,903	8
50	West Virginia	2,253	2,610	16

*Includes Washington, DC.

TOTAL VIOLENT CRIME RATE

As indicated above, violent crime includes: murder, forcible rape, robbery and aggravated assault. Generally, those states that ranked highest in this table contained large urban areas. Rural states were at the bottom of the ranking.

TABLE: Total Violent Crime Rate
DATE: 1992
SOURCE: U.S. Federal Bureau of Investigation, *Crime in the United States*, annual
DESCRIPTION: Violent crime rate per 100,000 population.

Rank		Violent crime rate per 100,000 population
	United States*	758
1	Florida	1,207
2	New York	1,122
3	California	1,120
4	Maryland	1,000
5	Louisiana	985
6	Illinois	977
7	South Carolina	944
8	New Mexico	935

Rank		Violent crime rate per 100,000 population
9	Alabama	872
10	Texas	806
11	Massachusetts	779
12	Michigan	770
13	Tennessee	746
14	Missouri	740
15	Georgia	733
16	Nevada	697
17	North Carolina	681
18	Arizona	671
19	Alaska	660
20	New Jersey	626
21	Oklahoma	623
22	Delaware	621
23	Colorado	579
24	Arkansas	577
25	Kentucky	535
26	Washington	535
27	Ohio	526
28	Kansas	511
29	Oregon	510
30	Indiana	508
31	Connecticut	495
32	Pennsylvania	427
33	Mississippi	412
34	Rhode Island	395
35	Virginia	375
36	Nebraska	349
37	Minnesota	338
38	Wyoming	320
39	Utah	291
40	Idaho	281
41	Iowa	278
42	Wisconsin	276
43	Hawaii	258
44	West Virginia	212
45	South Dakota	195
46	Montana	170
47	Maine	131
48	New Hampshire	126
49	Vermont	109
50	North Dakota	83

*Includes Washington, DC

MURDER RATE

The state rankings below generally mirror the previous table. The only exception was New Mexico, in the top 10 in violent crime, but ranked 18th here. Many of the southern states ranked higher in murder than in overall violent crime.

TABLE: Murder Rate
DATE: 1992

SOURCE: U.S. Federal Bureau of Investigation, *Crime in the United States*, annual
DESCRIPTION: Murder rate per 100,000 population.

Rank		Murder rate per 100,000 population**
	United States*	9.3
1	Louisiana	17.4
2	New York	13.2
3	Texas	12.7
4	California	12.7
5	Mississippi	12.2
6	Maryland	12.1
7	Illinois	11.4
8	Georgia	11.0
9	Alabama	11.0
10	Nevada	10.9
11	Arkansas	10.8
12	North Carolina	10.6
13	Missouri	10.5
14	South Carolina	10.4
15	Tennessee	10.4
16	Michigan	9.9
17	Florida	9.0
18	New Mexico	8.9
19	Virginia	8.8
20	Indiana	8.2
21	Arizona	8.1
22	Alaska	7.5
23	Ohio	6.6
24	Oklahoma	6.5
25	West Virginia	6.3
26	Pennsylvania	6.2
27	Colorado	6.2
28	Kansas	6.0
29	Kentucky	5.8
30	Connecticut	5.1
31	New Jersey	5.1
32	Washington	5.0
33	Oregon	4.7
34	Delaware	4.6
35	Wisconsin	4.4
36	Nebraska	4.2
37	Massachusetts	3.6
38	Rhode Island	3.6
39	Wyoming	3.6
40	Hawaii	3.6
41	Idaho	3.5
42	Minnesota	3.3
43	Utah	3.0
44	Montana	2.9
45	Vermont	2.1
46	North Dakota	1.9
47	Maine	1.7
48	New Hampshire	1.6
49	Iowa	1.6
50	South Dakota	0.6

*Includes Washington, DC.
**Includes nonnegligent manslaughter.

FORCIBLE RAPE

This table shows the rate of forcible rape in each state. Nationwide, in 1992 the forcible rape rate ranged among states from a high of 99 per 100,000 population in Alaska to a low of 19 per 100,000 population in Iowa, a five-to-one ratio. In 1992 forcible rape averaged 43 per 100,000 population nationwide. Regionally, with the exception of the Northeast (30 per 100,000 population) the rates in the rest of the country varied little. Three states ranked in the top 10 in forcible rape and in the top 10 in total violent crimes: New Mexico, South Carolina and Florida.

TABLE: Forcible Rape
DATE: 1992
SOURCE: U.S. Federal Bureau of Investigation, *Crime in the United States*, annual
DESCRIPTION: Forcible rape rate per 100,000 population.

Rank		Forcible rape rate per 100,000 population
	United States*	43
1	Alaska	99
2	Delaware	86
3	Michigan	80
4	Washington	72
5	New Mexico	63
6	Nevada	63
7	South Carolina	58
8	Florida	54
9	Texas	53
10	Oregon	53
11	Ohio	52
12	South Dakota	52
13	Oklahoma	48
14	Tennessee	47
15	Colorado	47
16	Maryland	46
17	Georgia	45
18	Mississippi	45
19	Utah	45
20	Arizona	43
21	Indiana	42
22	Louisiana	42
23	Minnesota	41
24	Kansas	41
25	Alabama	41
26	Arkansas	41
27	California	41
28	New Hampshire	38
29	Hawaii	38
30	Illinois**	37
31	Massachusetts	36
32	Missouri	36
33	North Carolina	36
34	Wyoming	35
35	Kentucky	32

Rank		Forcible rape rate per 100,000 population
36	Idaho	32
37	Rhode Island	31
38	New Jersey	31
39	Nebraska	31
40	Virginia	31
41	New York	28
42	Pennsylvania	28
43	Connecticut	27
44	Wisconsin	26
45	Vermont	25
46	Montana	25
47	Maine	24
48	North Dakota	23
49	West Virginia	22
50	Iowa	19

*Includes Washington, DC.
**Forcible rape figures furnished by the state-level uniform crime reporting (UCR) Program administered by the Illinois Department of State Police were not in accordance with the national UCR guidelines. The 1989 through 1992 forcible rape totals for Illinois were estimated using the national rate of forcible rapes when grouped by like agencies.

ROBBERY

As in the case of other violent crimes, states with large urban areas rank high in this table. Lowest ranks are associated with rural and farming states.

TABLE: Robbery
DATE: 1992
SOURCE: U.S. Federal Bureau of Investigation, *Crime in the United States*, annual
DESCRIPTION: Robbery rate.

Rank		Robbery rate per 100,000 population
	United States*	264
1	New York	597
2	Maryland	429
3	California	424
4	Illinois	412
5	Florida	367
6	Nevada	331
7	New Jersey	285
8	Louisiana	271
9	Texas	253
10	Georgia	250
11	Missouri	227
12	Michigan	221
13	Tennessee	218
14	Connecticut	211
15	Ohio	199
16	North Carolina	187
17	Massachusetts	184
18	Pennsylvania	181
19	South Carolina	171

Rank		Robbery rate per 100,000 population
20	Alabama	165
21	Arizona	153
22	Delaware	151
23	Oregon	151
24	Washington	140
25	New Mexico	139
26	Virginia	138
27	Oklahoma	136
28	Kansas	130
29	Arkansas	126
30	Mississippi	124
31	Indiana	122
32	Wisconsin	120
33	Colorado	120
34	Minnesota	110
35	Alaska	109
36	Hawaii	99
37	Rhode Island	95
38	Kentucky	87
39	Nebraska	57
40	Utah	56
41	West Virginia	43
42	Iowa	40
43	New Hampshire	33
44	Montana	27
45	Maine	23
46	Idaho	21
47	Wyoming	18
48	South Dakota	17
49	Vermont	9
50	North Dakota	8

*Includes Washington, DC.

TOTAL PROPERTY CRIME

Property crimes include burglary, larceny-theft and motor vehicle theft. Regionally in 1992, the West and the South ranked highest in property crime, followed by the Midwest and Northeast. Seven western states (Arizona, Texas, Hawaii, Washington, California, Nevada and New Mexico) and three southern states (Florida, Georgia and Louisiana) made up the top 10 cluster. Again, rural states were at the bottom of the list. It is interesting to note that the rate of property crime does not seem affected by the presence or absence of large urban areas.

TABLE: Total Property Crime
DATE: 1992
SOURCE: U.S. Federal Bureau of Investigation, *Crime in the United States*, annual
DESCRIPTION: Total property crime rate per 100,000 population.

Rank		Property crime rate per 100,000 population
	United States*	4,903
1	Florida	7,151
2	Arizona	6,358
3	Texas	6,252
4	Hawaii	5,854
5	Georgia	5,672
6	Washington	5,638
7	Louisiana	5,562
8	California	5,560
9	Nevada	5,507
10	New Mexico	5,499
11	Colorado	5,380
12	Utah	5,368
13	Oregon	5,311
14	Maryland	5,224
15	North Carolina	5,121
16	South Carolina	4,949
17	Alaska	4,909
18	Michigan	4,841
19	Kansas	4,809
20	Oklahoma	4,809
21	Illinois	4,788
22	New York	4,736
23	Connecticut	4,558
24	New Jersey	4,439
25	Montana	4,426
26	Alabama	4,396
27	Tennessee	4,390
28	Missouri	4,357
29	Wyoming	4,256
30	Minnesota	4,253
31	Delaware	4,227
32	Massachusetts	4,224
33	Arkansas	4,185
34	Rhode Island	4,183
35	Indiana	4,178
36	Ohio	4,140
37	Wisconsin	4,043
38	Nebraska	3,975
39	Virginia	3,924
40	Mississippi	3,871
41	Idaho	3,715
42	Iowa	3,679
43	Maine	3,393
44	Vermont	3,301
45	Pennsylvania	2,966
46	New Hampshire	2,955
47	North Dakota	2,820
48	South Dakota	2,804
49	Kentucky	2,788
50	West Virginia	2,398

*Includes Washington, DC.

BURGLARY

A burglary is an unlawful entry for the purpose of committing a felony or theft. The burglary rate was highest in the South and the West, followed by the Midwest and the Northeast. There is no clear urban vs. rural breakdown in the rankings.

TABLE: Burglary
DATE: 1992
SOURCE: U.S. Federal Bureau of Investigation, *Crime in the United States*, annual.
DESCRIPTION: Burglary rate.

Rank		Burglary rate per 100,000 population
	United States*	1,168
1	Florida	1,889
2	North Carolina	1,653
3	Texas	1,523
4	New Mexico	1,511
5	Georgia	1,443
6	Arizona	1,412
7	California	1,385
8	South Carolina	1,379
9	Louisiana	1,366
10	Oklahoma	1,360
11	Kansas	1,294
12	Nevada	1,289
13	Mississippi	1,283
14	Tennessee	1,267
15	Alabama	1,186
16	Maryland	1,131
17	Washington	1,122
18	Hawaii	1,121
19	Connecticut	1,109
20	Oregon	1,107
21	Missouri	1,100
22	Arkansas	1,093
23	Colorado	1,091
24	Illinois	1,077
25	Massachusetts	1,072
26	New York	1,068
27	Rhode Island	1,048
28	Michigan	1,041
29	New Jersey	969
30	Delaware	958
31	Indiana	952
32	Ohio	947
33	Minnesota	890
34	Utah	885
35	Alaska	881
36	Vermont	826
37	Maine	822
38	Iowa	754
39	Idaho	744
40	Kentucky	729
41	Nebraska	715

Rank		Burglary rate per 100,000 population
42	Virginia	709
43	Wisconsin	692
44	Wyoming	671
45	Montana	644
46	Pennsylvania	631
47	West Virginia	623
48	New Hampshire	622
49	South Dakota	541
50	North Dakota	391

*Includes Washington, DC.

MOTOR VEHICLE THEFT

Motor vehicle theft was concentrated in 11 states that had rates higher than the U.S. average. Regionally, theft was highest in the West and the Northeast, followed by the South and the Midwest.

TABLE: Motor Vehicle Theft
DATE: 1992
SOURCE: U.S. Federal Bureau of Investigation, *Crime in the United States*, annual
DESCRIPTION: Motor vehicle theft rate.

Rank		Motor vehicle theft rate per 100,000 population
	United States*	631
1	California	1,037
2	New York	932
3	Florida	828
4	Texas	822
5	Arizona	822
6	New Jersey	816
7	Massachusetts	791
8	Rhode Island	743
9	Maryland	726
10	Connecticut	722
11	Nevada	697
12	Louisiana	628
13	Michigan	626
14	Illinois	619
15	Georgia	576
16	Tennessee	576
17	Oregon	533
18	Oklahoma	517
19	Colorado	509
20	Missouri	497
21	Alaska	497
22	Ohio	471
23	Washington	471
24	Pennsylvania	468
25	Indiana	450
26	Wisconsin	431
27	New Mexico	378

Rank		Motor vehicle theft rate per 100,000 population
28	Hawaii	375
29	Alabama	362
30	Minnesota	355
31	South Carolina	345
32	Mississippi	337
33	Arkansas	329
34	Kansas	324
35	Delaware	306
36	Virginia	306
37	North Carolina	287
38	Utah	238
39	Montana	233
40	Kentucky	216
41	Nebraska	201
42	New Hampshire	195
43	West Virginia	164
44	Iowa	159
45	Idaho	157
46	Wyoming	150
47	North Dakota	149
48	Maine	144
49	Vermont	105
50	South Dakota	101

*Includes Washington, DC.

STATE AND LOCAL POLICE

The figures below combine both state and local police protection. No pattern emerges among those states at the top of the ranking. They include populous states with large urban areas such as New York and Illinois, but also rural states with small populations such as Wyoming. Washington, DC's first place is due to the fact that it is a city with a large population concentrated in a small geographic area rather than a state with population spread over a large region.

TABLE: State and Local Police
DATE: 1991
SOURCE: U.S. Bureau of the Census, *Public Employment*, annual, and *Government Finances*
DESCRIPTION: Total number of state and local police and number per 10,000 population. Table ranked by number per 10,000.

Rank		Total police	Police per 10,000 population
	United States	706,584	28.0
1	Washington, DC	5,320	89.0
2	New Jersey	30,536	39.4
3	New York	66,920	37.1
4	Illinois	39,890	34.6

Rank		Total police	Police per 10,000 population
5	Florida	45,036	33.9
6	Wyoming	1,527	33.2
7	Nevada	4,228	32.9
8	Maryland	14,754	30.4
9	Rhode Island	2,985	29.7
10	Arizona	11,105	29.6
11	New Mexico	4,536	29.3
12	Massachusetts	17,220	28.9
13	Hawaii	3,255	28.7
14	California	86,259	28.4
15	Missouri	14,578	28.3
16	Connecticut	9,258	28.1
17	Delaware	1,909	28.1
18	Louisiana	11,870	27.9
19	Georgia	18,288	27.6
20	Oklahoma	8,767	27.6
21	Alaska	1,572	27.6
22	Colorado	9,235	27.3
23	Texas	46,207	26.6
24	New Hampshire	2,939	26.6
25	Kansas	6,613	26.5
26	Idaho	2,681	25.8
27	Wisconsin	12,773	25.8
28	North Carolina	17,307	25.7
29	Alabama	10,418	25.5
30	Ohio	27,398	25.0
31	South Carolina	8,885	25.0
32	Tennessee	12,361	25.0
33	Pennsylvania	29,210	24.4
34	Montana	1,959	24.2
35	Virginia	15,224	24.2
36	Nebraska	3,832	24.1
37	Maine	2,945	23.8
38	Indiana	13,081	23.3
39	Michigan	21,634	23.1
40	Utah	3,967	22.4
41	Oregon	6,492	22.2
42	South Dakota	1,544	22.0
43	Mississippi	5,690	22.0
44	Vermont	1,231	21.7
45	Washington	10,872	21.7
46	Iowa	6,034	21.6
47	North Dakota	1,366	21.5
48	Arkansas	5,096	21.5
49	Kentucky	7,781	21.0
50	Minnesota	9,064	20.5
51	West Virginia	2,932	16.3

EMPLOYMENT IN CORRECTIONS

Corrections officers and support employees work in the nation's prisons and jails. The rankings in this table are similar to those for "State and Local Police" above. Again, the District of Columbia's high ranking is due to the fact that it is a city rather than a state. Corrections employees ranged from 31.9 per 10,000 population in New York to 7.5 employees per 10,000 population in West Virginia.

TABLE: Employment in Corrections
DATE: 1991
SOURCE: U.S. Bureau of the Census, *Public Employment*, annual, and *Government Finances*
DESCRIPTION: Total state and local government employees in corrections and rate per 10,000 population.

Rank		Total employed in corrections	Persons per 10,000 population
	United States	521,880	20.7
1	Washington, DC	4,643	77.6
2	New York	57,688	31.9
3	Florida	40,047	30.2
4	Nevada	3,551	27.7
5	Georgia	17,564	26.5
6	Arizona	9,602	25.6
7	South Carolina	8,685	24.4
8	Maryland	11,749	24.2
9	Delaware	1,634	24.0
10	Alaska	1,341	23.5
11	New Mexico	3,594	23.2
12	California	69,737	23.0
13	Louisiana	9,625	22.6
14	Texas	39,093	22.5
15	Virginia	14,100	22.4
16	North Carolina	14,958	22.2
17	New Jersey	17,223	22.2
18	Tennessee	10,078	20.3
19	Michigan	18,519	19.8
20	Oregon	5,406	18.5
21	Kentucky	6,867	18.5
22	Wyoming	850	18.5
23	Kansas	4,556	18.3
24	Washington	9,032	18.0
25	Rhode Island	1,777	17.7
26	Colorado	5,950	17.6
27	Oklahoma	5,544	17.5
28	Missouri	8,736	16.9
29	Illinois	19,343	16.8
30	Hawaii	1,886	16.6
31	Indiana	9,218	16.4
32	Connecticut	5,366	16.3
33	Nebraska	2,532	15.9
34	Arkansas	3,690	15.6
35	Alabama	6,244	15.3
36	Utah	2,629	14.9
37	Pennsylvania	17,519	14.6
38	Ohio	15,858	14.5
39	Idaho	1,491	14.4
40	Mississippi	3,675	14.2
41	Maine	1,751	14.2
42	Montana	1,136	14.1
43	Massachusetts	8,256	13.8

Rank		Total employed in corrections	Persons per 10,000 population
44	New Hampshire	1,421	12.9
45	Wisconsin	6,357	12.8
46	Vermont	676	11.9
47	Minnesota	5,152	11.6
48	South Dakota	798	11.4
49	Iowa	2,834	10.1
50	North Dakota	545	8.6
51	West Virginia	1,354	7.5

STATE AND LOCAL SPENDING ON POLICE PROTECTION AND CORRECTIONS

There is an obvious correlation between expenditures and number of employees in this sector. However, it is necessary to exercise caution in evaluating the ranking. A high ranking does not necessarily indicate a stronger commitment to protection than in other states. Cost of living is an important element in evaluating placement. This factor explains the number two ranking of Alaska. Again, Washington, DC's ranking is a result of its being a city rather than a state.

TABLE: State and Local Spending on Police Protection and Corrections
DATE: 1991
SOURCE: U.S. Bureau of the Census, *Public Employment*, annual and *Government Finances*
DESCRIPTION: State and local government expenditures on police protection and corrections.

Rank		Expenditures per capita ($)
	United States	299
1	Washington, DC	1,261
2	Alaska	600
3	New York	499
4	California	432
5	Nevada	417
6	Arizona	372
7	Maryland	358
8	Florida	354
9	New Jersey	349
10	Connecticut	346
11	Delaware	328
12	Hawaii	320
13	Massachusetts	315
14	Michigan	303
15	Wyoming	300
16	Colorado	290

Rank		Expenditures per capita ($)
17	Oregon	288
18	Rhode Island	287
19	New Mexico	284
20	Wisconsin	268
21	Georgia	266
22	Illinois	266
23	Washington	261
24	Virginia	260
25	Ohio	249
26	Louisiana	241
27	Kansas	239
28	Texas	237
29	New Hampshire	233
30	North Carolina	231
31	Pennsylvania	229
32	Minnesota	228
33	South Carolina	224
34	Tennessee	221
35	Utah	220
36	Idaho	197
37	Montana	196
38	Oklahoma	195
39	Iowa	190
40	Kentucky	190
41	Missouri	189
42	Maine	189
43	Vermont	185
44	Alabama	185
45	Nebraska	183
46	Indiana	173
47	South Dakota	161
48	North Dakota	143
49	Arkansas	142
50	Mississippi	134
51	West Virginia	118

ADULTS UNDER CORRECTIONAL SUPERVISION

More aggressive policing, higher crime rates and tougher sentencing laws have all contributed to the large number of persons under correctional supervision. The table below includes not only prison inmates, but also parolees and adults on probation. There are large state variations in this table. Georgia had almost eight times the number of adults under correctional supervision per 10,000 adults as North Dakota. Rates were highest in the South and followed by the Northeast and the Midwest. Georgia and Texas recorded almost twice the national rate.

TABLE: Adults Under Correctional Supervision
DATE: 1990

Rank		Total (thousands**)	Rate (per 10,000 adults)
45	Iowa	22.2	107.7
46	Utah	11.3	103.3
47	Kentucky	24.7	90.4
48	New Hampshire	6.0	72.8
49	West Virginia	9.4	69.9
50	North Dakota	2.8	59.6

*Includes Washington, DC.
**Includes persons in jail not shown separately.
***Jail population for Hawaii included with prison population.

SOURCE: U.S. Bureau of Justice Statistics, *Correctional Populations in the United States*, annual

DESCRIPTION: Total under correctional supervision and rate per 10,000 adults. Figures include prison inmates, parolees and adults on probation.

Figures do not include those incarcerated in mental health institutions in lieu of prison, persons held by the armed services, persons held on Indian reservations, parolees under county jurisdiction, parolees whose sentences were for one year and or court probationers.

INMATES IN PRISONS OR JAILS

The number of inmates in prisons or jails almost tripled from 1980 to 1992. This is not a reflection of a dramatic increase in crime during the same period. Instead, it is a result of a push toward sterner sentences and more aggressive law enforcement generated by a call for a "war on crime."

TABLE: Inmates in Prisons or Jails
DATE: 1992
SOURCE: U.S. Bureau of Justice Statistics, *Prisoners in 1992*, and earlier reports
DESCRIPTION: Prisoners under jurisdiction of state and federal correctional authorities 1980 and 1992.

Rank		Total (thousands**)	Rate (per 10,000 adults)
	United States*	4,349.8	235.0
1	Georgia	201.0	423.0
2	Texas	503.2	414.2
3	Maryland	119.9	331.4
4	Delaware	16.6	329.3
5	Washington	109.2	303.0
6	Florida	288.6	286.6
7	Michigan	190.7	278.9
8	Oregon	55.1	260.2
9	California	541.3	246.0
10	Rhode Island	18.1	232.2
11	North Carolina	114.6	228.3
12	Indiana	92.3	225.8
13	Connecticut	57.0	224.7
14	Louisiana	66.6	222.4
15	South Carolina	57.0	222.2
16	New Jersey	127.2	214.4
17	Nevada	19.2	212.7
18	Pennsylvania	193.1	212.5
19	Minnesota	68.1	212.4
20	Arizona	54.2	201.9
21	New York	272.5	198.5
22	Massachusetts	91.2	195.7
23	Kansas	35.3	194.2
24	Colorado	45.7	187.7
25	Hawaii***	15.5	187.0
26	Missouri	70.9	186.6
27	Alabama	55.4	185.7
28	Illinois	152.7	180.0
29	Oklahoma	41.1	178.2
30	Alaska	6.7	176.5
31	Tennessee	63.8	174.2
32	Vermont	7.2	171.5
33	Nebraska	19.3	168.2
34	Arkansas	28.9	166.8
35	Ohio	132.0	164.0
36	Wyoming	4.8	151.4
37	Wisconsin	47.0	130.3
38	Mississippi	23.3	127.7
39	Montana	7.3	126.1
40	New Mexico	13.2	123.7
41	Maine	11.1	121.2
42	Idaho	8.3	119.2
43	Virginia	55.4	118.3
44	South Dakota	5.7	113.5

Rank		1980	1992	Percent of change in rate 1980–1992
	United States	329,821	883,656	168
1	California**	24,569	109,496	346
2	New York	21,815	61,736	183
3	Texas**	29,892	61,178	105
4	Florida**	20,735	48,302	133
5	Michigan**	15,124	39,113	159
6	Ohio	13,489	38,378	185
7	Illinois**	11,899	31,640	166
8	Georgia**	12,178	25,290	108
9	Pennsylvania	8,171	24,974	206
10	New Jersey	5884***	22,653	285
11	Virginia	8,920	21,199	138
12	Louisiana	8,889	20,896	135
13	North Carolina**	15,513	20,454	32
14	Maryland	7,731	19,977	158
15	South Carolina	7,862	18,643	137
16	Alabama	6,543	17,453	167
17	Arizona**	4,372	16,477	277
18	Missouri	5,726	16,189	183
19	Oklahoma	4,796	14,821	209
20	Indiana**	6,683	13,945	109
21	Tennessee	7,022	11,849	89
22	Connecticut*	4,308	11,403	165
23	Washington, DC*/**	3,145	10,875	246

Rank		1980	1992	Percent of change in rate 1980–1992
24	Kentucky	3,588	10,364	189
25	Massachusetts**	3,185	10,053	216
26	Washington	4,399***	9,959	126
27	Colorado	2,629	8,997	242
28	Wisconsin	3,980	8,912	124
29	Mississippi	3,902	8,780	125
30	Arkansas	2,911	8,285	185
31	Oregon	3,177	6,583	107
32	Nevada	1,839	6,049	229
33	Kansas	2,494	6,028	142
34	Iowa	2,481	4,518	82
35	Delaware*/**	1,474	4,051	175
36	Minnesota	2,001	3,822	91
37	New Mexico	1,279	3,271	156
38	Hawaii*	985	2,926	197
39	Alaska*	822	2,865	249
40	Rhode Island*	813	2,775	241
41	Utah	932	2,699	190
42	Nebraska	1,446	2,514	74
43	Idaho	817	2,256	176
44	New Hampshire	326	1,777	445
45	West Virginia	1,257	1,674	33
46	Maine	814	1,519	87
47	Montana	739	1,498	103
48	South Dakota	635	1,487	134
49	Vermont*	480	1,254	161
50	Wyoming	534	1,063	99
51	North Dakota	253	477	89

*Includes both jail and prison inmates (State has combined jail and prison system).
**Numbers are custodial, not jurisdictional counts.
***Jurisdiction counts exclude prisoners held in jail because of crowding.

JUVENILE INMATES

Most states classify a juvenile offender as anyone under 18 years of age who has committed a crime or crimes. Twenty-two percent of the nation's juvenile inmates were incarcerated in Florida, which ranked first in the number of juvenile inmates. Connecticut, Illinois, North Carolina and New York accounted for another 39% of the total juvenile inmates incarcerated.

TABLE: Juvenile Inmates
DATE: 1990
SOURCE: U.S. Department of Justice, Bureau of Justice Statistics, *Correctional Population in the United States,* 1990
DESCRIPTION: Number of inmates and residents of state and federal correctional facilities under age 18 and percent of total. Percentages may not add to 100% because of rounding.

Rank		Total	Percent
	United States	3,600	
1	Florida	806	22.39
2	Connecticut	441	12.25
3	Illinois	326	9.06
4	North Carolina	312	8.67
5	New York	302	8.39
6	Maryland	156	4.33
7	Arkansas	143	3.97
8	Ohio	139	3.86
9	Michigan	128	3.56
10	Indiana	116	3.22
11	Wisconsin	93	2.58
12	Georgia	65	1.81
13	Oklahoma	64	1.78
14	Missouri	57	1.58
15	Texas	51	1.42
16	South Carolina	47	1.31
17	Virginia	38	1.06
18	Louisiana	33	0.92
19	Washington	28	0.78
20	Nebraska	21	0.58
21	Nevada	20	0.56
22	Pennsylvania	19	0.53
23	Kansas	19	0.53
24	Arizona	19	0.53
25	Minnesota	14	0.39
26	California	14	0.39
27	Colorado	12	0.33
28	Iowa	11	0.31
29	Tennessee	9	0.25
30	Hawaii	9	0.25
31	New Jersey	8	0.22
32	Vermont	7	0.19
33	Massachusetts	6	0.17
34	South Dakota	6	0.17
35	Wyoming	4	0.11
36	Washington, DC	3	0.08
37	Mississippi	3	0.08
38	Alaska	3	0.08
39	Oregon	3	0.08
40	Idaho	2	0.06
41	Montana	2	0.06
42	Kentucky	1	0.03
43	Utah	1	0.03
44	Maine	0	Less than .01
45	New Hampshire	0	Less than .01
46	Rhode Island	0	Less than .01
47	North Dakota	0	Less than .01
48	Alabama	0	Less than .01
49	Delaware	0	Less than .01
50	West Virginia	0	Less than .01
51	New Mexico	0	Less than .01

FEMALE INMATES

The states are ranked in this table according to the percentage of female inmates in the total female prison population. The table also shows the number of female inmates in each state. The percentage of female inmates among states ranged from a high of 8.8% in Rhode Island to a low of 3.1% in Vermont. (The District of Columbia ranked last 2.4%)

TABLE: Female Inmates
DATE: June 1990
SOURCE: U. S. Department of Justice, Bureau of Justice Statistics, *Correctional Populations of the United States*, 1990
DESCRIPTION: Total number of female prison inmates and percent of total female inmates. Percentage may not add up to 100% because of rounding.

Rank		Total	Percent of total female inmate population
	United States	35,846	
1	California	6,255	18.57
2	New York	2,715	8.06
3	Florida	2,505	7.44
4	Texas	2,214	6.57
5	Ohio	2,070	6.14
6	Michigan	1,479	4.39
7	Georgia	1,243	3.69
8	Illinois	1,120	3.32
9	Pennsylvania	991	2.94
10	North Carolina	968	2.87
11	South Carolina	894	2.65
12	Oklahoma	865	2.57
13	Arizona	820	2.43
14	Maryland	781	2.32
15	New Jersey	779	2.31
16	Missouri	750	2.23
17	Alabama	707	2.10
18	Indiana	632	1.88
19	Massachusetts	621	1.84
20	Connecticut	605	1.80
21	Virginia	599	1.78
22	Louisiana	547	1.62
23	Nevada	421	1.25
24	Tennessee	367	1.09
25	Mississippi	361	1.07
26	Colorado	331	0.98
27	Kentucky	330	0.98
28	Washington	321	0.95
29	Wisconsin	292	0.87
30	Kansas	290	0.86
31	Arkansas	286	0.85
32	Oregon	270	0.80
33	Iowa	257	0.76
34	Rhode Island	216	0.64
35	Delaware	207	0.61
36	New Mexico	187	0.56
37	Washington, DC	176	0.52
38	Hawaii	167	0.50
39	Nebraska	164	0.49
40	Minnesota	162	0.48
41	Utah	148	0.44
42	Alaska	121	0.36
43	Idaho	99	0.29
44	Wyoming	84	0.25
45	South Dakota	83	0.25
46	New Hampshire	79	0.23
47	West Virginia	78	0.23
48	Montana	71	0.21
49	Maine	49	0.15
50	North Dakota	44	0.13
51	Vermont	25	0.07

OPERATING EXPENDITURES PER INMATE

Prison costs differ dramatically across the nation. Minnesota, ranked first, spends almost four times as much per inmate as Arkansas, ranked last. There is no geographic pattern at the top of the list, but the southern states predominated at the bottom.

TABLE: Operating Expenditures Per Inmate
DATE: 1990
SOURCE: U.S. Department of Justice Bureau of Justice Statistics, *Census of State and Federal Correctional Facilities*, 1990
DESCRIPTION: Annual operating expenditures per inmate in state and federal correctional facilities.

Rank		Expenditure per inmate ($)
	United States	$15,513
1	Minnesota	30,302
2	Alaska	28,214
3	Maine	22,656
4	California	21,816
5	New Jersey	20,703
6	Tennessee	20,048
7	Washington	19,742
8	Hawaii	19,542
9	Wisconsin	18,965
10	New York	18,670
11	North Carolina	18,486
12	Iowa	18,304
13	Maryland	17,214

Rank		Expenditure per inmate ($)
14	New Hampshire	17,208
15	Connecticut	17,002
16	New Mexico	16,711
17	Michigan	16,649
18	Rhode Island	16,497
19	Virginia	16,145
20	Illinois	15,980
21	Vermont	15,905
22	Pennsylvania	15,438
23	Utah	15,251
24	Massachusetts	15,152
25	Indiana	14,822
26	Kansas	14,670
27	Montana	14,590
28	North Dakota	14,581
29	Colorado	14,180
30	Florida	13,902
31	Washington, DC	13,894
32	Nebraska	13,012

Rank		Expenditure per inmate ($)
33	Texas	12,988
34	Georgia	12,930
35	Wyoming	12,151
36	West Virginia	11,699
37	Oregon	11,561
38	Delaware	11,208
39	Kentucky	11,118
40	Ohio	11,028
41	South Dakota	10,859
42	Arizona	10,311
43	South Carolina	10,268
44	Oklahoma	9,919
45	Missouri	9,766
46	Idaho	9,450
47	Louisiana	9,337
48	Mississippi	9,133
49	Alabama	8,718
50	Nevada	8,630
51	Arkansas	7,557

EXECUTIONS

In 1972 the Supreme Court ruled that capital punishment as then practiced in the United States was unconstitutional because it was disproportionately imposed on individuals who were members of minority and lower socioeconomic groups. Four years later, however, the Court ruled that capital punishment for convicted murderers did not, as such, violate the constitutional restriction on cruel and unusual punishment. That ruling renewed controversy over the issue and sparked debates within the states that has generated varied responses to the demand for the resumption of executions.

There were no executions in the United States from 1968 through 1976. The death penalty was never authorized in Alaska, Hawaii, Maine, Minnesota or Wisconsin. Michigan abolished the death penalty in 1963, and North Dakota allowed its statute to lapse in 1975. During the 1980s and 1990s executions were carried out with far less frequency than in pervious periods. They were more likely to occur in the South than in other regions.

TABLE: Executions
DATE: 1992
SOURCE: United States Law Enforcement Assistance Administration; United States Department of Justice, Bureau of Justice Statistics, *Capital Punishment*, annual.
DESCRIPTION: Prisoners executed 1940–1992 and total prisoners executed. Table ranked by total executions.

Rank		1940–1949	1950–1959	1960–1969	1977–1989	1989–1992	Total
	United States*	1,284	717	191	120	84	2,396
1	Georgia	130	85	14	14	2	245
2	Texas	74	74	29	33	26	236
3	California	80	74	30	0	1	185
4	New York	114	52	10	0	0	176
5	Florida	65	49	12	21	10	157
6	North Carolina	112	19	1	3	1	136
7	Mississippi	60	36	10	4	1	111
8	South Carolina	61	26	8	2	2	99
9	Louisiana	47	27	1	18	2	95
10	Ohio	51	32	7	0	0	90
11	Alabama	50	20	5	7	7	89
12	Virginia	35	23	6	0	10	74
13	Pennsylvania	36	31	3	0	0	70
14	Arkansas	38	18	9	0	4	69
15	Maryland	45	6	1	0	0	52
16	Kentucky	34	16	1	0	0	51

Rank		1940–1949	1950–1959	1960–1969	1977–1989	1989–1992	Total
17	Tennessee	37	8	1	0	0	46
18	Missouri	15	7	4	1	7	34
19	New Jersey	14	17	3	0	0	34
20	Illinois	18	9	2	0	1	30
21	Oklahoma	13	7	6	0	3	29
22	Nevada	10	9	2	4	3	28
23	Washington	16	6	2	0	0	24
24	Arizona	9	8	4	0	1	22
25	Colorado	13	3	6	0	0	22
26	Washington, DC	16	4	0	0	0	20
27	West Virginia	11	9	0	0	0	20
28	Oregon	12	4	1	0	0	17
29	Connecticut	10	5	1	0	0	16
30	Utah	4	6	1	3	1	15
31	Kansas	5	5	5	0	0	15
32	Indiana	7	2	1	2	0	12
33	Iowa	7	1	2	0	0	10
34	Massachusetts	9	0	0	0	0	9
35	New Mexico	2	3	1	0	0	6
36	Delaware	4	0	0	0	1	5
37	Wyoming	2	0	1	0	1	4
38	Nebraska	2	2	0	0	0	4
39	Idaho	0	3	0	0	0	3
40	Vermont	1	2	0	0	0	3
41	Montana	1	0	0	0	0	1
42	South Dakota	1	0	0	0	0	1
43	Alaska	0	0	0	0	0	0
44	Hawaii	0	0	0	0	0	0
45	Maine	0	0	0	0	0	0
46	Michigan	0	0	0	0	0	0
47	Minnesota	0	0	0	0	0	0
48	New Hampshire	0	0	0	0	0	0
49	North Dakota	0	0	0	0	0	0
50	Rhode Island	0	0	0	0	0	0
51	Wisconsin	0	0	0	0	0	0

*Includes 23 federal executions not shown by states (1940–1949, 13; 1950–1959, 9; and 1960–1969, 1).

TRANSPORTATION*

This section is designed to offer an overview of America's dependence on motor vehicles, the cost of automobile insurance, the methods and problems associated with commuting, and air travel patterns. The primary sources for this information are the Federal Highway Administration, the U.S. Bureau of the Census, the National Association of Insurance Commissioners, the Texas Transportation Institute, the U.S. Federal Aviation Association and the Air Transport Association of America.

*Several tables on transportation are found in other sections. They include: transportation expenditures covered in Federal Aid for Highways and State Spending on Highways tables on pages 68 and 72, respectively. For data on gasoline taxes see Gasoline Tax Rates table on page 61. For the table on Motor Vehicle Deaths see page 80.

MOTOR VEHICLES

Unlike some countries in Europe with effective rail systems, the United States is highly dependent on motor vehicles for daily transportation and the transport of goods. As this table shows, the dependence is increasing. Nationwide, the number of registered vehicles increased by 22% between 1980 and 1992. In some states the increase was significant. Alaska, Georgia, Virginia and Arizona all had dramatic increases in vehicle ownership. Yet some states—Kansas, Arkansas, West Virginia and Massachusetts—actually experienced a decline. Population shifts, age of population and economic conditions may account for the trends.

TABLE: Motor Vehicles
DATE: 1992
SOURCE: U.S. Federal Highway Administration
DESCRIPTION: Registered motor vehicles. Table ranked by 1992 vehicles.

Rank		1980 (thousands)	1992 (thousands)	Percent increase: vehicles 1980–1992
	United States	155,796	190,362	22
1	California	16,873	22,202	32
2	Texas	10,475	12,767	22

Rank		1980 (thousands)	1992 (thousands)	Percent increase: vehicles 1980–1992
3	Florida	7,614	10,232	34
4	New York	8,002	9,780	22
5	Ohio	7,771	9,030	16
6	Pennsylvania	6,926	8,179	18
7	Illinois	7,477	7,982	7
8	Michigan	6,488	7,311	13
9	Georgia	3,818	5,899	55
10	New Jersey	4,761	5,591	17
11	North Carolina	4,532	5,307	17
12	Virginia	3,626	5,239	44
13	Tennessee	3,271	4,645	42
14	Indiana	3,826	4,516	18
15	Washington	3,225	4,466	38
16	Missouri	3,271	4,004	22
17	Wisconsin	2,941	3,735	27
18	Maryland	2,803	3,689	32
19	Massachusetts	3,749	3,663	(2)
20	Minnesota	3,091	3,484	13
21	Alabama	2,938	3,304	12
22	Louisiana	2,779	3,094	11
23	Kentucky	2,593	2,983	15
24	Colorado	2,342	2,915	24
25	Arizona	1,917	2,801	46
26	Oklahoma	2,583	2,737	6
27	Iowa	2,329	2,706	16
28	South Carolina	1,996	2,601	30
29	Oregon	2,081	2,583	24
30	Connecticut	2,147	2,569	20
31	Mississippi	1,577	1,954	24
32	Kansas	2,007	1,921	(4)
33	Arkansas	1,574	1,501	(5)
34	Nebraska	1,254	1,355	8
35	New Mexico	1,068	1,352	27
36	West Virginia	1,320	1,273	(4)
37	Utah	992	1,252	26
38	Idaho	834	1,034	24
39	Maine	724	978	35
40	Nevada	655	921	41
41	Montana	680	907	33

Rank		1980 (thousands)	1992 (thousands)	Percent increase: vehicles 1980–1992
42	New Hampshire	704	894	27
43	Hawaii	570	774	36
44	South Dakota	601	720	20
45	North Dakota	627	655	5
46	Rhode Island	623	622	0
47	Delaware	397	545	37
48	Alaska	262	486	86
49	Wyoming	467	483	3
50	Vermont	347	465	34
51	Washington, DC	268	256	(4)

AUTOMOBILES

Automobiles account for the vast majority of motor vehicles in the United States, over 75%. Seventy-six percent of all registered motor vehicles were automobiles in 1992. Not surprisingly, the percentage was highest in states with large suburban populations, where the family car was a necessity. The percentage was lowest in rural and farming states, where trucks would be needed for daily activity.

TABLE: Automobiles
DATE: 1992
SOURCE: U.S. Federal Highway Administration
DESCRIPTION: Registered automobiles and automobiles as a percent of total motor vehicles. Table ranked by number of vehicles.

Rank		Automobiles	Percent of motor vehicles (automobiles)
	United States	144,213	76
1	California	17,219	78
2	Texas	8,689	68
3	New York	8,467	83
4	Florida	8,131	83
5	Ohio	7,304	81
6	Illinois	6,622	81
7	Pennsylvania	6,535	82
8	Michigan	5,680	78
9	New Jersey	5,136	87
10	Georgia	4,121	74
11	Virginia	3,961	75
12	North Carolina	3,778	72
13	Tennessee	3,726	80
14	Indiana	3,301	73
15	Massachusetts	3,156	71
16	Washington	3,140	78
17	Maryland	3,075	82
18	Missouri	2,821	76

Rank		Automobiles	Percent of motor vehicles (automobiles)
19	Minnesota	2,736	75
20	Wisconsin	2,463	71
21	Connecticut	2,429	74
22	Alabama	2,196	71
23	Colorado	2,165	73
24	Louisiana	2,006	69
25	Arizona	1,994	71
26	Oregon	1,955	71
27	South Carolina	1,948	72
28	Kentucky	1,939	75
29	Iowa	1,931	75
30	Oklahoma	1,758	68
31	Mississippi	1,496	77
32	Kansas	1,258	65
33	Arkansas	974	65
34	Nebraska	893	66
35	New Mexico	838	62
36	Utah	810	64
37	West Virginia	778	62
38	Maine	754	73
39	New Hampshire	694	71
40	Hawaii	668	73
41	Nevada	621	68
42	Idaho	610	68
43	Montana	541	70
44	Rhode Island	517	72
45	South Dakota	427	65
46	Delaware	419	67
47	North Dakota	394	72
48	Vermont	346	71
49	Alaska	308	64
50	Wyoming	249	54
51	Washington, DC	238	93

HOUSEHOLDS WITH MOTOR VEHICLES

The table below is an indication of how dependent certain states are on motor vehicles. In most rural and farming states, the majority of households had two or more vehicles. States with large urban areas and mass transit systems generally reported one or no vehicles.

TABLE: Households with Motor Vehicles
DATE: 1990
SOURCE: U.S. Bureau of the Census, *Census of Population and Housing*, 1990
DESCRIPTION: Total and percent of households with motor vehicles. Table ranked by total households with vehicles. Percentages may not add to 100% due to rounding.

Rank		None	Percent of households with no vehicles	Households with one vehicle (thousands)	Percent of households with one vehicle	Households with two or more vehicles (thousands)	Percent of households with two or more vehicles	Total households with motor vehicles (thousands)
	United States	10,602	11	31,039	34	50,306	55	81,345
1	California	923	9	3,452	33	6,006	58	9,458
2	Texas	489	8	2,190	36	3,392	56	5,582
3	Florida	474	9	2,106	41	2,555	50	4,661
4	New York	1,994	30	2,153	32	2,492	38	4,646
5	Pennsylvania	681	15	1,589	35	2,226	50	3,815
6	Ohio	416	10	1,351	33	2,320	57	3,672
7	Illinois	588	14	1,476	35	2,138	51	3,614
8	Michigan	344	10	1,133	33	1,943	57	3,076
9	New Jersey	360	13	966	35	1,468	53	2,435
10	North Carolina	242	10	786	31	1,489	59	2,275
11	Georgia	244	10	730	31	1,393	59	2,123
12	Virginia	205	9	717	31	1,370	60	2,087
13	Massachusetts	321	14	819	36	1,107	49	1,926
14	Indiana	175	8	670	32	1,221	59	1,891
15	Missouri	191	10	652	33	1,118	57	1,770
16	Washington	141	8	582	31	1,149	61	1,732
17	Tennessee	181	10	593	32	1,079	58	1,672
18	Wisconsin	170	9	600	33	1,052	58	1,652
19	Maryland	216	12	554	32	979	56	1,533
20	Minnesota	142	9	517	31	988	60	1,506
21	Alabama	156	10	466	31	885	59	1,351
22	Louisiana	209	14	542	38	749	50	1,291
23	Arizona	107	8	532	39	730	53	1,262
24	Kentucky	159	12	447	32	773	56	1,221
25	Colorado	89	7	412	32	781	61	1,193
26	South Carolina	137	11	402	32	720	57	1,122
27	Oklahoma	91	8	414	34	701	58	1,115
28	Connecticut	124	10	386	31	721	59	1,107
29	Oregon	88	8	355	32	660	60	1,015
30	Iowa	75	7	332	31	657	62	989
31	Kansas	60	6	302	32	583	62	885
32	Arkansas	88	10	303	34	501	56	804
33	Mississippi	111	12	307	34	494	54	801
34	West Virginia	94	14	247	36	347	50	595
35	Nebraska	43	7	182	30	377	63	559
36	Utah	29	5	153	28	355	66	508
37	New Mexico	38	7	185	34	320	59	505
38	Nevada	36	8	174	37	256	55	430
39	Maine	40	9	159	34	266	57	425
40	New Hampshire	26	6	132	32	254	62	385
41	Idaho	17	5	101	28	243	67	344
42	Rhode Island	40	11	132	35	206	54	338
43	Hawaii	35	10	129	36	193	54	321
44	Montana	20	10	91	30	194	64	286
45	South Dakota	17	6	76	29	166	64	242
46	Delaware	20	8	80	33	147	59	227
47	North Dakota	16	7	73	30	152	63	225
48	Vermont	17	8	72	34	122	58	194
49	Alaska	23	12	64	34	102	54	166
50	Wyoming	8	5	48	28	113	67	161
51	Washington, DC	93	37	103	41	53	21	156

Rank		1991 ($)	1992 ($)
34	Missouri	469	493
35	Wisconsin	463	492
36	Vermont	474	484
37	Tennessee	466	478
38	Kentucky	435	473
39	Maine	484	468
40	Utah	436	463
41	Oklahoma	422	448
42	North Carolina	432	448
43	Arkansas	387	424
44	Idaho	386	402
45	Montana	370	393
46	Kansas	368	392
47	Iowa	359	379
48	Wyoming	330	366
49	Nebraska	346	352
50	South Dakota	309	333
51	North Dakota	329	319

AUTOMOBILE INSURANCE

Nationwide, it cost $617 dollars to insure a vehicle. The cost ranged from a high of $974 in Hawaii to a low of $319 in North Dakota. Regionally, the Midwest and the Plains states had the lowest cost. High cost is frequently an indication of the existence of large urban areas or high motor theft rates.

TABLE: Automobile Insurance
DATE: 1992
SOURCE: Reprinted by permission of the National Association of Insurance Commissioners, Kansas City, MO, *State Average Expenditures and Premiums for Personal Automobile Insurance*, annual, (copyright)
DESCRIPTION: Average expenditure on automobile insurance per insured vehicle in dollars.

Rank		1991 ($)	1992 ($)
	United States	596	617
1	Hawaii	874	974
2	New Jersey	984	957
3	Washington, DC	863	880
4	Connecticut	841	878
5	Massachusetts	814	860
6	Rhode Island	823	837
7	California	783	800
8	New York	681	799
9	Delaware	718	745
10	Louisiana	679	724
11	Maryland	689	702
12	Alaska	643	685
13	Florida	669	684
14	Nevada	640	673
15	Arizona	647	667
16	Michigan	606	661
17	Colorado	588	653
18	Texas	612	646
19	Pennsylvania	610	642
20	New Hampshire	646	638
21	Washington	549	588
22	Minnesota	530	566
23	West Virginia	519	557
24	New Mexico	517	543
25	Oregon	529	535
26	Illinois	552	534
27	South Carolina	491	528
28	Mississippi	482	519
29	Georgia	541	514
30	Alabama	475	510
31	Virginia	506	503
32	Ohio	494	503
33	Indiana	474	497

TRANSPORTATION TO WORK

Nationwide, 84 million people drove alone to work, another 15 million drove to work in car-pools and 3 million worked at home. Five percent used public transportation. Not surprisingly, the states that encompassed or bordered large urban areas had the highest percentage of people traveling to work via public transportation. Densely populated metropolitan areas have fostered the use, development and maintenance of public transportation systems.

It took Americans 22 minutes on average to get to work. In 1990 the average travel time was lowest in rural states, where large portions of the population worked at home. Highway and road congestion contributed to long travel times. New York had the longest average travel time, followed by Washington, DC and Maryland, New Jersey, Illinois and California. These times reflect the high cost of housing in metropolitan areas that has forced families to travel long distances for affordable housing.

TABLE: Transportation to Work
DATE: 1990
SOURCE: U.S. Bureau of the Census, *Census of Population and Housing*, 1990
DESCRIPTION: Type of transportation to work and average commuting time. Table ranked by "drove alone."

Rank		Drove alone (thousands)	Car-pooled (thousands)	Worked at home (thousands)	Percent using public transportation	Average travel time to work (minutes)
	United States	84,215	15,378	3,406	5.3	22.4
1	California	9,982	2,036	453	4.9	24.6
2	Texas	5,821	1,134	185	2.2	22.2
3	Florida	4,468	819	132	2.0	21.8
4	New York	4,461	861	213	24.8	28.6
5	Ohio	3,889	521	119	2.5	20.7
6	Pennsylvania	3,818	690	145	6.4	21.6
7	Illinois	3,742	653	144	10.1	25.1
8	Michigan	3,328	429	100	1.6	21.2
9	New Jersey	2,731	472	80	8.8	25.3
10	North Carolina	2,528	530	71	1.0	19.8
11	Georgia	2,379	468	65	2.8	22.7
12	Virginia	2,281	500	103	4.0	24.0
13	Massachusetts	2,148	318	75	8.3	22.7
14	Indiana	2,040	332	73	1.3	20.4
15	Missouri	1,816	312	84	2.0	21.6
16	Tennessee	1,763	324	52	1.3	21.5
17	Wisconsin	1,751	270	114	2.5	18.3
18	Maryland	1,733	376	65	8.1	27.0
19	Washington	1,701	282	86	4.5	22.0
20	Minnesota	1,593	247	116	3.6	19.1
21	Alabama	1,374	267	31	0.8	21.2
22	Connecticut	1,301	187	45	3.9	21.1
23	Louisiana	1,239	247	31	3.0	22.3
24	South Carolina	1,235	277	31	1.1	20.5
25	Colorado	1,217	210	67	2.9	20.7
26	Kentucky	1,195	229	47	1.6	20.7
27	Arizona	1,178	239	48	2.1	21.6
28	Oklahoma	1,079	191	41	0.6	19.3
29	Iowa	971	157	89	1.2	16.2
30	Oregon	949	165	56	3.4	19.6
31	Kansas	929	136	49	0.7	17.2
32	Mississippi	777	184	19	0.8	20.6
33	Arkansas	765	153	28	0.5	19.0
34	Nebraska	590	87	44	1.2	15.8
35	Utah	541	111	26	2.3	18.9
36	West Virginia	493	107	16	1.1	21.0
37	New Mexico	472	96	24	1.0	19.1
38	Nevada	444	94	12	2.7	19.8
39	New Hampshire	443	70	20	0.7	21.9
40	Maine	424	80	24	0.9	19.0
41	Rhode Island	376	58	10	2.5	19.2
42	Hawaii	344	116	19	7.4	23.8
43	Idaho	330	53	21	1.9	17.3
44	Delaware	258	43	8	2.4	20.0
45	Montana	250	41	22	0.6	14.8
46	South Dakota	233	33	31	0.3	13.8
47	North Dakota	210	31	24	0.6	13.0
48	Vermont	200	36	17	0.7	18.0
49	Alaska	165	40	11	2.4	16.7
50	Wyoming	154	28	9	1.4	15.4
51	Washington, DC	107	37	9	36.6	27.1

ROADWAY CONGESTION

The table below shows the economic and personal impact traffic delays cause. Delays and costs were highest around crowded urban areas, particularly where the rate of highway construction has not kept pace with population growth.

TABLE: Roadway Congestion
DATE: 1990
SOURCE: Texas Transportation Institute, College Station, Texas, *Roadway Congestion in Major Urban Areas,* annual (copyright)
DESCRIPTION: Vehicle hours of delay per 1,000 persons and cost per capita for one year. Various Federal, State, and local information sources were used to develop the data base with the primary source being the Federal Highway Administration's Highway Performance Monitoring System

Rank		Delay (per 1,000 persons in hours)	Per capita cost ($)
	United States	80	340
1	San Bernardino-River, CA	200	880
2	San Francisco-Oakland, CA	180	760
3	Washington, DC	180	770
4	Los Angeles, CA	160	670
5	San Jose, CA	160	690
6	Seattle-Everett, WA	150	660
7	Dallas, TX	130	570
8	Houston, TX	130	570
9	Atlanta, GA	120	530
10	Miami, FL	120	520
11	Boston, MA	110	490
12	Austin, TX	90	410
13	Denver, CO	90	370
14	Detroit, MI	90	380
15	New York, NY	90	390
16	Phoenix, AZ	90	400
17	Charlotte, NC	80	320
18	Fort Worth, TX	80	350
19	Honolulu, HI	80	360
20	Jacksonville, FL	80	330
21	Norfolk, VA	80	350
22	Orlando, FL	80	360
23	Portland, OR	80	330
24	Chicago, IL	70	300
25	Nashville, TN	70	310
26	Philadelphia, PA	70	270
27	Sacramento, CA	70	320
28	San Diego, CA	70	290
29	St. Louis, MO	70	290
30	Tampa, FL	70	290
31	Baltimore, MD	60	270
32	Ft. Lauderdale, FL	60	240
33	New Orleans, LA	60	270

Rank		Delay (per 1,000 persons in hours)	Per capita cost ($)
34	Pittsburgh, PA	60	270
35	Columbus, OH	50	200
36	Hartford, CT	50	220
37	Minneapolis-St. Paul, MN	50	220
38	San Antonio, TX	50	220
39	Albuquerque, NM	40	170
40	Cincinnati, OH	40	160
41	Milwaukee, WI	40	160
42	Cleveland, OH	30	120
43	Louisville, KY	30	110
44	Oklahoma City, OK	30	120
45	El Paso, TX	20	80
46	Indianapolis, IN	20	80
47	Kansas City, MO	20	100
48	Memphis, TN	20	100
49	Salt Lake City, UT	20	80
50	Corpus Christi, TX	10	40

TOP 10 AIRPORTS

This table ranks the nation's top 10 airports according to the total number of airline departures. During the 1980s and early 1990s airlines moved away from large numbers of direct flights to a hub system, forcing passengers to transfer at a central location. The rankings below are, in part, an indication of the airport's importance as a hub. They also are influenced by the number of cargo flights.

TABLE: Top 10 Airports
DATE: 1992
SOURCE: U.S. Federal Aviation Administration and Research and Special Programs Administration, *Airport Activity Statistics,* annual
DESCRIPTION: Departures from top 10 airports and percent of total U.S. airport departures. For scheduled carriers only.

Rank		Departures* (thousands)	Percent of total departures
	All airports**	6,607	
1	Chicago, O'Hare	378	6
2	Dallas/Ft. Worth International	281	4
3	Atlanta, Hartsfield International	217	3
4	Los Angeles International	197	3
5	San Francisco International	169	3
6	Denver, Stapleton International	161	2
7	Phoenix, Sky Harbor International	144	2
8	Newark International	134	2
9	St. Louis International	178	3
10	Detroit, Metro Wayne	137	2

*Includes completed scheduled and unscheduled.
**Includes other airports, not shown separately.

TOP DOMESTIC AIRLINE MARKETS

This table shows the top 30 domestic airline markets in each metropolitan area according to the number of passengers traveling in 1992. New York dominated the market, as the departure point for seven of the 10 major markets.

TABLE: Top Domestic Airline Markets

DATE: 1992

SOURCE: Air Transport Association of America, Washington, DC, *Air Transport*, annual

DESCRIPTION: Data are for the 30 top markets and include all commercial airports in each metro area. Data do not include connecting passengers.

Rank	Market	Passengers
1	New York to—from Los Angeles	2,904,060
2	New York to—from Boston	2,350,240
3	New York to—from Chicago	2,330,750
4	New York to—from Washington	2,282,480
5	Los Angeles to—from San Francisco	2,153,360

Rank	Market	Passengers
6	New York to—from Miami	2,142,690
7	Dallas/Ft. Worth to—from Houston	2,090,390
8	Honolulu to—from Kahului, Maui	2,035,100
9	New York to—from San Francisco	2,010,350
10	New York to—from Orlando	1,727,260
11	New York to—from Ft. Lauderdale	1,547,970
12	New York to—from San Juan	1,524,400
13	Los Angeles to—from Phoenix	1,402,160
14	Chicago to—from Detroit	1,339,600
15	New York to—from Atlanta	1,330,730
16	Honolulu to—from Lihue, Kauai	1,273,460
17	Los Angeles to —from Las Vegas	1,217,420
18	Chicago to—from Los Angeles	1,188,980
19	New York to—from West Palm Beach	1,187,110
20	Los Angeles to—from Honolulu	1,165,470
21	San Francisco to—from San Diego	1,058,870
22	Honolulu to—from Kona, Hawaii	1,055,760
23	Los Angeles to—from Oakland	1,042,880
24	New York to—from Dallas/Ft. Worth	1,029,860
25	Honolulu to—from Hilo, Hawaii	1,019,250
26	Chicago to—from St. Louis	973,580
27	Boston to—from Washington	952,450
28	Los Angeles to—from Washington	925,220
29	San Francisco to—from Honolulu	880,390
30	Chicago to—from Washington	875,740

POLITICS

This section summarizes the positions of the two major parties at the congressional level before the 1994 election and after the one in 1996. It also includes a table on the popular vote in the 1992 and 1996 presidental elections. The 1994 election witnesses a dramatic turnover in Congress as the Republicans became the majority party in both houses. The Republicans maintained control in the 1996 election, but the White House remained Democratic. President Clinton, however, did not receive a majority of the popular vote.

The primary source for the material below is the United States Congress, which tallied House and Senate figures.

PARTY AFFILIATION IN THE HOUSE OF REPRESENTATIVES

Democrats were the majority party in the 103rd Congress, maintaining their 40-year control of the House. However, in the 1994 elections for the 104th Congress, Republicans took control of the House for the first time since the 83rd Congress (1935–55). The Republicans maintained their majority in the 1996 elections. In the 105th Congress Republicans held 226 seats and the Democrats held 207. (There were two independents.)

TABLE: Party Affiliation in the House of Representatives
DATE: 1994, 1997
SOURCE: U.S. Congress, Joint Committee on Printing, *Congressional Directory*, and unpublished data
DESCRIPTION: Political composition of the House of Representatives in the last session of the 103rd Congress and the first session of the 105th Congress. Table ranked by 105th Congress.

United States	103rd Congress (1994)	105th Congress (1997)	Change 1994–1997
Democrats	257	207	-50
Republicans	176	226	50

State*	103rd Congress (1994)**	105th Congress (1997)	Change 1994–1997
Democrats			
California	30	29	-1
New York	18	18	0
Texas	21	17	-4
Pennsylvania	11	11	0
Illinois	12	10	-2
Massachusetts	8	10	2
Michigan	10	10	0
Florida	10	8	-2
Ohio	10	8	-2
Minnesota	6	6	0
New Jersey	7	6	-1
North Carolina	8	6	-2
Virginia	7	6	-1
Missouri	6	5	-1
Wisconsin	4	5	1
Connecticut	3	4	1
Indiana	7	4	-3
Maryland	4	4	0
Oregon	4	4	0
Tennessee	6	4	-2
Georgia	7	3	-4
Washington	8	3	-5
West Virginia	3	3	0
Alabama	4	2	-2
Arkansas	2	2	0
Colorado	2	2	0
Hawaii	2	2	0
Louisiana	4	2	-2
Maine	1	2	1
Mississippi	5	2	-3
Rhode Island	1	2	1
South Carolina	3	2	-1
Arizona	3	1	-2
Iowa	1	1	0
Kentucky	4	1	-3
New Mexico	1	1	0
North Dakota	1	1	0
Alaska	0	0	0
Delaware	0	0	0

State*	103rd Congress (1994)**	105th Congress (1997)	Change 1994–1997
Idaho	1	0	-1
Kansas	2	0	-2
Montana	1	0	-1
Nebraska	1	0	-1
Nevada	1	0	-1
New Hampshire	1	0	-1
Oklahoma	3	0	-3
South Dakota	1	0	-1
Utah	2	0	-2
Vermont*	0	0	0
Wyoming	0	0	0

Republicans

State*	103rd Congress (1994)**	105th Congress (1997)	Change 1994–1997
California	22	23	1
Florida	13	15	2
New York	13	13	0
Texas	9	13	4
Ohio	9	11	2
Illinois	8	10	2
Pennsylvania	10	10	0
Georgia	4	8	4
New Jersey	6	7	1
Indiana	3	6	3
Michigan	6	6	0
North Carolina	4	6	2
Oklahoma	2	6	4
Washington	1	6	5
Alabama	3	5	2
Arizona	3	5	2
Kentucky	2	5	3
Louisiana	3	5	2
Tennessee	3	5	2
Virginia	4	5	1
Colorado	4	4	0
Iowa	4	4	0
Kansas	2	4	2
Maryland	4	4	0
South Carolina	3	4	1
Wisconsin	5	4	-1
Mississippi	0	3	3
Missouri	3	3	0
Nebraska	2	3	1
Utah	1	3	2
Arkansas	2	2	0
Connecticut	3	2	-1
Idaho	1	2	1
Minnesota	2	2	0
Nevada	1	2	1
New Hampshire	1	2	1
New Mexico	2	2	0
Alaska	1	1	0
Delaware	1	1	0
Montana	0	1	1
Oregon	1	1	0
South Dakota	0	1	1
Wyoming	1	1	0

State*	103rd Congress (1994)**	105th Congress (1997)	Change 1994–1997
Hawaii	0	0	0
Maine	1	0	-1
Massachusetts	2	0	-2
North Dakota	0	0	0
Rhode Island	1	0	-1
Vermont	0	0	0
West Virginia	0	0	0

*Vermont had one Independent-Socialist Representative in the 103rd and 105th Congress. Missouri had one independent in the 105th Congress. Oklahoma had one vacancy in the second session of the 103rd Congress.

**1994 103rd Congress as of beginning of second session (January 25).

PARTY AFFILIATION IN THE SENATE

Prior to the 1994 election, the Democrats controlled the Senate, holding 56 seats. Republicans gained control of the chamber that fall, winning 52 seats. It was the first time the Republicans had been in the majority in the Senate since the 99th Congress, beginning in 1985. The Republicans increased their majority in 1996, with 55 seats to the Democrats' 45.

TABLE: Party Affiliation in the Senate
DATE: 1994, 1997
SOURCE: U.S. Congress, Joint Committee on Printing, *Congressional Directory*, and unpublished data
DESCRIPTION: Political composition of the Senate in the last session of the 103rd Congress and the first session of the 105th Congress.

United States	103rd Congress (1994)	105th Congress (1997)	Change 1994–1997
Democrats	56	45	-11
Republicans	44	55	11

Democrats

	103rd Congress (1994)	105th Congress (1997)	Change 1994–1997
Alabama	2	0	-2
Alaska	0	0	0
Arizona	1	0	-1
Arkansas	2	1	-1
California	2	2	0
Colorado	1	0	-1
Connecticut	2	2	0
Delaware	1	1	0
Florida	1	1	0
Georgia	1	1	0

State	103rd Congress (1994)	105th Congress (1997)	Change 1994–1997
Hawaii	2	2	0
Idaho	0	0	0
Illinois	2	2	0
Indiana	0	0	0
Iowa	1	1	0
Kansas	0	0	0
Kentucky	1	1	0
Louisiana	2	2	0
Maine	1	0	-1
Maryland	2	2	0
Massachusetts	2	2	0
Michigan	2	1	-1
Minnesota	1	1	0
Mississippi	0	0	0
Missouri	0	0	0
Montana	1	1	0
Nebraska	2	1	-1
Nevada	2	2	0
New Hampshire	0	0	0
New Jersey	2	2	0
New Mexico	1	1	0
New York	1	1	0
North Carolina	0	0	0
North Dakota	2	2	0
Ohio	2	1	-1
Oklahoma	1	0	-1
Oregon	0	1	1
Pennsylvania	1	0	-1
Rhode Island	1	1	0
South Carolina	1	1	0
South Dakota	1	2	1
Tennessee	2	0	-2
Texas	0	0	0
Utah	0	0	0
Vermont	1	1	0
Virginia	1	1	0
Washington	1	1	0
West Virginia	2	2	0
Wisconsin	2	2	0
Wyoming	0	0	0

Republicans

State	103rd Congress (1994)	105th Congress (1997)	Change 1994–1997
Alabama	0	2	2
Alaska	2	2	0
Arizona	1	2	1
Arkansas	0	1	1
California	0	0	0
Colorado	1	2	1
Connecticut	0	0	0
Delaware	1	1	0
Florida	1	1	0
Georgia	1	1	0
Hawaii	0	0	0
Idaho	2	2	0
Illinois	0	0	0
Indiana	2	2	0
Iowa	1	1	0
Kansas	2	2	0
Kentucky	1	1	0
Louisiana	0	0	0
Maine	1	2	1
Maryland	0	0	0
Massachusetts	0	0	0
Michigan	0	1	1
Minnesota	1	1	0
Mississippi	2	2	0
Missouri	2	2	0
Montana	1	1	0
Nebraska	0	1	1
Nevada	0	0	0
New Hampshire	2	2	0
New Jersey	0	0	0
New Mexico	1	1	0
New York	1	1	0
North Carolina	2	2	0
North Dakota	0	0	0
Ohio	0	1	1
Oklahoma	1	2	1
Oregon	2	1	-1
Pennsylvania	1	2	1
Rhode Island	1	1	0
South Carolina	1	1	0
South Dakota	1	0	-1
Tennessee	0	2	2
Texas	2	2	0
Utah	2	2	0
Vermont	1	1	0
Virginia	1	1	0
Washington	1	1	0
West Virginia	0	0	0
Wisconsin	0	0	0
Wyoming	2	2	0

THE PERCENTAGE OF POPULAR VOTE CAST FOR PRESIDENT, BY POLITICAL PARTY IN 1996

The percentage of votes cast by party is shown in this table. In 1996 Bill Clinton was reelected president of the United States with 49% of the popular vote, becoming the first Democrat since Franklin D. Roosevelt to win a second term. Senator Bob Dole of Kansas, the Republican presidential nominee, received 41% of the popular vote.

President Clinton carried 31 states and received 379 electoral votes. Bill Clinton carried the northeastern, midwestern and western states. A significant victory for Clinton was Florida, with 25 elctoral votes; it ranked fourth nationwide in number of electoral votes. No Democratic presidental canndidate had won in Florida since Jimmy Carter in 1976.

Senator Dole won 19 states and 159 electoral votes. Dole won a swath of states stretching from North Dakota to Texas. Texas with 32 electoral votes was an impressive Dole victory. Only California (54) and New York (33) claim more electoral votes. Dole also won in several southern states: Virginia (13), North Carolina (14), South Carolina (8), Georgia (13), Alabama (9) and Mississippi (7).

Billionaire businessman and third-party candidate Ross Perot received 8.5% of the popular vote. The Reform Party candidate received no electoral votes, a much weaker showing than that of four years earlier. Details of the 1992 election follow.

In 1992 the incumbent Republican president, George Bush, ran against Bill Clinton, then governor of Arkansas. However, what made this presidential election year uncus-tomary was the introduction of billionaire businessman and third-party candidate Ross Perot. Bill Clinton became the 41st president, winning the election with 43% of the vote. Former President George Bush received 38% of the popular vote and Ross Perot received 19% of the vote. This was an unusually strong showing for a third-party candidate. The Perot vote was particularly high in some of the western states: Alaska (28%), Idaho and Utah (27%), Montana and Nevada (26%), Arizona, Oregon and Washington (24%). In Maine (30%) and Kansas (27%) the percentage of Perot voters was also substantial.

TABLE: The Percentage of Popular Vote Cast for President, by Political Party in 1996
DATE: 1997
SOURCE: *Facts On File*
DESCRIPTION: Percent of popular vote cast for president by political party. Percentages will not add up to 100% because of voting for minor party candidates.

	1992 percent Democratic Party	1992 percent Republican Party	1992 percent Perot Reform Party	1996 percent Democratic Party	1996 percent Republican Party	1996 percent Perot Reform Party
United States	43.0	37.4	18.9	49.2	40.8	8.5
Alabama	41	48	11	43	51	6
Alaska	30	39	28	33	51	11
Arizona	37	38	24	47	44	8
Arkansas	53	35	10	54	37	8
California	46	33	21	51	38	7
Colorado	40	36	23	44	46	7
Connecticut	42	36	22	52	35	10
Delaware	44	35	20	52	37	11
Florida	39	41	20	48	42	9
Georgia	43	43	13	46	47	6
Hawaii	48	37	14	57	32	8
Idaho	28	42	27	34	52	13
Illinois	49	34	17	54	37	8
Indiana	37	43	20	42	47	10
Iowa	43	37	19	50	40	9
Kansas	34	39	27	36	54	9
Kentucky	45	41	14	46	45	9
Louisiana	46	41	12	52	40	7
Maine	39	30	30	52	31	14
Maryland	50	36	14	54	38	7
Massachusetts	48	29	23	62	28	9
Michigan	44	36	19	52	38	9
Minnesota	43	32	24	51	35	12
Mississippi	41	50	9	44	49	6
Missouri	44	34	22	48	41	10
Montana	38	35	26	41	44	14
Nebraska	29	47	24	35	53	11
Nevada	37	35	26	44	43	9
New Hampshire	39	38	23	50	40	10
New Jersey	43	41	16	53	36	9
New Mexico	46	37	16	49	41	6

	1992 percent Democratic Party	1992 percent Republican Party	1992 percent Perot Reform Party	1996 percent Democratic Party	1996 percent Republican Party	1996 percent Perot Reform Party
New York	50	34	16	59	31	8
North Carolina	43	43	14	44	49	7
North Dakota	32	44	23	40	47	12
Ohio	40	38	21	47	41	11
Oklahoma	34	43	23	40	48	11
Oregon	42	33	24	47	37	11
Pennsylvania	45	36	18	49	40	10
Rhode Island	47	29	23	60	27	11
South Carolina	40	48	12	44	50	6
South Dakota	37	41	22	43	46	10
Tennessee	47	42	10	48	46	6
Texas	37	41	22	44	49	7
Utah	25	43	27	33	54	10
Vermont	46	30	23	54	31	12
Virginia	41	45	14	45	47	7
Washington	43	32	24	51	36	9
West Virginia	48	35	16	51	37	11
Wisconsin	41	37	22	49	39	10
Wyoming	34	40	26	37	50	12
Washington, DC	85	9	4	85	9	2

GOVERNMENT

This section presents statistics on the configuration of federal and state legislative bodies and on federal, state and local government employees.

The primary sources are the United States Congress, the National Conference of State Legislatures, the U.S. Office of Personnel Management and the U.S. Bureau of the Census.

In 1980 approximately 16.2 million Americans were employed in the public sector, by either the federal, state or local governments. Despite the emphasis on downsizing government during the 1980s, by 1992, the number had grown to 16.5 million Americans. Between 1960 and 1992 civilian government employment accounted for approximately 17% of employment nationwide.

The first two tables in this section focus on U. S. House of Representatives reapportionment in light of the 1990 census and detail the number of legislators in the states and state legislative bodies. The following tables assess government employment and earnings.

CONGRESSIONAL APPORTIONMENT

One of the primary tasks of the census is to determine the distribution of population for the purpose of assigning a proportional number of House seats to each state. The House of Representatives is comprised of 435 members. However, the number of representatives from a given state changes as the result of population shifts.

As a result of the 1990 census, 19 seats were reapportioned. The biggest gains were in the western states and in southern states. Several northeastern and midwestern states lost seats. Not all southern states gained seats. Kentucky, Louisiana and West Virginia each lost a seat.

TABLE: Congressional Appportionment
DATE: 1997

SOURCE: U.S. Congress, Joint Committee on Printing, *Congressional Directory*, biennial, and unpublished data
DESCRIPTION: Congressional apportionment in the U.S. House of Representatives and changes in number of representatives in each state between 1987 and 1997. Table ranked by 105th Congress.

Rank		100th Congress 1987	105th Congress 1997	Change 1987–1997
	United States	435	435	
1	California	45	52	7
2	New York	34	31	-3
3	Texas	27	30	3
4	Florida	19	23	4
5	Pennsylvania	23	21	-2
6	Illinois	22	20	-2
7	Ohio	21	19	-2
8	Michigan	18	16	-2
9	New Jersey	14	13	-1
10	North Carolina	11	12	1
11	Georgia	10	11	1
12	Virginia	10	11	1
13	Indiana	10	10	0
14	Massachusetts	11	10	-1
15	Missouri	9	9	0
16	Tennessee	9	9	0
17	Washington	8	9	1
18	Wisconsin	9	9	0
19	Maryland	8	8	0
20	Minnesota	8	8	0
21	Alabama	7	7	0
22	Louisiana	8	7	-1
23	Arizona	5	6	1
24	Colorado	6	6	0
25	Connecticut	6	6	0
26	Kentucky	7	6	-1
27	Oklahoma	6	6	0
28	South Carolina	6	6	0
29	Iowa	6	5	-1
30	Mississippi	5	5	0
31	Oregon	5	5	0
32	Arkansas	4	4	0

Rank		100th Congress 1987	105th Congress 1997	Change 1987–1997
33	Kansas	5	4	-1
34	Nebraska	3	3	0
35	New Mexico	3	3	0
36	Utah	3	3	0
37	West Virginia	4	3	-1
38	Hawaii	2	2	0
39	Idaho	2	2	0
40	Maine	2	2	0
41	Nevada	2	2	0
42	New Hampshire	2	2	0
43	Rhode Island	2	2	0
44	Alaska	1	1	0
45	Delaware	1	1	0
46	Montana	2	1	-1
47	North Dakota	1	1	0
48	South Dakota	1	1	0
49	Vermont	1	1	0
50	Wyoming	1	1	0

COMPOSITION OF STATE LEGISLATURES

Each state autonomously determines the size and composition of its legislature. New Hampshire's House of Representatives was the largest at 399 members or approximately one for 25,000 citizens, the highest quotient in the nation.

Nebraska's single chamber, or unicameral system, is unique. In 1934 the state shifted from a bicameral to a unicameral 49-member legislative body.

TABLE: Composition of State Legislatures
DATE: 1992
SOURCE: National Conference of State Legislatures, Denver, CO, unpublished data (copyright)
DESCRIPTION: Number of state legislators by chamber. Table ranked by total seats.

Rank	State	Members of the State House of Representatives*	Members of the State Senate**	Total seats
1	New Hampshire	399	24	423
2	Pennsylvania	203	49	252
3	Georgia	179	56	235
4	New York	150	61	211
5	Minnesota	134	67	201
6	Massachusetts	158	40	198
7	Missouri	163	34	197
8	Maryland	141	47	188
9	Maine	151	35	186
10	Connecticut	149	36	185
11	Texas	149	31	180
12	Vermont	150	30	180

Rank	State	Members of the State House of Representatives*	Members of the State Senate**	Total seats
13	Illinois	118	59	177
14	Mississippi	122	52	174
15	North Carolina	120	50	170
16	South Carolina	124	46	170
17	Kansas	125	40	165
18	Florida	120	40	160
19	Indiana	100	50	150
20	Iowa	100	50	150
21	Montana	100	50	150
22	Rhode Island	100	50	150
23	Oklahoma	101	48	149
24	Michigan	110	38	148
25	North Dakota	98	49	147
26	Washington	98	49	147
27	Louisiana	105	39	144
28	Alabama	105	35	140
29	Virginia	100	40	140
30	Kentucky	100	38	138
31	Arkansas	101	35	136
32	West Virginia	100	34	134
33	Ohio	99	33	132
34	Tennessee	99	33	132
35	Wisconsin	98	33	131
36	New Jersey	80	40	120
37	California	80	39	119
38	New Mexico	70	42	112
39	Idaho	70	35	105
40	South Dakota	70	35	105
41	Utah	75	29	104
42	Colorado	65	35	100
43	Arizona	61	30	91
44	Oregon	60	30	90
45	Wyoming	60	30	90
46	Hawaii	51	25	76
47	Delaware	41	21	62
48	Nevada	39	21	60
49	Alaska	38	20	58
50	Nebraska	Single chamber 49 members.		49

*Excludes one vacancy each for GA, NH, TX, and WI; two vacancies each for CT and MA; and three vacancies for NV.
**Excludes one vacancy each for CA and PA.

CIVILIAN EMPLOYEES IN THE FEDERAL GOVERNMENT

This table shows the total number of civilian employees in the federal government and federal employees as a percentage of total government employees in each state. Not surprisingly, the highest percentage of federal workers were located in Washington, DC, Maryland and Virginia. Among the states that exceeded or matched the national average were Hawaii and Alaska and several western states: Utah, Colorado and New Mexico.

Thirty-nine percent of all federal employees were located in five states (California, Virginia, Texas, Maryland, New York, and Washington, DC). Federal employees tallied 4% or less of total government employees in the remaining 45 states.

TABLE: Civilian Employees in the Federal Government
DATE: 1992
SOURCE: U.S. Office of Personnel Management, *Biennial Report of Employment by Geographic Area*
DESCRIPTION: Paid civilian employees in the federal government and federal government employees as a percentage of total state, local, and federal employees.

Rank		Total federal employees (thousands)	Federal employees as percent of total government employees
	United States	2,988	18
1	Washington, DC*	223	80
2	Maryland	136	36
3	Virginia	168	33
4	Hawaii	25	28
5	Utah	35	27
6	Alaska	16	26
7	Colorado	57	24
8	New Mexico	28	22
9	Missouri	66	21
10	Pennsylvania	132	21
11	Alabama	58	20
12	Maine	16	20
13	Oklahoma	46	20
14	South Dakota	10	20
15	Washington	69	20
16	Georgia	93	19
17	California	312	18
18	Massachusetts	62	18
19	Montana	12	18
20	North Dakota	8	18
21	Tennessee	54	18
22	Arizona	40	17
23	Oregon	31	17
24	Rhode Island	10	17
25	Illinois	106	16
26	Kentucky	38	16
27	Vermont	6	16
28	Wyoming	7	16
29	Florida	114	15
30	Idaho	11	15
31	Nevada	12	15
32	New Jersey	74	15
33	Ohio	94	15
34	Texas	179	15
35	West Virginia	17	15
36	Arkansas	21	14
37	Connecticut	24	14

Rank		Total federal employees (thousands)	Federal employees as percent of total government employees
38	Kansas	26	14
39	Mississippi	26	14
40	Nebraska	16	14
41	South Carolina	33	14
42	Indiana	43	13
43	New Hampshire	8	13
44	Delaware	5	12
45	Louisiana	35	12
46	Minnesota	34	12
47	North Carolina	51	12
48	Iowa	20	11
49	Michigan	59	11
50	New York	149	11
51	Wisconsin	30	10

*Figures based on federal government and local government employees.

STATE GOVERNMENT EMPLOYMENT

Hawaii and Alaska lead the rest of the nation in state government employment per 10,000 population. Hawaii, Alaska and Delaware were the only states in which state government workers outnumbered local government workers (see Local Government Employment table on page 208).

Two types of states rank high in this table. One type—represented by Alaska, New Mexico, North Dakota and Wyoming—were characterized by comparatively small populations, settled sparsely over vast territories. A second type—Hawaii, Delaware and Rhode Island—were characterized by comparatively small land areas. In this situation the state government supplies services that local governments usually perform in states that are larger in both area and population. The states that ranked lowest according to the rate of government employment were the big states with large populations.

TABLE: State Government Employment
DATE: 1992
SOURCE: U.S. Bureau of the Census, *Public Employment*, annual
DESCRIPTION: Number of state government employees and state employees per 10,000 population. Table ranked by employment per 10,000 people.

Rank		1992 government employment (thousands)	1992 government employment (per 10,000 people)
	United States	3,856	151
1	Hawaii	51	437
2	Alaska	24	413

Rank		1992 government employment (thousands)	1992 government employment (per 10,000 people)
3	Delaware	20	293
4	New Mexico	42	267
5	North Dakota	16	259
6	Wyoming	12	242
7	Vermont	13	227
8	Utah	40	219
9	South Carolina	78	216
10	Oklahoma	67	209
11	Louisiana	89	207
12	Montana	17	207
13	Kentucky	76	203
14	Rhode Island	20	198
15	Alabama	81	196
16	Arkansas	47	194
17	Washington	98	191
18	Idaho	20	190
19	Kansas	48	190
20	South Dakota	14	190
21	West Virginia	34	185
22	Virginia	116	182
23	Mississippi	47	181
24	Nebraska	29	179
25	Maine	22	178
26	Georgia	114	170
27	Indiana	95	168
28	Iowa	47	168
29	Maryland	82	167
30	Oregon	50	167
31	Connecticut	54	165
32	North Carolina	109	159
33	Colorado	53	153
34	Tennessee	76	151
35	Minnesota	67	150
36	New Jersey	116	149
37	New York	267	148
38	New Hampshire	16	147
39	Michigan	138	146
40	Wisconsin	73	145
41	Nevada	19	144
42	Missouri	74	143
43	Massachusetts	85	142
44	Arizona	54	141
45	Texas	240	136
46	Ohio	140	127
47	Florida	164	122
48	Pennsylvania	143	119
49	Illinois	137	117
50	California	323	104

STATE GOVERNMENT EMPLOYEES' AVERAGE EARNINGS

Nationally, on average state employees earned $2,621 a month or $31,452 a year in 1992, a 29% increase over 1986 earnings. Top states in this ranking were generally found in the Northeast, Mid-Atlantic and West. Southern states were found at the bottom of the list. State employees ranged from those employed in higher education and the public welfare system to highway crews and hospital service workers.

TABLE: State Government Employees' Average Earnings
DATE: 1992
SOURCE: U.S. Bureau of the Census, *Public Employment*, annual
DESCRIPTION: Average earnings of full-time state government employees. Table ranked by 1992 earnings.

Rank		1986 average monthly earnings ($)	1992 average monthly earnings ($)	Percent change 1986-1992
	United States	2,025	2,621	29
1	California	2,751	3,420	24
2	Connecticut	2,336	3,286	41
3	Alaska	3,228	3,258	1
4	Wisconsin	2,128	3,216	51
5	New York	2,355	3,143	33
6	Michigan	2,541	3,134	23
7	Minnesota	2,428	3,101	28
8	New Jersey	2,278	3,100	36
9	Colorado	2,368	3,016	27
10	Iowa	2,049	2,895	41
11	Rhode Island	2,041	2,817	38
12	Washington	2,231	2,760	24
13	Nevada	1,990	2,738	38
14	Maryland	2,046	2,720	33
15	Pennsylvania	1,915	2,696	41
16	Ohio	1,984	2,691	36
17	Massachusetts	2,034	2,645	30
18	Illinois	2,165	2,642	22
19	Oregon	1,975	2,607	32
20	Hawaii	1,844	2,554	39
21	Vermont	1,842	2,514	36
22	Indiana	2,056	2,506	22
23	Delaware	1,795	2,463	37
24	Maine	1,714	2,437	42
25	New Hampshire	1,759	2,416	37
26	North Carolina	1,935	2,413	25
27	Arizona	2,126	2,361	11
28	Texas	1,927	2,351	22
29	Kentucky	1,651	2,349	42
30	Montana	1,864	2,300	23

Rank		1986 average monthly earnings ($)	1992 average monthly earnings ($)	Percent change 1986-1992
31	Virginia	1,895	2,270	20
32	Idaho	1,766	2,265	28
33	New Mexico	1,792	2,253	26
34	Alabama	1,884	2,243	19
35	North Dakota	1,805	2,231	24
36	Louisiana	1,673	2,227	33
37	Florida	1,748	2,202	26
38	Arkansas	1,724	2,195	27
39	Kansas	1,687	2,191	30
40	Nebraska	1,509	2,185	45
41	South Dakota	1,684	2,166	29
42	Tennessee	1,746	2,153	23
43	Utah	1,654	2,100	27
44	South Carolina	1,705	2,098	23
45	Georgia	1,811	2,075	15
46	Missouri	1,621	2,075	28
47	Wyoming	1,924	2,055	7
48	Oklahoma	1,733	2,044	18
49	Mississippi	1,430	2,000	40
50	West Virginia	1,574	1,969	25

LOCAL GOVERNMENT EMPLOYMENT

Nationwide, local governments employed twice as many people as state governments. The ratio between local and state government employment indicates the apportionment of state and local responsibilities in each state. Hawaii, which ranked lowest in local government employees, carried out its functions primarily via the state government with comparatively little assistance from local entities. By comparison, Alaska maintained support for both local and state governments, evidenced by high numbers of employees in both sectors.

TABLE: Local Government Employment
DATE: 1992
SOURCE: U.S. Bureau of the Census, *Public Employment*, annual
DESCRIPTION: Local government full-time employment. Table ranked by government employment per 100,000 people.

Rank		1992 government employment (thousands)	1992 government employment (per 10,000 people)
	United States	9,513	373
1	Washington, DC	55	928
2	Wyoming	25	543
3	New York	884	488
4	Montana	37	451
5	Nebraska	71	441
6	Kansas	109	433
7	Texas	748	424
8	Georgia	283	419
9	Mississippi	108	412
10	New Jersey	302	387
11	Iowa	108	386
12	Minnesota	173	385
13	Colorado	132	381
14	New Mexico	60	381
15	North Carolina	260	380
16	Arizona	145	379
17	Wisconsin	189	377
18	Oklahoma	121	376
19	Louisiana	161	375
20	Alabama	154	373
21	Idaho	40	373
22	Alaska	22	371
23	Florida	500	370
24	Illinois	431	370
25	Ohio	399	363
26	South Dakota	26	361
27	California	1,108	359
28	Virginia	229	359
29	Indiana	202	358
30	Oregon	106	354
31	Tennessee	178	354
32	Nevada	47	353
33	Maine	43	349
34	Washington	177	345
35	South Carolina	124	344
36	Arkansas	82	342
37	Michigan	323	342
38	Missouri	174	334
39	North Dakota	21	331
40	West Virginia	59	324
41	Kentucky	121	322
42	Maryland	158	321
43	Massachusetts	192	321
44	New Hampshire	36	320
45	Vermont	18	309
46	Pennsylvania	367	305
47	Connecticut	97	296
48	Utah	53	294
49	Rhode Island	28	276
50	Delaware	18	254
51	Hawaii	14	120

LOCAL GOVERNMENT EMPLOYEES' AVERAGE EARNINGS

On average, local employees earned $2,539 or $30,468 a year in 1992. Government employee earnings increased 27% nationwide from 1986 to 1992, or slightly less than state employees (see State Government Employees' Average Earnings table on page 207). The disparity in earnings between states was greater at the local level than it was at the state level. Local government workers in Alaska made an average of $3,590 per month. On the other hand, in Mississippi workers made almost half that figure, $1,608. Mississippi may not be generous to its workers, but part of the disparity is a result of the extremely high cost of living in Alaska. Local employees include teachers, police officers, maintenance workers and garbage collectors

TABLE: Local Government Employees' Average Earnings
DATE: 1992
SOURCE: U.S. Bureau of the Census, *Public Employment*, annual.
DESCRIPTION: Average earnings of full-time local government employees. Table ranked by 1992 earnings.

Rank		1986 average monthly earnings ($)	1992 average monthly earnings ($)	Percent change 1986–1992
	United States	1,992	2,539	27
1	Alaska	3,324	3,590	8
2	California	2,535	3,281	29
3	Washington, DC	2,594	3,175	22
4	Connecticut	2,089	3,160	51
5	New York	2,266	3,147	39
6	New Jersey	2,146	3,062	43
7	Hawaii	2,010	3,031	51
8	Michigan	2,329	2,906	25
9	Maryland	2,233	2,892	30
10	Rhode Island	2,215	2,832	28
11	Massachusetts	2,082	2,775	33
12	Nevada	2,140	2,772	30
13	Washington	2,134	2,738	28
14	Minnesota	2,318	2,673	15
15	Illinois	2,166	2,672	23
16	Delaware	1,991	2,669	34
17	Pennsylvania	1,976	2,622	33
18	Oregon	2,018	2,599	29
19	Wisconsin	2,035	2,594	27
20	Arizona	2,185	2,557	17
21	New Hampshire	1,701	2,456	44
22	Colorado	2,017	2,450	21
23	Ohio	1,911	2,417	26
24	Virginia	1,787	2,322	30

Rank		1986 average monthly earnings ($)	1992 average monthly earnings ($)	Percent change 1986–1992
25	Florida	1,872	2,294	23
26	North Dakota	2,017	2,269	12
27	Vermont	1,653	2,240	36
28	Utah	1,900	2,204	16
29	Wyoming	1,967	2,202	12
30	Indiana	1,686	2,199	30
31	Nebraska	1,785	2,198	23
32	Iowa	1,735	2,179	26
33	Kansas	1,700	2,133	25
34	Missouri	1,826	2,133	17
35	Texas	1,748	2,107	21
36	Maine	1,590	2,101	32
37	North Carolina	2,092	2,092	0
38	Tennessee	2,004	2,004	0
39	West Virginia	2,002	2,002	0
40	Montana	1,995	1,995	0
41	Kentucky	1,980	1,980	0
42	South Carolina	1,970	1,970	0
43	Georgia	1,968	1,968	0
44	Idaho	1,943	1,943	0
45	Oklahoma	1,903	1,903	0
46	New Mexico	1,858	1,858	0
47	South Dakota	1,833	1,833	0
48	Alabama	1,830	1,830	0
49	Louisiana	1,800	1,800	0
50	Arkansas	1,724	1,724	0
51	Mississippi	1,608	1,608	0

CITY GOVERNMENT EMPLOYMENT

The nation's cities display no strong geographic pattern in size of government. Cities in both the Northeast and the South have large numbers of employees in proportion to total population. Those in the Midwest tend to be in the middle or bottom of the ranking. The numbers below are distorted by varying reporting methods. New York and Washington, DC, include employees of the city's schools, colleges and university system in their count. Other cities do not.

TABLE: City Government Employment
DATE: 1992
SOURCE: U.S. Bureau of the Census, *City Employment*, annual, and unpublished data
DESCRIPTION: Total full-time city government employment and city government employment per 10,000 people in the largest cities. Table ranked by employment per 10,000 people.

Rank	City***	1992 full-time employment (thousands)	1992 full-time employment (per 10,000 people)
1	Washington, DC***	46	763
2	New York, NY***	415	557
3	Norfolk, VA*	10	394
4	Buffalo, NY*	13	390
5	Baltimore, MD*	27	372
6	Memphis, TN*	22	366
7	Boston, MA*	21	361
8	Virginia Beach, VA*	14	356
9	San Francisco, CA	26	354
10	Nashville-Davidson, TN	17	340
11	Denver, CO	12	266
12	Austin, TX	11	246
13	Seattle, WA	10	197
14	Atlanta, GA	8	197
15	Cincinnati, OH	7	191
16	Philadelphia, PA	30	189
17	St. Louis, MO	7	188
18	Colorado Springs, CO	5	181
19	Detroit, MI	19	180
20	Indianapolis, IN	13	172
21	Cleveland, OH	8	167
22	Minneapolis, MN	6	161
23	Louisville, KY	4	160
24	Jacksonville, FL	10	156
25	New Orleans, LA	10	149
26	Chicago, IL	41	148
27	Albuquerque, NM	6	147
28	Kansas City, MO	6	146
29	Pittsburgh, PA	5	145
30	Birmingham, AL	4	145
31	Los Angeles, CA	50	140
32	San Antonio, TX	13	140
33	Tampa, FL	54	140
34	Newark, NJ	4	139
35	Dallas, TX	14	137
36	Milwaukee, WI	8	133
37	Oakland, CA	5	130
38	Houston, TX	21	129
39	Columbus, OH	8	125
40	Long Beach, CA	5	123
41	Tulsa, OK	4	120
42	St. Paul, MN	3	119
43	Tucson, AZ	5	118
44	Charlotte, NC	5	115
45	Fort Worth, TX	5	114
46	Honolulu, HI	9	111
47	Phoenix, AZ	11	110
48	Sacramento, CA	4	107
49	Oklahoma City, OK	5	104
50	Portland, OR	5	104
51	Miami, FL	4	101
52	El Paso, TX	5	99
53	Anaheim, CA	3	98
54	Wichita, KS	3	97

Rank	City***	1992 full-time employment (thousands)	1992 full-time employment (per 10,000 people)
55	San Diego, CA	9	93
56	Toledo, OH	3	86
57	Mesa, AZ	2	82
58	Omaha, NE	3	81
59	San Jose, CA	6	76
60	Fresno, CA	3	73
61	Arlington, TX	2	73
62	Santa Ana, CA	2	64

*Includes city-operated elementary and secondary schools.
**Includes city-operated university or college.
***Kansas City and Portland 1991 data; San Jose, Boston, Long Beach, Tulsa, 1979 data; Jacksonville, Fort Worth, Albuquerque, Arlington 1978 data; New Orleans, Pittsburgh 1977 data.
Nashville-Davidson: noneducation data are for 1979; Newark operated elementary schools prior to 1983.

CITY GOVERNMENT EMPLOYEES' AVERAGE EARNINGS

Average pay ranged from a high in Santa Ana, California, of $5,162 (or $61,944 a year) to a low in New Orleans, Louisiana, of $1,632 (or $19,584 a year). California cities in general reported comparatively high earnings. High earnings are a function of both the cost of living and the strength of municipal unions in the area.

TABLE: City Government Employees' Average Earnings
DATE: 1992
SOURCE: U.S. Bureau of the Census, *City Employment*, annual, and unpublished data
DESCRIPTION: Average one-month earnings for full-time government employees in the largest cities. Table ranked by 1990 earnings.

Rank	City***	1980 ($)	1990 ($)	1980–1990 percent change
1	Santa Ana, CA	1,819	5,162	184
2	Anaheim, CA	1,616	4,235	162
3	San Jose, CA	1,714	4,206	145
4	Miami, FL	1,408	3,994	184
5	Oakland, CA	2,011	3,985	98
6	San Francisco, CA	1,761	3,881	120
7	Los Angeles, CA	1,806	3,815	111
8	Long Beach, CA	1,678	3,627	116
9	Seattle, WA	1,830	3,494	91
10	St. Paul, MN	1,734	3,429	98
11	Sacramento, CA	1,762	3,384	92
12	Portland, OR	1,916	3,363	76

Rank	City***	1980 ($)	1990 ($)	1980–1990 percent change	Rank	City***	1980 ($)	1990 ($)	1980–1990 percent change
13	Chicago, IL	1,569	3,269	108	42	Oklahoma City, OK	1,323	2,567	94
14	Newark, NJ	1,387	3,220	132	43	Austin, TX	1,515	2,496	65
15	New York, NY***	1,587	3,154	99	44	Kansas City, MO	1,368	2,485	82
16	Honolulu, HI	1,401	3,139	124	45	San Antonio, TX	1,282	2,472	93
17	Omaha, NE	1,684	3,138	86	46	Tulsa, OK	1,184	2,463	108
18	Phoenix, AZ	1,517	3,104	105	47	Charlotte, NC	1,290	2,436	89
19	Minneapolis, MN	1,821	3,097	70	48	Nashville-Davidson, TN	1,295	2,430	88
20	Philadelphia, PA	1,611	3,092	92	49	Wichita, KS	1,327	2,429	83
21	Pittsburgh, PA	1,116	3,092	177	50	St. Louis, MO	1,279	2,405	88
22	Cincinnati, OH	1,527	3,092	102	51	Houston, TX	1,499	2,404	60
23	Fresno, CA	1,607	3,043	89	52	Atlanta, GA	1,230	2,373	93
24	Washington, DC***	1,761	3,022	72	53	Memphis, TN*	1,335	2,361	77
25	Buffalo, NY*	1,475	2,986	102	54	Norfolk, VA*	1,222	2,349	92
26	Toledo, OH	1,758	2,955	68	55	Birmingham, AL	1,333	2,293	72
27	Boston, MA*	1,398	2,949	111	56	Fort Worth, TX	1,198	2,277	90
28	Mesa, AZ	1,592	2,908	83	57	Virginia Beach, VA*	1,204	2,275	89
29	San Diego, CA	1,773	2,894	63	58	El Paso, TX	942	2,220	136
30	Jacksonville, FL	1,031	2,888	180	59	Indianapolis, IN	1,098	2,164	97
31	Tampa, FL	1,178	2,861	143	60	Albuquerque, NM	1,135	2,100	85
32	Denver, CO	1,540	2,859	86	61	Louisville, KY	1,358	1,965	45
33	Milwaukee, WI	1,631	2,782	71	62	New Orleans, LA	919	1,623	77
34	Cleveland, OH	1,460	2,742	88					
35	Arlington, TX	1,180	2,721	131					
36	Detroit, MI	1,852	2,700	46					
37	Tucson, AZ	1,474	2,645	79					
38	Dallas, TX	1,465	2,642	80					
39	Baltimore, MD*	1,172	2,613	123					
40	Columbus, OH	1,498	2,607	74					
41	Colorado Springs, CO	1,445	2,594	80					

*Includes city-operated elementary and secondary schools.
**Includes city-operated university or college.
***Kansas City and Portland 1991 data; San Jose, Boston, Long Beach, Tulsa, 1979 data; Jacksonville, Fort Worth, Albuquerque, Arlington 1978 data; New Orleans, Pittsburgh 1977 data.
Nashville-Davidson: noneducation data are for 1979; Newark operated elementary schools prior to 1983.

CULTURE AND LEISURE

This section presents statistics covering the arts, newspaper circulation, public libraries, and the use of national forests, state parks and public lands. Sources include the National Assembly of State Arts Agencies Annual Surveys, the U.S. Department of Education, the U.S. Forest Service, the U.S. Bureau of Land Management and the National Association of State Park Directors.

Americans pursue such a vast range of cultural and leisure activities that it is impossible to include even all major activities here. The following tables represent only a sampling of the total. The section is designed to give an indication of a state's commitment to the arts and to libraries and offer an overview of library usage. It closes with an overview of state and national park usage.

STATE FUNDING FOR THE ARTS

Strong support for the arts is found in only a few states, largely in the Northeast. Florida, Michigan, Utah and Minnesota, which have strong arts communities, also ranked high. The lowest levels of support generally prevailed in the West and South.

TABLE: State Funding for the Arts
DATE: 1997
SOURCE: National Assembly of State Arts Agencies, Washington, DC Legislative Appropriations Annual Survey Fiscal Years 1996 and 1997 (copyright)
DESCRIPTION: State art agencies' legislative appropriations per capita. Table ranked by per capita spending.

Rank		Spending per capita ($)	Total spending
	United States	1.02	275,404,367
1	Hawaii	5.18	6,429,988
2	Washington, DC	3.19	1,575,000

Rank		Spending per capita ($)	Total spending
3	Delaware	3.18	2,315,600
4	Massachusetts	2.45	14,646,811
5	Michigan	2.26	21,730,100
6	New York	1.96	35,690,000
7	Florida	1.89	27,299,672
8	Missouri	1.88	10,016,130
9	Maryland	1.51	7,726,374
10	Minnesota	1.49	6,936,395
11	New Jersey	1.46	11,657,000
12	Utah	1.29	2,561,700
13	Connecticut	1.11	3,626,152
14	West Virginia	1.09	2,000,000
15	New Mexico	1.07	1,822,700
16	Ohio	1.05	11,867,073
17	Louisiana	0.95	4,176,375
18	South Carolina	0.95	3,568,364
19	Oklahoma	0.92	3,036,037
20	Kentucky	0.87	3,392,200
21	Nebraska	0.77	1,281,981
22	Pennsylvania	0.75	9,100,000
23	North Carolina	0.74	5,370,606
24	Alabama	0.70	3,008,423
25	Alaska	0.70	456,400
26	Vermont	0.70	410,000
27	Idaho	0.68	808,500
28	Wyoming	0.67	331,561
29	Illinois	0.63	7,502,300
30	Rhode Island	0.62	617,439
31	Arizona	0.61	2,547,100
32	Georgia	0.61	4,420,782
33	Tennessee	0.58	3,093,000
34	Kansas	0.53	1,384,093
35	South Dakota	0.53	395,943
36	Arkansas	0.52	1,286,651
37	Indiana	0.51	3,002,971
38	Iowa	0.50	1,430,229
39	Wisconsin	0.49	2,551,600
40	Mississippi	0.48	1,283,457
41	Colorado	0.47	1,791,077
42	North Dakota	0.45	288,309
43	Maine	0.42	524,567
44	Nevada	0.42	648,060

Rank		Spending per capita ($)	Total spending
45	New Hampshire	0.42	482,911
46	Virginia	0.40	2,668,552
47	California	0.38	12,432,000
48	Oregon	0.36	1,142,322
49	Washington	0.36	2,025,409
50	Texas	0.18	3,323,816
51	Montana	0.14	121,233

CHANGE IN STATE ARTS FUNDING

Over half the states increased their funding to the arts from 1996 to 1997. Delaware, Alabama, Illinois and Missouri in particular, saw dramatic rises. Spending increased nationally, on average 5%, and 16 states recorded a decline in spending.

TABLE: Change in State Arts Funding
DATE: 1997
SOURCE: National Assembly of State Arts Agencies, Washington, DC
Legislative Appropriations Annual Survey Fiscal Years 1996 and 1997 (copyright)
DESCRIPTION: Change in state arts funding total appropriations from fiscal year 1996 to fiscal year 1997.

Rank		Percent change 1996–1997
	United States	5.02
1	Delaware	77.05
2	Alabama	49.79
3	Illinois	35.34
4	Missouri	17.52
5	Connecticut	15.11
6	New York	12.63
7	South Carolina	6.15
8	Colorado	5.91
9	Hawaii	5.02
10	Utah	4.88
11	Florida	3.83
12	New Mexico	3.55
13	Massachusetts	3.42
14	Kansas	3.06
15	Ohio	2.86
16	Tennessee	2.76
17	Kentucky	2.54
18	Maine	2.18
19	Washington, DC	1.86
20	Iowa	1.64
21	Nevada	1.41
22	Maryland	1.32
23	Arkansas	0.87
24	Nebraska	0.74
25	Montana	0.70
26	Georgia	0.55

Rank		Percent change 1996–1997
27	Texas	0.23
28	Louisiana	0.01
29	Indiana	0
30	Minnesota	0
31	North Dakota	0
32	Oregon	0
33	Pennsylvania	0
34	Virginia	0
35	Wyoming	0
36	Michigan	-0.02
37	Oklahoma	-0.07
38	California	-0.51
39	New Hampshire	-0.65
40	North Carolina	-0.75
41	Rhode Island	-1.46
42	Arizona	-1.66
43	South Dakota	-1.78
44	West Virginia	-2.94
45	Mississippi	-3.01
46	Idaho	-3.35
47	Vermont	-4.65
48	Wisconsin	-5.26
49	Washington	-10.55
50	New Jersey	-14.64
51	Alaska	-19.08

PUBLIC LIBRARIES

Five states accounted for approximately 30% of all the nation's libraries: New York, Illinois, Iowa, Texas and Pennsylvania. All are large states with a historically strong commitment to libraries and education. Thirty-two states and the District of Columbia fell below the national average of 176. The lowest rankings could be found in the Mountain states and in the South.

TABLE: Public Libraries
DATE: 1990
SOURCE: U.S. Department of Education, *Public Libraries in the United States: 1990*
DESCRIPTION: Number of public libraries by state and percentage of total libraries. Totals may be underestimated because some public libraries did not respond to the census.

Rank		Libraries	Percent of total libraries
	United States	8,978	
1	New York	760	8.47
2	Illinois	603	6.72
3	Iowa	500	5.57
4	Texas	478	5.32
5	Pennsylvania	445	4.96
6	Wisconsin	377	4.20
7	Michigan	376	4.19
8	Massachusetts	374	4.17

Rank		Libraries	Percent of total libraries
9	Kansas	318	3.54
10	New Jersey	311	3.46
11	Nebraska	264	2.94
12	Ohio	250	2.78
13	Indiana	238	2.65
14	Maine	238	2.65
15	New Hampshire	228	2.54
16	Alabama	206	2.29
17	Vermont	205	2.28
18	Connecticut	194	2.16
19	California	168	1.87
20	Missouri	155	1.73
21	Tennessee	135	1.50
22	Minnesota	130	1.45
23	Oregon	125	1.39
24	Colorado	124	1.38
25	Florida	119	1.33
26	South Dakota	117	1.30
27	Kentucky	115	1.28
28	Idaho	107	1.19
29	Oklahoma	106	1.18
30	West Virginia	98	1.09
31	North Dakota	95	1.06
32	Arizona	91	1.01
33	Virginia	90	1.00
34	Montana	82	0.91
35	Alaska	81	0.90
36	North Carolina	73	0.81
37	Washington	70	0.78
38	Utah	69	0.77
39	New Mexico	68	0.76
40	Louisiana	64	0.71
41	Georgia	53	0.59
42	Rhode Island	51	0.57
43	Mississippi	46	0.51
44	South Carolina	40	0.45
45	Arkansas	37	0.41
46	Delaware	29	0.32
47	Nevada	26	0.29
48	Maryland	24	0.27
49	Wyoming	23	0.26
50	Hawaii	1	0.01
51	Washington, DC	1	0.01

LIBRARY BOOKS

The number of library books per capita is a general indicator of a state's commitment to its library system. However, the numbers should be used with caution. The figures do not give an indication of current policy. Systems that have been historically well funded may currently receive little or no money.

TITLE: Library Books
DATE: 1990

SOURCE: U. S. Department of Education, *Public Libraries in the U.S: 1990*

DESCRIPTION: Number of books and serial volumes, per capita, available through public libraries and total number of books and serial volumes. Table ranked per capita.

Rank		Total books	Per capita books
	United States	613,345,216	2.53
1	Maine	4,911,537	4.88
2	Massachusetts	26,862,504	4.32
3	Wyoming	1,868,623	4.28
4	Vermont	2,262,370	4.14
5	South Dakota	2,322,388	4.13
6	Kansas	8,051,902	4.04
7	New Hampshire	4,418,498	3.98
8	Iowa	10,352,297	3.82
9	Nebraska	4,880,092	3.75
10	New York	64,985,916	3.56
11	New Jersey	27,333,925	0.56
12	Connecticut	11,881,552	3.42
13	Indiana	17,772,853	3.39
14	Missouri	15,088,238	3.38
15	Idaho	2,766,445	3.37
16	Ohio	36,604,570	3.37
17	Illinois	31,630,482	3.31
18	Alaska	1,585,223	3.13
19	Wisconsin	15,179,169	3.11
20	Montana	2,293,363	3.01
21	Washington, DC	1,727,203	2.77
22	North Dakota	1,301,707	2.76
23	Rhode Island	3,434,194	2.74
24	Colorado	8,619,456	2.62
25	Minnesota	11,266,942	2.58
26	Washington	11,703,450	2.56
27	Utah	4,256,992	2.47
28	Michigan	22,256,992	2.43
29	New Mexico	2,844,458	2.41
30	Maryland	10,721,139	2.34
31	Virginia	13,721,139	2.33
32	Oregon	5,890,745	2.32
33	Texas	34,393,902	2.22
34	Hawaii	2,391,704	2.15
35	West Virginia	4,149,676	2.15
36	Pennsylvania	23,765,597	2.08
37	Louisiana	8,505,554	2.03
38	Oklahoma	5,472,398	2.01
39	Arkansas	4,392,467	1.97
40	California	55,955,644	1.95
41	Mississippi	4,948,989	1.88
42	Kentucky	6,769,261	1.87
43	Arizona	6,817,429	1.86
44	Alabama	6,953,671	1.81
45	North Carolina	11,796,506	1.74
46	Georgia	11,328,400	1.7
47	Delaware	1,148,037	1.68
48	Tennessee	7,613,673	1.56
49	Florida	18,634,745	1.54

Rank		Total books	Per capita books
50	Nevada	2,016,644	1.51
51	South Carolina	5,193,479	1.49

LIBRARY CIRCULATION

The number of library materials circulating per capita is a general indicator of library usage and readership in each state. Usage is heaviest in the Midwest and Northwest and lightest in the South.

TABLE: Library Circulation
DATE: 1990
SOURCE: U. S. Department of Education, *Public Libraries in the U.S: 1990*
DESCRIPTION: Total circulation and interlibrary loans and per capita circulation and interlibrary loans.

Rank		Total circulation	Per capita circulation
	United States	1,394,374	5.75
1	Ohio	110,703,857	10.21
2	Maryland	44,100,048	9.63
3	Washington	43,933,078	9.46
4	Minnesota	39,337,847	9.00
5	Wyoming	3,956,044	8.72
6	Indiana	44,098,156	8.42
7	Iowa	22,589,435	8.33
8	Kansas	16,538,417	8.31
9	Oregon	21,314,362	8.21
10	Wisconsin	38,292,185	7.83
11	Nebraska	9,924,812	7.63
12	Utah	12,870,510	7.48
13	Idaho	5,839,932	7.12
14	Virginia	40,730,348	6.93
15	Illinois	69,301,179	6.85
16	Missouri	30,409,756	6.84
17	South Dakota	3,833,451	6.82
18	Maine	6,770,307	6.73
19	New Hampshire	7,256,231	6.54
20	Connecticut	22,631,324	6.50
21	New York	113,607,622	6.47
22	Colorado	21,247,975	6.45
23	North Dakota	2,882,427	6.13
24	Alaska	3,098,729	6.12
25	Massachusetts	36,944,008	5.94
26	New Mexico	7,006,262	5.94
27	Arizona	21,228,979	5.82
28	Vermont	3,011,701	5.62
29	Hawaii	6,225,224	5.60
30	Oklahoma	15,078,132	5.53
31	New Jersey	39,264,793	5.12
32	Montana	3,849,249	5.06
33	California	144,447,249	5.04
34	Kentucky	17,781,463	4.91
35	Michigan	44,716,146	4.82
36	North Carolina	31,207,603	4.60

Rank		Total circulation	Per capita circulation
37	Rhode Island	5,749,558	4.59
38	Florida	52,611,138	4.27
39	Louisiana	17,484,964	4.20
40	Texas	63,959,816	4.13
41	West Virginia	7,953,145	4.08
42	Pennsylvania	46,306,455	4.04
43	Alabama	15,850,473	3.95
44	Arkansas	8,784,954	3.95
45	Delaware	2,608,812	3.82
46	Nevada	5,004,097	3.75
47	Georgia	24,428,797	3.68
48	Tennessee	16,854,652	3.46
49	Washington, DC	2,070,739	3.33
50	South Carolina	11,341,280	3.25
51	Mississippi	7,849,653	2.98

NATIONAL FOREST RECREATION USE

Nationwide, visitor days totaled 288 million in 1992. Categorized into five major activities, visitor hours were spent accordingly: vehicles driving through National Forest and sightseeing (35%); camping, picnicking and swimming (27%); hiking, horseback riding and water travel (8%); winter sports (6%); and hunting (6%).

TABLE: National Forest Recreation Use
DATE: 1992
SOURCE: U.S. Forest Service, unpublished data
DESCRIPTION: Represents recreational use of National Forest land and water in states that have a forest recreation program.

Rank		Recreation use: visitor days (thousands)*	Percent of total recreational use
	United States	287,691	
1	California	67,614	24.02
2	Colorado	29,053	10.10
3	Arizona	25,544	8.87
4	Oregon	19,898	6.91
5	Washington	18,740	6.51
6	Utah	18,413	6.40
7	Idaho	13,087	4.54
8	Montana	11,046	3.83
9	New Mexico	8,603	2.99
10	Wyoming	7,516	2.61
11	Alaska	5,888	2.05
12	North Carolina	5,767	2.00
13	Minnesota	5,739	1.99
14	Michigan	4,755	1.65
15	Virginia	4,269	1.48
16	Nevada	3,360	1.17
17	South Dakota	3,244	1.13
18	Florida	3,104	1.10

Rank		Recreation use: visitor days (thousands)*	Percent of total recreational use
19	New Hampshire	3,037	1.10
20	Georgia	2,993	1.04
21	Tennessee	2,978	1.04
22	Pennsylvania	2,942	1.02
23	Texas	2,273	0.79
24	Wisconsin	2,185	0.76
25	Arkansas	2,153	0.75
26	Kentucky	2,113	0.73
27	Missouri	1,803	0.63
28	Vermont	1,565	0.54
29	Mississippi	1,298	0.45
30	West Virginia	1,264	0.44
31	South Carolina	950	0.33
32	Illinois	900	0.31
33	Alabama	701	0.24
34	Ohio	672	0.23
35	Indiana	552	0.19
36	Louisiana	507	0.18
37	Oklahoma	369	0.13
38	North Dakota	142	0.05
39	Kansas	76	0.03
40	Massachusetts	61	0.02
41	New York	31	0.01

*One day is the recreation use that aggregates 12 visitor-hours. This may entail one person for 12 hours, 12 persons for one hour, or any equivalent combination of individual or group use, either continuous or intermittent.

STATE PARKS AND RECREATION AREAS

State park systems developed at the beginning of the 20th century in an effort to remove chosen land from development and preserve it for posterity. Today these systems range from large areas in states such as Alaska to only a few acres in small states such as Delaware and Rhode Island. Some states that have large tracts of land designated as National Parks have only small amounts in the state park system.

Alaska's state parks and recreation areas accounted for 27% of the nation's total. California ranked first in the nation in total number of visitors.

TABLE: State Parks and Recreation Areas
DATE: 1991
SOURCE: National Association of State Park Directors, Tallahassee, FL, Annual Information Exchange
DESCRIPTION: Number of acres in and visitors to state parks and recreation areas. In some states the figures below include forests and fish and wildlife areas as well as state parks. Table ranked by acreage.

Rank		Acreage (thousands)	Total visitors (thousands)*
	United States	11,148	736,897
1	Alaska	3,169	6,815
2	California	1,314	70,444
3	Texas	499	23,957
4	Florida	444	13,087
5	Illinois	405	34,594
6	Colorado	307	8,653
7	New Jersey	303	10,945
8	Pennsylvania	277	36,311
9	Massachusetts	273	11,975
10	Michigan	264	25,260
11	New York	260	60,744
12	Washington	241	46,813
13	Minnesota	231	7,981
14	Maryland	226	7,828
15	Ohio	208	67,222
16	West Virginia	202	8,278
17	Connecticut	172	6,743
18	Nevada	142	2,563
19	Nebraska	142	9,215
20	Wisconsin	139	12,252
21	North Carolina	134	9,463
22	Tennessee	133	26,974
23	New Mexico	123	4,251
24	Wyoming	120	2,018
25	Missouri	117	14,998
26	Utah	97	4,940
27	South Dakota	92	5,894
28	Oregon	90	39,479
29	Vermont	90	982
30	Iowa	82	12,111
31	South Carolina	80	7,970
32	Oklahoma	77	16,031
33	Maine	75	2,448
34	Virginia	59	3,862
35	Georgia	57	16,262
36	Indiana	57	10,536
37	Alabama	50	6,084
38	Arkansas	47	6,949
39	Kentucky	42	27,272
40	Arizona	42	2,236
41	Idaho	42	2,500
42	Louisiana	39	1,107
43	Montana	32	1,652
44	New Hampshire	31	2,815
45	Kansas	30	4,117
46	Hawaii	25	19,112
47	Mississippi	23	3,912
48	North Dakota	19	954
49	Delaware	13	3,212
50	Rhode Island	9	5,075

*Includes overnight visitors.

STATE
RANKINGS

ALABAMA

Total area:	30
Mean elevation:	40
Federally owned land:	33
Hazardous waste sites:	26
Social Security beneficiaries:	19
Disposable personal income:	41
Population in poverty:	12
Public Assistance recipients:	19
Food Stamp recipients:	10
Homeless:	27
Federal aid to state:	22
Percent of state revenues from sales taxes:	37
Percent of state revenues from income taxes:	33
Per capita state debt:	37
Death rate:	10
Health expenditures:	22
Medicare enrollment:	20
Medicaid recipients:	21
Per capita energy expenditures:	13
Funding on public education:	28
Expenditures per pupil:	49
College enrollment:	20
Population:	23
Population growth:	25
Population density:	26
Non-metropolitan population:	20
Urban population:	38
Non-English-speaking population:	46
Immigrant population:	37
Marriage rate:	15
Divorce rate:	9
Married couples:	21
Single parent families headed by women:	1
Teenage mothers:	3
Births to unmarried mothers:	15
Owner-occupied housing:	6
Christian church adherents:	4
Number of farms:	18
Total crime rate:	23
Violent crime rate:	9
Property crime rate:	26
State parks:	37

ALASKA

Total area:	1
Mean elevation:	15
Federally owned land:	2
Hazardous waste sites:	41
Social Security beneficiaries:	51
Disposable personal income:	7
Population in poverty:	44
Public Assistance recipients:	27
Food Stamp recipients:	49
Homeless:	38
Federal aid to state:	2
Percent of state revenues from sales taxes:	47
Percent of state revenues from income taxes:	45
Per capita state debt:	1
Death rate:	51
Health expenditures:	49
Medicare enrollment:	51
Medicaid recipients:	49
Per capita energy expenditures:	1
Funding on public education:	42
Expenditures per pupil:	2
College enrollment:	49
Population:	48
Population growth:	12
Population density:	51
Non-metropolitan population:	10
Urban population:	30
Non-English-speaking population:	15
Immigrant population:	41
Marriage rate:	12
Divorce rate:	17
Married couples:	49
Single parent families headed by women:	8
Teenage mothers:	39
Births to unmarried mothers:	29
Owner-occupied housing:	46
Christian church adherents:	49
Number of farms:	50
Total crime rate:	20
Violent crime rate:	19
Property crime rate:	17
State parks:	1

ARIZONA

Total area:	6
Mean elevation:	7
Federally owned land:	7
Hazardous waste sites:	36
Social Security beneficiaries:	24
Disposable personal income:	38
Population in poverty:	20
Public Assistance recipients:	28
Food Stamp recipients:	14
Homeless:	11
Federal aid to state:	34
Percent of state revenues from sales taxes:	10
Percent of state revenues from income taxes:	38
Per capita state debt:	43
Death rate:	35
Health expenditures:	24
Medicare enrollment:	24
Medicaid recipients:	25
Per capita energy expenditures:	41
Funding on public education:	22
Expenditures per pupil:	44
College enrollment:	13
Population:	21
Population growth:	2
Population density:	38
Non-metropolitan population:	40
Urban population:	6
Non-English-speaking population:	6
Immigrant population:	11
Marriage rate:	18
Divorce rate:	4
Married couples:	24
Single parent families headed by women:	51
Teenage mothers:	15
Births to unmarried mothers:	5
Owner-occupied housing:	39
Christian church adherents:	41
Number of farms:	40
Total crime rate:	3
Violent crime rate:	18
Property crime rate:	2
State parks:	40

ARKANSAS

Total area:	28
Mean elevation:	36
Federally owned land:	20
Hazardous waste sites:	29
Social Security beneficiaries:	30
Disposable personal income:	49
Population in poverty:	11
Public Assistance recipients:	24
Food Stamp recipients:	19
Homeless:	39
Federal aid to state:	21
Percent of state revenues from sales taxes:	13
Percent of state revenues from income taxes:	30
Per capita state debt:	42
Death rate:	3
Health expenditures:	32
Medicare enrollment:	30
Medicaid recipients:	28
Per capita energy expenditures:	14
Funding on public education:	32
Expenditures per pupil:	48
College enrollment:	36
Population:	33
Population growth:	19
Population density:	35
Non-metropolitan population:	12
Urban population:	41
Non-English-speaking population:	48
Immigrant population:	42
Marriage rate:	4
Divorce rate:	3
Married couples:	32
Single parent families headed by women:	39
Teenage mothers:	2
Births to unmarried mothers:	21
Owner-occupied housing:	14
Christian church adherents:	16
Number of farms:	19
Total crime rate:	30
Violent crime rate:	24
Property crime rate:	33
State parks:	38

CALIFORNIA

Total area:	3
Mean elevation:	11
Federally owned land:	8
Hazardous waste sites:	3
Social Security beneficiaries:	1
Disposable personal income:	13
Population in poverty:	14
Public Assistance recipients:	3
Food Stamp recipients:	27
Homeless:	1
Federal aid to state:	28
Percent of state revenues from sales taxes:	24
Percent of state revenues from income taxes:	15
Per capita state debt:	26
Death rate:	47
Health expenditures:	1
Medicare enrollment:	1
Medicaid recipients:	1
Per capita energy expenditures:	49
Funding on public education:	1
Expenditures per pupil:	37
College enrollment:	1
Population:	1
Population growth:	18
Population density:	14
Non-metropolitan population:	49
Urban population:	2
Non-English-speaking population:	2
Immigrant population:	1
Marriage rate:	44
Divorce rate:	35
Married couples:	1
Single parent families headed by women:	48
Teenage mothers:	29
Births to unmarried mothers:	9
Owner-occupied housing:	47
Christian church adherents:	43
Number of farms:	9
Total crime rate:	4
Violent crime rate:	3
Property crime rate:	8
State parks:	2

COLORADO

Total area:	8
Mean elevation:	1
Federally owned land:	9
Hazardous waste sites:	22
Social Security beneficiaries:	32
Disposable personal income:	16
Population in poverty:	40
Public Assistance recipients:	41
Food Stamp recipients:	39
Homeless:	20
Federal aid to state:	47
Percent of state revenues from sales taxes:	38
Percent of state revenues from income taxes:	5
Per capita state debt:	41
Death rate:	48
Health expenditures:	26
Medicare enrollment:	31
Medicaid recipients:	33
Per capita energy expenditures:	48
Funding on public education:	24
Expenditures per pupil:	31
College enrollment:	19
Population:	25
Population growth:	5
Population density:	39
Non-metropolitan population:	34
Urban population:	13
Non-English-speaking population:	16
Immigrant population:	19
Marriage rate:	28
Divorce rate:	15
Married couples:	27
Single parent families headed by women:	32
Teenage mothers:	28
Births to unmarried mothers:	40
Owner-occupied housing:	42
Christian church adherents:	45
Number of farms:	30
Total crime rate:	12
Violent crime rate:	23
Property crime rate:	11
State parks:	6

CONNECTICUT

Total area:	48
Mean elevation:	41
Federally owned land:	51
Hazardous waste sites:	24
Social Security beneficiaries:	27
Disposable personal income:	2
Population in poverty:	47
Public Assistance recipients:	32
Food Stamp recipients:	44
Homeless:	14
Federal aid to state:	17
Percent of state revenues from sales taxes:	18
Percent of state revenues from income taxes:	31
Per capita state debt:	6
Death rate:	29
Health expenditures:	23
Medicare enrollment:	25
Medicaid recipients:	29
Per capita energy expenditures:	23
Funding on public education:	20
Expenditures per pupil:	4
College enrollment:	32
Population:	28
Population growth:	49
Population density:	5
Non-metropolitan population:	47
Urban population:	16
Non-English-speaking population:	10
Immigrant population:	15
Marriage rate:	35
Divorce rate:	46
Married couples:	28
Single parent families headed by women:	16
Teenage mothers:	48
Births to unmarried mothers:	25
Owner-occupied housing:	33
Christian church adherents:	20
Number of farms:	45
Total crime rate:	27
Violent crime rate:	31
Property crime rate:	23
State parks:	17

DELAWARE

Total area:	49
Mean elevation:	51
Federally owned land:	38
Hazardous waste sites:	21
Social Security beneficiaries:	47
Disposable personal income:	19
Population in poverty:	51
Public Assistance recipients:	39
Food Stamp recipients:	36
Homeless:	48
Federal aid to state:	39
Percent of state revenues from sales taxes:	48
Percent of state revenues from income taxes:	14
Per capita state debt:	2
Death rate:	30
Health expenditures:	44
Medicare enrollment:	47
Medicaid recipients:	47
Per capita energy expenditures:	12
Funding on public education:	47
Expenditures per pupil:	12
College enrollment:	44
Population:	46
Population growth:	16
Population density:	8
Non-metropolitan population:	35
Urban population:	19
Non-English-speaking population:	27
Immigrant population:	43
Marriage rate:	40
Divorce rate:	31
Married couples:	47
Single parent families headed by women:	25
Teenage mothers:	27
Births to unmarried mothers:	14
Owner-occupied housing:	8
Christian church adherents:	36
Number of farms:	47
Total crime rate:	29
Violent crime rate:	22
Property crime rate:	31
State parks:	49

FLORIDA

Total area:	23
Mean elevation:	49
Federally owned land:	19
Hazardous waste sites:	7
Social Security beneficiaries:	3
Disposable personal income:	17
Population in poverty:	17
Public Assistance recipients:	23
Food Stamp recipients:	23
Homeless:	3
Federal aid to state:	49
Percent of state revenues from sales taxes:	2
Percent of state revenues from income taxes:	46
Per capita state debt:	40
Death rate:	4
Health expenditures:	4
Medicare enrollment:	3
Medicaid recipients:	4
Per capita energy expenditures:	51
Funding on public education:	5
Expenditures per pupil:	27
College enrollment:	5
Population:	4
Population growth:	11
Population density:	12
Non-metropolitan population:	45
Urban population:	9
Non-English-speaking population:	8
Immigrant population:	4
Marriage rate:	10
Divorce rate:	8
Married couples:	4
Single parent families headed by women:	33
Teenage mothers:	20
Births to unmarried mothers:	12
Owner-occupied housing:	27
Christian church adherents:	42
Number of farms:	22
Total crime rate:	1
Violent crime rate:	1
Property crime rate:	1
State parks:	4

GEORGIA

Total area:	24
Mean elevation:	37
Federally owned land:	30
Hazardous waste sites:	27
Social Security beneficiaries:	14
Disposable personal income:	31
Population in poverty:	9
Public Assistance recipients:	11
Food Stamp recipients:	13
Homeless:	13
Federal aid to state:	42
Percent of state revenues from sales taxes:	15
Percent of state revenues from income taxes:	8
Per capita state debt:	45
Death rate:	36
Health expenditures:	11
Medicare enrollment:	14
Medicaid recipients:	9
Per capita energy expenditures:	24
Funding on public education:	14
Expenditures per pupil:	39
College enrollment:	16
Population:	10
Population growth:	7
Population density:	21
Non-metropolitan population:	21
Urban population:	35
Non-English-speaking population:	39
Immigrant population:	14
Marriage rate:	20
Divorce rate:	12
Married couples:	11
Single parent families headed by women:	5
Teenage mothers:	11
Births to unmarried mothers:	7
Owner-occupied housing:	36
Christian church adherents:	25
Number of farms:	20
Total crime rate:	7
Violent crime rate:	15
Property crime rate:	5
State parks:	35

Hawaii

Total area:	47
Mean elevation:	10
Federally owned land:	14
Hazardous waste sites:	47
Social Security beneficiaries:	43
Disposable personal income:	9
Population in poverty:	36
Public Assistance recipients:	34
Food Stamp recipients:	18
Homeless:	28
Federal aid to state:	16
Percent of state revenues from sales taxes:	7
Percent of state revenues from income taxes:	25
Per capita state debt:	4
Death rate:	49
Health expenditures:	40
Medicare enrollment:	43
Medicaid recipients:	41
Per capita energy expenditures:	35
Funding on public education:	41
Expenditures per pupil:	18
College enrollment:	39
Population:	35
Population growth:	20
Population density:	9
Non-metropolitan population:	29
Urban population:	4
Non-English-speaking population:	4
Immigrant population:	17
Marriage rate:	2
Divorce rate:	27
Married couples:	42
Single parent families headed by women:	49
Teenage mothers:	37
Births to unmarried mothers:	33
Owner-occupied housing:	49
Christian church adherents:	47
Number of farms:	44
Total crime rate:	11
Violent crime rate:	43
Property crime rate:	4
State parks:	46

Idaho

Total area:	14
Mean elevation:	6
Federally owned land:	4
Hazardous waste sites:	36
Social Security beneficiaries:	42
Disposable personal income:	37
Population in poverty:	21
Public Assistance recipients:	51
Food Stamp recipients:	46
Homeless:	42
Federal aid to state:	40
Percent of state revenues from sales taxes:	27
Percent of state revenues from income taxes:	13
Per capita state debt:	28
Death rate:	41
Health expenditures:	46
Medicare enrollment:	42
Medicaid recipients:	42
Per capita energy expenditures:	32
Funding on public education:	44
Expenditures per pupil:	47
College enrollment:	40
Population:	41
Population growth:	3
Population density:	45
Non-metropolitan population:	4
Urban population:	39
Non-English-speaking population:	30
Immigrant population:	40
Marriage rate:	5
Divorce rate:	7
Married couples:	41
Single parent families headed by women:	40
Teenage mothers:	21
Births to unmarried mothers:	49
Owner-occupied housing:	10
Christian church adherents:	30
Number of farms:	33
Total crime rate:	41
Violent crime rate:	40
Property crime rate:	41
State parks:	41

ILLINOIS

Total area:	25
Mean elevation:	38
Federally owned land:	36
Hazardous waste sites:	10
Social Security beneficiaries:	7
Disposable personal income:	11
Population in poverty:	18
Public Assistance recipients:	14
Food Stamp recipients:	21
Homeless:	6
Federal aid to state:	35
Percent of state revenues from sales taxes:	26
Percent of state revenues from income taxes:	23
Per capita state debt:	20
Death rate:	24
Health expenditures:	6
Medicare enrollment:	7
Medicaid recipients:	6
Per capita energy expenditures:	31
Funding on public education:	9
Expenditures per pupil:	29
College enrollment:	4
Population:	6
Population growth:	37
Population density:	13
Non-metropolitan population:	39
Urban population:	10
Non-English-speaking population:	12
Immigrant population:	6
Marriage rate:	38
Divorce rate:	38
Married couples:	7
Single parent families headed by women:	26
Teenage mothers:	23
Births to unmarried mothers:	11
Owner-occupied housing:	38
Christian church adherents:	23
Number of farms:	7
Total crime rate:	17
Violent crime rate:	6
Property crime rate:	21
State parks:	5

INDIANA

Total area:	38
Mean elevation:	34
Federally owned land:	40
Hazardous waste sites:	12
Social Security beneficiaries:	13
Disposable personal income:	32
Population in poverty:	31
Public Assistance recipients:	42
Food Stamp recipients:	32
Homeless:	21
Federal aid to state:	37
Percent of state revenues from sales taxes:	11
Percent of state revenues from income taxes:	24
Per capita state debt:	39
Death rate:	21
Health expenditures:	16
Medicare enrollment:	13
Medicaid recipients:	19
Per capita energy expenditures:	6
Funding on public education:	11
Expenditures per pupil:	20
College enrollment:	15
Population:	14
Population growth:	28
Population density:	17
Non-metropolitan population:	28
Urban population:	34
Non-English-speaking population:	40
Immigrant population:	29
Marriage rate:	22
Divorce rate:	50
Married couples:	13
Single parent families headed by women:	17
Teenage mothers:	16
Births to unmarried mothers:	22
Owner-occupied housing:	9
Christian church adherents:	34
Number of farms:	13
Total crime rate:	31
Violent crime rate:	30
Property crime rate:	35
State parks:	36

IOWA

Total area:	26
Mean elevation:	22
Federally owned land:	46
Hazardous waste sites:	19
Social Security beneficiaries:	28
Disposable personal income:	39
Population in poverty:	34
Public Assistance recipients:	40
Food Stamp recipients:	48
Homeless:	33
Federal aid to state:	45
Percent of state revenues from sales taxes:	34
Percent of state revenues from income taxes:	12
Per capita state debt:	44
Death rate:	9
Health expenditures:	29
Medicare enrollment:	28
Medicaid recipients:	32
Per capita energy expenditures:	29
Funding on public education:	30
Expenditures per pupil:	28
College enrollment:	30
Population:	30
Population growth:	42
Population density:	34
Non-metropolitan population:	11
Urban population:	37
Non-English-speaking population:	42
Immigrant population:	34
Marriage rate:	33
Divorce rate:	37
Married couples:	29
Single parent families headed by women:	27
Teenage mothers:	38
Births to unmarried mothers:	45
Owner-occupied housing:	11
Christian church adherents:	17
Number of farms:	3
Total crime rate:	42
Violent crime rate:	41
Property crime rate:	42
State parks:	30

KANSAS

Total area:	15
Mean elevation:	14
Federally owned land:	47
Hazardous waste sites:	36
Social Security beneficiaries:	33
Disposable personal income:	22
Population in poverty:	37
Public Assistance recipients:	44
Food Stamp recipients:	43
Homeless:	22
Federal aid to state:	43
Percent of state revenues from sales taxes:	20
Percent of state revenues from income taxes:	32
Per capita state debt:	50
Death rate:	23
Health expenditures:	31
Medicare enrollment:	33
Medicaid recipients:	34
Per capita energy expenditures:	9
Funding on public education:	31
Expenditures per pupil:	25
College enrollment:	27
Population:	32
Population growth:	36
Population density:	41
Non-metropolitan population:	15
Urban population:	25
Non-English-speaking population:	33
Immigrant population:	31
Marriage rate:	30
Divorce rate:	23
Married couples:	31
Single parent families headed by women:	28
Teenage mothers:	26
Births to unmarried mothers:	42
Owner-occupied housing:	22
Christian church adherents:	29
Number of farms:	12
Total crime rate:	22
Violent crime rate:	28
Property crime rate:	19
State parks:	45

KENTUCKY

Total area:	37
Mean elevation:	33
Federally owned land:	28
Hazardous waste sites:	19
Social Security beneficiaries:	22
Disposable personal income:	45
Population in poverty:	6
Public Assistance recipients:	5
Food Stamp recipients:	9
Homeless:	31
Federal aid to state:	18
Percent of state revenues from sales taxes:	36
Percent of state revenues from income taxes:	26
Per capita state debt:	17
Death rate:	13
Health expenditures:	25
Medicare enrollment:	22
Medicaid recipients:	15
Per capita energy expenditures:	16
Funding on public education:	25
Expenditures per pupil:	33
College enrollment:	26
Population:	24
Population growth:	29
Population density:	24
Non-metropolitan population:	13
Urban population:	44
Non-English-speaking population:	51
Immigrant population:	35
Marriage rate:	6
Divorce rate:	11
Married couples:	22
Single parent families headed by women:	9
Teenage mothers:	8
Births to unmarried mothers:	32
Owner-occupied housing:	13
Christian church adherents:	18
Number of farms:	4
Total crime rate:	46
Violent crime rate:	25
Property crime rate:	49
State parks:	39

LOUISIANA

Total area:	31
Mean elevation:	50
Federally owned land:	37
Hazardous waste sites:	29
Social Security beneficiaries:	21
Disposable personal income:	46
Population in poverty:	2
Public Assistance recipients:	4
Food Stamp recipients:	2
Homeless:	29
Federal aid to state:	5
Percent of state revenues from sales taxes:	29
Percent of state revenues from income taxes:	39
Per capita state debt:	11
Death rate:	26
Health expenditures:	21
Medicare enrollment:	23
Medicaid recipients:	12
Per capita energy expenditures:	3
Funding on public education:	21
Expenditures per pupil:	43
College enrollment:	24
Population:	22
Population growth:	40
Population density:	23
Non-metropolitan population:	30
Urban population:	28
Non-English-speaking population:	17
Immigrant population:	26
Marriage rate:	27
Divorce rate:	51
Married couples:	23
Single parent families headed by women:	3
Teenage mothers:	6
Births to unmarried mothers:	3
Owner-occupied housing:	32
Christian church adherents:	5
Number of farms:	29
Total crime rate:	5
Violent crime rate:	5
Property crime rate:	7
State parks:	42

MAINE

Total area:	39
Mean elevation:	39
Federally owned land:	48
Hazardous waste sites:	36
Social Security beneficiaries:	37
Disposable personal income:	30
Population in poverty:	26
Public Assistance recipients:	15
Food Stamp recipients:	11
Homeless:	46
Federal aid to state:	12
Percent of state revenues from sales taxes:	19
Percent of state revenues from income taxes:	21
Per capita state debt:	13
Death rate:	22
Health expenditures:	41
Medicare enrollment:	37
Medicaid recipients:	37
Per capita energy expenditures:	10
Funding on public education:	38
Expenditures per pupil:	15
College enrollment:	42
Population:	40
Population growth:	45
Population density:	37
Non-metropolitan population:	7
Urban population:	49
Non-English-speaking population:	18
Immigrant population:	44
Marriage rate:	23
Divorce rate:	33
Married couples:	38
Single parent families headed by women:	34
Teenage mothers:	33
Births to unmarried mothers:	39
Owner-occupied housing:	7
Christian church adherents:	46
Number of farms:	41
Total crime rate:	43
Violent crime rate:	47
Property crime rate:	43
State parks:	33

MARYLAND

Total area:	42
Mean elevation:	43
Federally owned land:	35
Hazardous waste sites:	29
Social Security beneficiaries:	23
Disposable personal income:	6
Population in poverty:	33
Public Assistance recipients:	33
Food Stamp recipients:	31
Homeless:	17
Federal aid to state:	36
Percent of state revenues from sales taxes:	40
Percent of state revenues from income taxes:	6
Per capita state debt:	18
Death rate:	40
Health expenditures:	17
Medicare enrollment:	21
Medicaid recipients:	26
Per capita energy expenditures:	45
Funding on public education:	17
Expenditures per pupil:	11
College enrollment:	17
Population:	19
Population growth:	22
Population density:	6
Non-metropolitan population:	44
Urban population:	14
Non-English-speaking population:	20
Immigrant population:	12
Marriage rate:	21
Divorce rate:	44
Married couples:	19
Single parent families headed by women:	18
Teenage mothers:	40
Births to unmarried mothers:	18
Owner-occupied housing:	35
Christian church adherents:	37
Number of farms:	35
Total crime rate:	8
Violent crime rate:	4
Property crime rate:	14
State parks:	14

MASSACHUSETTS

Total area:	45
Mean elevation:	42
Federally owned land:	44
Hazardous waste sites:	13
Social Security beneficiaries:	11
Disposable personal income:	4
Population in poverty:	45
Public Assistance recipients:	16
Food Stamp recipients:	34
Homeless:	8
Federal aid to state:	13
Percent of state revenues from sales taxes:	44
Percent of state revenues from income taxes:	2
Per capita state debt:	15
Death rate:	16
Health expenditures:	10
Medicare enrollment:	11
Medicaid recipients:	14
Per capita energy expenditures:	37
Funding on public education:	10
Expenditures per pupil:	9
College enrollment:	23
Population:	13
Population growth:	46
Population density:	4
Non-metropolitan population:	48
Urban population:	11
Non-English-speaking population:	11
Immigrant population:	7
Marriage rate:	41
Divorce rate:	49
Married couples:	14
Single parent families headed by women:	13
Teenage mothers:	50
Births to unmarried mothers:	38
Owner-occupied housing:	45
Christian church adherents:	14
Number of farms:	43
Total crime rate:	28
Violent crime rate:	11
Property crime rate:	32
State parks:	9

MICHIGAN

Total area:	11
Mean elevation:	29
Federally owned land:	16
Hazardous waste sites:	5
Social Security beneficiaries:	8
Disposable personal income:	21
Population in poverty:	25
Public Assistance recipients:	8
Food Stamp recipients:	15
Homeless:	15
Federal aid to state:	26
Percent of state revenues from sales taxes:	23
Percent of state revenues from income taxes:	35
Per capita state debt:	33
Death rate:	32
Health expenditures:	8
Medicare enrollment:	8
Medicaid recipients:	8
Per capita energy expenditures:	36
Funding on public education:	7
Expenditures per pupil:	13
College enrollment:	6
Population:	8
Population growth:	39
Population density:	15
Non-metropolitan population:	36
Urban population:	21
Non-English-speaking population:	28
Immigrant population:	13
Marriage rate:	39
Divorce rate:	34
Married couples:	8
Single parent families headed by women:	10
Teenage mothers:	22
Births to unmarried mothers:	28
Owner-occupied housing:	4
Christian church adherents:	31
Number of farms:	16
Total crime rate:	19
Violent crime rate:	12
Property crime rate:	18
State parks:	10

MINNESOTA

Total area:	12
Mean elevation:	21
Federally owned land:	17
Hazardous waste sites:	8
Social Security beneficiaries:	20
Disposable personal income:	20
Population in poverty:	27
Public Assistance recipients:	35
Food Stamp recipients:	40
Homeless:	24
Federal aid to state:	23
Percent of state revenues from sales taxes:	31
Percent of state revenues from income taxes:	9
Per capita state debt:	38
Death rate:	37
Health expenditures:	19
Medicare enrollment:	19
Medicaid recipients:	24
Per capita energy expenditures:	42
Funding on public education:	18
Expenditures per pupil:	22
College enrollment:	18
Population:	20
Population growth:	21
Population density:	32
Non-metropolitan population:	25
Urban population:	23
Non-English-speaking population:	35
Immigrant population:	18
Marriage rate:	46
Divorce rate:	43
Married couples:	20
Single parent families headed by women:	36
Teenage mothers:	49
Births to unmarried mothers:	44
Owner-occupied housing:	2
Christian church adherents:	9
Number of farms:	5
Total crime rate:	34
Violent crime rate:	37
Property crime rate:	30
State parks:	13

MISSISSIPPI

Total area:	32
Mean elevation:	45
Federally owned land:	27
Hazardous waste sites:	45
Social Security beneficiaries:	31
Disposable personal income:	51
Population in poverty:	1
Public Assistance recipients:	2
Food Stamp recipients:	1
Homeless:	41
Federal aid to state:	15
Percent of state revenues from sales taxes:	8
Percent of state revenues from income taxes:	41
Per capita state debt:	46
Death rate:	8
Health expenditures:	33
Medicare enrollment:	32
Medicaid recipients:	20
Per capita energy expenditures:	25
Funding on public education:	34
Expenditures per pupil:	50
College enrollment:	31
Population:	31
Population growth:	26
Population density:	33
Non-metropolitan population:	5
Urban population:	48
Non-English-speaking population:	49
Immigrant population:	45
Marriage rate:	29
Divorce rate:	13
Married couples:	33
Single parent families headed by women:	4
Teenage mothers:	1
Births to unmarried mothers:	2
Owner-occupied housing:	3
Christian church adherents:	6
Number of farms:	23
Total crime rate:	40
Violent crime rate:	33
Property crime rate:	40
State parks:	47

MISSOURI

Total area:	21
Mean elevation:	32
Federally owned land:	26
Hazardous waste sites:	17
Social Security beneficiaries:	12
Disposable personal income:	27
Population in poverty:	16
Public Assistance recipients:	25
Food Stamp recipients:	17
Homeless:	25
Federal aid to state:	32
Percent of state revenues from sales taxes:	14
Percent of state revenues from income taxes:	18
Per capita state debt:	27
Death rate:	6
Health expenditures:	14
Medicare enrollment:	12
Medicaid recipients:	17
Per capita energy expenditures:	33
Funding on public education:	19
Expenditures per pupil:	40
College enrollment:	21
Population:	16
Population growth:	33
Population density:	28
Non-metropolitan population:	24
Urban population:	27
Non-English-speaking population:	44
Immigrant population:	25
Marriage rate:	24
Divorce rate:	19
Married couples:	15
Single parent families headed by women:	14
Teenage mothers:	17
Births to unmarried mothers:	19
Owner-occupied housing:	16
Christian church adherents:	26
Number of farms:	2
Total crime rate:	25
Violent crime rate:	14
Property crime rate:	28
State parks:	25

MONTANA

Total area:	4
Mean elevation:	8
Federally owned land:	12
Hazardous waste sites:	41
Social Security beneficiaries:	44
Disposable personal income:	42
Population in poverty:	24
Public Assistance recipients:	36
Food Stamp recipients:	33
Homeless:	45
Federal aid to state:	9
Percent of state revenues from sales taxes:	49
Percent of state revenues from income taxes:	29
Per capita state debt:	12
Death rate:	27
Health expenditures:	48
Medicare enrollment:	44
Medicaid recipients:	48
Per capita energy expenditures:	7
Funding on public education:	45
Expenditures per pupil:	26
College enrollment:	46
Population:	44
Population growth:	14
Population density:	49
Non-metropolitan population:	1
Urban population:	43
Non-English-speaking population:	37
Immigrant population:	50
Marriage rate:	34
Divorce rate:	21
Married couples:	44
Single parent families headed by women:	37
Teenage mothers:	31
Births to unmarried mothers:	36
Owner-occupied housing:	26
Christian church adherents:	38
Number of farms:	31
Total crime rate:	33
Violent crime rate:	46
Property crime rate:	25
State parks:	43

NEBRASKA

Total area:	16
Mean elevation:	12
Federally owned land:	42
Hazardous waste sites:	36
Social Security beneficiaries:	35
Disposable personal income:	24
Population in poverty:	42
Public Assistance recipients:	47
Food Stamp recipients:	47
Homeless:	37
Federal aid to state:	31
Percent of state revenues from sales taxes:	17
Percent of state revenues from income taxes:	22
Per capita state debt:	34
Death rate:	15
Health expenditures:	36
Medicare enrollment:	35
Medicaid recipients:	38
Per capita energy expenditures:	15
Funding on public education:	36
Expenditures per pupil:	32
College enrollment:	33
Population:	38
Population growth:	34
Population density:	43
Non-metropolitan population:	14
Urban population:	31
Non-English-speaking population:	41
Immigrant population:	38
Marriage rate:	47
Divorce rate:	36
Married couples:	35
Single parent families headed by women:	29
Teenage mothers:	43
Births to unmarried mothers:	46
Owner-occupied housing:	29
Christian church adherents:	12
Number of farms:	15
Total crime rate:	37
Violent crime rate:	36
Property crime rate:	38
State parks:	19

NEVADA

Total area:	7
Mean elevation:	5
Federally owned land:	1
Hazardous waste sites:	50
Social Security beneficiaries:	39
Disposable personal income:	10
Population in poverty:	23
Public Assistance recipients:	49
Food Stamp recipients:	38
Homeless:	32
Federal aid to state:	50
Percent of state revenues from sales taxes:	6
Percent of state revenues from income taxes:	47
Per capita state debt:	21
Death rate:	42
Health expenditures:	39
Medicare enrollment:	40
Medicaid recipients:	43
Per capita energy expenditures:	26
Funding on public education:	39
Expenditures per pupil:	30
College enrollment:	38
Population:	39
Population growth:	1
Population density:	44
Non-metropolitan population:	42
Urban population:	5
Non-English-speaking population:	13
Immigrant population:	22
Marriage rate:	1
Divorce rate:	1
Married couples:	40
Single parent families headed by women:	50
Teenage mothers:	24
Births to unmarried mothers:	10
Owner-occupied housing:	48
Christian church adherents:	51
Number of farms:	48
Total crime rate:	9
Violent crime rate:	16
Property crime rate:	9
State parks:	18

NEW HAMPSHIRE

Total area:	44
Mean elevation:	25
Federally owned land:	15
Hazardous waste sites:	23
Social Security beneficiaries:	41
Disposable personal income:	8
Population in poverty:	50
Public Assistance recipients:	50
Food Stamp recipients:	51
Homeless:	47
Federal aid to state:	48
Percent of state revenues from sales taxes:	50
Percent of state revenues from income taxes:	43
Per capita state debt:	5
Death rate:	39
Health expenditures:	43
Medicare enrollment:	41
Medicaid recipients:	45
Per capita energy expenditures:	40
Funding on public education:	40
Expenditures per pupil:	21
College enrollment:	45
Population:	42
Population growth:	32
Population density:	19
Non-metropolitan population:	17
Urban population:	45
Non-English-speaking population:	21
Immigrant population:	39
Marriage rate:	25
Divorce rate:	25
Married couples:	39
Single parent families headed by women:	41
Teenage mothers:	51
Births to unmarried mothers:	50
Owner-occupied housing:	17
Christian church adherents:	44
Number of farms:	46
Total crime rate:	47
Violent crime rate:	48
Property crime rate:	46
State parks:	44

NEW JERSEY

Total area:	46
Mean elevation:	46
Federally owned land:	34
Hazardous waste sites:	1
Social Security beneficiaries:	9
Disposable personal income:	3
Population in poverty:	46
Public Assistance recipients:	31
Food Stamp recipients:	41
Homeless:	7
Federal aid to state:	19
Percent of state revenues from sales taxes:	25
Percent of state revenues from income taxes:	28
Per capita state debt:	10
Death rate:	18
Health expenditures:	9
Medicare enrollment:	9
Medicaid recipients:	13
Per capita energy expenditures:	11
Funding on public education:	6
Expenditures per pupil:	1
College enrollment:	11
Population:	9
Population growth:	38
Population density:	2
Non-metropolitan population:	50
Urban population:	3
Non-English-speaking population:	7
Immigrant population:	5
Marriage rate:	48
Divorce rate:	48
Married couples:	9
Single parent families headed by women:	35
Teenage mothers:	47
Births to unmarried mothers:	31
Owner-occupied housing:	37
Christian church adherents:	27
Number of farms:	39
Total crime rate:	26
Violent crime rate:	20
Property crime rate:	24
State parks:	7

NEW MEXICO

Total area:	5
Mean elevation:	4
Federally owned land:	10
Hazardous waste sites:	34
Social Security beneficiaries:	36
Disposable personal income:	47
Population in poverty:	4
Public Assistance recipients:	12
Food Stamp recipients:	7
Homeless:	36
Federal aid to state:	11
Percent of state revenues from sales taxes:	9
Percent of state revenues from income taxes:	40
Per capita state debt:	36
Death rate:	44
Health expenditures:	38
Medicare enrollment:	36
Medicaid recipients:	36
Per capita energy expenditures:	19
Funding on public education:	37
Expenditures per pupil:	36
College enrollment:	35
Population:	37
Population growth:	8
Population density:	46
Non-metropolitan population:	16
Urban population:	20
Non-English-speaking population:	1
Immigrant population:	27
Marriage rate:	36
Divorce rate:	24
Married couples:	37
Single parent families headed by women:	42
Teenage mothers:	12
Births to unmarried mothers:	4
Owner-occupied housing:	25
Christian church adherents:	22
Number of farms:	36
Total crime rate:	6
Violent crime rate:	8
Property crime rate:	10
State parks:	23

NEW YORK

Total area:	27
Mean elevation:	26
Federally owned land:	49
Hazardous waste sites:	4
Social Security beneficiaries:	2
Disposable personal income:	5
Population in poverty:	19
Public Assistance recipients:	7
Food Stamp recipients:	8
Homeless:	2
Federal aid to state:	4
Percent of state revenues from sales taxes:	45
Percent of state revenues from income taxes:	3
Per capita state debt:	7
Death rate:	17
Health expenditures:	2
Medicare enrollment:	2
Medicaid recipients:	2
Per capita energy expenditures:	50
Funding on public education:	2
Expenditures per pupil:	3
College enrollment:	3
Population:	3
Population growth:	47
Population density:	7
Non-metropolitan population:	43
Urban population:	12
Non-English-speaking population:	5
Immigrant population:	2
Marriage rate:	26
Divorce rate:	47
Married couples:	3
Single parent families headed by women:	19
Teenage mothers:	45
Births to unmarried mothers:	8
Owner-occupied housing:	50
Christian church adherents:	28
Number of farms:	24
Total crime rate:	14
Violent crime rate:	2
Property crime rate:	22
State parks:	11

NORTH CAROLINA

Total area:	29
Mean elevation:	35
Federally owned land:	22
Hazardous waste sites:	18
Social Security beneficiaries:	10
Disposable personal income:	35
Population in poverty:	15
Public Assistance recipients:	18
Food Stamp recipients:	28
Homeless:	18
Federal aid to state:	41
Percent of state revenues from sales taxes:	41
Percent of state revenues from income taxes:	10
Per capita state debt:	48
Death rate:	25
Health expenditures:	12
Medicare enrollment:	10
Medicaid recipients:	10
Per capita energy expenditures:	28
Funding on public education:	13
Expenditures per pupil:	35
College enrollment:	9
Population:	11
Population growth:	13
Population density:	18
Non-metropolitan population:	19
Urban population:	46
Non-English-speaking population:	43
Immigrant population:	20
Marriage rate:	45
Divorce rate:	20
Married couples:	10
Single parent families headed by women:	11
Teenage mothers:	13
Births to unmarried mothers:	16
Owner-occupied housing:	21
Christian church adherents:	19
Number of farms:	14
Total crime rate:	16
Violent crime rate:	17
Property crime rate:	15
State parks:	21

NORTH DAKOTA

Total area:	18
Mean elevation:	16
Federally owned land:	29
Hazardous waste sites:	49
Social Security beneficiaries:	46
Disposable personal income:	40
Population in poverty:	30
Public Assistance recipients:	46
Food Stamp recipients:	37
Homeless:	49
Federal aid to state:	8
Percent of state revenues from sales taxes:	21
Percent of state revenues from income taxes:	42
Per capita state debt:	19
Death rate:	19
Health expenditures:	45
Medicare enrollment:	46
Medicaid recipients:	50
Per capita energy expenditures:	4
Funding on public education:	51
Expenditures per pupil:	41
College enrollment:	43
Population:	47
Population growth:	48
Population density:	48
Non-metropolitan population:	8
Urban population:	42
Non-English-speaking population:	22
Immigrant population:	49
Marriage rate:	49
Divorce rate:	42
Married couples:	46
Single parent families headed by women:	47
Teenage mothers:	46
Births to unmarried mothers:	47
Owner-occupied housing:	34
Christian church adherents:	2
Number of farms:	28
Total crime rate:	49
Violent crime rate:	50
Property crime rate:	47
State parks:	48

OHIO

Total area:	34
Mean elevation:	31
Federally owned land:	45
Hazardous waste sites:	11
Social Security beneficiaries:	6
Disposable personal income:	26
Population in poverty:	28
Public Assistance recipients:	9
Food Stamp recipients:	12
Homeless:	10
Federal aid to state:	27
Percent of state revenues from sales taxes:	28
Percent of state revenues from income taxes:	17
Per capita state debt:	32
Death rate:	20
Health expenditures:	7
Medicare enrollment:	6
Medicaid recipients:	7
Per capita energy expenditures:	18
Funding on public education:	8
Expenditures per pupil:	16
College enrollment:	7
Population:	7
Population growth:	41
Population density:	10
Non-metropolitan population:	33
Urban population:	18
Non-English-speaking population:	36
Immigrant population:	16
Marriage rate:	32
Divorce rate:	26
Married couples:	6
Single parent families headed by women:	12
Teenage mothers:	18
Births to unmarried mothers:	17
Owner-occupied housing:	24
Christian church adherents:	32
Number of farms:	10
Total crime rate:	32
Violent crime rate:	27
Property crime rate:	36
State parks:	15

OKLAHOMA

Total area:	20
Mean elevation:	20
Federally owned land:	41
Hazardous waste sites:	34
Social Security beneficiaries:	26
Disposable personal income:	44
Population in poverty:	8
Public Assistance recipients:	29
Food Stamp recipients:	16
Homeless:	23
Federal aid to state:	38
Percent of state revenues from sales taxes:	39
Percent of state revenues from income taxes:	27
Per capita state debt:	31
Death rate:	11
Health expenditures:	28
Medicare enrollment:	27
Medicaid recipients:	27
Per capita energy expenditures:	22
Funding on public education:	29
Expenditures per pupil:	45
College enrollment:	25
Population:	27
Population growth:	31
Population density:	36
Non-metropolitan population:	18
Urban population:	29
Non-English-speaking population:	38
Immigrant population:	28
Marriage rate:	16
Divorce rate:	2
Married couples:	26
Single parent families headed by women:	15
Teenage mothers:	9
Births to unmarried mothers:	24
Owner-occupied housing:	19
Christian church adherents:	8
Number of farms:	11
Total crime rate:	21
Violent crime rate:	21
Property crime rate:	20
State parks:	32

OREGON

Total area:	10
Mean elevation:	9
Federally owned land:	5
Hazardous waste sites:	29
Social Security beneficiaries:	29
Disposable personal income:	33
Population in poverty:	35
Public Assistance recipients:	37
Food Stamp recipients:	26
Homeless:	16
Federal aid to state:	29
Percent of state revenues from sales taxes:	51
Percent of state revenues from income taxes:	1
Per capita state debt:	14
Death rate:	28
Health expenditures:	30
Medicare enrollment:	29
Medicaid recipients:	31
Per capita energy expenditures:	44
Funding on public education:	27
Expenditures per pupil:	14
College enrollment:	29
Population:	29
Population growth:	9
Population density:	40
Non-metropolitan population:	27
Urban population:	22
Non-English-speaking population:	24
Immigrant population:	21
Marriage rate:	31
Divorce rate:	16
Married couples:	30
Single parent families headed by women:	43
Teenage mothers:	25
Births to unmarried mothers:	30
Owner-occupied housing:	40
Christian church adherents:	50
Number of farms:	25
Total crime rate:	15
Violent crime rate:	29
Property crime rate:	13
State parks:	28

PENNSYLVANIA

Total area:	33
Mean elevation:	23
Federally owned land:	39
Hazardous waste sites:	2
Social Security beneficiaries:	5
Disposable personal income:	15
Population in poverty:	32
Public Assistance recipients:	22
Food Stamp recipients:	22
Homeless:	5
Federal aid to state:	25
Percent of state revenues from sales taxes:	35
Percent of state revenues from income taxes:	34
Per capita state debt:	35
Death rate:	5
Health expenditures:	5
Medicare enrollment:	4
Medicaid recipients:	5
Per capita energy expenditures:	30
Funding on public education:	4
Expenditures per pupil:	6
College enrollment:	8
Population:	5
Population growth:	44
Population density:	11
Non-metropolitan population:	41
Urban population:	26
Non-English-speaking population:	25
Immigrant population:	9
Marriage rate:	50
Divorce rate:	45
Married couples:	5
Single parent families headed by women:	20
Teenage mothers:	34
Births to unmarried mothers:	20
Owner-occupied housing:	5
Christian church adherents:	21
Number of farms:	17
Total crime rate:	45
Violent crime rate:	32
Property crime rate:	45
State parks:	8

RHODE ISLAND

Total area:	50
Mean elevation:	47
Federally owned land:	50
Hazardous waste sites:	29
Social Security beneficiaries:	40
Disposable personal income:	18
Population in poverty:	29
Public Assistance recipients:	13
Food Stamp recipients:	25
Homeless:	43
Federal aid to state:	6
Percent of state revenues from sales taxes:	30
Percent of state revenues from income taxes:	16
Per capita state debt:	3
Death rate:	12
Health expenditures:	42
Medicare enrollment:	39
Medicaid recipients:	35
Per capita energy expenditures:	39
Funding on public education:	43
Expenditures per pupil:	8
College enrollment:	41
Population:	43
Population growth:	50
Population density:	3
Non-metropolitan population:	46
Urban population:	8
Non-English-speaking population:	9
Immigrant population:	32
Marriage rate:	42
Divorce rate:	39
Married couples:	43
Single parent families headed by women:	21
Teenage mothers:	42
Births to unmarried mothers:	26
Owner-occupied housing:	44
Christian church adherents:	3
Number of farms:	49
Total crime rate:	35
Violent crime rate:	34
Property crime rate:	34
State parks:	50

SOUTH CAROLINA

Total area:	40
Mean elevation:	44
Federally owned land:	31
Hazardous waste sites:	15
Social Security beneficiaries:	25
Disposable personal income:	43
Population in poverty:	7
Public Assistance recipients:	26
Food Stamp recipients:	24
Homeless:	35
Federal aid to state:	30
Percent of state revenues from sales taxes:	16
Percent of state revenues from income taxes:	19
Per capita state debt:	25
Death rate:	31
Health expenditures:	27
Medicare enrollment:	26
Medicaid recipients:	23
Per capita energy expenditures:	20
Funding on public education:	26
Expenditures per pupil:	38
College enrollment:	28
Population:	26
Population growth:	23
Population density:	22
Non-metropolitan population:	26
Urban population:	40
Non-English-speaking population:	45
Immigrant population:	36
Marriage rate:	3
Divorce rate:	30
Married couples:	25
Single parent families headed by women:	6
Teenage mothers:	10
Births to unmarried mothers:	6
Owner-occupied housing:	12
Christian church adherents:	13
Number of farms:	32
Total crime rate:	13
Violent crime rate:	7
Property crime rate:	16
State parks:	31

SOUTH DAKOTA

Total area:	17
Mean elevation:	13
Federally owned land:	25
Hazardous waste sites:	45
Social Security beneficiaries:	45
Disposable personal income:	36
Population in poverty:	22
Public Assistance recipients:	45
Food Stamp recipients:	42
Homeless:	44
Federal aid to state:	14
Percent of state revenues from sales taxes:	4
Percent of state revenues from income taxes:	48
Per capita state debt:	9
Death rate:	7
Health expenditures:	47
Medicare enrollment:	45
Medicaid recipients:	46
Per capita energy expenditures:	34
Funding on public education:	49
Expenditures per pupil:	42
College enrollment:	48
Population:	45
Population growth:	30
Population density:	47
Non-metropolitan population:	6
Urban population:	47
Non-English-speaking population:	29
Immigrant population:	48
Marriage rate:	11
Divorce rate:	40
Married couples:	45
Single parent families headed by women:	38
Teenage mothers:	32
Births to unmarried mothers:	37
Owner-occupied housing:	31
Christian church adherents:	7
Number of farms:	27
Total crime rate:	48
Violent crime rate:	45
Property crime rate:	48
State parks:	27

TENNESSEE

Total area:	36
Mean elevation:	30
Federally owned land:	32
Hazardous waste sites:	24
Social Security beneficiaries:	16
Disposable personal income:	34
Population in poverty:	13
Public Assistance recipients:	10
Food Stamp recipients:	5
Homeless:	26
Federal aid to state:	20
Percent of state revenues from sales taxes:	3
Percent of state revenues from income taxes:	44
Per capita state debt:	47
Death rate:	14
Health expenditures:	15
Medicare enrollment:	17
Medicaid recipients:	11
Per capita energy expenditures:	27
Funding on public education:	23
Expenditures per pupil:	46
College enrollment:	22
Population:	17
Population growth:	15
Population density:	20
Non-metropolitan population:	22
Urban population:	36
Non-English-speaking population:	47
Immigrant population:	30
Marriage rate:	7
Divorce rate:	6
Married couples:	16
Single parent families headed by women:	7
Teenage mothers:	4
Births to unmarried mothers:	13
Owner-occupied housing:	20
Christian church adherents:	15
Number of farms:	6
Total crime rate:	24
Violent crime rate:	13
Property crime rate:	27
State parks:	22

TEXAS

Total area:	2
Mean elevation:	17
Federally owned land:	43
Hazardous waste sites:	14
Social Security beneficiaries:	4
Disposable personal income:	28
Population in poverty:	10
Public Assistance recipients:	30
Food Stamp recipients:	6
Homeless:	4
Federal aid to state:	46
Percent of state revenues from sales taxes:	5
Percent of state revenues from income taxes:	49
Per capita state debt:	49
Death rate:	43
Health expenditures:	3
Medicare enrollment:	5
Medicaid recipients:	3
Per capita energy expenditures:	5
Funding on public education:	3
Expenditures per pupil:	34
College enrollment:	2
Population:	2
Population growth:	10
Population density:	30
Non-metropolitan population:	38
Urban population:	15
Non-English-speaking population:	3
Immigrant population:	3
Marriage rate:	14
Divorce rate:	14
Married couples:	2
Single parent families headed by women:	30
Teenage mothers:	14
Births to unmarried mothers:	48
Owner-occupied housing:	43
Christian church adherents:	11
Number of farms:	1
Total crime rate:	2
Violent crime rate:	10
Property crime rate:	3
State parks:	3

UTAH

Total area:	13
Mean elevation:	3
Federally owned land:	3
Hazardous waste sites:	27
Social Security beneficiaries:	38
Disposable personal income:	50
Population in poverty:	49
Public Assistance recipients:	48
Food Stamp recipients:	35
Homeless:	34
Federal aid to state:	44
Percent of state revenues from sales taxes:	12
Percent of state revenues from income taxes:	11
Per capita state debt:	29
Death rate:	50
Health expenditures:	37
Medicare enrollment:	38
Medicaid recipients:	39
Per capita energy expenditures:	47
Funding on public education:	35
Expenditures per pupil:	51
College enrollment:	34
Population:	34
Population growth:	4
Population density:	42
Non-metropolitan population:	31
Urban population:	7
Non-English-speaking population:	23
Immigrant population:	33
Marriage rate:	9
Divorce rate:	22
Married couples:	36
Single parent families headed by women:	22
Teenage mothers:	35
Births to unmarried mothers:	51
Owner-occupied housing:	18
Christian church adherents:	1
Number of farms:	37
Total crime rate:	18
Violent crime rate:	39
Property crime rate:	12
State parks:	26

VERMONT

Total area:	43
Mean elevation:	27
Federally owned land:	24
Hazardous waste sites:	41
Social Security beneficiaries:	48
Disposable personal income:	29
Population in poverty:	41
Public Assistance recipients:	17
Food Stamp recipients:	20
Homeless:	50
Federal aid to state:	10
Percent of state revenues from sales taxes:	43
Percent of state revenues from income taxes:	20
Per capita state debt:	8
Death rate:	33
Health expenditures:	50
Medicare enrollment:	49
Medicaid recipients:	44
Per capita energy expenditures:	17
Funding on public education:	46
Expenditures per pupil:	7
College enrollment:	50
Population:	49
Population growth:	35
Population density:	31
Non-metropolitan population:	2
Urban population:	51
Non-English-speaking population:	31
Immigrant population:	47
Marriage rate:	13
Divorce rate:	28
Married couples:	48
Single parent families headed by women:	44
Teenage mothers:	44
Births to unmarried mothers:	41
Owner-occupied housing:	15
Christian church adherents:	40
Number of farms:	42
Total crime rate:	44
Violent crime rate:	49
Property crime rate:	44
State parks:	29

VIRGINIA

Total area:	35
Mean elevation:	28
Federally owned land:	23
Hazardous waste sites:	15
Social Security beneficiaries:	15
Disposable personal income:	14
Population in poverty:	48
Public Assistance recipients:	43
Food Stamp recipients:	30
Homeless:	19
Federal aid to state:	51
Percent of state revenues from sales taxes:	42
Percent of state revenues from income taxes:	4
Per capita state debt:	30
Death rate:	38
Health expenditures:	13
Medicare enrollment:	15
Medicaid recipients:	18
Per capita energy expenditures:	38
Funding on public education:	12
Expenditures per pupil:	24
College enrollment:	10
Population:	12
Population growth:	17
Population density:	16
Non-metropolitan population:	32
Urban population:	24
Non-English-speaking population:	26
Immigrant population:	8
Marriage rate:	8
Divorce rate:	32
Married couples:	12
Single parent families headed by women:	23
Teenage mothers:	30
Births to unmarried mothers:	23
Owner-occupied housing:	30
Christian church adherents:	35
Number of farms:	21
Total crime rate:	39
Violent crime rate:	35
Property crime rate:	39
State parks:	34

WASHINGTON

Total area:	19
Mean elevation:	18
Federally owned land:	11
Hazardous waste sites:	6
Social Security beneficiaries:	18
Disposable personal income:	12
Population in poverty:	38
Public Assistance recipients:	21
Food Stamp recipients:	29
Homeless:	9
Federal aid to state:	24
Percent of state revenues from sales taxes:	1
Percent of state revenues from income taxes:	50
Per capita state debt:	24
Death rate:	45
Health expenditures:	20
Medicare enrollment:	18
Medicaid recipients:	16
Per capita energy expenditures:	43
Funding on public education:	15
Expenditures per pupil:	23
College enrollment:	14
Population:	15
Population growth:	6
Population density:	27
Non-metropolitan population:	37
Urban population:	17
Non-English-speaking population:	19
Immigrant population:	10
Marriage rate:	19
Divorce rate:	10
Married couples:	18
Single parent families headed by women:	45
Teenage mothers:	36
Births to unmarried mothers:	34
Owner-occupied housing:	41
Christian church adherents:	48
Number of farms:	26
Total crime rate:	10
Violent crime rate:	26
Property crime rate:	6
State parks:	12

WEST VIRGINIA

Total area:	41
Mean elevation:	19
Federally owned land:	21
Hazardous waste sites:	44
Social Security beneficiaries:	34
Disposable personal income:	48
Population in poverty:	3
Public Assistance recipients:	6
Food Stamp recipients:	3
Homeless:	40
Federal aid to state:	7
Percent of state revenues from sales taxes:	22
Percent of state revenues from income taxes:	36
Per capita state debt:	23
Death rate:	2
Health expenditures:	35
Medicare enrollment:	34
Medicaid recipients:	30
Per capita energy expenditures:	8
Funding on public education:	33
Expenditures per pupil:	19
College enrollment:	37
Population:	36
Population growth:	43
Population density:	29
Non-metropolitan population:	9
Urban population:	50
Non-English-speaking population:	50
Immigrant population:	46
Marriage rate:	51
Divorce rate:	18
Married couples:	34
Single parent families headed by women:	24
Teenage mothers:	5
Births to unmarried mothers:	27
Owner-occupied housing:	1
Christian church adherents:	39
Number of farms:	34
Total crime rate:	38
Violent crime rate:	44
Property crime rate:	50
State parks:	16

WISCONSIN

Total area:	22
Mean elevation:	24
Federally owned land:	18
Hazardous waste sites:	9
Social Security beneficiaries:	17
Disposable personal income:	25
Population in poverty:	39
Public Assistance recipients:	20
Food Stamp recipients:	50
Homeless:	30
Federal aid to state:	33
Percent of state revenues from sales taxes:	32
Percent of state revenues from income taxes:	7
Per capita state debt:	22
Death rate:	34
Health expenditures:	18
Medicare enrollment:	16
Medicaid recipients:	22
Per capita energy expenditures:	46
Funding on public education:	16
Expenditures per pupil:	10
College enrollment:	12
Population:	18
Population growth:	27
Population density:	25
Non-metropolitan population:	23
Urban population:	32
Non-English-speaking population:	32
Immigrant population:	24
Marriage rate:	37
Divorce rate:	41
Married couples:	17
Single parent families headed by women:	31
Teenage mothers:	41
Births to unmarried mothers:	35
Owner-occupied housing:	28
Christian church adherents:	10
Number of farms:	8
Total crime rate:	36
Violent crime rate:	42
Property crime rate:	37
State parks:	20

WYOMING

Total area:	9
Mean elevation:	2
Federally owned land:	6
Hazardous waste sites:	47
Social Security beneficiaries:	50
Disposable personal income:	23
Population in poverty:	43
Public Assistance recipients:	38
Food Stamp recipients:	45
Homeless:	51
Federal aid to state:	3
Percent of state revenues from sales taxes:	33
Percent of state revenues from income taxes:	51
Per capita state debt:	16
Death rate:	46
Health expenditures:	51
Medicare enrollment:	50
Medicaid recipients:	51
Per capita energy expenditures:	2
Funding on public education:	48
Expenditures per pupil:	17
College enrollment:	47
Population:	51
Population growth:	24
Population density:	50
Non-metropolitan population:	3
Urban population:	33
Non-English-speaking population:	34
Immigrant population:	51
Marriage rate:	17
Divorce rate:	5
Married couples:	50
Single parent families headed by women:	46
Teenage mothers:	19
Births to unmarried mothers:	43
Owner-occupied housing:	23
Christian church adherents:	33
Number of farms:	38
Total crime rate:	50
Violent crime rate:	38
Property crime rate:	29
State parks:	24

WASHINGTON, DC

Total area:	51
Mean elevation:	48
Federally owned land:	13
Hazardous waste sites:	X
Social Security beneficiaries:	49
Disposable personal income:	1
Population in poverty:	5
Public Assistance recipients:	1
Food Stamp recipients:	4
Homeless:	12
Federal aid to state:	1
Percent of state revenues from sales taxes:	46
Percent of state revenues from income taxes:	37
Per capita state debt:	X
Death rate:	1
Health expenditures:	34
Medicare enrollment:	48
Medicaid recipients:	40
Per capita energy expenditures:	21
Funding on public education:	50
Expenditures per pupil:	5
College enrollment:	51
Population:	50
Population growth:	51
Population density:	1
Non-metropolitan population:	51
Urban population:	1
Non-English-speaking population:	14
Immigrant population:	23
Marriage rate:	43
Divorce rate:	29
Married couples:	51
Single parent families headed by women:	2
Teenage mothers:	7
Births to unmarried mothers:	1
Owner-occupied housing:	51
Christian church adherents:	24
Number of farms:	X
Total crime rate:	X
Violent crime rate:	X
Property crime rate:	X
State parks:	X

X Not Available

INDEX

D

rental housing 160–161
retail trade, employees in 31–32
Roman Catholics 165–166
rural land 10–11

for public welfare 71–72
suicide 79–80
sunshine 15–16
Supplemental Security Income 45–46, 47–48

S

sales tax 58
sales tax rates 60–61
school lunch program 50–51
self-employed workers 34
Senate, U.S. 200
service jobs, employees in 32–33
Seventh-Day Adventists 170
single parent families 145–146
snowfall 21–22
Soviet Union 136
Spanish-speaking population 126
state government
    composition of legislatures 205
    debt 74
    employees in 206–207 *see also* state revenue;
      state spending
state legislatures 205
state parks
    state area in 13–14
    visitors to 216
state profiles 219–244
state revenue
    from alcoholic beverages 60
    from corporate income tax 59
    from federal government 54
    from local government 54
    from local taxes 55
    from sales tax 58
    from state taxes 57
    from tobacco products 60
    general 53
state spending
    for corrections 73–74
    for education 70–71
    for health and hospitals 72–73
    for highways 72

T

tax rates
    cigarettes 62
    gasoline 61–62
    sales 62
taxes
    alcoholic beverages 60
    corporate income tax 59–60
    federal income tax returns 62–63
    federal revenue 54–55
    local revenue 54–57
    sales tax 58
    state income tax 58–59
    state revenue 53–54
    state tax collections 57
    tobacco 60
teachers
    number of 107–108
    salaries 108
teenage mothers 153–154
temperature 16–20
tobacco 60, 62
transportation
    airlines 198
    airports 197
    employees in 30–31
    highways, state spending for 72
    roadway congestion to work 195–196 *see also*
      motor vehicles; pollution

U

U.S. Congress 199–200